DOMESTIC VIOLENCE

INTERVENTION, PREVENTION, POLICIES, AND SOLUTIONS

DOMESTIC VIOLENCE

INTERVENTION, PREVENTION, POLICIES, AND SOLUTIONS

RICHARD L. DAVIS

Vincennes University
Shake Learning Resources Center
Vincennes, In 47591-9986

CRC Press
Taylor & Francis Group
Boca Raton   London   New York

CRC Press is an imprint of the
Taylor & Francis Group, an **informa** business

CRC Press
Taylor & Francis Group
6000 Broken Sound Parkway NW, Suite 300
Boca Raton, FL 33487-2742

© 2008 by Taylor & Francis Group, LLC
CRC Press is an imprint of Taylor & Francis Group, an Informa business

No claim to original U.S. Government works
Printed in the United States of America on acid-free paper
10 9 8 7 6 5 4 3 2 1

International Standard Book Number-13: 978-1-4200-6139-0 (Hardcover)

Library of Congress Cataloging-in-Publication Data

Davis, Richard L., 1941-
Domestic violence : intervention, prevention, policies, and solutions / Richard L. Davis.
p. cm.
Includes bibliographical references and index.
ISBN 978-1-4200-6139-0 (alk. paper)
1. Family violence--United States. 2. Victims of family violence--United States. 3. Family violence--Government policy--United States. I. Title.

HV6626.2.D394 2008
362.82'920973--dc22   2007045310

Visit the Taylor & Francis Web site at
http://www.taylorandfrancis.com

and the CRC Press Web site at
http://www.crcpress.com

Dedication

To Helen Elizabeth Davis

Contents

Preface	**xiii**
Acknowledgments	**xxi**
Author	**xxiii**

1   Introduction   1

Background	2
Gender Equality	3
An Unnecessary Schism	4
Ideologically Held Beliefs Become Reality	5
The Criminalization of All Acts of Family Conflict	6
A Good Idea Gone Bad	6
What Is Domestic Violence?	7
The Children	8
The 21st Century	8
The Beat Goes On	10
An Objective View	10
A Chance To Be Heard	11
Discussion	12

2   Domestic Violence and Violent Behavior in General   13

Introduction	13
A Blind Eye	14
A Deaf Ear	15
Domestic Violence	16
Why They Do It	17
Crime Statistics	19
Homicides	20
A Distinct Model for Murder	22
Power and Control	22
Opportunity and Ability	24
It Is Not Always One Or the Other	25
The Fallacious Argument	25
The Wellspring of Violent Behavior	26

Victims and Offenders 27
Time for Change 28
Where Violence Occurs 29
Conclusion 30
Discussion Questions 31

3 Battered Statistics Harm All Victims   33

How Non-Facts Become Facts 33
A Non-Fact 35
The Facts 36
The Numbers Game 37
Do These Numbers Help or Hinder? 38
Some Measuring Tools 39
Time to Stop and Think 40
Domestic Violence Homicides 42
Marginalizing Victims 42
Conclusion 43
Discussion Questions 44

4 Dating Abuse   47

The Massachusetts Constitution 47
    Article I 47
    Article I 47
Valentine's Day in America's Hometown 48
An Overview 49
Battering Behavior 50
Dating Violence or Family Conflict 50
Risk Factors for Dating Abuse 51
One-Solution-Fits-All 52
Women's Rights Research 52
Jane Doe 54
Definition 55
Liz Claiborne Inc. 56
    Findings 57
    Power and Control Issues 58
    Emotional Abuse 59
    It's Time to Talk Day 59
    Keeping the Silence 61
Is There a Gender Agenda? 61
Gender Symmetry 63
The Violence Against Women Act 64
Juvenile Violent and Non-Violent Crime Rate 66

The 2004 Boston Youth Survey 67
The College Campus 68
Self-Defense and Aggression 70
Avoiding the Obvious 74
Senator Joseph Biden 75
Circumstances and Context 75
Ideology Skews Public Policy 76
The National Center for Victims of Crime 77
The Centers for Disease Control and Prevention 78
Safety First 79
Conclusion 82
Discussion Questions 85

5   The California Conundrum: Keeping the Promise   87

Introduction 87
Keeping the Promise (KtP) 89
Permeating the System 90
One-Solution-Fits-All 91
Domestic Violence Is Not Treated the Same as Other Crimes 91
Battering Behavior 93
Family Conflict 93
The Domestic Violence Problem 93
The Fear Factor Gender Differential 94
Reporting 94
Dating Relationships 96
Domestic Violence Homicides 97
Limited Understanding and a Lack of Knowledge 98
Research Ignored 99
Mandatory 99
Helpful for Some, Harmful for Others 100
One Size Does Not Fit All 101
Why Ignore These NIJ-Sponsored Reports 102
The National Research Council 102
Justice for All 103
Restraining Orders 104
    The Facts 104
    The Premise 105
    Deterrence 106
    Connecting the Dots 106
    The Cart and the Horse 107

Prosecuting Domestic Violence Misdemeanors: Ignoring the
Obvious   109
   An Imperfect Idea   110
   It's All about Choice   110
   What Not to Do   111
   Read the Studies   112
Holding Batterers Accountable: Batterer Intervention
Programs, Probation Departments, and the Courts   114
   The Nexus of the Problem   114
   It Gets Worse   114
   The Duluth or Cognitive-Behavioral Model   116
   The Family Conflict Model   116
   The Psychotherapeutic Model   116
   And Worse Still   117
Law Enforcement's Response to Health Practitioner Reports
of Domestic Violence   118
   Empirical Data, Not Hunches and Hopes   118
   Look before You Leap   118
   Leaping without Looking   119
   Autonomy and Confidentiality   120
   California Mandatory Reporting Law: A Summary   120
   Why Confusion Reigns   121
   The Letter of the Law   122
Recommendations for KtP Change   123
   Criminal Justice Data   124
   A Central Premise   125
   An Emerging Awareness   126
Recommendations for the California Attorney General   126
   Recommendation One   126
   Recommendation Two   128
   Recommendation Three   128
   Recommendation Four   128
Conclusion   129
Discussion Questions   130

6   Rape and Sexual Assault   **133**

Introduction   133
Those That Stand Accused   133
Engaging Men   134
A Crime That Spawned a Center   135
Experts   136
Law Enforcement Intervention   138

Educational Intervention   139
Invisible Victims   140
Further Complications   141
Rape Statistics   141
Conclusion   144
Discussion Questions   144

7   Mandatory Domestic Violence Arrest Policies   145

What Is *Domestic Violence?*   145
Battering   146
Family Conflict   146
A False Premise   147
The Rise in Arrests for Females   148
Questioning Mandatory Arrest   149
Outcomes   150
Conclusion   151
Discussion Questions   152

8   The Colorado Star Chamber   155

Introduction   155
The U.S. Department of Justice   156
The Star Chamber   157
The Fifth Amendment   157
The Sixth Amendment   157
The Fourteenth Amendment—Section 1   158
Moral and Legal Rights   158
Injustice Indeed   159
Plea Bargain   160
The 2002 Colorado Star Chamber   161
    Thinking and Nonthinking   164
Unsubstantiated Beliefs   167
Logic and Common Sense   168
Discussion Questions   169

9   Ain't I a Victim   171

Introduction   171
Domestic Violence Awareness   171
Equality and Equity   172
Abusive Not Violent Behavior   173
The "Experts" Cannot See Them   173
Why Male Victims Seem Invisible   176

Facts Ignored   177
The Search for the Whole Truth   177
Can't They Handle the Truth?   178
And What about Our Children?   179
The Patriarchy Makes Them Do It   179
The Invisible Victim   180
And The Truth Shall Set Us Free   182
Discussion Questions   183

10   In Memoriam   185

Introduction   185
Implicit Bias   185
The 2003 Massachusetts Domestic Violence Homicide Report   186
The Silent Voices   186
    January 14, 2003   186
    February 7, 2003   187
    March 25, 2003   187
    March 31, 2003   187
    April 19, 2000   187
    April 19, 2003   187
    June 1, 2003   188
    June 11, 2003   188
    June 16, 2003   188
    June 26, 2003   188
    June 29, 2003   188
    July 23, 2003   189
    October 2, 2003   189
    October 28, 2003   189
    November 2, 2003   189
    November 26, 2003   189
    December 1, 2003   190
Implicit Bias   190
Lessons Ignored   191
Domestic Violence Homicide Is Preventable   192
Conclusion   193
Discussion Questions   194

11   Rethinking Victimization   195

Some Perspective   195
Differing Domestic Violence Data   196
Compromise   197
    The Duluth Model   198

The Family Conflict Model   198
The Psychological Model   198
A Complex and Multifaceted Issue   198
Batterers   200
Family Conflict   201
Assessments Needed   202
The Value of Assessments   202
The Need for a More Objective View   203
Unbiased Reporting of Facts   204
Conclusion   204
Discussion Questions   206

12   Afterword   207

Introduction   207
The Resolution   208
   Resolution   208
Thinking about Thinking   210
   "Advancing the Federal Research Agenda on Violence
   Against Women"   211
   "The Exposure Reduction or Backlash? The Effects of
   Domestic Violence Resources on Intimate Partner
   Homicide"   211
   Controlling Violence against Women: A Research
   Perspective on the 1994 VAWA's Criminal Justice Impacts   211
   Intimate Partner Violence (IPV): Overview   212
Conclusion   213

References   215

Recommendations   255
Recommendation One   255
Recommendation Two   257
Recommendation Three   257
Recommendation Four   259
Recommendation Five   260
Recommendation Six   261
Recommendation Seven   261
Recommendation Eight   263
Recommendation Nine   263
   The Family Violence Act   263
Recommendation Ten   264
Unaware of the Data?   264

Selected Resources   **267**

Index   **281**

Preface

Rigorous inquiry into violence against women is precluded when scholars fail to distinguish among what constitutes an act of violence, abuse or battering.

—Kruttschnitt, McLaughlin and Petrie, p. 56

Errors of fact follow from the failure to make distinctions among types of violence.

—Michael P. Johnson, p. 1129

To understand the nature of intimate partner violence, it is important to make a distinction between common couple violence and chronic battering.

—Hendricks, McKean and Hendricks, p. 228

The lack of agreement in defining family violence has led to confusion and disarray in attempts to determine factors that cause or contribute to family violence.

—Harvey Wallace, p. 3

In sum, the labeling of all acts of physical aggression as violent can have unintended social implications.

—K. Daniel O'Leary, p. 8

Deborah Capaldi, PhD, an acknowledged domestic violence expert and senior scientist at the Oregon Social Learning Center in Eugene, Oregon, is currently the principal investigator of three studies for the National Institutes of Health: (1) the cause and consequences of antisocial behavior; (2) young couples' relationships and (3) intergenerational influences on risk. Some of Capaldi's most recent research focuses on understanding the dynamics of romantic relationships in early adulthood with a particular interest concerning the development of aggression in romantic-styled relationships.

Andy Klein, PhD, also an acknowledged domestic violence expert, is a senior research analyst at Advocates for Human Potential, Inc.; a domestic violence consultant; and the former chief probation officer for the Quincy, Massachusetts District Court, one of the first courts in the nation to recognize the unique problem domestic violence presents to the criminal justice system. Klein is an author and a columnist for the *National Bulletin on Domestic Violence Prevention*.

A recent study coauthored by Capaldi documents that many of the young women in that particular subgroup of the population (at-risk young couples who have displayed frequent physical aggression toward their intimate partner) were more likely than the young men to initiate assaultive behavior or to engage in mutual aggression with their dating partner. Further, the study concludes that the behavior of these young women increases the chance of their being injured (Capaldi, Kim and Shortt, 2004).

On June 24, 2005, Capaldi and Klein appeared on the MSNBC show *Scarborough Country* (Soler, 2007). In their interview, Klein asserted that the Capaldi study is a misrepresentation of what domestic violence is all about. Klein notes that domestic violence, as seen by Klein in the criminal courts, is not about two people engaged in mutual fights and pushing, slapping, or hitting each other. The violent behavior Klein had seen as a chief probation officer is the type that often can land females (primarily the injured victim) in the hospital with serious injuries or in the morgue (usually at the hands of males).

The truth is that both Capaldi and Klein are correct. However, each of them, at least concerning the *Scarborough Country* interview, is describing a different and individual subdivision of a very complex and multifaceted phenomenon as if it represents the entire phenomena. I do not believe that either Capaldi or Klein should suppose that their individual "expertise" concerning any particular subgroup of a population is representative of the population in general.

Capaldi's view of domestic violence primarily involves at-risk young people living at the lower end of the socioeconomic educational strata of society—those who have social or behavioral factors that can increase the risk that they will hurt or harm their partners (Capaldi, Kim and Shortt, 2004).

Klein's view is that domestic violence involves men and women who, more often than not, have been engaged in the criminal justice system as juveniles or adults (Klein, 1996). Neither Capaldi nor Klein presents any evidence that his or her particular subgroup is representative of the majority of the population.

The Nexus of the Confusion and Disarray

Ester Soler (another acknowledged domestic violence expert) is the founder and president of the nationally recognized domestic violence organization, the Family Violence Prevention Fund (FVPF) (www.endabuse.org).

Soler believes that the debate between Capaldi and Klein gets to the root of the domestic violence problem. Soler claims that the problem with the

Capalidi study is with the definition of domestic violence. In an article entitled "Backlash Study," Soler writes:

> Certainly, all violence is wrong regardless who the perpetrator is. But domestic violence is not one person pushing another person one time. *Domestic violence* occurs when there is an ongoing pattern of fear, intimidation and violent assault [italics added] (Soler, 2007).

I agree that the definition offered by Soler *should be* the accepted definition of domestic violence, but Soler knows that it is not. The FVPF website, similar to the vast majority of the nationally recognized domestic violence websites, agrees that not one of these organizations, including Soler's FVPF, believes the above Soler definition is or should be the accepted definition of domestic violence. The FVPF "Get the Facts" section (http://www.endabuse.org/resources/facts/) documents domestic victims.

As their websites document, not a single domestic violence organization—or any state—accepts the Soler definition as the definition of domestic violence. In fact, nowhere on her own FVPF website does it appear that Soler's own organization accepts the Soler definition as *the* definition of domestic violence.

What is also very troubling for scholars and researchers (as presented in the Soler "Backlash Study" article on the FVPF website) is that both Klein and Soler appear to have disagreed with Capaldi and then challenged data in her study after reading only media reports about it. It appears that neither Klein nor Soler had actually read the Capaldi study, as it had yet to be released.

The National Violence Against Women Survey (NVAWS)

The NVAWS documents that 1.3 million women and 835,000 men are physically assaulted annually by intimate partners in domestic violence incidents (Tjaden and Thoennes, 2000b, p. iv). Forty percent of women and 53.8% of surveyed men report they were physically assaulted by an adult caretaker as a child (p. 35).

Data from the NVAWS are routinely accepted by nationally recognized domestic violence organizations as the definition of domestic violence and NVAWS domestic violence data often appear on their websites and in their literature.

It is my contention that the reason there is so much confusion and disarray surrounding domestic violence is due to the misleading depiction of the dynamics of abuse portrayed by Soler, the majority of domestic violence organizations and most public policy makers.

As O'Leary notes above and this book will document, the legislating and labeling of all acts of family physical aggression and emotional distress as acts of domestic violence have had unintended negative social implications.

Is There a Legal Definition?

While there is variance among the states concerning the legal definition of domestic violence, *none of their definitions match that proffered by Soler.* Most of the states' legal definitions of domestic violence are similar to those of the state of Delaware, the home state of Senator Joseph R. Biden, Jr. Delaware law defines domestic violence as the occurrence of one or more of the following acts of "abuse" between "family" or "household members":

- Actual physical injury or sexual offenses
- Threatening physical injury or sexual offense
- Damaging, destroying, or taking property
- Trespassing
- Child abuse
- Kidnapping
- Unlawful imprisonment
- Interference with custody
- Causing fear or emotional distress
- Any other conduct that a reasonable person would find threatening or harmful.

A state-by-state search of the definition of domestic violence reveals that no state definition requires that domestic violence be an *ongoing pattern* of fear, intimidation or *repeat violent assaults* between intimate partners (www. Womenslaw.org).

The Experts

How can there be any domestic violence experts if the experts refuse to agree just what "it" is they are agreeing or disagreeing about? How are physicians, nurses, psychiatrists, psychologists, family counselors, educators, social workers, attorneys, judges, law enforcement, domestic violence offenders and most importantly domestic violence victims going to become aware of the dynamics and dangers of domestic violence when so many experts offer very different theories and definitions to our public policy makers (Wallace, 2003)?

Without consistency of definition, how can experts present interventions, prevention programs, policies and solutions to those in need? Most experts accept their individually held theories as fact and many often ignore or minimize the theories of others. This lack of agreement has ceased or slowed the glimmer of hope for an emerging consensus regarding domestic violence as the 20th century closed (Dobash and Dobash, 1979, 1992; Dutton, 2006; Mills, 2003; Young, 1999).

I believe, as Soler writes in her article, that *the problem is with the definition of* domestic violence. Harvey Wallace clearly defines the dilemma faced by laypersons and scholars alike: "How does one accurately study or research a phenomenon if a definition cannot be agreed on because the definition of any act both sets limits and focuses research within certain boundaries?" (Wallace, 2002, p.3).

The process of placing the entitlements of one group of victims—adult heterosexual women—above all others has caused the majority of domestic violence organizations and public policy makers, as this book will document, to minimize, marginalize or ignore sibling, same-sex and elder abuse, and the victimization of adult heterosexual males at the hands of adult heterosexual females.

The claim that one person is the primary victim (Tjaden and Thoennes, 2000b) in effect reduces the other victims to a minor victimization status and minimizes the needs of those "minor" victims, proving to be detrimental to all victims as it has replaced a growing consciousness and concern about family violence with a schism over gender symmetry and primary victimization (Straus and Medeiros, 2002).

Conclusion

The greatest obstacle to the discovery of the truth is the illusion that the truth has already been discovered. That being said, I do believe that the truth lies in evidence-based empirical studies. I believe that domestic violence is a problem for both females and males. However, it is not my intent to present only studies that favor my conclusion; I hope that this book in general and the reference section in particular will be used by domestic violence advocates and public policy makers to discover what they believe to be the truth.

It should be the collective goal of researchers, domestic violence advocates, public policy makers and in fact anyone concerned about the issue of domestic violence to research and read all of the studies concerning domestic violence before they conclude that any single theory is absolutely right and everyone else's theory is absolutely wrong.

To accomplish this, readers will need to set aside, at least temporarily, the fact that they believe they have already discovered the truth concerning the cause and consequence of domestic violence.

Most importantly for researchers and scholars, many of the studies and articles in the reference section of this book contain websites that allow them to view the studies online. The Taylor & Francis website (http://www.taylorandfrancis.com) will allow readers to use the Internet interactive reference of this book to connect directly to those studies.

Acknowledgments

Here I must thank (no possession intended) my daughter Bridget, son Ian, and niece Lynda for their invaluable assistance.

Author

Richard L. Davis is a retired police lieutenant. He has graduate degrees from Anna Maria College and Harvard University. He is an instructor for Quincy College at Plymouth, Massachusetts, and is the president of www.Family-nonviolence.org. He is the author of *Domestic Violence: Facts and Fallacies,* and has published numerous articles for newspapers, journals, and magazines concerning the issue of domestic violence and its intersection with the criminal justice system. He is a columnist for www.PoliceOne.com. He can be reached at rldavis@post.harvard.edu.

Introduction

1

Pitting the suffering of one group against the suffering of another in a bid for the moral high ground is as old and as odious as injustice itself.

—Eileen McNamara, *Boston Globe,* **Mar. 14, 2004**

Most importantly, this book must provide a definition of domestic violence that the majority of the nationally recognized domestic violence agencies and advocates will accept. The greatest failing in the debate about domestic violence is that it remains different things to different people (Wallace, 2002). Hence, this book will use the definition found on June 1st, 2007 on the National Domestic Violence Hotline (NDVH) (http://www.ndvh.org/educate/what_is_dv.html).

- Domestic violence can be defined as a pattern of behavior in any relationship that is used to gain or maintain power and control over an intimate partner.
- Abuse is physical, sexual, emotional, economic or psychological actions or threats of actions that influence another person. This includes any behaviors that frighten, intimidate, terrorize, manipulate, hurt, humiliate, blame, injure or wound someone.
- Domestic violence can happen to anyone of any race, age, sexual orientation, religion or gender. It can happen to couples who are married, living together or who are dating. Domestic violence affects people of all socioeconomic backgrounds and educational levels (NDVH, 2007).

The NDVH is funded with millions of dollars from the Violence Against Women Act. It is vital that the reader note that the NDVH definition, similar to the majority of the nationally recognized domestic violence organizations, does not require that an act of domestic "violence" be a "violent physical assault."

The NDVH website, for reasons I do not understand, limits its definition of domestic violence to behavior between couples in romantic or intimate relationships. The vast majority of the states, as noted in the Preface, recognize domestic violence as incidents that occur between family or household members. To meet 21st century standards, the NDVH website needs to change its name to the National Intimate Partner Hotline or change its definition of domestic violence to meet the definitions set by the vast majority of states.

The dual concepts of unequal power and control are not limited to romantic relationships and there is little doubt that the issues of power and control are not the only cause of domestic violence (Chalk and King, 1998; Felson, 2002).

The data documents that in families, both males and females, young and old, are abused by other males and females. It states that children are vulnerable to economic and physical abuse from adult males and females; smaller and weaker siblings, regardless of gender, are vulnerable to larger and stronger siblings; and the weak, infirm and elderly, regardless of gender, are vulnerable to abuse from those who are young and strong (Chalk and King, 1998; Crowell and Burgess, 1996; Davis, 1996; Dutton, 2006; Felson, 2002; Gelles and Loseke, 1993; Hendricks, McKean, and Hendricks, 2003; Hamel and Nicholls, 2007; Jackson, 2007; Reiss and Roth, 1993; Straus and Gelles, 1990; and Wallace, 2002).

Background

For thousands of years of written history people did not write about the reasons that those who professed to love one another would often abuse each other. Physical assaults were—and perhaps among siblings still are—more often than not accepted if not approved behavior in families (Wallace, 2002). No one that I am aware of has yet to claim that each and every physical assault between siblings should be treated as a crime and that restraining orders should be issued to prevent further assaultive behavior between siblings. However, many advocates in our contemporary society believe that each and every physical assault between adult males and females should be considered a criminal act.

After centuries of not addressing the abusive behavior by those in familial or intimate partner relationships, near the middle of the 20th century important progress came about. It is now recognized that the majority of physical assaults are not between strangers, they occur between family members and acquaintances.

Marvin Wolfgang's (1958) landmark study *Patterns in Criminal Homicide* documented that, from 1948 to 1952, only 12.2% of the 550 homicides with known suspects were committed against "strangers." The Wolfgang study confirmed the fact that most murders are familial or by acquaintances of the family. As in sexual assaults, it is not the strangers among us who wreak the most havoc.

Until the 20th century, violence between family members, regardless of gender, more often than not was considered to be a private family matter rather than a social problem or a criminal justice concern. In mid-20th century, three social events occurred:

1. The child advocacy movement
2. The civil rights movement
3. The feminist movement

The intent of all these events was to bring equitable opportunity and behavior to everyone. That was, and, I believe, is the core intent of a progressive feminist movement (Chesney-Lind, 2002). However, a small number of ideological domestic violence advocates (people who are as much or more concerned with women's rights than victim's rights) have attempted to turn the feminist movement, a movement that was once and should remain primarily concerned with equal rights, into a "women's rights" movement. This turns the concept of *equal rights* on its head, because by its very nature a women's rights movement must be concerned exclusively with women's rights and not necessarily equal rights.

An attempt to pass the Equal Rights Amendment was three states short of enactment in 1982. I voted for that amendment and to this day have no idea why it did not pass. The 21st century amendment, however, has a new name: It is now the Women's Equality Amendment (Eilperin, 2007).

Gender Equality

In the early 1960s, Dr. C.H. Kempe produced a series of studies that called the attention of society to the fact that parents, caretakers and siblings physically and sexually assaulted children more that did strangers. Kempe and his colleagues coined the term "battered child syndrome" and reported that child abuse was not a problem primarily or specifically for those who live a the lower end of the socioeconomic educational strata of society (Wallace, 2002, p. 30).

The people most often found guilty of physically abusing their children proved to be their parents, caretakers or siblings in the home. Society began to understand that the enemy was not some other group of "them"; rather, as a famous possum once said, "the enemy is us" (Kelly, 1998).

Concerning the issue of child abuse, change came quickly and, within just a few years, all 50 states had passed various forms of mandated child abuse laws. However, the criminalization of child abuse does not include yelling at a child or spanking the child on the hand, the face or the buttocks, as long as those acts do not cause physical injury that can be documented (Wallace, 2002). No laws mandate the reporting of each abusive incident or mandatory arrest for every physically assaultive incident, regardless of severity, that occurs within the family. Child abuse arrests and mandated governmental intervention are confined to acute or serious cases only. There is also universally agreement concerning the fact that men, women, and siblings, regardless of gender, could be the offender.

It is generally recognized that children, regardless of gender, can be a victim of neglect, psychological or physical abuse. It is generally agreed that, concerning sexual assaults and rapes of children, males are the primary but not exclusive offenders and females the primary yet not exclusive victims. This universal agreement about offending and victimization, rather than dividing the issue along lines of gender, brought with it a solidarity of purpose and not the dividedness and disarray that is so often found today among so many domestic violence advocates.

An Unnecessary Schism

Strengthened by civil rights legislation the feminist movement of the 1970s became politically empowered and women, along with a great many men, began to speak out concerning the issue of equality or at least equitable behavior. At first, the most important issues of the feminist movement were women's reproductive rights, sexual discrimination, education and employment (Brinkley, 2008).

In her book *Battered Wives*, Del Martin (1976), a pioneering lesbian-rights activists, concluded that the issue of "wife beating" could be traced to the unequal power relations between men and women—in marriage in particular—and the unequal gender power relations of society in general. Martin and other domestic violence advocates who were deeply concerned with the dilemma of wife beating seemed to conclude that patriarchy (the man is the head of the family or society) was the primary cause of wife beating. However, few advocates seemed to notice that nowhere in the Martin book is there any objective empirical data that documents her subjective claim.

Many domestic violence advocates thought the two ideas—wife beating and patriarchy—might be a natural fit for their agenda of the issue of women's rights and of opposing the victimization of females. Hence, without any empirical documentation, the theory that the patriarchy actually did "cause" wife beating became an accepted "fact" by many if not most, domestic violence advocates. Thus, the origin of the theory that violence against women is singularly, exclusively, and dramatically different from all other forms of violence was born from the power and control theory.

It seems odd that Martin and many domestic violence advocates seemed to be unaware that coercion, physical power and economic control are fundamental concerns of anyone, regardless of age or gender, who wants to change or control the behavior of another person, whether a family member or not. In fact, history documents that nations use coercion, physical power and economic control to change or alter the behavior of other nations.

The differences in physically power and economic control are obvious in child, sibling, intimate partner and elder abuse. The same dynamics of power and control are not exclusive to the heterosexual community; they are prevalent in the lesbian, gay, bisexual, and transgendered community (Mills, 2003). These same issues of coercion, physical power and economic control are also fundamental to criminal behavior (Brownstein, 2000; Felson, 2002), and they are often at the center of differences between nations (Brinkley, 2008). However, it is rather surprising to me that Martin would claim that male dominance and the suppression of women's right are the primary causes of domestic violence.

It is difficult to believe that Martin would be unaware that the National Coalition of Anti-Violence Programs (NCAVP) consistently has reported that the rate of domestic violence in the homosexual community is approximately the same as in the heterosexual community (NCAVP, 2006). How can Martin and other advocates believe that the cause of intimate partner violence in the homosexual community has little to do with coercion, physical power and economic control?

To the surprise of many sociologists and researchers, the "patriarchy causes domestic violence theory" was born, nurtured, and became a "fact" to a great many domestic violence advocates (Dutton, 2006). Few public policy makers seem to be aware that the theory remains a theory and that the claim that the cause of domestic violence is patriarchy is without a single scientific empirical study (Ford, Bachman, Friend, and Meloy, 2002).

Ideologically Held Beliefs Become Reality

The National Coalition Against Domestic Violence (NCADV) (http://www.ncadv.org/) suggests that domestic violence is caused by men because they are men. The NCADV website documents that the NCADV believes that men objectify women, that they do not see women as people and do not respect women as a group, and that contemporary mores and norms cause men in general to view women as property or sexual objects.

The NCADV and the majority of domestic violence organizations, as their websites document, believe that America continues to be a patriarchal society where men are expected to be the dominant figure in the family. Further, they believe that this patriarchal dominance naturally leads men to believe it is their right, if not their duty, to control women. These fundamental feminists believe that men have to use violence to control women in our contemporary democratic, if patriarchal, society, and they believe that the majority of other men condone and support that use of violence.

On the NCADV website is a long list of national public policy makers who, because they apparently approve of the NCADV philosophy, must agree with NCADV. What the NCADV and these public policy makers must ignore is the fact that almost each and every scientific empirical study, including the National Violence Against Women Survey, documents that the issue of domestic violence is far more complicated than any single grandstand theory alone. Again, very few or no empirical scientifically controlled studies can support that the theory that patriarchy makes them do it is factual.

The vast majority of physicians, nurses, psychiatrists, psychologists, family counselors, educators, social workers, attorneys, judges, and law enforcement officials nationwide do not necessarily agree with NCADV (Wallace, 2002). These professionals understand that domestic violence is an extremely complex and multifaceted phenomenon. They understand that the reasons for and causes of child, sibling, spousal, intimate partner, and elder abuse, regardless of sexual orientation, are most often the same reasons for and causes of violence against adult heterosexual women (Chalk and King, 1998). The majority of professionals understand that offenders and victims of domestic violence are not limited by age or gender (Wallace, 2002). What is it that NCADV and the majority of are public policy makers are missing or do not understand about the issue of domestic violence?

The Criminalization of All Acts of Family Conflict

In the 1970s, domestic violence advocates in rape crisis centers were aware that children now had legislation that protected them from violent family members. These advocates demanded the same type of legal protection for adult women. They adapted the "battered child syndrome" for battered women. Many advocates believed that the male-dominated criminal justice system was ignoring the perpetuation of violence against wives in particular and women in general. The advocates were right to note, when they examined violence against women in a familial context, that physical and sexual assaults were treated differently by law enforcement and the courts. However, examination of all victims of family violence, regardless of gender, revealed that law enforcement officers and the courts did not enforce family violence in the same manner as they did violence by strangers. It was not until 1977 in Pennsylvania that the victims of domestic violence assaults could obtain legal protection from violent husband or wife in the form of specific domestic violence legislation. During the 1970s and into the 1980s, this specific form of legislation was expanded to include all family members and would include both minor and severe forms of violence (Barlow and Kauzlarich, 2002; Brownstein, 2000; Cole, 1999; Donziger, 1996; Flowers, 1996, 2000; Roberson, 2000; Schmalleger; 2005; Sherman, 1992).

A Good Idea Gone Bad

In 1981, the Minnesota's Duluth Abuse Intervention Project (DAIP) seemed to demonstrate that if the entire community worked together concerning the issue of women who were "beaten and battered," those women could be helped. DIAP and law enforcement agreed that when the police were called to a "family dispute" and discovered that a woman had been physically injured and there was probable cause concerning who actually assaulted whom, the police should have the power to make an arrest. Under those specific circumstances there should be no officer discretion concerning arrest. After the arrest, depending on the circumstances, the offender might be given the choice of going to jail or being allowed to enter a batterer's counseling program.

The theory was that if the police did make arrests, district attorneys did prosecute, and judges did pass sentences, domestic violence would then be ended or at least minimized. The fact that there were few to no studies to document that the arrest process actually did prevent any other types of crimes was either overlooked or ignored by advocates and public policy makers alike (Buzawa and Buzawa, 1996). And there is another problem that makes many contemporary domestic violence interventions a difficult process: Domestic violence was and remains different things to different people.

What Is Domestic Violence?

All 50 states now have in place various models of domestic violence statutes, laws, and intervention policies. However, few if any states have a process where there is a constant and consistent protocol between the criminal justice system and social service agencies. In fact, the majority of those in the criminal justice system do not have community-wide protocols that mandate in writing what the responsibilities of each agency should be.

Approximately half the states have mandatory arrest laws, and in those that do not the majority do have preferred arrest laws (Miller, 2004, 2005). This has not only caused the arrests of men to rise; it has caused the numbers of women arrested and charged with domestic violence to skyrocket (Wells and DeLeon-Granados, 2002).

This arrest process continues to today, despite the fact that there is still not a single definition of domestic violence that satisfies or has been agreed upon by scholars, academics, law enforcement professionals, or advocates.

What we do have in place is laws against domestic violence in all 50 states and a national condemnation of domestic violence, yet, at the same time, disagreement concerning just what we are condemning and attempting to prevent continues. Is it any wonder that numerous myths, misunderstandings, and outright denials continue to fragment and divide proper understanding of the issue?

What began as the honest effort to end wife beating and other serious forms of family violence has morphed into the criminalization of any and all forms of familial abuse among adults. In Duluth, offenders who hit, assaulted, and injured a victim were arrested. Today, someone who so much as looks at or appears in a public place near a plaintiff after a court-ordered restraining order has been issued can be arrested. Restraining orders can be so all encompassing as to demand that a suspected offender not enter a county. People who are arrested for domestic violence appear in court and are issued orders that allow them to return home and live together but are ordered not to swear or yell at each other. People are issued restraining orders that inform them if they do not pay the phone bill they will be arrested. And victims who are truly beaten and battered are becoming just another one of the thousands upon thousands of people streaming to the court system to settle many "family disputes" and divorce cases (Davis, 1998).

The Children

As in the past, children still are often not protected from physical assaults. The exception to domestic violence laws is that it continues to be lawful to beat with implements (belts, sticks, paddles) and physically assault children, familial or not, at will, while almost any act of abuse against adults, regardless of how minor (in some states just being in fear that some form of abuse might happen is sufficient), are now criminalized (RADAR, 2007).

In all 50 states, laws ensure that adults will be allowed to continue to use physical assaults (spankings, hitting with belts, etc.) to change the behavior of children. In most states, children are legally considered children until the age of 18. Thus, the legalized beating of some people (children) continues to be condoned by society and sanctioned by the courts until children reach the magic age of 18, when that same behavior is criminalized and an arrest for that same act is mandated in almost half the states (Miller, 2004; Miller, 2005; Straus, 1991).

The 21st Century

Domestic violence advocates who work in battered-women shelters, as their websites document, often claim that 95% of domestic violence victims are women. It is true that some criminal justice data from the National Institute of Justice does document that 85% of victims are women. The National Violence against Women Survey records that approximately two thirds of women and one third of men are physically assaulted by an intimate partner annually. National studies by the Family Research Laboratory at the University of New Hampshire in 1975, 1985, and 1992 details that physical abuse rates are approximately equal between husbands and wives (Finkelhor and Straus, 2006).

Many advocates and agencies individually view domestic violence victims through their own particular and singular lens. Different advocates and agencies provide different definitions of what domestic violence is and often reach conclusions based on their personal experience and perspective (Mills, 2003). Hence, domestic violence, for many, is more subjective than objective.

There continues heated disagreement among many domestic violence victim advocates concerning just what domestic violence is or is not, and they often choose to present disparate data. This disagreement has spurned what seems at times to be an endless and specious debate that domestic violence occurs (1) because of sexism and the power and control men have over women; and (2) because men and women are equally violent.

Each contention is, at least to me, a counterproductive red herring that impedes proper progress concerning assistance for victims and understanding the causes of this aberrant behavior. Why does conflicting data continue to proliferate? Who is right and who is wrong?

It should be clear to everyone that domestic violence, as the laws in all 50 states document, is not singularly and specifically violence against women, nor is it only and exclusively abusive behavior between heterosexual adult male and female intimate partners.

By statute in all 50 states, domestic violence is child, sibling, spousal, intimate partner and elder abuse. This is true, regardless of what the National Domestic Violence Hotline claims and regardless of that fact the Federal Violence Against Women Act (VAWA) continues to sponsor and fund gender-isolated and age-specific domestic violence interventions.

Although the laws are often clearly written in gender-neutral language so as not to exclude men as victims, because of their philosophic beliefs, as their websites document and similar to NICAD, the vast majority of domestic violence agencies do continue to serve adult heterosexual females primarily. And laws continue to be passed that purposely exclude children from protections provided adults under domestic violence laws.

Advocates for all victims of domestic violence deserve to have their voices heard. Is it not logical to believe that a positive inclusion of all victims, not a negative exclusion of some, will cause advocates, both male and female, to display a more compassionate and empathic response to victims and in particular to those who are most in need of resources and support? Will not the recognition that more than "just a very small number" of men are victims of domestic violence cause more men to become concerned, compassionate and supportive of all victims?

How can there be a productive debate concerning the percentage of male domestic violence victims while at the same time advocates and researchers do not agree on just what it is they are debating? It should be an undisputed fact that men should be eligible under VAWA grant funding. While some women's rights advocates deny that men are discriminated against, VAWA funding documents that of the billions that have been spent on domestic violence interventions for heterosexual women, not one dime has been spent on a specific heterosexual adult male victim intervention program.

The Beat Goes On

The majority of Americans still believe that it is appropriate for men and women—people who are big and strong—to spank children—people who are small and weak—and unnecessary to change or alter their behavior. Some other acts of violence such as hitting children with belts or other objects, corporal punishment using paddles in our schools and the almost universal condoning of sibling violence are considered legal and socially accepted as only the acts of "children being children." It is difficult for me to understand how or why most domestic violence advocates—and in fact, most Americans—do not understand that violence does beget violence and that there can be no magic age or circumstances that condone the use of violence to alter or change the behavior of others (Douglas and Straus, 2003).

An Objective View

As their websites state, many women's rights activists profess that ambition is and should be gender-neutral. Most sociologists agree that, while some "needs" may differ, females have no less a power and control "need" than males (Barnett and Rivers, 2004; Glasser, 1984; Macionis, 1997). It should be apparent that most women can be just as tough and demanding as some men.

The majority of data records and most researchers agree that, in domestic violence incidents, the more serious and injurious assaults are suffered by women (Wallace, 2002). Many studies note that more women than men suffer emotionally and economically (Straus and Ramirez, 2002). Society should focus on protecting victims of chronic violence and particularly those at the lower end of the socioeconomic educational ladder who lack resources and family support. However, this should not be interpreted to mean that women are the exclusive or primary victims of domestic violence nor should the nationally recognized domestic violence organizations, as their websites say they do, continue to minimize or ignore the victimization of men.

All data does verify that some women are abusers and some men their victims. Despite the differences and severity of abuse or the lack of agreement concerning percentages of abusers or victims, and regardless of age or gender, should not all victims receive our sympathy and compassion? Do not all victims deserve access to services and funding (Kimmel, 2002)?

Is it not time that an agreement is reached that no one, regardless of age or gender, is immune to family or intimate partner violence? Progress will be rediscovered through the inclusion not exclusion of all abusers and victims, regardless of age or gender.

A Chance To Be Heard

The vast majority of books concerning domestic violence are authored by, for example, sociologists, criminologists, attorneys, college professors, psychologists, child development specialists, psychiatrists, women's studies specialists, human development and family violence specialists, and child and adult sexual abuse prevention specialists. In short, those in academe who study the issue are considered the experts.

Police officers are often still considered by many domestic violence advocates to be their adversaries rather than their partners. Most of what has been written about law enforcement departments and officers stems from studies conducted by research concerning past events; it is extremely rate for any studies to actually listen to law enforcement officers (Buzawa and Buzawa, 2002).

One of the rare studies that took the time and effort to sit down and listen to law enforcement officers was conducted by Peter G. Sinden and B. Joyce Stephens (1999). Sinden and Stephens concluded that police officers are most often just as human and little different from anyone else. As I was then a law enforcement officer responding to domestic-violence calls, I know firsthand that many law enforcement officers in 1975 knew that violence in families was then and is now one of the most difficult calls for law enforcement to resolve.

Regardless of the facts, many advocates continue to believe that law enforcement departments systematically ignore domestic violence perpetrated by their own officers. Some advocates claim that law enforcement departments often deny protection to women who are domestic violence victims at the hands of law enforcement officers (Wallace, 2002). Some advocates continue to profess that law enforcement officers routinely ignore domestic violence, that they are trained to be deceptive and manipulative, and that law enforcement officers are trained to beat and batter without leaving any bruises or broken bones (Wetendorf, 2007).

While it is true that some officers within law enforcement do fit these criteria, to claim that departments train their officers in this behavior or that this behavior is exhibited simply because these abusive officers are law enforcement officers is without empirical justification.

The majority of law enforcement officers agree that their intervention in domestic violence is a formidable but necessary process. Most law enforcement departments have multidisciplinary policies, procedures, and training concerning domestic violence that far exceed most other vocations—public or private. Most law enforcement officers, including myself, are married and have a deep and abiding love and concern for their wives, daughters, and sons.

Discussion

1. Explain why and what you believe should be the nationally accepted definition of domestic violence.
2. Should domestic violence interventions be limited to the aberrant behavior exhibited between couples in romantic or intimate relationships?
3. Should the feminist movement focus on equal rights or women's rights?
4. Are men and women equally violent? State specifically what your definition of *violence* is.
5. What is the greatest failing in the debate about domestic violence?

Domestic Violence and Violent Behavior in General

2

Criminality refers to the propensity to use force and fraud in the pursuit of self-interest.

—**Barlow and Kauzlarich**

Introduction

Similar to criminality in general, domestic violence varies in seriousness, chronicity, and frequency (Hendricks, McKean, and Hendricks, 2002, p. 185). Not only criminals use coercive behavior—compulsion, force, intimidation, bullying, oppression, cruelty or duress—in the pursuit of self-interest. If society is honest enough, a mirror will reveal that often many of us, regardless of age, gender, or sexual orientation, put our own self-interest ahead of the interest of others (Myers, 2004).

The degrees of force or fraud are often in the eyes of the beholder and can become subject to interpretation by others. Adults, often as unwitting role models, teach children at a tender age how to use coercion or physical force to get their own way. As adults, the children will then replicate that behavior and pass it on to their own offspring.

After centuries of condoning or ignoring the physical and sexual assaultive behavior by those in familial or intimate relationships, important progress was made toward the end of the 20th century. However, there continue numerous half-truths, misconceptions, and outright denial that fragment consensus and impede progress (Wallace, 2002).

Many ideological red herrings hinder progress concerning resources and assistance for all victims. There is now a schism between men's and women's rights groups regarding agreement on the cause and consequences of this aberrant behavior. This separation hurts all victims of domestic violence regardless of age, gender, or sexual orientation and needs to be set aside (Dutton, 2006).

Holding on to one position and disregarding all others not only causes one to ignore reality, it requires that one must make the conscious choice to disregard reams of national studies, research, and data that disavows and disputes all single stand-alone grand theories. The issue of domestic violence should not be one of women's or men's rights but rather of victim's rights regardless of age, gender, or sexual orientation.

A Blind Eye

In *Understanding Violence Against Women*, (Crowell and Burgess, 1996, p. 4) the authors note, "Although there appear to be some similarities and some differences between generally violent behavior and violence directed at women, the extent of the similarities and differences remain unknown." Contemporarily, the studies that do document violence against males by females are not reflected in public policy in general and in batterer-intervention programs in particular.

By virtue of its specific goal, the Violence Against Women Office explores only or primarily violence against women, not violence against intimate partners, family members, acquaintances, or violence in general. Neither the similarities nor the differences will be discovered through the efforts of the Violence Against Women Office. One only needs to read the name to understand that the Violence Against Women Office has little interest in violence against men.

The on-line Federal Bureau of Investigation (FBI) Supplemental Homicide Report (FBI, 2006) defines intimate or family members as relatives, step-relatives, in-laws, and common-law or ex-spouses. This definition is similar to the majority of state statute law definitions of domestic violence. Neither the federal government nor any of the states define domestic violence as only violence against adult heterosexual women by adult heterosexual men (Miller, 2005).

The ideals of objectivity (personal neutrality), value-free scientific research, and relationships among variables are compromised and ignored by many researchers because of VAWA "gender-specific" funding (Macionis, 1997). It also appears that, because of the billions in federal funding, domestic violence advocates, as their websites clearly document, are concerned about violence against females and not males.

Most, if not all, of the $4.9 billion under VAWA is being spent on efforts to create a safer society only for women and girls (Kruttschnitt, McLaughlin, and Petrie, 2004). The fact that violence against women and girls is being addressed by the federal government is laudable and deserving of praise. However, the expenditure of the $4.9 billion is being allotted thus despite the findings from the National Violence Against Women Survey (NVAWS) that document that 40% of women and 53.8% of men report they were physically assaulted by a parent, stepparent, or other adult caretaker as a child.

This data concerning male victimization would not have been known if the authors of the NVAWA had their way. It was the original intent of the authors of this survey, as the title notes, to be inclusive of women and to exclude men (Dutton, 2006).

The NVAWS estimates that 1.9 million women and 3.2 million men are physically assaulted annually (Tjaden and Thoennes, 2000b, p. ii). It also documents the annual rate of intimate partner assaults was 44.2 per 1,000 women and 31.5 per 1,000 men (ibid., p. iii). From 1976 to 1996, 31,260 women and 20,311 men were murdered by an intimate partner. During that same time period, more African Americans males were murdered by an intimate partner than African American females (Greenfeld, 1998).

Regardless of these facts, the majority of domestic violence advocates and public policy makers claim that males commit from 85% to 95% of all domestic violence assaults. The previous facts also do not prevent the National Domestic Violence Hotline (NDVH) website from claiming that 92% of all victims of domestic violence are women. This and similar websites state that the vast majority of domestic violence organizations and agencies similar to the NDVH have decided to place the interests of adult heterosexual women ahead of the interests of all victims regardless of age, gender, or sexual orientation. While the NDVH claims it is concerned about all victims, the exclusion of male victimization on its website speaks volumes about its real agenda and lack of empathy for male victimization.

A Deaf Ear

The National Conference on Family Violence: Health and Justice convened in March of 1994, 10 years after the first Attorney General's Task Force on Family Violence, noted that the problem of family violence in the United States is epidemic (Witwer and Crawford, 1995). The conference estimated that the annual incidence of abuse of family members is at 2 to 4 million for children, nearly 4 million for women, and 1 to 2 million for elder adults. An inference can be drawn that among the children and elder statistics that some of the victims are male. An inference might also be drawn that if there are 4 million women who are victims there must be 4 million men who are offenders and no men who are victims.

At this conference there were 400 professionals and 80 national experts. And, while data from the criminal justice system and many public and private studies document that men can be victims of domestic violence, these professionals or national "experts" seemed unwilling or unable to note a single adult male as being a victim of domestic violence.

Too often when domestic violence advocates and public policy makers are confronted with data that is not consistent with what they believe (men are the perpetrators and women their victims) the domestic violence organization websites and legislation passed by our public policy makers indicate that data that is inclusive of all victims is simply ignored. Too often, public perception causes public policy makers to disregard reality and thus ideological desires and assumptions continue to drive domestic violence public policy (Kruttschnitt et al., 2004).

In fact, Tjaden and Thoennes (2000b, p. iii) note, "The data shows that violence is more widespread and injurious to women's and men's health than previously thought, an important finding for legislators, policymakers, intervention planners, and researchers as well as the public health and criminal justice communities." Why is it then that the majority of domestic violence public policy does not reflect the effect domestic violence victimization has on men?

It should be profoundly troubling that so many domestic violence advocates and our public policy makers continue to ignore research that could contribute to a safer world for everyone regardless of age, gender, or sexual orientation. It is more troubling that so many continue to use ideological-based, rather than evidence-based, research, to make our daughters safe and at the same time continue to paint our sons with the single large brush of abusers.

Domestic Violence

Reams of data document that the vast majority of men and women are not violently abusive toward each other. Most interactions between strangers or family members are devoid of violence (Fletcher, 2002).

Domestic violence advocates used to claim (in fact, some still do) that 95% of domestic violence was committed by men against women. This figure is from the old version of the National Crime Victimization survey (NCVS), which was flawed and is no longer used. Domestic violence advocates now claim that 85% of domestic violence abusers are males. This figure, based on crime data from the new NCVS, appears in federal documents and on many federally sponsored domestic violence websites. It is both enlightening and troubling to note that domestic violence advocates and our public policy makers readily accept the 85% figure from the NCVS while at the same time they ignore the assault data of 44.2 per 1,000 women and 31.5 per 1,000 men from the same survey.

The National Institute of Justice (NIJ) is the lead agency involved with the research and presentation of the NCVS and the NVAWS. Why is it that domestic violence advocates and public policy makers do not recognize and question those dramatic differences?

What is also ignored by both is that the NCVS records that between January 1992 and June 1998, half of 1% of 529,829 households report at least one incident of domestic violence (Dugan, 2003). Domestic violence advocates and public policy makers cannot rationally claim that domestic violence is a problem of epidemic proportions and worthy of $4.9 billion if they accept the half of 1% finding, so it is simply ignored.

Perhaps it is time for the NIJ to sponsor a study that can document the reason that some NCVS data is accepted as fact by the majority of domestic violence advocates and public policy makers and other NCVS data is ignored.

Most of the aforementioned victims are reporting physical assaults. Women are more likely than men to report physical assaults in general or domestic violence physical assaults. A recent study reveals that men are far more reluctant than women to report assaults by their intimate partners (Felson and Cares, 2005). Other studies show that the majority of serious (injurious and lethal) domestic violence is perpetrated by men and the majority of the injuries and deaths are suffered by women. However, most studies also document that women are as—or more—likely than men to use assertive, aggressive, coercive behavior, and physical assaults in domestic disputes. (Archer, 2000; Barnett and Rivers, 2004).

Most professionals and ideological advocates agree that psychological pain can hurt as much as physical pain, regardless of age, gender, or sexual orientation. The majority of domestic violence advocates understand that one does not necessarily need to have a broken nose or blackened eyes to be considered a victim of domestic violence. Data clearly documents that domestic violence is not, as many domestic violence advocates continue to proclaim, a rare event for males.

Why They Do It

People use violent behavior (the use of physical force or coercion) for three basic reasons (Felson, 2002):

1. To change or alter the behavior of another in order to suit their own purposes
2. Revenge, retribution, jealousy, or seeking justice for a real or perceived wrong
3. To defend or advance their perceived standing in the family or community

A few examples are as follows:

- Violence or coercion is used by all members of families and intimate partners regardless of age, gender, or sexual orientation, as well as bank robbers or other criminals to force other people to act against their will.

- Violence or coercion is used by jealous persons for real or perceived wrongs to "get even" for crimes committed by others as well as by members of gangs or others in the community.
- Violence or coercion is used by individuals, regardless of age, gender, or sexual orientation to maintain or advance their real or perceived "role" in the family or community.

The relative risk of offending and the percentage of victimization of intimate partners and strangers is not equal for everyone (Kruttschnitt et al., 2004). Risk factors significantly rise and fall with the socioeconomic and educational status of either the victim or the offender (Flowers, 2000). Risk factors are habits, traits, conditions, or characteristics that are likely to increase, yet not cause, the occurrence of any event. The more empirically based risk factors (they must be real and statistically relevant) that are present the more likely the event will occur.

The risk factors of offending and victimization differ by age. This is true for both domestic violence and violence in general. Younger people experience more nonfatal violence in general than older people (Klaus and Rennison, 2002). However, it is the risk factors present for some at that age and not the age in general that is of most importance.

Data from the NVAWS reveals that people are just as likely to report incidents of domestic violence assaults as they are to report assaults by other people they know but are not related to or involved with in an intimate relationship (Felson and Pare, 2005).

All NIJ data clearly documents that the rate for both offending and victimization for most crimes is higher and more severe in economically disadvantaged neighborhoods. The NIJ report "When Violence Hits Home" clearly documents that it is the same for intimate partner violence (Benson and Fox, 2004). The report also finds that, similar to street crimes, African Americans are more likely than whites in these neighborhoods to be offenders and victims of intimate partner violence (ibid.). However, the same report notes, as do many others from the NIJ website, that socioeconomic and educational demographics are often far more important then ethnic or racial differences.

The majority of criminologists acknowledge that more men than women commit crimes, however, they also understand that crime rates for both crime in general and domestic violence in particular are strongly correlated (Moffit, Krueger, Caspi, and Fagan, 2000). In so-called high-crime neighborhoods both crime in general and domestic violence in particular increase proportionally for both men and women (Zuger, 1998).

Crime Statistics

Male vs. Female Involvement in Crimes

Crime	Male (%)	Female (%)
Rape	98.5	1.5
Robbery	89.0	11.0
Murder/Manslaughter	88.4	11.6
Burglary	85.7	14.3
Motor Vehicle Theft	82.9	17.1
Arson	83.5	16.5
Aggravated Assault	79.3	20.7
Forgery/Counterfeiting	60.2	39.8
Larceny/Theft	61.7	38.3
Fraud	55.1	44.9
Embezzlement	50.4	49.6

Source: Federal Bureau of Investigation Uniform Crime Report (2004) (http://www.fbi.gov/ucr/cius_04/documents/CIUS_2004_Section4.pdf)

Such crime data show that *males* are more likely than females to be arrested for violent or serious crimes such as murder, rape, robbery and burglary and that males exhibit more "violent" behavior than females. The data also show that the less violent the crime, the more likely females are to become involved in criminal behavior. It may be that the criminality differential between males and females has been defined more by size, strength, a belief that they can succeed and peer acceptance of that behavior than it is by ethical and moral reasoning.

It also appears that, as the societal role of females has changed over the last few decades, so has the propensity of females to commit crimes. Between 1970 and 2000, the number of crimes in general committed by men increased by 46%, while crimes committed by women increased by 144%. Violent crimes by men increased by 85% during that same period, and violent crimes by women increased by 260% (Schmalleger, 2007, p.110).

Contemporarily, as the National Violence Against Women Survey (NVAWS) shows, most domestic violence incidents consist of minor physical assaults and, as the majority of the nationally recognized domestic violence organizations note, domestic violence incidents can be verbal, emotional, or financial acts.

The table shows that males are more *violent* than females. However, domestic *violence* often involves verbal abuse or coercive behavior. Domestic violence is not always about *physically violent* behavior. And the crime data also shows that females in increasing numbers seem more willing and able to exhibit some aberrant criminal behavior in numbers equal to those of males.

Ellen Goodman (2004) wonders:

> How long will it take us to get over the stereotypes of women as exclusively peaceful, nurturing, empathic ... . Only when the stereotype becomes dangerous to society? When the social constraints are off—surely when women are rewarded for violence—they can mimic the worst behavior of men.

Caryl Rivers, the co-author of *Same Difference* (Barnett and Rivers, 2004), presents data that show that, "It's a fantasy that women are so much more caring and empathetic than men. In all the systematic research, men and women come out about equal."

Homicides

Most murders are not committed by strangers; they are committed by intimates, family members, or acquaintances. This is true for both men and women. From 1981 to 2,000, 149,510 males and 61,198 females were murdered by an intimate, a family member, or an acquaintance. During that same time period 49,424 males and 8,518 females were murdered by a stranger.

In 1980, the on-line FBI Supplementary Homicide Reports (FBI, 2006) documents that 2,094 males and 1,609 females were murdered by a family member or intimate. In 2,000, 928 males and 1,133 females were murdered by a family member or intimate.

Females account for 24% of the total number of all homicide victims. Of that general total, approximately 30% of females are murdered by a husband or intimate partner (FBI Supplementary Homicide Reports, 1976–2000). The majority of males and females are not murdered by a spouse or intimate partner.

Approximately one third of family murders involved a female as the murderer. In sibling murders, females account for 15% and in the murder of parents they account for 18%. In spousal killings, women represent 41% of the murders. In the murder of their biological children, women account for 55%. Among black spouses, wives were just as likely to kill their husbands as the other way around (Dawson and Lagan, 1994).

National Institute of Justice data document that the highest rate of intimate partner murders—similar to murder rates in general—are in the South and Southwest. The highest number of acquaintance murders, murders by strangers, and murders where the offender is unknown are also higher in the South and Southwest.

In the NIJ study *Homicide in Eight U.S. Cities: Trends, Context, and Policy Implications* (Lattimore, Riley, Trudeau, Leiter, and Edwards, 1997), the researchers report that female homicide victimization occurred at such low rates relative to male homicide victimization that the changes in female victimization over the period of the study accounted for little of the overall fluctuation of the homicide trends.

Between 1976 and 1996, 64% of female intimate partner victims were killed by their husbands, 5% by ex-husbands and 32% by partners or boyfriends. Of male victims, 62% were killed by their wives, 4% by ex-wives and 34% by partners or girlfriends. From 1976 to 1996 31,260 women and 20,311 men were murdered by an intimate partner (Greenfeld, 1998).

The SHC documents that between 1980 and 2000, 28,586 females were the victims of a homicide by a family member or intimate. During that same period, there were 31,509 male victims. The yearly decrease in intimate or family homicides during this period for both males and females is reflective of the decrease in the total number of all homicides, regardless of relationship, nationwide.

While the percentage of intimate partner homicide victimization for males appears to be much smaller than females, it is because the total male victimization of homicides in general is so much higher. In fact, the total of male intimate or family homicides is often higher than that of females in urban settings. For example, in Washington, D.C. the percent of all homicides for males was 2% and for females it was 15%. However, the average number of intimate or family homicides for males was 7.3 and females 6.7 (Lattimore et al., 1997).

While murder is the most serious of crimes, it is also the least common (Hendricks et al., 2003). The Bureau of Justice Statistics report "Family Violence Statistics: Including Statistics on Strangers and Acquaintances" (Durose et. al, 2005) reports that murder accounts for less than half of 1% of all family violence between 1998 and 2002). The Bureau of Justice Statistics factbook "Violence by Intimates" documents that intimate partner violence accounts for about one fifth of the total violence against females (Greenfeld, 1998).

The total number of men who murder is statistically insignificant when compared with the total population of males. What the homicide and suicide data do document is that men kill other men and themselves in numbers far greater than they kill women.

The data clearly indicate that a small subgroup of men commit homicides far more often than a small subgroup of women. However, it is both illogical and irrational to attempt to generalize the behavior of a very small subgroup of any population toward the behavior of the population in general. Men who murder their intimate partners cannot be used to generalize or infer that their behavior is representative of the behavior of the majority of men anymore than criminals who murder can be used to generalize the behavior of the majority of criminals.

A Distinct Model for Murder

Most, but certainly not all, domestic violence homicides are committed by individuals who have histories of criminal behavior, long histories of violent and aberrant behavior inside and outside the family, were abused as children, or suffer from alcohol or substance abuse (Greenfeld, 1998). NIJ data reveals that the same is true for murders by acquaintances, strangers, and where the offender is unknown.

Individuals who do not have histories of criminal behavior and commit a much smaller number of domestic violence homicides often appear to be people who display extreme narcissistic behavior or pathological jealousy, become extremely depressed at the prospect of losing their partner, and blame their intimate partners for the loss of their economic standing or professional and personal esteem in the community (Daly and Wilson, 1988). Approximately one out of every four domestic violence homicides also involves a suicide.

On the last day of each year, the *Boston Globe* lists the names of people who lost their lives as a result of domestic violence. Each year the *Globe* excludes those lives lost at their own hands. In 2003 there were 13 incidents in Massachusetts that resulted in domestic violence homicides. Five of the 13 involved homicide-suicides (*Boston Globe*, Dec. 31, 2003).

The editors of the *Globe* do acknowledge that the homicide-suicides involve many people who feel helpless and hopeless and are profoundly troubled. However, the editors and the domestic violence advocates who provide the *Globe* with the names of those who die as a result of domestic violence ignore these deaths. Despite the fact that these offenders took the lives of others along with their own, their suicides are the direct results of domestic violence and they will be mourned and missed by those who loved them.

Power and Control

It is generally recognized that the issues of unequal power, control, and economic resources can influence any violent act, not just violence against women. While there continues to be an ongoing effort to explain violence against women as being caused by gender inequality, data show that it most often shares the same common community characteristics and variables as violence in general (Kruttschnitt et al., 2004). Power and control issues are not unique to violence against women. It is generally agreed that the issue of unequal power, control, and resources affects abuse of child, sibling, spouse, intimate partner, or elders, regardless of the age, gender, or sexual orientation of the offender (Chalk and King, 1998).

These same issues of power and control affect violence in general (Brownstein, 2000). A robber uses the power of a gun to control the behavior of the store clerk to get the money the robber wants. In crime in general and in family violence, power and control are most often the means to a goal, not the goal itself.

Both men and women have an equal interest in power. In fact, the feminist movement is founded on the belief of establishing "an equal playing field" (i.e., equal power for both males and females). An equal playing field allows women to have the same "power" men do in society. As societies became more complex and structured, a small number of men and some women gained power over most other men and the majority of women. However, at the same time, in all hierarchal societies many women held positions of power over many men. Power in these societies was not equally distributed and, while it is true most women remained subservient to some men, a great many men were subservient to those women. As history texts reveal, the belief that all women have been subservient to all men is a historical myth.

Simply because history records that some men have retained the majority of social and economic power, most often because of their physicality, this does not mean that women will behave any differently from men once they become more powerful (Glasser, 1984). History documents that most often when some women do have power they behave much the same as some men (Barnett and Rivers, 2004).

Most violence in general and family violence acts in particular involve power, domination, and threats to harm that indicate that the offender intends to impose predetermined outcomes on strangers or family members (Felson, 2002). Obviously, those predetermined outcomes are designed to be beneficial for the offender. Those who are successful with this behavior will use it more often than those who are not.

The reasons or causes for violence within the family most often reflect the various theories concerning violence in general (Brownstein, 2000). The majority of characteristics and variables of domestic violence are similar to those of violence in general (Hendricks et al., 2003).

The vast majority of risk factors for offending and victimization for domestic violence and violence in general are strikingly similar. In fact, many researchers, criminologists, and law enforcement professionals question whether any risk factors are exclusive to intimate-partner violence or are specific to violence in general (Moffitt and Caspi, 1999).

Opportunity and Ability

The issues that most often cause one to decide to use force to achieve a goal are opportunity and ability coupled with the chances of success (Barlow and Kauzlarich, 2002). The reasons for the use of violent behaviors are little different regardless of relationships or the gender of either the offender or the victim.

Women are less successful using physical assaults and violence than men to achieve specific goals. Women, as the Bureau of Justice statistics document, rarely use violence concerning sexually assertive behavior. Most women understand that, because of their lack of physical strength and size, violent behavior may not produce positive outcomes for them. However, many studies now show that females are as likely as males to use low level forms of physical aggression or coercive behavior to achieve their goals (Mills, 2003).

Criminal justice data show that men in general are not violent against women in particular. In fact, criminal justice data indicate that men are far more violent against other men than against women. Some men are more violent than others and some women are more violent than some men (Ghiglieri, 1999). When confronted with the reality that far more women physically assault and maltreat children than men, the reason most often offered is that more children reside with women than with men (Flowers, 2000). Women abuse children because the children are there. The "there factor" and the fact that women are often bigger and stronger than their children and control the resources in the family provides women with both the opportunity and ability coupled with the chance of success.

In 1968, sociologist William Goode, when asked why relatives, spouses, lovers, and close friends commit violence against each other, he replied, "Perhaps the most powerful if crude answer is that they are there" (Daly and Wilson, p. 21, 1988). A folk lore or an urban myth is that when Willie Sutton was asked why he robbed banks, he replied because that is where the money is.

Both women and men are more physically violent against the opposite sex in the home than in public. Similarly, both groups are more physically violent toward children and elders in the home than they are in public.

The on-line National Archive of Criminal Justice Data (NACJD) at the University of Michigan documents that, by percentage of total violent crime, men are victims more often than women. Criminal justice data from the above site also indicates that women report being victims in the home more than men. However, given the totality of crime by women, women commit a greater percentage of their violence in the home than do men.

NACJD data documents that males resort to physical assaults more than females do to settle disputes and conflicts. Few researchers argue against the fact that in domestic violence incidents women suffer more serious injuries and sexual assaults than men.

Many studies show that women suffer more serious injuries psychologically and economically than men (Crowell and Burgess, 1996). However, this should not mean that violence against men and boys should be ignored or that the use of violence by women should be minimized, legitimatized, or excused simply because male offenders suffer—percentage-wise—from less serious injury (Kelly, 2003).

It Is Not Always One Or the Other

Violence by strangers, friends, family or intimate partners can be expressive, instrumental, or a combination of both. Expressive or affective violence rises from feelings of anger, rage, or hate. Instrumental or cognitive violence is when an offender uses force to achieve short- or long-term goals.

Spanking is often presented by parents and others who approve of it as an instrumental or cognitive decision. The majority of its proponents claim that spanking is used only for compliance or behavioral modification. However, most studies report that parents are most often "upset and angry" when they spank a child (expressive or affective). Is it not logical to believe that regardless of the age, gender, or sexual orientation of the offender or victim, that violence can be expressive and affective or instrumental and cognitive; in fact, it can often be a combination of both (Hendricks et al., 2003).

Violence intervention and prevention efforts must be based on the fact that domestic violence can present itself in a number of different shapes and forms. History records that any belief system that proclaims it alone holds the "single and ultimate truth" breeds intolerance and extremism. Remaining stuck at either end of any paradigm serves only to hinder a balanced and proper understanding of the issue.

The Fallacious Argument

Since the late 1970s an argument has continued over studies that may or may not document how women and men are equally victimized by their intimate partners (Tjaden and Thoennes, 2000b). This argument is fallacious because few domestic violence advocates, researchers, and scholars agree on just what *domestic violence* is, what *violence* is, or what an *injury* is. It is inconceivable how this argument, lacking any agreed upon definition of terms, continues unabated.

Domestic violence advocates do an injustice to all victims when they claim that one out of every three women is abused or half of all married women will be abused. They lump together victims of chronic and severe beatings with surveys that document whether a woman has ever suffered any emotional or physical abuse. The number of women and men who believe they have been emotional abused, pushed, or slapped by an intimate partner differs dramatically from those who suffer broken noses and blackened eyes.

The vast majority of researchers and scholars agree with Deborah Capaldi, Donald Dutton, Jeffery Fagan, Richard Gelles, Linda Mills, and Terrie Moffitt, to name only a few, that both women and men can be domestic violence offenders, victims and sometimes both. These researchers and scholars also agree that a substantial number of women's assaultive acts against their male partners cannot be explained away only or primarily as acts of self-defense (Dutton, 1996). Those researchers who do attempt to explain away women's assaultive acts as self-defense can only note that studies *suggest* that theory is true and they do not provide empirical data (White and Smith, 2001).

The measuring tool used by most researchers and scholars for violent acts is the Conflict Tactics Scales (CTS), which can be found on the Internet (Straus, 2007). The CTS measures the physical abuse from minor to severe. Most researchers and scholars, including those above, agree that, in chronic and severe relationship violence, men are more likely to be the primary perpetrators and women the primary victims (Kwong, Bartholomew, and Dutton, 1999).

Concerning sexual violence, the NVAWS estimates that 302,091 women and 92,748 men were raped in the 12 months prior to the survey administration (Tjaden and Thoennes, 2000b). According to a survey of high school students, the Youth Risk Behavior Surveillance System (YRBSS) documents that 11.9% of female students and 6.1% of male students report having been sexually assaulted (Grunbaum et al., 2004).

The Wellspring of Violent Behavior

A society that often condones and legitimizes the use of physical force, violence, and economic dominance as a proper means of behavior modification should not be surprised that many of its children will find rationalizations for that same type of behavior as adults. Approximately 97% of 3-year-olds, 49% of 13-year-olds, and 34% of 15- to 17-year-olds experience physical abuse for behavioral modification at the hands of their parents (Straus and Gelles, 1990).

The first lesson children often learn, both inside and outside of the home, is that power and control, both physical and economic, do matter. Studies show that physical bullying or emotionally abusive incidents are equally engaged in by both boys and girls (Thompson, Grace, and Cohen, 2001).

Researchers need to explore the link between violent victimization of boys and girls by adults and similar violent offending as adults (Kruttschnitt, McLaughlin, and Petrie, 2004). Regardless of age, some of the domestic violence and violent behavior in general is deliberate and instrumental while others are spontaneous and irresponsible (Daly and Wilson, 1988).

In the early 1970s Samuel Yochelson and Stanton E. Samenow, who were not researching information about domestic violence, produced their classic multivolume work titled *The Criminal Personality* (Yochelson and Samenow, 1976). They were concerned with determining what behaviors chronic criminals shared. And, as it often happens in empirical studies, the results surprised researchers as much as others.

Yochelson and Samenow (1976) identified 53 patterns of thought and action that they said were present in all 255 offenders they studied: "They described criminals as untrustworthy, demanding and exploitive of others, with little capacity for love. Habitual offenders were said to harbor a persistent anger, which could boil over at any time" (Schmalleger, 1999 p. 113). Most, but not all, criminals and domestic violence abusers exhibit similar behavior. They believe their needs are more important than the needs of others. Many demonstrate a lack of empathy and compassion for others.

Most criminals and domestic violence abusers exhibit different behavior in private from what they show in public. Many have learned when not to exhibit their aggression, violence, and anger. Most criminals and domestic violence abusers do not exhibit antisocial or violent behavior unless they have reason to believe that the results will be positive and beneficial for them.

Victims and Offenders

In the classic study of criminal violent behavior of adult males, *Delinquency in a Birth Cohort* (Wolfgang, Figlio, and Sellin, 1987), it was revealed that approximately 6% of violent chronic criminals account for about 70% of all violent crime in America (Ghiglieri, 1999).

A survey of criminal offenders (both men and women) documents that .05% of those who reported assaults accounted for 68% of the total number of reported physical and sexual assaults (Fletcher, 2002). A Massachusetts Department of Probation study reports that almost one out of every four people who have restraining orders issued against them are repeat offenders who often abuse multiple victims. Approximately 91% of these serial or chronic domestic violence abusers have appeared before juvenile or adult courts for past criminal behavior (Adams, 1999).

An NIJ report, "The Effects of Arrest on Intimate Partner Violence: New Evidence From the Spouse Assault Replication Program," documents that 8% of victims of domestic violence reported repeat victimization that accounted for more than 82% of the 9,000 incidents studied (Maxwell, Garner, Fagan, 2001).

Small numbers of offenders account for the majority of the offenses and small numbers of victims account for most of the victimization. Concentration of specific sanctions and programs concerning this small number of offenders and victims could cause a dramatic decrease in the total number of incidents.

Time for Change

Nations, communities, and individuals will use force and fraud to ensure their basic needs are met. Research concerning domestic violence must examine more closely how human behavior is affected from a Darwinian (the powerful over the weak) perspective and explore Maslow's hierarchy of needs (Maslow, 1971; Macionis, 1997). Following the need of water and food is the need for safety and security. Maslow's hierarchy of needs is gender neutral.

At the heart and core of the 2004 American presidential election was the issue of who could best provide for the safety of the nation. It appeared that for many millions of Americans all other issues paled in importance. There is a need to further explore the connection between our genes and our behavior (Burnham and Phelan, 2000). This is true for violence in general and domestic violence in particular. History and science document that the strong most often exhibit behavior that is intended to dominate the weak, probably to ensure that their particular group has sufficient food and water and is safe and secure.

The National Research Council (NRC), in its report to Congress, concludes that there is no evidence that shows that violence between intimates is dramatically different from violence in general (Kruttschnitt et al., 2004). Public policy makers need to understand that gender-specific ideology explores only half an issue and provides only half an answer. Domestic violence policies are needed that reflect the causes and consequences found in numerous empirical research studies and findings (Felson and Pare, 2005).

The NRC report agrees with the vast majority of scientific empirical studies and concludes that while there are some distinctions in the context and consequences of the violence, the patterns of behavior that cause the violence are little different from violence in general. The racial, cultural, socioeconomic, and educational backgrounds of different groups of people have the same dramatic effects on whether people will be offenders or victims of domestic violence and violence in general (Benson and Fox, 2004).

The NRC report, as well as most researchers and scholars, concludes that much of the violence women perpetrate cannot and should not be dismissed as primarily defensive. There is little doubt that some women can be and are just as assertive and aggressive and violent as some men (Barnett and Rivers, 2004). The majority of the perpetrators of domestic violence, regardless of gender, have histories of violence and behavioral problems both inside and outside of intimate relationships (Kruttschnitt et al., 2004). Quibbling over the percentage differences between males and females concerning domestic violence is more harmful than helpful for all victims of all forms of violence.

The NRC concludes, as have many other researchers and scholars, that until the civil and criminal justice systems agree on just what is an *injury*, what is an act of *violence*, what is an act of *abuse*, and what is *battering*, the contemporary contentious disagreement, confusion, discussion, and disarray about who does what will continue unabated.

Given all of these facts it is time to create a common non-gender-specific understanding that domestic violence encompasses child, sibling, spousal, intimate partner, and elder abuse. All anti-violence efforts need to explore both the lethal and non-lethal risk factors faced by females and males, both as offenders and victims (Lauritsen and White, 2001).

Because of their commonalities, interventions for both crime in general and domestic violence in particular should focus sanctions and programs first and foremost toward the small number of chronic offenders who account for the preponderance of violent incidents. Very small numbers of chronic repeat offenders of crime in general and domestic violence in particular can and do wreak havoc inside and outside of their homes (Fletcher, 2002).

Because of limited resources, assistance should be provided first for high-risk individuals, regardless of age, gender, or sexual orientation, who are marginalized by their socioeconomic and educational status and who lack familial resources and support.

Where Violence Occurs

The definitive domestic violence crime is domestic violence homicide. For the year 2,000 the Supplemental Homicide Report (SHR) documents that among intimates or family members the number of females murdered by another intimate or family member is 1,133 and males is 928. The report, because of its finality, is absolutely and completely bias-free data, and it documents that the home can be a dangerous place for both females and males.

For the same year, among acquaintances the number of females murdered is 1,320 and males 3,581 and the number of females murdered by strangers is 274 and males 1,759. The majority of all these murders of females or males are committed by people who have histories of criminal behavior. These people, whether intimates or family, acquaintance or strangers, represent the minority not the majority of males and females in our society.

For the total number of intimate, family, acquaintance and stranger murders, a male is more likely to be the murderer than a female. However, males murder other males and themselves far more than they murder females. And the SHR documents that females murder males more often than they murder females.

The intimate or family relationship appears to be an equally safe place for both males and females. The family is where, by far, the smallest numbers of murders are committed. However, Bureau of Justice (BJS) data show the majority of female murderers will murder an intimate or family member far more often than a stranger or casual acquaintance (Durose et al., 2005).

Some people use homicide statistics to claim that because more women are murdered by intimates or family members or acquaintances than strangers, then the home must be the most dangerous place for females. The data seems to indicate that women are safer on the streets of our communities than in their homes. This brings to mind the old adage, "There are lies, greater lies and then there are statistics."

More people each year will fall and injure themselves in their homes than in hotel rooms. Most automobile accidents each year occur in state rather than out of state. More Americans will be killed in airplane accidents in the United States than overseas.

Do these statistics mean that our homes are more dangerous than hotel rooms, is driving in state is more dangerous than driving out of state, or that flying in the United States is more dangerous than flying overseas? Similar to all of these incidents, murder is all about the frequency of venue and opportunity.

One very apparent behavioral distinction is murder-suicides. A suicide following an acquaintance or stranger murder is exceptionally rare. However, one out of every four domestic violence homicides results in a suicide. Those who murder and then take their own lives are almost always men.

The *Bureau of Justice Statistics Sourcebook* (Maguire and Pastore, 2002) clearly documents that men are engaged in crime and violent activity in the community far more often than most women. It then only stands to reason that men will violently physically assault and murder at rates higher than women both inside and outside the home (Barkan and Snowden, 2001). In both crime in general and domestic violence in particular a small number of offenders will account for the vast majority of offenses, regardless of gender. These violent people do not alter or change their behavior once they are behind the closed doors of their homes (Maguire and Pastore, 2002).

The home is the venue of domestic violence incidents, not the cause. NIJ data documents that in 74% of familial murders, the murderer has a prior criminal record of arrest or conviction. In fact, 44% of the victims also had a prior criminal record. Women and children suffer far fewer physical assaults and murders because they, far more often than men, do not have the ability or the frequency of successful opportunity.

Conclusion

Just as there is with crime in general, there are dramatic differences in the reporting of domestic violence between affluent and educated victims and victims with little education and who are impoverished. The causal factors for crime in general and domestic violence are far more similar than they are different (Moffit et al., 2000).

Domestic violence advocates claim that the primary reason for those dramatic differences in the reporting of domestic violence is that affluent or educated people have the economic resources or educational wherewithal to deal privately with the issue of being abused. Some advocates believe that the abuse is about the same for the affluent and educated as it is for the impoverished and less educated.

However, the victims of domestic violence homicides regardless of social or economic standing, reflect the same dramatic differences found in the reporting of non-fatal abuse. Such victims have no choice in reporting their victimization. This homicide data is a hard cold fact and is the numbers are very similar to those of non-fatal victimization.

In fact, NIJ data shows that, given the total percentage of violence women commit, both in the home and in the community, women commit more violence in the home and against males than they do in the community. NIJ data also documents that, given the total percentage of violence, men commit most of their violence against other males and in the community rather than in the home against females.

Other than venue or place and the fact that family and intimate partner murders most often occur after a history of violent or emotionally volatile behavior between family members, there appear to be far more similarities than difference in the dynamics or the reasons for the use and purpose of violent behavior in general and domestic violence in particular. The claim that women are being murdered because of sexism and the power and control men want to exert over women lacks even a single empirical study that can document data to prove that claim.

Very simply put, people use violent behavior in general and domestic violence behavior in particular because they want to change or alter the behavior of others to benefit themselves. The data from the NIJ documents that the vast majority of people who use violent behavior in general and domestic violence behavior in particular represent a subgroup of population and not the population in general, regardless of age, gender, or sexual orientation.

Discussion Questions

1. Statistics are often distorted to promote a specific agenda. The National Violence Against Women Survey and the National Domestic Violence Hotline use dramatically different statistics to portray the same intimate partner abuse phenomenon. What policy implications does this divergence have for local, state, and federal legislators? What can be done to move the domestic violence scholars, researchers, and advocates

away from bickering over statistics to constructive dialogue focused on finding actionable solutions?

2. So much of the focus of the domestic violence scholars, researchers, and advocates is directed toward those abuses perpetrated by adult men against adult women. However, as the National Conference on Family Violence in 1994 documents, a significant proportion of the victims of domestic abuse are children, males, same-sex couples and the elderly (Witwer and Crawford, 1995). Why is it that these victims are forced to suffer from this inattention? What can be done to readjust the focus of the domestic violence policy-making community to account for this deficiency?

3. The NIJ notes that the rates for both offending and victimization for most crimes are higher and more severe in economically disadvantaged neighborhoods. Assuming this is true, apply the model of the "three basic reasons for using violent behavior" to postulate why these reasons would be amplified or more pronounced in these neighborhoods? To what extent do you believe that rates of domestic violence abuse are affected by socio-economic factors (education, per capita income)?

4. The hypothesis that those who are most likely to commit domestic violence homicides are those individuals with histories of criminal behavior, long histories of violent and aberrant behavior inside and outside the family, and those abused as children or who suffer from alcohol or substance abuse. Because the criminal justice system can, with some degree of accuracy, identify individuals with histories of violent or aberrant criminal behavior, should all of these individuals, once arrested, be "assessed" by psychologists or advocates in the domestic violence community for proactive intervention to prevent or minimize re-offending or re-victimization?

5. *Delinquency in a Birth Cohort* (Wolfgang et al., 1987) found that approximately 6% of violent chronic criminals account for about 70% of all violent crime in America. Should tax dollars that are meant to be spent on domestic violence prevention focus primarily on the treatment of a small group of individuals that Wolfgang and colleagues identify, or should they be spent on general education measures, such as teaching school children about gender equity and the merits of displaying compassion and empathy toward members of the opposite sex? What are the benefits and drawbacks of both?

Battered Statistics
Harm All Victims

3

The test of a first-rate intelligence is the ability to hold two opposed ideas in mind at the same time and still retain the ability to function.

—**F. Scott Fitzgerald,** *The Crack-up* **(1936)**

It is not the intent of this book to have the readers believe what I believe. The intent is to provide the readers with research that will allow them to reach their own conclusions. Too often, too many organizations simply parrot conclusions reached by others.

Following in the footsteps of Sugarman, I expect that any reasonable and prudent person will read all the research data before deciding what is right and what is wrong concerning domestic violence public policy.

How Non-Facts Become Facts

Not long ago the editors of a prominent journal decided not to accept a manuscript I submitted because it lacked enough "empirical support" for its premise. In fact, others who reviewed the article agreed. While I can accept the right of any publication to believe that there is not enough "empirical support" for an article, there remain questions about just how empirical some of the empirical support in domestic violence research is.

Is scientific research in respected journals always "factual?" Or is it possible, as Benjamin Disraeli reportedly observed, "There are three kinds of lies: lies, damned lies, and statistics?" Is it possible that a journal or a researcher's bias and political agenda might be more important than objectivity and that some researchers set objectivity aside in favor of their concern about gender equality (Macionis, 1997)?

The fact is, as this chapter documents, some empirical citations do not provide empirical support. It is important that professionals, researchers, and domestic violence advocates understand that sometimes scientific evidence presented in prestigious journals may not always be synonymous with the facts.

Author and researcher Donald Dutton and other researchers believe that, concerning domestic violence research, there is now a scholarly paradigm where one group of researchers will cite only data that supports their position and that they purposely ignore data that conflicts with their theory or hypotheses (Dutton, 2006).

In the search for the truth there needs to be scientific objectivity and a lack of bias. Few researchers manage to be completely objective or lack any bias whatsoever, however, to reach the truth, most researchers agree, the researcher must be or at least attempt to be, objective and bias free. However, it seems that some researchers, because of the hypotheses they hold about patriarchy and sexism believe that historically scientific research has ignored women, and, because of past inequities, their contemporary research must always include that women's rights were historically suppressed by men (Macionis, 1997).

Hence, ideological research cannot be objective because it requires that the researchers must be biased. Ideological researchers, because of their social and political beliefs and their personal and professional objectives, provide research that is primarily in pursuit of data that supports their theories and hypotheses, and this bias hinders, not helps, the search for the truth (Dutton, 2007; Macionis, 1997; Myers, 2004; Straus and Scott, 2007).

Central to the domestic violence research by ideological researchers is the need to marginalize and minimize heterosexual male victimization at the hands of heterosexual females. This is most often accomplished in U.S. Department of Justice-sponsored studies where the authors cite the National Crime Victimization data that records the predominance of female victimization: The same researchers simply ignore the NVAWS, which documents that women perpetrate approximately 40% of the intimate partner incidents (Straus and Scott, 2007). The search for the truth for some ideological researchers and many, if not most, domestic violence advocates begins and ends with the belief, as their websites show, that women are the victims of domestic violence and men their victimizers.

My personal experience reveals that many domestic violence advocates will acknowledge homosexual domestic violence. However, in gay domestic violence incidents, both the victim and perpetrator are male and, in lesbian incidents, the female perpetrator, some advocates have claimed, is simply acting like a male. The advocates believe that in child, sibling, and elder abuse the female perpetrators are acting out their violence against others because of their past victimization at the hands of males or their witnessing victimization of other females at the hands of males (Belknap and Melton, 2005; Swan, Gambone, and Fields, 2005; Swan and Snow, 2002).

Rather than observe, recognize, or understand data to the contrary, ideological researchers minimize, marginalize, or ignore facts that are contrary to their political and social agenda (Dutton, 2005; Gelles, 1980). Ideological researchers recognize only data that agree with their theories and hypotheses (Straus and Scott, 2007).

A Non-Fact

In the article "Risk Factors for Injury to Women from Domestic Violence," the New England Journal of Medicine (NEJM) shows how non-facts can become "facts." The following sentence appears twice on the first page of article, which was presented in the December 16, 1999 issue: "Domestic violence is the most common cause of nonfatal injury to women in the United States."

This domestic violence injury non-fact has been written many times and so often presented as fact by the electronic and print media, it has actually become accepted as a fact by the general public. This NEJM article documents how non-fact can become accepted as fact by many professionals, researchers, and domestic violence advocates. Once published in a respectable journal, the non-fact will also be cited by many professionals as "fact" and hence it is the first step in the cycle of a non-fact becoming a fact.

The NEJM article has three citations for its "most common injury" claim. The first citation is "Current Trends and Other Intimate Assaults—Atlanta, 1984" (Elsea, Napper, and Sikes, 1990). This study provides little data to support the NEJM researchers' claim. It is a small study and the majority of the participants are African Americans living in an urban setting. These offenders and perpetrators represent only a small subset of the general population. The information is gleaned from police reports and presents no comparison with other nonfatal injury reports. This subgroup of women from an inner-city African American community *cannot* accurately represent a cross section of America women. In fact, the rate for injuries, the Morbidity and Mortality Weekly Report (MMWR) study notes, is that African America women were injured three times more often than white women.

The second citation in the NEJM article is "A Population-Based Study of Injuries in Inner-City Women" (Grisso et al., 1991). The abstract concludes that more work is needed to understand the nature of injuries to women.

NEJM researchers appear unaware that the study they use to document their claim that the most common cause of injury to women is domestic violence actually demonstrates that the major cause of injury to women was falls, not domestic violence. What the article does claim is that very little is known about nonfatal injuries to women.

This study also does not provide a cross-section of American women. The majority of the participants are, as the authors of the study note, from a poor, urban, African American community. For any study to be relevant nationally, it must collect data from a sample that represents the entire population. These two studies clearly do not meet that very basic random sampling standard needed to produce accurate results that can be used to be representative of the general population (Macionis, 1997).

It is difficult to understand how this NEJM article can be used to conclude that the information in either of these first two studies is empirical scientific data that provide "support" that domestic violence is the most common injury claim.

In fact, the third citation the article cites is less empirical than the first two: Stark and Flitcraft (1985). This motor vehicle accidents, rape, and mugging combined claim is based on a small study that took place in an inner-city emergency room where the population is almost exclusively African American women. This small subgroup of women from an urban minority community cannot accurately represent a generalized cross section of American women. In fact, there is no data that documents this often repeated claim. In the original study, the authors simply make an *assumption* that their claim may be true (Gelles, 2005).

In fact, as Gelles notes, the Centers for Disease Control and Prevention (CDC) is on record that it will not recognize this claim as being presented by the agency or the attorney general.

The Facts

All that researchers and others who are concerned about this domestic violence nonfatal injury claim have to do is to visit the CDC at the Web-based Injury Statistics Query and Reporting System to find out that the claim that domestic violence is the most common cause of nonfatal injury to women in the United States is simply not true (http://www.cdc.gov/ncipc/wisqars/). The CDC table "Estimated Number of Nonfatal Injuries Treated in Hospital Emergency Departments" is available on line (CDC, Office of Statistics and Programming, National Center for Injury Prevention and Control, 2001).

The CDC website documents that domestic violence is not the most common cause of nonfatal injury to women in the United States. Just a cursory view of CDC data reveals that falls cause the most injuries to women. In fact, a number of unintentional injuries are listed before any type of intentional injury, intimate partner or not, are listed.

The findings from the NVAWS, the "Full Report of the Prevalence, Incidence, and Consequences of Violence Against Women" (Tjaden and Thoennes, 2000b, p. 57), show that men and women are nearly twice as likely to be injured on the job than during a rape or physical assault.

The Bureau of Justice Statistics Special Report "Violence-Related Injuries Treated in Hospital Emergency Departments" (Rand, 1997, p. 1) documents that an estimated total of 1.4 million people were treated in U.S. hospital emergency departments for injuries that were confirmed or suspected to have occurred from interpersonal violence. The total of all interpersonal violence patients represent about 1.5% of all visits to hospital emergency departments and 3.6% of all injury-related visits.

For violence-related injuries, 7% were inflicted by a spouse or ex-spouse and 10% by a current or former boyfriend or girlfriend. Parents, children, siblings, and others were responsible for 8% and friends or acquaintances for 23%. Strangers accounted for about 23%. In almost 30% of the cases, the relationship between the patient and the victim was reported as unknown (Rand, 1997).

The Numbers Game

Which of these numbers present the correct number of female victims of domestic violence? Is it 188,000, 876,340, 1.3 million, 1.8 million, 4.8 million, 18 million, 27 million, 60 million or 2 billion?

The 188,000 and 1.8 million are from the 1975 "National Family Violence Survey." That landmark study estimates that 84% of American families are not violent and that 16% do engage in some form of physical assault against each other. The 188,000 is the number of women who are injured severely enough to seek medical attention. The 1.8 million are women who suffer from violent behavior such as kicking, punching, or assault by some type of a weapon (Straus, Gelles, and Steinmetz, 1980).

The 876,340 number is reported by Callie Marie Rennison and Sarah Welchans (2000) in the Bureau of Justice Statistics Special Report "Intimate Partner Violence." These data are from a study by the National Crime Victimization Survey (NCVS). The survey estimates that about 1 million violent crimes were committed against people by their current or former spouse, boyfriend, or girlfriend. About 85% of the victims who reported they were assaulted were women and 15% were men (ibid., p. 1). This same study on the same page also reveals that the vast majority of violent crimes against women (78%) are not committed by intimate partners.

Both the 1.3 million and the 4.8 million come from Patricia Tjaden and Nancy Thoennes in the findings from the NVAWS; their numbers vary depending on which of their two reports you read. The "Full Report of the Prevalence, Incidence, and Consequences of Violence Against Women" (Tjaden and Thoennes, 2000b) reports the 1.3 million number. The 4.8 million is from "Extent, Nature, and Consequences of Intimate Partner Violence" (Tjaden and Thoennes, 2000a).

The 18 million number can be attributed to the National Coalition Against Domestic Violence, which, on its website, estimates that annually more than one third of all married women are being "battered." The 27 million is another estimate by NCDV that more than half of all married women will experience "violence" during their marriage. These numbers are often reported on many domestic violence websites and by the electronic and print media (http://www.ncadv.org).

Miami talk show host Pat Stevens conjured up the 60 million number. Stevens appeared on CNN's "Crossfire" show and made the claim that all the numbers concerning battered women are incorrect and in fact, Stevens claimed, when the real numbers are adjusted for underreporting, the true number for battered women is 60 million. The trouble with Stevens is that his guesstimate is more than the total number of women in the United States who are married or living with a man in some form of spousal relationship. Nevertheless, this number went undisputed on that respectable and nationally televised show (Young, 1994).

The 2 billion number can be attributed to the report "Ending Violence Against Women" (Heise, Ellsbert, and Gottemoeller, 1999). The authors of this report claim that one of every three women around the world has been beaten, coerced into sex, or otherwise abused in her lifetime. Although the majority of domestic violence organizations report this, the data is not limited to domestic violence. The abuse in this report includes acts that result in or are likely to result in threats, psychological violence in the family, sexual harassment, or intimidation at work and in school.

Do These Numbers Help or Hinder?

In a study sponsored by the U.S. Department of Justice, "Violence and Victimization: Exploring Women's Histories of Survival," Postmus and Severson (2006) claim that their research discovered that 98% of the women they interviewed reported some type of psychological, physical, or sexual abuse during their lifetime. It is almost impossible for me to fathom how Postmus or Severson, or in fact any researcher, can actually believe that only 2% of the women they interviewed were not victims of intimate partner violence.

Constantly and consistently producing numbers has caused the majority of Americans, both women and men, to become skeptical concerning any and all numbers about the real number of victims who are actually being battered.

James Ptacek argues that painting millions of women as being equally at risk of domestic violence has marginalized many battered women, particularly those at the lower end of the socioeconomic educational ladder. Ptacek (1998) suggests that it is these women who lack family support that often suffer the most.

The "equal risk" theory proffered by so many advocates ignores reality. In fact, some advocates believe that "a woman who experienced one episode of violence could have suffered equal or greater harm than another woman who experienced multiple episodes over longer periods of her lifespan" (Postmus and Severson, 2006, p. 195).

These advocates seem unwilling or unable to acknowledge that there is a dramatic difference between victims who are chronically "beaten" and "battered" and someone who has been psychologically abused once in her lifetime.

Ptacek (1998) not once mentions that a male can suffer from family violence and be mistreated by the court system. That reminds me of an old adage my grandmother used to repeat to me: If you don't look for it, you can't see it. Although Ptacek's book is myopic (Ptacek is concerned only about the abuse of women and not men) it is an excellent book concerning victimization and the court system.

It should be obvious to anyone, researcher or otherwise, that presenting someone who has somehow been abused, mistreated, or insulted once during their lifetime as a "victim" of "abuse" may mean an endless list of "victims" and siphon off limited resources from chronically "battered victims" who are in dire need of assistance (Ptacek, 1998).

Some Measuring Tools

One measuring tool for "abused women" is called the Woman Abuse Screening Tool (WAST). It is used in the medical field to measure women who report being abused emotionally or physically by a partner (Brown, 2001). It seems logical that this tool would be useful and beneficial for the health and well being of both women and men if these same screening questions, whatever they chose the questions to be, are asked of both females and males.

An "abused woman" tool that is now an abused victim tool is HITS, which is an acronym for Hurt, Insulted, Threaten, Scream. The exact wording of this tool is: In the last year how often did your partner hurt you physically, insult or talk down to you, threaten you with physical harm, scream or curse at you (Shakil, Smith, Sinacore, and Krepcho, 2005). This instrument has recently been redesigned to extend the application of HITS to the male population as well as female. However, it seems to me that it is difficult for anyone to claim that, regardless of gender, their partner, another family member, or in fact themselves, has never been guilty of displaying at least one form of the HITS behavior.

The majority of studies used to measure the number of "battered or abused victims" use some form of the Conflict Tactics Scale (CTS), first developed by the University of New Hampshire in 1971 (Straus, 2007). The majority of domestic violence websites use this tool when it serves their purpose to measure the number of women they claim are victims and then the same advocates rail against it when it can be used to document the number of men who claim to be victims.

CTS and CTS2 are the most common measure of non-sexual family violence (Straus, Hamby, Boney-McCoy, and Sugarman, 1996). They measure three styles of intimate-partner conflict in familial-styled relationships. They measure, most often through telephone interview, the use of rational verbal agreement and disagreement, the use of verbal and nonverbal aggressive behavior, and the use of physical force or violent behavior. They are not designed to measure in any context the reason or motivation for the behavior of either offender or victim.

Almost all versions of the CTS ask questions such as the following:

- Did you have something thrown towards you that could hurt if it hit you?
- Were you grabbed, pushed, or shoved?
- Were you slapped, hit, bitten, or kicked?
- Were you hit with a fist, object, choked, or beaten up?
- Were you threatened with a knife, gun, or other weapon?
- Was a knife, gun, or other weapon used against you?

The too obvious question begged here is, how many people can claim, at least once during their lifetime, that they have not been an offender or on the receiving end of some form of the behavior described by the CTS scales? How does a single answer in the affirmative to any one of the above questions document that a person who has been on the receiving end of behavior, of what may be a once-in-a-life-time isolated event, is a "domestic violence victim"?

Time to Stop and Think

No one, not the most ardent women's or men's rights advocate, can argue with any degree of reason or certainty that some of this self-reported behavior may or may not have been motivated by an isolated argument, anger, jealousy, or revenge for some perceived prior behavior or fueled by an excessive use of alcohol or drugs.

There is almost always some validity and commonality in most seemingly opposite positions. An unbiased review of most domestic violence research allows for the understanding that many of the seemingly opposite positions are in reality intertwined and linked together. Most seemingly polarized positions often contain as many similar characteristics as contradictions.

What is proffered in this chapter is that the continued and constant attempt to inflate the number of victims and to paint all men as batterers and all women equally at risk of being battered has resulted in driving many women and men away from the issue. It is also as wrong to claim that domestic violence occurs equally among the all the socioeconomic educational strata as it is to claim that domestic violence is confined to those at the lower end of the socioeconomic educational strata (Hendricks, McKean, and Hendricks, 2003).

I, similar to many other law enforcement officers, believe that most people recognize that many of the numbers of "victims" of domestic violence
are inflated and do not honestly represent the number of people who exhibit
"battering behavior." I believe that these constant misrepresentations of what
a "domestic violence victim" is have caused many people not to believe *any*
of the numbers. The actual victims of "battering behavior" (the data clearly
documents that the majority of them are at the lower end of the socioeconomic and educational ladder without family support), are being marginalized because of the continued claim that all women are equally at risk of
"domestic violence."

Many families that are involved in domestic violence want solutions, not
only and always punitive criminal sanctions. Much too often civil and criminal court solutions are based on legal precedents that display an increasing
lack of compassion and empathy for the victims because of "mandatory policies" and the adversarial nature of the criminal court process (Mignon, Larson, and Holmes, 2002).

There can be no national domestic violence intervention system until
there is agreement about what domestic violence is or is not. There can be
no agreement about what should be done because there is no agreement on
just what domestic violence is (Wallace, 2002). Almost everyone in the civil
and criminal court system recognizes that they lack the resources to properly
resolve the numbers of domestic disputes that appear on their doorsteps. The
courts in general and the criminal courts in particular should not and cannot be the accepted forum to resolve each and every familial-styled domestic
dispute (Buzawa and Buzawa, 2002).

Many domestic violence advocates, with an almost complete absence
of any data that documents that claim to be true, believe that the educated
and affluent victims often seek private care. These advocates believe the only
reason domestic violence appears so often in the lower strata of society is
because educated and affluent women do not report their abusive incidents
to the police.

The very same advocates who willingly accept as fact the 85% to 15%
differential victimization and offending rate that the NCVS documents
between males and females, as their websites show, almost always ignore the
fact that the NCVS records both reported and unreported crimes. The NCVS
shows that approximately half of the domestic violence incidents reported
to the NCVS survey were not reported to law enforcement. Thus, this documentation of unreported victimization clearly disputes the claim made by
some advocates that there is a vast number of unreported domestic violence
incidents is not based in any empirical data (Dugan, 2003, p. 299). These
85% to 15% differential advocates are also, most often, the same advocates
who ignore the NCVS statistics that show of the 529,829 households reviewed

between January 1992 and June 1998, only 0.5%—that is, one half of 1%—reported at least one incident of domestic violence (Dugan, 2003, p. 299).

Domestic Violence Homicides

Domestic violence homicides are difficult to misrepresent. Bureau of Justice Statistics data show quite clearly that the majority of domestic violence homicides are highly concentrated in lower socioeconomic and educational strata of society.

Victims who live at the lower end of the socioeconomic educational strata often have little family support, live in communities where violence is common, and are at much greater risk of being murdered by an intimate partner. The number one risk factor for domestic violence homicide is living with someone who has a history of violent criminal behavior (Domestic Violence Fatality Review Teams, 2006; Hirschel et al., 2007.)

Many studies note quite clearly that the majority of both perpetrators and victims suffer social, economic, and educational deprivation, have few resources, exhibit a variety of behavioral disorders, and lack the family support that puts them at greater risk than those with such benefits (Kruttschnitt, McLaughlin, and Petrie, 2004, pp. 38–43). These victims, regardless of gender, are the ones who need help first, and their abusers need sure, swift, and just interventions or sanctions.

Marginalizing Victims

As difficult as it may be, the importance of becoming more understanding concerning abusers must be recognized and understood. Certainly many feminist criminologists now recognize the need for different interventions for different female domestic violence offenders. Their studies show that many of the female offenders are also victims. It is important that this is also recognized concerning many male offenders. Abusers are, after all, essential to our ability to prevent or minimize future and further violence (Mignon, Larson, and Holmes, 2002).

In some communities, more than one in every four domestic violence abusers arrested are women. These women are now being placed in batterer intervention programs. Professor Jeffrey L. Edleson (1998), a domestic violence intervention researcher, notes—and rightly so—that female abusers should be carefully assessed and then categorized into three distinct groups and placed into programs tailored to fit their needs. Is it not logical that this assessment process and tailored programs replace contemporary state standards that now mandate the "one-size-fits-all" programs (Macmillan and Kruttschnitt, 2005)?

Today, when someone suspects a friend might be displaying either violent or minor forms of abusive behavior toward an intimate partner, many may hesitate to report these behaviors because all family conflict acts, regardless of how minor, have become criminalized. Laura Dugan, a domestic violence researcher from the National Consortium on Violence Research, in the March 2003 issue of *Criminology and Public Policy,* suggests that mandatory arrest laws keep people from calling the police, and third parties are *significantly* less likely to report incidents. In that same issue in an article that focuses on domestic violence arrests, Davis, Smith, and Taylor (2003, p. 280) write, "But to ignore victims' wishes as an important piece of data in deciding whether to prosecute invites a caseload of unwinnable cases, disgruntled victims, and (potentially) prosecution of innocent defendants."

Many families who need and seek solutions are provided with false hopes (a restraining order will protect you; Klein, 2004), broken promises (after an arrest the offender will be prosecuted; Buzawa and Buzawa, 1996, 2002) and the deterrent effect of criminal sanctions (court data show that offenders with histories of criminal sanctions are often not deterred by such sanctions; Sherman, 1992).

The findings from the NVAWS show quite clearly that most forms of domestic violence are minor and that most victims, whether female or male, are not "battered victims" (Tjaden and Thoennes, 2000b). The mandatory arrest or preferred arrest laws in all 50 states and the "one-size-fits-all" criminal justice interventions do little or nothing to distinguish between the violent and controlling behavior that is "battering" and other many minor forms of family conflict abuse (Miller, 2004, 2005).

Violence in families or between people who profess to love one another is not a new problem. However, the resolve of many contemporary efforts to define what is actually domestic violence is central to implementing proper solutions. Contemporary public policy and interventions ignore the complexities of the issue and are most often placed in a one-size-fits-all package (Fagan, 1996).

Conclusion

Misinformation harms *all victims* as it breeds mistrust concerning the "real" number concerning domestic violence, intimate partner abuse, and battering behavior. In Canada in 1999 the General Social Survey (GSS), which documents the severity, frequency, and consequences of domestic violence for both men and women (Laroche, 2005) had 11,607 male and 14,269 female respondents. The GSS records that more women (40%) were injured than men

(13%). It also reveals that more women (15%) were likely to receive medical attention than men (3%) and notes that more women (32%) than men (10%) reported that the incident disrupted their normal everyday activities (ibid., p. 8). Few domestic violence agencies or advocates would dispute this data.

The GSS also shows that more women (37%) than men (15%) brought the incident to the attention of law enforcement, and notes that more women (48%) than men (17%) sought support services for the incident (Laroche, 2005, p. 9). The GSS, as do more than 100 empirical studies (Fiebert, 2005), documents that men and women report spousal or intimate partner abuse in similar numbers (Laroche, 2005, p. 6). Few domestic violence agencies or advocates concerned about male victimization will dispute this data. As the survey notes, while there very well may be similar numbers of men and women who report they are victims of domestic violence incidents, it is clear that women report suffering more physically and emotionally than men.

It is difficult for me to understand why the majority of ideological domestic violence advocates attack the findings from the 1975 "National Family Violence Survey" that document that a similar number of women hit their husbands as husbands hit their wives when the findings also note that women will suffer more "… pain, injury and harm …" than a man (Straus, Gelles and Steinmetz, 1980).

Gelles and Straus (1988) also agree that more women than men use violence in self-defense. Increasingly many researchers, similar to Gelles and Straus, who are concerned about the victimization of both men and women, and a growing number of advocates like myself, agree that an unbiased understanding of the data shows that all victims, regardless of age, gender, or sexual orientation, deserve our compassion and empathy (Kimmel, 2002). The compassion for male victims does not have to be "equal" to that of women, however, minimizing or ignoring male victimization and pitting the rights of one victim against those of another, as do the majority of domestic violence organizations, as their websites clearly document they do, hinders all victims of domestic violence.

Discussion Questions

1. Why do so many domestic violence advocates purposely mislead the media and society in general concerning the number of women who are "battered?"
2. Does everyone, regardless of what percentage or form of victimization they represent, deserve access to services and funding?
3. Do all victims, regardless of age, gender, or sexual orientation, deserve our sympathy and compassion?

4. Why has the Violence Against Women Act, (politicians proclaim the act is gender neutral) not spent a single penny for a specific heterosexual male domestic violence program?

5. Is it time for our public policy makers, the media, and society in general to demand and receive answers to these questions?

Dating Abuse

4

> Above all thought, children are linked to adults by the simple fact that they are in the process of turning into them.

> **—Phillip Larkin, (1922–1986)**

The Massachusetts Constitution

The constitution of the Commonwealth of Massachusetts was written by John Adams, Samuel Adams, and James Bowdoin. Formally accepted in 1780, it is the oldest acknowledged written constitution in continuous effect. Its formal structure was adopted and replicated by the U.S. Constitution. In its original version, Article I was as follows:

Article I

All men are born free and equal, and have certain natural, essential, and unalienable rights; among which may be reckoned the right of enjoying and defending their lives and liberties; that of acquiring, possessing, and protecting property; in fine, that of seeking and obtaining their safety and happiness.

Similar to the U.S. Constitution, "All men are created equal," the Massachusetts article was originally written as *men* rather than as *people*. It was later amended to substitute the word *people* in place of *men* and equality under the law was expanded. Article I now reads as follows:

Article I

All people are born free and equal, and have certain natural essential and unalienable rights among which may be reckoned the right of enjoying and defending their lives and liberties; that of acquiring, possessing, and protecting property; in fine, that of seeking and obtaining their safety and happiness. Equality under the law shall not be denied or abridged because of sex, race, color, creed or national origin.

Without a doubt, I believe it is right to be inclusive of all citizens regardless of sex, race, color, creed, or national origin. In this 21st century we should all remain vigilant about continuing to be inclusive of all citizens and avoid the mistakes of past centuries, when the rights of some citizens were placed above others.

Valentine's Day in America's Hometown

Plymouth South High School, in Plymouth, Massachusetts, for the last seven years has been celebrating Valentine's Day by having the boys stand in the bleachers and raise their right arms to pledge that they will never commit, condone, or remain silent about violence against women. The girls remain seated and silent.

The health education teacher began this White Ribbon Valentine's Day tradition in 2000 to demonstrate that the men in Plymouth respect and love their women. The White Ribbon Campaign website (http://www.whiterib-bon.ca/) claims to recognize that most men are not violent; however, on that website, the White Ribbon Campaign suggests that the silence of men about domestic or dating violence implies that most men do condone such violence against women (Harbert, 2006, p. A1).

In a newspaper article, the county's district attorney told the students, "Someone you know right now is the victim of violence. Someone in this room, a boyfriend, girlfriend, husband or wife, is or has been a victim. It's there. It's not just on the front page of the paper, it's on the back page too" (Harbert, 2006, p. A1). The county's sheriff advised the students not to tolerate the myths and excuses that so often accompany incidents of domestic violence and said that claims of accidental injuries and cultural differences simply cannot go unchallenged. Another speaker told the students that he never spoke out against the abusive relationships his sister endured when they were growing up in Fall River, Massachusetts, and a school administrator noted that he is reminded of the need to stand against violence every time he visits his mother.

The director of the South Shore Women's Center told the students, "It [this Valentine's celebration] represents equal and peaceful relationships. We're trying to send a message of what it's like to have respect for the women we care for and for this joining together as equals" (Harbert, 2006, p. A1). The boys of the sophomore and junior classes who stood to take this pledge received a standing ovation from the other students and teachers in the school gym. One student commented, "The only way to lead is by example. People want to be good people. Sometimes it takes people to show them how" (ibid.).

Perhaps this campaign might be more equitable and successful if it became more inclusive of all the students of Plymouth South High School. Perhaps it might be right to follow the lead of the Massachusetts Constitution and have all the boys and girls stand and pledge to equally respect each other.

Important messages are being missed in this celebration of male pledges. Respect does not appear on demand. Respect does not reveal itself when one person makes a pledge. Respect must be earned; respect must be shared; respect is a two-way street.

Despite the fact that the district attorney noted that boys and husbands could be the victims of domestic or dating violence, it appears that no one thought to have the girls stand and pledge their respect and love for men. Although the sheriff told the students not to tolerate the myths and excuses that so often accompany incidents of domestic or dating violence, the sheriff is involved in a celebration that addresses the violence by boys and men, but he remains silent about the violence and abuse perpetrated by girls and women (Harbert, 2006).

It should be apparent to everyone involved that the message from this Plymouth South High School celebration is one of neither equal responsibility nor equal respect. The message of this Valentine's Day celebration is that boys and men are the violent aggressive perpetrators of dating or domestic violence and that girls and women are their passive docile victims.

Does the data show that girls and women are most often the passive and docile victims of violence or abuse at the hands of boys and men, or is the Plymouth South High School celebration actually tolerating female offending while perpetuating the myth of female passivity?

An Overview

All dating and domestic violence incidents must be taken seriously as they may be precursors of more dangerous and violent events. When not confronted early and properly addressed, many of these apparently minor incidents may evolve into more violent forms of abuse (O'Leary, 2000).

It is important to remember that this chapter's purpose is to examine dating violence and family conflict behavior rather than violent long-term battering behavior (Kruttschnitt, McLaughlin, and Petrie, 2004). The National Violence Against Women Survey reports, as do most dating and domestic violence surveys, that more than 90% of domestic violence incidents are relatively minor and consist of pushing, grabbing, shoving, slapping, and hitting (Rennison, 2003; Tjaden and Thoennes, 2000b). The authors of "Advancing the Federal Research Agenda on Violence Against Women" conclude that it is vital that researchers, domestic violence advocates, and all intervenors distinguish what constitutes an act of violence, abuse, or battering (Kruttschnitt et al., 2004).

The authors of the college text *Crisis Intervention* write that it is crucial, as this chapter will explore, that all intervenors understand both the causes and consequences of intimate partner violence and recognize the importance of making the distinction between common couple violence (family conflict) and chronic battering (Hendricks, McKean, and Hendricks, 2003).

Battering Behavior

As noted elsewhere in this book, most researchers agree that a "batterer" is a family member or intimate partner who repeatedly uses force or physical violence for the express purpose of manipulating and controlling the behavior of another family member or intimate partner (Wallace, 2002).

Battering can occur without physical assaults as the constant threat of a violent physical assault can be enough to change or alter another's behavior. Unwanted injurious sexual acts and violent episodes destroying property or harming pets can be considered battering behaviors. Having absolute and complete control of even the most minor of family finances is deemed by some researchers as battering behavior (Dutton, 1995).

The behavior of a batterer is not that of someone who is out of control. On the contrary, it is the specific long-term intent and goal of a batterer to willfully control an intimate partner or family member by repeatedly using or threatening the use of force and violent physical assaults (Wallace, 2002).

Dating Violence or Family Conflict

Research shows that the majority of dating violence and family conflict is minor. It can occur when a family member, regardless of age or gender, employs psychological and minor physical assaults (shoving, slapping, or throwing objects) to "get their way" in a specific or a single general disagreement. This behavior is not usually repeated over a long span of time, nor does it involve excessively violent physical or injurious sexual behavior (Tjaden and Thoennes, 2000b).

Dating violence and family conflict are most often not long-term controlling behaviors. They both can evolve from or be exacerbated by a number of factors such as sudden or chronic illness, special-needs children, anger, anxiety, grief, alcohol or drug abuse, stress, work issues, depression, or any number of psychological reasons.

Some form of dating violence or family conflict will occur in most relationships (Wallace, 2002). I believe that it is time to question the use of criminal justice intervention and the arrest process for each and every act of family conflict, as an every growing number of studies now show that there can are often be negative unintended consequences for many family members following such intervention (Eng, 2003).

At the very least it should be time to change mandatory law enforcement arrest policies that allow for little to no discretion between minor and severe acts and that do no allow law enforcement officers to respond to the needs and desires of individual families and victims (O'Leary, 2000). In fact, one National Institute of Justice (NIJ) study shows that arrest rates for domestic violence are higher in those states that do not have mandatory arrest policies. In mandatory arrest states, the rate of arrest increased by 95%, and in states with discretionary arrest polices arrest increased 177% (Hirschel, Buzawa, Pattavina, Faggiani, and Reuland, 2007).

Risk Factors for Dating Abuse

There are few to no studies that report which behavior actually occurs first, the dating behavior or the violent behavior. Certainly it is apparent that many boys and girls do physically and psychologically assault each other, regardless of gender, before they date.

As the many studies cited in this chapter record, there appears to be no significant differences in offending or victimization concerning dating violence. There do appear to be some risk factors that can increase the risk of offending or victimization (Selekman and Praeger, 2006, p. 934):

- Alcohol, tobacco, and cocaine use
- Unhealthy weight control activities
- First intercourse before the age of 15 years
- Multiple sexual partners
- Pregnancy
- Seriously considered or attempted suicide
- A need for power and control
- Demonstration of threats, verbal abuse, and aggression
- Violence in the home
- Owning a weapon

It is important to remember that any single risk factor cannot and should not be considered to be the primary cause of dating violence. Certainly not everyone who displays a single risk factor will be an abuser or victimized by a dating partner.

Data clearly detail that the vast majority of females who become pregnant do not experience dating nor intimate partner violence. Data also report that the vast majority of homes where there is a weapon present do not report incidents of dating or intimate partner offending or victimization. However, some studies do seem to verify that as the numbers of risk factors increase within a household there is a greater likelihood of a dating or intimate partner violence incident. As the numbers increase so does the likelihood of offending or victimization.

One-Solution-Fits-All

It is now recognized that the issue of unequal power and control can influence dating violence and family violence, not only violence against women. The issue of unequal power, control, and resources affects child, sibling, spousal, intimate partner, and elder abuse (Chalk and King, 1998). Psychologists and sociologists clearly recognize that the issues of power and control are not gender based (Myers, 2004).

The reasons for violence within relationships often reflect the various theories concerning violence in general (Moffitt and Caspi, 1999). Many evidence-based empirical studies report that the origins and patterns of the use of violence may be similar for males and females and that violence prevention and public policies should reflect those similarities (Kruttschnitt et al., 2004).

This chapter demonstrates that the majority of dating violence intervention programs assume that females are most often victims and only rarely are they perpetrators. There is an inherent danger for all victims in concluding that one gender is violent and aggressive whereas the other is passive and docile (Graham-Kevan and Archer, 2005).

Rather than contemporary "one-solution-fits-all" criminal justice policies, procedures and programs need to be interventions, programs, and sanctions that consider the context and circumstances of individual incidents and needs of specific families (Fagan, 1996). Impediments to multiple and equitable interventions for specific individual incidents were created when it was proffered that the violence suffered by most if not all adult heterosexual women is different and distinct from all of the other forms of familial or intimate partner relationships (Kruttschnitt et al., 2004). Most researchers now agree that there is no single correct theory concerning the factors that cause dating or domestic violence (Wallace, 2002).

Women's Rights Research

In 1966 the National Organization for Women (NOW) declared that women must seek equality "…not in pleas for special privilege, nor in enmity toward men, who are also victims of the current half-equality between the sexes—but in an active, self-respecting partnership with men" (Young, 2006, op ed page).

Contemporarily, the goal of many women's rights researchers and the Violence Against Women Act (VAWA) is to primarily or exclusively concern themselves with the violence against women by men. This sociological perspective has caused many contemporary researchers to charge that feminist researchers are less concerned about science than they are political activism (Macionis, 1997).

I have three daughters and two sons, and I agree with the 1966 goal of NOW and expect that all five of my children be treated equitably. This chapter details that the majority of dating and domestic violence organizations are only or primarily concerned with violence against women and that most dating and domestic violence organizations do not provide nor proffer equitable dating and domestic violence intervention and education for males and females.

Most dating and domestic violence advocates, because they have linked feminism and domestic violence as the same issue, see any and all attempts to address the issue of male victimization as a concealed agenda to undermine and to turn back the progress many women have made concerning efforts to provide services and programs to battered women. This chapter, respecting NOW's 1966 statement of equality, only requests equitable programs and resources for males and females and should not be viewed as an attack on feminism.

Data show that there is a need for programs and interventions to end the use of physical assaults and psychological abuse among family members and intimate partners regardless of age gender or sexual orientation. Age, gender, or sexual orientation should never be used as a general measuring tool concerning individual rights. It is ill advised—and I believe that it has become counterproductive—to generalize which gender is the most violent while not defining violence. It is without question that men commit more murders than women. However, it is also a fact that men murder men and kill themselves at rates that far exceed their murders of women.

It is counterproductive and irresponsible to provide interventions and policies that presume that men in general are guilty and arresting and sanctioning men without first exploring the context and circumstances of the specific events will resolve individual problems. The willingness of each gender to accept its share of responsibility of the use of abusive behavior creates much progress concerning child abuse. As this chapter shows, such is not the case concerning dating violence.

The eagerness of each gender to blame the other has proven to be as dangerous as it is divisive. It will prove to be far more productive for the safety of all victims to determine which specific individual in each specific incident initiates, causes, or creates the violence and then to provide interventions based on those incidents, one incident and one individual at a time.

It is counterproductive to minimize, marginalize, or ignore some victims or to paint one gender as always passive and the other as always aggressive. All physical assaults or coercive behavior specifically used to change or alter the behavior of another family member or intimate partner are wrong. All psychologically abusive behaviors, direct or indirect, used to change or alter the behavior of a dating partner, family member, or intimate partner are wrong.

It is divisive to proclaim one gender to be the primary victim. This gender-specific classification begins anew the old and odious process of placing the rights of one gender against those of another. It is also divisive to pass public policy that proclaims one alleged theory superior to the other when there is no empirical evidence to document that to be a fact.

Dating and domestic violence intervention must be free of stereotypical gender bias and become more positive and inclusive and less negative and exclusive. Promoting equality and eradicating stereotypical gender bias was and should remain the heart and soul of the feminist movement. Too many advocates are concerned only with or about their victim, and many advocates seem unable or unwilling to recognize that their behavior is the very same behavior they once railed against. Everyone, as feminists once claimed, regardless of age, gender, sexual orientation, or percentage of victimization, deserves to have their needs and concerns heeded not hidden.

Jane Doe

The Massachusetts Coalition Against Sexual Assault and Domestic Violence (Jane Doe, Inc.) notes on its website that its goal is to bring together organizations and people who are committed to ending domestic violence and sexual assault (Jane Doe Inc., 2007). There is an expectation that Jane Doe, Inc., a Massachusetts-based domestic violence coalition, as a domestic violence organization should or would be committed to ending domestic violence and sexual assaults against everyone regardless of gender. However, it appears that Jane Doe believes that domestic and dating violence is primarily a problem for heterosexual women.

"Men are sometimes victims of domestic violence," said Nancy Scannell, legislative director of Jane Doe. "But the attempt to be inclusive [of male victims] should never be interpreted to mean that the issue is gender-neutral. It does not change our mind about why [domestic violence] happens. It happens because of sexism and power and control of men over women in our society" (Stockman, 2002).

A visit to the Jane Doe website reveals that their concerns for our daughters do seem to differ when compared with their concerns about our sons. It appears, at least to me, that Jane Doe's primary concern about our sons is that someday our sons will abuse someone's daughter.

The Jane Doe website notes that 1 in 5 female high school students report being physically or sexually abused by a dating partner. The Jane Doe website excludes any information about the victimization of boys despite the fact that data about the victimization of boys appear in the very same database showing that 1 in 5 high school female students report being physically or sexually abused by a dating partner. Jane Doe is or should be aware that the survey it cites giving proof that the victimization of female high school students also shows the victimization of male high school students.

Jane Does clearly focuses on female victimization and male perpetration. The Jane Doe website notes that in homes where domestic violence occurs, children are at high risk of suffering physical assaults and other types of abuse. The Jane Doe website claims that 95% of the domestic violence children observe is that of men abusing women. However, there is no citation for their claim because it simply is not true. The Jane Does website ignores the report "Estimating the Number of American Children Living in Partner-Violent Families" (McDonald, Caetano, Green, Jouriles, and Ramisetty-Mikler, 2006). This report shows that intimate partner violence is reported by 21.45% of the couples in the study. Male-to-female violence is estimated at 13.66%, and female-to-male violence is 18.20%. Severe male-to-female violence is 3.63%, and severe female-to-male violence is 7.52%.

The Jane Doe website does not report that data from the U.S. Department of Health and Human Services Administration for Children and Families (2004) verifies that women neglect and abuse their children more often than men. Data also reveal that more children live with single mothers than with single fathers. However, simply because the children are there and the opportunity is greater for mothers to abuse their children is no reason for that differential any more than men abuse women because they can.

The Jane Doe website, similar to the majority of other domestic violence organizations, claims that the U.S. Department of Justice estimates that more than 90% of all domestic violence victims are women. Jane Doe and most advocates are or should be aware that the NIJ, Office of Justice Programs, U.S. Department of Justice and the Centers for Disease Control and Prevention (CDC) report the NVAWS (NVAWS) and that the NVAWS does not substantiate the Jane Doe Inc. claim that 90 to 95% of victims are women (Tjaden and Thoennes, 2000b).

Definition

There is not a solitary nationally accepted definition of dating violence and abuse (O'Keefe, 2005). However, dating violence and abuse is defined by the National Center for Injury Prevention and Control (www.cdc.gov/ncipc) as the physical, sexual, or psychological and emotional violence within a dating relationship (CDC, 2006a).

Using the 2005 Youth Risk Behavior Survey (YRBS), 9.3% of females and 9.0% of males reported being a victim of physical dating abuse (CDC, YRBS, 2005). The YRBS also reports that 10.8% of girls and 4.2% of boys say they were forced to have sexual intercourse when they did not want to. Researchers believe that many of these incidents can be prevented by helping adolescents (both boys and girls) develop skills for healthy relationships with others (Foshee et al. 2005).

This definition is a guideline and not a mandate. The definition varies between violence and abuse and somewhat differently from state to state. Some of the behavior, as defined already, is viewed as abuse or coercive behavior rather than as violence. The National Domestic Violence Hot Line (NDVH, 2007) defines abuse as a pattern of coercive control that one person exercises over another (Texas Council on Family Violence, n.d.).

It is just as important to recognize that the nature and scope of the problem often lies in the definition of the problem and the methodology of the study. Dating violence studies range from as low as 9% to as high as 57% (Cascardi and Avery-Leaf, 2003; O'Keefe, 2005).

When verbal aggression against a partner is included as abuse, one study records that 95% of women and 86% of men reported using verbal abuse at least once during the study period (Grauwiler and Mills, 2004, p. 5). It is generally recognized that the distinct methodologies used in different surveys are the main factors that account for the dramatic differences in the collection of data (Tjaden and Thoennes, 2000a).

Liz Claiborne Inc.

In fall 2005, the U.S. Congress reauthorized the Violence Against Women Act (VAWA III). The newspaper article "Domestic Violence Starting in Teenage Years" states, "Senator Hillary Rodham Clinton wants to be assured that VAWA provides intervention and prevention programs that address violence against young women. However, Senator Clinton, similar to the majority of our public policy makers, did not inquire or want to be assured about interventions and prevention programs for young men" (Janelle, 2006).

In the same article, the chief executive officer (CEO) and chair of Liz Claiborne Inc. (LCI) is quoted as saying that it is time to stop teen dating abuse and to ensure that the young people (one would assume the CEO means both girls and boys) receive the assistance they need so that abusive lifestyles as teenagers and young adults do not follow them into adulthood (Janelle, 2006).

Starting the week of April 25, 2006, 350 high schools began teaching the LCI curriculum, "Love Is Not Abuse." LCI hopes this program will help teenagers to recognize and stop abusive relationships (LCI, 2006).

In February 2005, LCI commissioned a "Teen Dating Abuse Survey" (TRAS) (Liz Claiborne, Inc., 2007). The findings of the LCI survey reveal that an overwhelming majority of teens—both girls and boys—claim that physical and verbal abuse is a serious issue for them.

The TRAS data document the need for education, intervention, support, and services for both boys and girls. However, LCI provides a curriculum in 39 states that primarily portray our sons as offenders and our daughters as their victims.

The data verify that LCI, similar to most high school and college dating violence intervention programs, ignores evidence-based dating violence data. LCI primarily refers to males as abusers and to females as victims. It appears that LCI has ignored the results of its own survey. On the LCI website is the following:

Abuser = He
Why?
Victim = She

When the reader uses a computer mouse and clicks on this section of the LCI website a box emerges that claims the following:

The U.S. Department of Justice (DOJ) estimates that more than 90% of all domestic violence victims are female and that most abusers are male. Because of this we use he when referring to abusers. Whether the victim is female or male, violence of any kind is unacceptable.

LCI should be aware that the U.S. Department of Justice does not claim, estimate, or document that 90% of domestic violence victims are females at the hands of males. In fact, the LCI TRAS shows this claim not to be accurate. In reality the LCI key findings appear to minimize and ignore both the offenses by our daughters and the victimization of our sons.

Findings

One LCI (2007) key finding is this:

FACT: 1 in 3 girls who have been in a serious relationship say they've been concerned about being physically hurt by their partner.

The TRAS survey provides no definition of just what is a serious relationship when it provides information about serious relationships. Hence, the differences reported between a relationship and a serious relationship is left to be viewed and reported differently by girls and boys. And given the different cultural norms and mores between girls and boys, it appears that girls and boys will view and report their relationships differently.

LCI (2007) reports that 1 in 3 (35%) of our daughters report a fear of being concerned about their safety. What LCI does not include in this facts section is that their survey documents that one in four (25%) of our sons also report being concerned about their safety (LCI, 2007).

In bold at the top of page 11 (LCI, 2007) is this:

Of teens that have been in a relationship, a troublesome 30% (including more girls than guys) said they've been concerned for their physical safety.

Does LCI consider that the fear of our daughters' safety is unacceptable violence while our sons actually being physically assaulted should be considered as acceptable violence? Why is the data about our sons ignored?

On page 11 (LCI, 2007), the TRAS provides evidence that 17% of boys and 13% of females report that their partner hit, slapped, or pushed them. Is it possible that LCI has concluded that the fear of victimization by our daughters is a key finding and that the actual physical victimization of our sons is inconsequential? Why did LCI ignore the actual physical victimization of our sons? What is the reason that LCI ignores the fact that the findings of the LCI TRAS clearly dispute their criminal justice-based claim that 90% of the abusers are male?

Power and Control Issues

On the top of page 3 of the TRAS survey (LCI, 2007) it notes the following:

Power and control actions and attitudes are pervasive in teen relationships—many young people have dealt with a boyfriend or girlfriend who tried to control their whereabouts.

The survey asks if the boys or girls had partners who want to know the following:

- Who were they with all the time, 32% of boys and 39% of girls responded yes.
- Where they were all the time, 31% of boys and 35% of girls responded yes.
- Tried to tell them what to do a lot, 33% of boys and 31% of girls responded yes.
- Asked them to only spend time with him/her, 24% of boys and 24% of girls responded yes.
- Tried to prevent them from spending time with family or friends, 22% of boys and 21% of girls responded yes.

Hence, the LCI-sponsored TRAS (2007) clearly details that boys and girls equally attempt to control or monitor the whereabouts of their partner. The

TRAS on page 4 attempts to demonstrate that there is a greater difference in relationships that are serious as compared with nonserious relationships.

However, as previously noted, without any accepted or defined differential between serious and nonserious relationships or an understanding that both girls and boys agree how serious their relationships are, that difference reported by TRAS is clearly one of perception and not an empirical evidence-based reality.

Even if one would accept that perceptions are reality, in the instances that LCI (2007) claims are "serious" instances, boys reported that their partner attempted to control their behavior half or more than half as often as did girls in the "perceived serious" relationships. Clearly, as the TRAS shows, power and control are issues that are relevant to the behavior of both boys and girls, as victims and as offenders. However, it is just as clear that LCI is determined, for reasons LCI should explain, to show the victimization of our daughters while minimizing or ignoring the victimization of our sons.

Emotional Abuse

On page 15 of the TRAS (LCI, 2007) it explores relationships between boys and girls who have had to endure emotional abuse from their partner:

- 59% of boys and 64% of girls report that their partner made them feel bad or embarrassed about themselves.
- 28% of boys and 26% of girls report that their partner called them names or put them down.
- 8% of boys and 10% of girls report that their partner became physically or verbally abusive when drunk or high.

On their website, LCI (2007) notes, "It's not easy being a guy these days. Society puts all kinds of pressure on boys, right from the day they're born." LCI then, similar to VAWA, proceeds to minimize or ignore the difficulties boys have.

LCI appears to be either unwilling or unable to accept its own survey data concerning the offenses by our daughters and the victimization of our sons. In fact when you compare the data in the TRAS with the data on the LCI website, it appears that LCI intends to keep silent about the victimization of our sons and provide few to no solutions for their victimization.

It's Time to Talk Day

On October 11, 2005 *Marie Claire* magazine and LCI joined forces for an "It's Time to Talk Day" as a way to encourage public dialogue about domestic violence. The "It's Time to Talk Day" is a part of a national campaign that is intended *to break the silence* and get people talking about the issue of domestic violence (LCI, 2006).

When most people think about a domestic violence victim they think of a woman who has been beaten and battered by a man. Law enforcement officers know full well that some women are beaten and battered by some men. However, contemporary domestic violence is more broadly defined and is often characterized as verbal, emotional, manipulative, and coercive behavior as well as physical abuse.

Abuse is a pattern of coercive control that one person exercises over another. Battering is a behavior that physically harms, arouses fear, prevents a partner from doing what they wish, or forces them to behave in ways they do not want (Texas Council on Family Violence, n.d.). It is universally accepted that adult heterosexual domestic violence does not begin the day girls become women or boys become men. It is generally agreed that girls and boys who initiate or experience dating violence are at a higher risk of abusive behavior toward each other when they are adults as victims or perpetrators (O'Keefe, 2005).

Although LCI claims, "It's Time to Talk," data on the LCI website reveals that, rather than breaking the silence about dating/domestic violence, LCI and the majority of nationally recognized domestic violence organizations, by excluding data concerning male victimization, choose to remain silent about the victimization of boys and men.

The National Coalition Against Domestic Violence (NCADV) makes it quite clear on their website that the NCADV is only or primarily concerned about the victimization of women. The NCADV minimizes or ignores male victimization. What should be clear to NCADV, as the "National Center for Injury Prevention and Control: Intimate Partner Violence: Overview" (CDC, n.d.) website article records, is that male victimization is an issue that needs to be addressed, not minimized and ignored.

Though the NCADV claims that it is concerned about the children of battered women, one would assume that children would include both girls and boys. The NCADV website shows that the NCADV, similar to the majority of domestic violence organizations, is only or primarily concerned about our daughters, not our sons. The NCADV "Dating Abuse Fact Sheet" (CDC, 2006) minimizes, marginalizes, and ignores data concerning the victimization of our sons.

The LCI survey (2007) notes that its own research reveals that a significant number of today's teens are victims of dating abuse. What should be a really troubling concern for all parents is the fact that LCI, the NDVH, the NCADV, and, in fact, the majority of domestic violence organizations are unable or unwilling to acknowledge the victimization of our sons.

Keeping the Silence

Why is it that LCI has decided to ignore or minimize the data about female offenses and male victimization that is documented in the survey it commissioned in 350 schools nationwide?

Perhaps the LCI is concerned that if it accepts its survey data about dating and domestic violence, their theory that domestic violence happens because of sexism and power and control of men over women in our society will be revealed as a theory with little to no empirical evidence-based foundation.

The data in the TRAS (LCI, 2007) leaves no doubt that many girls often behave as badly as many boys concerning verbal, emotional, manipulative, coercive, and physically abusive behavior toward their partners.

It is difficult to understand how or why so many domestic violence organizations, in the 21st century, do not recognize that they are replicating the very behavior they railed against in the 20th century. Oppressive and prejudiced assumptions concerning gender are unfair, unwarranted, and, in fact, are dangerous concerning the well-being of girls and women and boys and men.

Is There a Gender Agenda?

Whereas girls and young women have received considerable attention concerning dating violence victimization, the victimization of boys and young men and the offending by girls and young women is most often minimized or ignored by the majority of researchers and domestic violence organizations (Howard and Wang, 2003a).

The National Center for Victims of Crime (NCVC) and the National Council on Crime and Delinquency (NCCD) jointly prepared the report "Our Vulnerable Teenagers: Their Victimization, Its Consequences, and Directions for Prevention and Intervention" (Wordes and Nunez, 2002).

Despite the fact that the NCVC acknowledges that boys are victimized more often than girls and that the NCVC report is about teenagers, the cover of the report portrays only a girl. Sometimes pictures do speak a thousand words. In fact, the cover of the report about teenagers might be considered a metaphor for the collective minimization and marginalization of the victimization of our sons concerning dating violence by the media, public policy makers, researchers, and domestic violence organizations.

On page i of the executive summary, Wordes and Nunez (2002) write, "Teenagers are disproportionately represented as victims of crime." Wordes and Nunez then produce a report that disproportionately represents boys as the victims of dating violence. The disproportionate representation of our daughters as offenders and the minimization or exclusion of the victimization of our sons is an accepted and common practice among many researchers and domestic violence organizations (Howard and Wang, 2003a).

On page 6 Wordes and Nunez (2002) play an active role in the minimization and marginalization of male victimization:

> While studies have found that males and females are at equal risk of dating violence, the motivation for women is usually self-defense (White and Koss, 1991). Studies however, report that women are anywhere from two to six times (Bachman and Saltzman, 1995; White and Koss, 1991) more likely to be victims—it is generally believed that about 85% of dating violence is perpetrated by men and boys.

Wordes and Nunez (2002) may believe that is true; however, the White and Koss (1991) study provides no data that can show that the motivation for the use of violence by females in dating violence incidents is usually self-defense. Perhaps Wordes and Nunez actually do believe their claim to be a fact. It may be possible that someone told Wordes and Nunez that the White and Koss study made such a claim. Nevertheless, had Wordes and Nunez read the White and Koss study they would have been aware that there is no data in the White and Koss study to document the self-defense claim. In fact, White and Koss clearly show on page 253, "… and the partner's perceptions of the act were not addressed in the present study."

The White and Koss (1991) study does cite Saunders (1988): "Wife abuse, husband abuse or mutual combat? A feminist perspective on the empirical findings." Saunders makes the claim that battered women often use physical assaults in self-defense. However, Saunders also does not provide any empirical evidence-based data showing the reasons for the use of self-defense in dating violence.

What Saunders (1988) provides is a hypothesis concerning studies of battered women in violent incidents. It is disingenuous and dangerous not to recognize or understand the difference between abusive behavior in dating relationships and the violent battering behavior between a small subsection of violent married or intimate partner adults.

More misleading than the White and Koss (1991) study is the Bachman and Saltzman (1995) citation that the White and Koss study offers as documentation that women are anywhere from two to six times more likely to be victims of dating violence. However, the fact is that the Bachman and Saltzman report is criminal justice data that have little to nothing to do with the victimization of girls and young women during dating violence incidents.

The Bachman and Saltzman (1995) report is criminal justice data drawn from the redesign of the National Crime Victimization Survey (NCVS). It is difficult if not impossible to understand how Wordes and Nunez (2002) can

sent a larger proportion of female assaultive offending than male assaultive offending. The National Incident Based Reporting System data report that 18% of aggravated assaults committed by juvenile males were against family members as compared with 33% for juvenile females (ibid.).

The report (Snyder and Sickmund, 2006) reveals that 23% of males and females have used alcohol, 34.9% of males and 26.9% of females have been drunk, 10% of males and 9% of females have used marijuana, and 9% of males and 6% of females have sold drugs. The report also verifies that 33% of teenage boys and 21% of teenage girls claim they have assaulted someone with the intent to seriously hurt them. In 1980, the violent crime index rate for boys was 8.3 times the female rate. By 2003 the male rate was just 4.2 times the female rate. The report also notes that the arrest rate for juvenile violent crimes committed by boys fell by 26% whereas the rate for girls rose by 47%.

The National Survey on Drug Use and Health (2007) reports that 1.5 million girls ages 12 to 17 started drinking alcohol in 2004 compared with 1.28 million boys. Among the same age group 730,000 girls compared with 565,000 boys started smoking cigarettes, and 675,000 girls compared with 577,000 boys started using marijuana. The survey also reports that 14.4% of girls and 12.5% of boys reported misusing prescription drugs.

The 2004 Boston Youth Survey

On page B3 of the April 16, 2006 *Boston Globe* a story in the *Boston Globe* about a group of girls attacking one young woman and stabbing her in the chest; in a separate incident on the same night, a story was printed about another girl who was stabbed in her left side and left bleeding after fighting with a group of girls.

In the same article, a youth worker notes that most of the recent brutal fights have been between girls using razors, box cutters, and knives. On the same date, 54% of girls awaiting court appearances in Boston were being held for violent crimes The 2004 Boston Youth Survey (BYS) survey reports the aggressive behavior by both boys and girls in the Boston school system (Hemenway, Prothrow-Stith, and Browne, 2005).

The survey is the result of a collaborative effort between the Harvard Youth Violence Prevention Center and the Boston Office of Human Services and Boston Youth and Families. The mayor's office hopes the BYS report (Hemenway et al., 2005) can help schools, parents, and other professionals discover how they can best serve our daughters and sons.

The "Sexual Abuse and Dating Violence" section of the BYS survey (Hemenway et al., 2005) paints a dramatically different picture than the one presented (passive females and aggressive males) by Jane Doe, Inc. and most domestic violence organizations.

The BYS shows (Hemenway et al., 2005, p. 74) that 8% of girls and 7% of boys experienced physical violence during the last 12 months by a dating partner. The report also notes that 7% of girls and 5% of boys over their lifetime report experiencing sexual violence by their dating partner. These data are inconsistent with the claims of Jane Doe and the majority of domestic violence organizations and brings into serious question the issue of female passivity. The BYS (Hemenway et al., 2005, p. 54) report also says that 48% of girls and 54% of boys hit back when someone hits them first. The BYS notes that 35% of girls and 39% of boys pushed, shoved, kicked, or slapped another student. The BYS notes that 19% of girls and 26% of boys got into a physical fight when they got angry and that 28% of girls and 32% of boys threatened to hit or hurt another student.

The behavior of many of the girls and boys in this BYS report (Hemenway et al., 2005) seems to contrast with the claims made by the majority of domestic violence organizations, as their websites show, that females—girls or women—are most often passive and docile and that males—boys or men—are violent and aggressive.

In fact, the BYS (Hemenway et al., 2005) data are consistent with national data that have been available for years from the National Youth Risk Behavior Survey (YRBS) (CDC, 2005). The YRBS on page 44 shows 9.3% of girls and 9.0% of boys report that they were hit, slapped, or physically hurt on purpose by a boyfriend or girlfriend. The same page of the YRBS shows that 10.8% of girls and 4.2% of teenage boys were physically forced to have sexual intercourse against their will with a dating partner.

Is it that Jane Doe, Inc., and the other national domestic violence organizations are completely ignorant about the results of the report by Snyder and Sickmund (2006), the YRBS (CDC, 2005), and the BYS (Hemenway et al., 2005) surveys, or is it possible, similar to adult domestic violence interventions, that these organizations purposely present data concerning the victimization of girls and women and suppress the documentation of the victimization of boys and men?

And most telling and more dangerous for both girls and boys as offenders or victims is the fact that if these organizations continue to ignore the offenses by girls they may actually be placing girls at a greater, not less, risk of their own victimization and factors concerning their offending.

The College Campus

A survey by White and Koss (1991) of 2,600 women and 2,100 men attending college in the United States reports that 85% of the men and 88% engaged in what it labeled verbal aggression against a dating partner, 37% of men and 35% of women reported physically assaulting their dating partner and 39% of men and 32% of women report their were physically assaulted by a dating partner. It seems to be apparent to me after reviewing the data that those who are offenders are very often also victims in these incidents (White and Smith, 2001).

The American College Health Association report "Campus Violence White Paper" (Carr, 2005) documents that 15.0% of females and 9.2% of males report being in an emotionally abusive relationship. Also 2.4% of females and 1.3% of males have been in a physically abusive relationship and 1.7% of females and 1.0% of males have been in a sexually abusive relationship within the last school year.

A report by the American Association of University Women (AAUW, 2006) titled "Drawing the Line: Sexual Harassment on Campus" shows that women and men are equally likely (35% female v. 29% male) to be sexually harassed on college campuses. The study reports that 62% of college students experienced sexual harassment and 32% reported being victims of physical harassment. The study found that male students were more likely to sexually harass someone than women were (51% v. 31%).

The AAUW held a press conference in Washington, D.C., on January 24, 2006, where Barbara O'Connor, the AAUW educational foundation president, said, "Because our research shows that sexual harassment takes an especially heavy toll on young women, we are concerned that sexual harassment may make it harder for them to get the education they need to take care of themselves and their families in the future" (AAUW, 2006).

The Academy for Educational Development (AED) is a national organization that supports non-biased education. Its study "Raising and Educating Healthy Boys: A Report on the Growing Crisis in Boys' Education" (AED, 2005) says, "... Boys lag behind girls in reading and writing, they are more likely to be referred to a school psychologist, and they are more likely to be diagnosed with attention deficit disorder with or without hyperactivity."

A recent *Newsweek* article (Tyre, 2006) details by every benchmark that boys, not girls, across the nation and in every demographic are the ones falling behind in school. Women account for 56% and men 44% of the college undergraduates. The single parent mother of one boy worries, "... It's hard to see doors close and opportunities fall away" (ibid.). The U.S. secretary of education, Margaret Spelling, believes that gap "... has profound implications for the economy, society, families and democracy" (ibid.).

Title III, section 303, of VAWA provides grants to combat violent crimes against women on college campuses. This VAWA also directs the U.S. attorney general to issue and to make available minimum standards of training relating to violent crimes against women on campus. There is no mention of violence against men on campus.

The Bureau of Justice Statistics report "Violent Victimization of College Students, 1995–2002" (Baum and Klaus, 2005) reveals that male college students were twice as likely as female college students to be the victim of a violent crime on campus.

Apparently, most of our public policy makers agree with the AAUW, as Title III ignores any mention of the abuse of men on college campuses. It appears that in educational settings our public policy makers are ensuring that our sons lag behind our daughters in more than just reading and writing.

Self-Defense and Aggression

Jane Doe, as well as the vast majority of domestic violence organizations, expects that U.S. public policy makers and the general public should also believe that most of the aggression or assaultive behavior used by girls and women is defensive in nature.

These organizations proffer that females often use physical assaults only in a response to assaults by boys and men. Girls and women are far more passive and docile, in dating or intimate partner relationships, than are boys and men—at least this is the tale that is contemporarily weaved.

The National Youth Violence Prevention Resource Center (2007) website has a section that offers "Facts for Teen: Youth Violence." This section claims, "… Teenage boys are much more likely to use force in order to control their girlfriends, while girls more often act violently in self-defense" (ibid.). O'Keefe (1997) is used as the citation to document this alleged fact.

O'Keefe (1997) writes on page 562 as a reason for females using dating violence: "For females, the second main reason was reported as self-defense, whereas for males it was to gain control over their partner." However, when you carefully read O'Keefe you will discover that the self-defensive act is only O'Keefe's perception of what females were reporting and it is not the actual reported reason by females. It appears that O'Keefe reports what she believes females thought without an empirical data set that actually proves that females did act in self-defense.

O'Keefe (1997, p. 562) writes, "… It is also possible that females may inflict more violence than males in self-defense or in retaliation for the sexual assault." Hence, the O'Keefe subjective "possible" and "may" are transformed into objective facts that are not objective facts.

O'Keefe (1997, p. 563) goes on to say, "Whereas being a victim of dating violence was a stronger predictor for females compared with males suggesting that females are more likely than males to hit in self-defense or retaliation, it is important for both sexes to realize that every violent action creates a risk for a violent response or future violent acts." Perhaps because O'Keefe intuitively believes that females often use violence only in self-defense has caused her to misinterpret her own data sets. Nevertheless O'Keefe should know better and that suggestions and possibilities are not empirically based evidences of fact.

What is a fact is that on page 556, O'Keefe (1997) shows that there is no statistical significance reported in the study that can document that males initiated violence more often than females. If the initiation of violence is statistically equal, how is it possible to believe that the person who initiates the violence is acting in self defense?

O'Keefe (1997, pp. 556–557) writes, "Among males, the most frequently chosen reason for their use of violence was anger, followed by the desire to get control over their partner. Among females anger was also the most frequently chosen reason for their use of violence followed by self-defense." Somehow what is in reality only "possible" and "suggested" has become a fact. However, nowhere is self-defense by girls documented in the O'Keefe study. The use of self-defense by girls is only O'Keefe's belief that it is possible self-defense may be a reason for the use of violence by girls.

The O'Keefe (1997) claim that boys use violence because of a desire to get control over their partner is also without documentation. There are four tables presented in the O'Keefe study, and not one of them provided any empirical evidence of O'Keefe asking the boys and girls to report that they use either self-defense or the desire to control their partner as a reason for their violence.

In fact, in the O'Keefe and Treister study (1998, p. 214) the authors report, "Also, of interest is the finding of *no gender differences* (italics added) in the amount of *interpersonal control* exhibited by males and females in dating relationships, suggesting that interpersonal control may not be gender-specific and that despite women's subordinate position in the larger social structure, they are just as likely to act to control their dating partner." In fact, there are only a few studies where the researchers actually and specifically inquire about and empirically provide evidence for the issue of self-defense by girls. One of those is a nationally recognized study by V. A. Foshee (1996, p. 284), "Another strength is that, unlike most other dating violence studies, the measure of victimization and perpetration used distinguished violence perpetrated or received in self-defense from that not in self-defense."

O'Keefe (2005) claims, "... Much of the dating violence research overlooks whether female use of violence was in self-defense or in response to male physical or sexual violence." When O'Keefe cites studies by Foshee (1996), she seems to overlook the Foshee study's documentation that even when controlling for violence perpetrated in self-defense, girls perpetrated more violence than boys. Further, why does the O'Keefe paper also exclude Foshee's (1996) record of the fact that 28% of girls and 15% of boys say they had engaged in some act of physical aggression against their partner? Do VAWnet and O'Keefe really believe that the willful exclusions of female dating violence offending are actually in the best interest of dating violence intervention programs for girls and boys?

When examining the context of dating violence, it is important to understand who initiated the violence and the reason or motivation given for that initiation. The reason or motivation most often given by girls is that they used violence to demonstrate their anger or in retaliation for emotional hurt. Males are more likely to indicate their use of violence was caused because of jealousy (O'Keefe, 1997). Neither of these two motivations by boys or girls are reasons; they are only excuses for the use of violent behavior.

O'Keefe (1997, p. 556) reveals that there is no statistically significant difference in the initiation of dating violence between boys and girls. O'Keefe shows that girls are more likely than males to slap, kick, bite, or hit with a fist or hit with an object. Regardless of the type of assaultive behavior, how can O'Keefe believe that the initiation of an assaultive act can become an act of self-defense?

O'Keefe (1997, p. 558) notes that inflicting a physical assault is the best predictor of receiving a physical assault. If domestic violence organizations want to protect victims, regardless of gender, the message they must present is that neither boys nor girls should initiate physical assaults. The fact that boys and girls initiate physical assaults are an important and vital message that is rarely presented by the majority of the nationally recognized domestic violence organizations. What is the reason these organizations ignore or minimize male victimization and female offending?

One of the few studies that actually and factually explore the issues of gender differences in adolescent dating abuse prevalence, types, and injuries and asks specific questions about self-defense reports the following (Foshee, 1996):

- Females perpetrate more mild, moderate, and severe violence than males toward partners even when controlling for violence perpetrated in self-defense.
- Females perpetrate more violence than males out of self-defense.
- Males perpetrate more sexual dating violence than females.
- Males and females sustain equal amounts of mild, moderate, and severe dating violence.
- Females sustain more sexual dating violence than males.
- Females sustain more psychological abuse than males from their partners.
- Females receive more injuries than males from dating violence.

Another study often cited as showing that girls most often use violence in self-defense is Makepeace (1986). However, what the Makepeace study actually documented was that girls were more likely to feel that they were acting in self-defense to an emotional hurt and not a physical assault by a boy-friend. The Makepeace study did not show that girls were actually physically assaulted and that girls only hit back in self-defense.

A dating violence study of 207 male and 288 female college students reported that more males who used force also reported they were using physical assaults in retaliation after being hit first by their female dating partner. Both the males and females reported that getting control and reacting out of jealousy were important factors in their use of physical assaults (Follingstad, Wright, and Sebastian, 1991).

There appears to be enough blame to go around for both boys and girls concerning the initiation of physical assaults (Chrisler, 2005; Straus, 2006). Some of this behavior seems to continue into adulthood. An NIJ report reveals that 56% of women admit that they were the first to use force in an intimate partner violence incident (NIJ, 2004). These women also admit that their use of force was not primarily or exclusively used to protect themselves. The report notes that their behavior increased their risk of being severely abused by their partner; hence, for their own safety it is important that the use of initiation by females be documented and examined.

The O'Keefe (1997) study reports that the number one reason for some-one becoming the recipient of dating violence is that they are the person who initiates the violence. This number one risk factor, initiation of assaults by females is rarely, if ever, mentioned in prevention and intervention programs.

O'Keefe (2005, p. 4) says, "One of the most consistent and strongest fac-tors associated with inflicting violence against a dating partner is the belief that it is acceptable to use violence." And O'Keefe (1997, p. 563) writes, "It is interesting to note that the mean scores of for both males and females of justification of female-to-male violence, indicating that both sexes are more accepting of females' use of violence compared with males." This study also says, "Whereas adolescents are taught that a man should never hit a woman, the portrayal of a woman slapping a man is frequently roman-ticized in the media."

Hence, the O'Keefe (1997) study shows that the best way to ensure that anyone, regardless of gender, who does not want to become a recipient of dating violence is not to initiate the dating violence incident. Further, ignor-ing the fact that females initiate and perpetrate dating violence, regardless of severity, as often or more often than males is actually placing girls in danger and not protecting them.

Despite these facts, lay people, domestic violence advocates, public policy makers, and many professionals continue to believe and publish that girls and women are far more passive and docile in dating and domestic violence inci-dents than are boys and men. For the safety of both girls and boys these incon-sistencies in dating violence intervention programs need to be explored.

Avoiding the Obvious

Does Jane Doe, Inc., similar to the vast majority of nationally sponsored and federally funded domestic violence organizations, really expect that our public policy makers are so naïve that somehow they will believe that the similarities in the abusive and aggressive behavior between girls and boys in high schools somehow magically evaporate the day girls become women and boys become men? Is it possible that our public policy makers are completely and absolutely ignorant of all of the data concerning the fact that both girls and women will often use dating and domestic violence to control or manipulate the behavior of boys and men?

Data from a wide variety of studies concerning Intimate Partner Violence (IPV) are noted in the National Research Council report "Advancing the Federal Research Agenda on Violence Against Women" (Kruttschnitt et al., 2004, pp. 36–40) (see also recommendation #10 of this book).

Apparently the majority of domestic violence advocates and public policy makers are either unaware—they rarely mention male victimization perhaps because they believe it is a rare event—of the aforementioned studies. It is difficult to understand why the majority of advocates and public policy maker have chosen to ignore all of these studies (with the single exception of the National Crime Victimization Survey) that document male victimization is quite common.

U.S. public policy makers have, for the third time, passed a Violence Against Women Act that minimizes female offending and male victimization. What public policy makers need to put in place is a Family Violence Act that is concerned with all victims regardless of age, gender, or sexual orientation.

In fact, in VAWA III, U.S. public policy makers have increased the funding for the NDVH. This is a hotline that claims, knowing that data does not support their claim, that in 95% of abusive relationships men abuse women. The NDVH, largely funded by VAWA funds, continues to minimize or ignore the victimization of boys and men and the offenses by girls and women.

In the "Abuse in America" section of the NDVH website, it is apparent that the intent of the NDVH is to minimize or ignore the victimization of men. There is not a single representation of a male victim, regardless of age, anywhere on the NDVH website. Not presenting one pictorial representation of the victimization of males appears to be a less than subtle attempt at reinforcing negative male stereotyping and implicit bias and leads other organizations, public policy makers, and the public in general to continue to ignore the plight of male victimization, regardless of age.

Senator Joseph Biden

Senator Joseph Biden is the architect of the Violence Against Women Act. Biden noted at the July 2005 Committee on the Judiciary Senate hearings that the primary regret he has about the VAWA is that so many men think it doesn't apply to them. Biden insists that he truly believes that men are included and covered.

Somehow Biden did not notice, as he sat at the July 2005 Committee on the Judiciary Senate hearings for the reauthorization of VAWA, that not one of the domestic violence advocates mentioned the issue of male victimization (Cooney, 2003). It is apparent that these advocates also do not think that VAWA applies to men.

Perhaps Biden has never looked at the obvious bias and implicit discrimination created through the minimization and ignoring of male victimization on the NDVH website, which is funded by millions of federal dollars. Perhaps Biden is not aware of the fact that as of August 13, 2007, there has never been a single picture of a heterosexual male victim, boy or man, anywhere on the NDVH website.

Biden seems unaware of the fact that the majority of domestic violence advocates, public policy makers, criminal justice professionals, and the general public believe that VAWA is intended for women, not men, simply because the act is titled the Violence Against Women Act. Perhaps Biden has not noticed the fact that of the billions spent on VAWA not a single dime has been allocated to a domestic violence intervention or program that specifically focuses on heterosexual male victimization.

Biden seems unwilling or unable to recognize that these are just some of the reasons there are a growing number of organizations similar to the California Men's Centers San Diego that know that men are minimized and ignored and that VAWA does not properly address their concerns about male victimization.

Circumstances and Context

When researchers move beyond the collection of raw data and explore the circumstances and context of individual events, it is obvious that girls report suffering more from dating violence than do boys. Many studies now report that girls experience more emotional problems, injuries, and fear. Domestic and dating violence organizations claiming that boys are not bothered emotionally, that boys report moderate rather than severe injury, and that boys only rarely express fear of girls are organizations that are implicitly minimizing the victimization of boys. Because of contemporary

Table 4.1   Victimization of Boys and Girls

	Victimization of Boys (%)	Victimization of Girls (%)
Overall Violence	38.1	34.9
Severe Physical Violence	13.1	22.5
Moderate Violence	32.9	21.0

cultural gender expectations, the disparity of physical strength and the differences in gender mores and gender norms, the fact that boys report victimization less than girls should be no surprise. Given the expectations of both parents and their peers, there should be little expectation that a boy is going to self-report in a survey that he was beaten up and injured by a girl, and there is even less of a chance that a boy will report he fears being beaten up and injured by a girl.

Table 4.1 shows results from the study "Gender and Contextual Factors in Adolescent Dating Violence" (Molidor and Tolman, 1998). When examining for context it is important to note that most non-sexual-related dating violence studies document that more boys than girls report initiating the incident; however, they also conclude that although there is a difference in the physicality, there is little to no difference in the attempts of coercive control exhibited by boys or girls (O'Keefe, 2005). The studies also report that there is a much greater acceptance for justification of girl-to-boy assaults than boy-to-girl assaults (Cascardi and Avery-Leaf, 2003).

Ideology Skews Public Policy

On November 1, 2001, the first issue of *Criminology and Public Policy* appeared. It was introduced, as it notes in the first issue, as a result of scholars and researchers observing that contemporary criminal justice policy far too often did not reflect the insight and knowledge provide by contemporary science. An important reason for the gap between policy relevant research findings and policy in action is that most policy-related research does not make its way into the hands of policy makers (Clear and Frost, 2001, p. 1).

The National Research Council (NRC) was organized by the National Academy of Sciences for the purpose of gathering research to advise Congress concerning the proper implementation of public policy. As noted elsewhere in this book, the NRC report "Advancing the Federal Research Agenda on Violence Against Women" (Kruttschnitt et al., 2004, p. 6) notes the following:

As previous National Research Council committee found, the design of prevention and control strategies—programs and services available to victims and offenders that aim to decrease the number of new cases of assault or abusive behavior, reduce the risk of death or disability from violence, and extend life after a violent event—frequently is driven by ideology and stakeholders interest rather than by plausible theories and scientific evidence of causes.

Although the behavior of ideological domestic violence advocates is not equitable concerning victims services, it is understandable how ideologically held beliefs would cause LIC, the NCADV, or the AAUW to be unwilling or unable to acknowledge male victimization. The ideology of these organizations is driven by the fact that they are primarily concerned with the welfare of females and their belief that sexism and the oppression of women by men is the exclusive or primary cause of domestic violence. Female victimization is their specific goal.

However, it is neither acceptable nor understandable why or how the U.S. Department of Health and Human Services, Office for the Victims of Crime, CDC, or in fact any federal agency or any public policy maker who will also minimize or ignore male victimization. By their very nature these organizations and public policy makers must be concerned with all victims regardless of age, gender, or sexual orientation.

The National Center for Victims of Crime

The National Center for Victims of Crime (NCVC) claims that information on its website is intended to improve the U.S. response to dating violence. The natural assumption by all parents should be that the NCVC will include all victims of dating violence, regardless of gender. However, the information on the NCVC website minimizes, marginalizes, and ignores the victimization of boys. At one time, not long ago, the NCVC dating violence did present a fair and balanced approach.

The NCVC dating violence section once noted that 45% of females and 43% of males reported being the victim of violence from a dating partner at least once. Why did they remove that information from the website?

Similar to the majority of dating violence advocates, the NCVC ignores information or resources for our boys. On their website is the following: "Twenty percent of teenage girls and young women have experienced some form of dating violence—controlling, abusive, and aggressive behavior in a romantic relationship" (NCVC, 2004). There is no similar information concerning the percentage of boys who have experienced some form of dating violence.

The Centers for Disease Control and Prevention

A CDC weekly report titled "Physical Dating Violence Among High School Students—United States 2003" (Black, Noonan, Legg, Eaton, and Breiding, 2006) details that similar numbers of girls and boys report engaging in physical dating violence incidents. It outlines that 8.9% of boys and 8.8% of girls reported that they were the victims of physical dating violence. Then, apparently without reason or logic, the report notes the following:

> Dating violence victimization can be a precursor for intimate partner violence (IPV) victimization in adulthood, most notably among women. Among adult women in the United States, an estimated 5.2 million IPV incidents occur each year, resulting in approximately 2 million injuries and 1,300 deaths.

The report (Black et al., 2006) does note that the data concerning the nonfatal IPV were collected from the NVAWS and the data about IPV homicides were obtained from the FBI's Uniform Crime Reports Supplementary Homicide Reports. However, what can be the reason that the report chose to ignore the relevant data concerning male victimization in the survey and explanation of results? Is it possible that Black and colleagues are unaware that the CDC National Center for Injury Prevention and Control acknowledges that intimate partner violence appears to be widely underreported by men?

Tjaden and Thoennes (2000a) report the following:

> Nearly 5.3 million incidents of IPV occur each year among U.S. women ages 18 and older, and 3.2 million occur among men. Most assaults are relatively minor and consist of pushing, grabbing, shoving, slapping, and hitting.

In the United States every year, about 1.5 million women and more than 800,000 men are raped or physically assaulted by an intimate partner. This translates into about 47 IPV assaults per 1,000 women and 32 assaults per 1,000 men (Tjaden and Thoennes, 2000a).

What, other than ideology, could cause Black et al. (2006) to believe that it is productive and positive to ignore the data concerning male victimization? The CDC also acknowledges that the differential just noted is far smaller because of the underreporting by male victims. It appears that the information about male victimization was purposely ignored by Black et al., as it is improbable to impossible to believe they are not aware of male victimization. If it is not ideologically held beliefs that cause this painting of male victimization as invisible, what is it?

Further, it appears to be quite possible that this continued and constant marginalization, minimization, and exclusion of any mention of male victimization in many dating, domestic violence, and intimate partner violence studies, similar to Black et al.'s (2006) report, is what causes the media, public policy makers, and the general public to so often simply dismiss male victimization.

Safety First

In a cart-before-the-horse leap of logic, many domestic violence advocates attempt to show that female and male domestic and dating violence offenders cannot be equally guilty of offending by presenting data that report the following (O'Keefe, 2005):

- Females are injured more often than males.
- Females seek medical treatment more often than males.
- Females fear for their safety more often than males.
- Females are hurt emotionally more often than males.

Somehow many, if not most, advocates, as their websites show, are unwilling or unable to recognize or acknowledge that the majority of dating violence incidents are not chronic violent beatings or battering behavior. And the NVAWS and all of the other studies record that most dating and family violence incidents are minor.

Primary and empirically based research in the reference section of this book outlines that the vast majority of studies clearly demonstrate that females often can be equally as guilty as males in exhibiting coercive and manipulative behavior. Also, most studies in the reference section show that that females and males initiate domestic and dating violence incidents on an equal basis. The reference section provides the website or URLs for these studies.

Also, most studies (Fiebert, 2005, list more than 200) show that females and males initiate domestic and dating violence incidents on an equal basis.

The four reasons listed above are the results or the effects of an incident and are not informative concerning what behavior affects or causes those incidents. And as O'Keefe explains, the primary predictor of getting physically assaulted is to physically assault someone else first (Health Inc, 2006).

It appears that if domestic violence organizations similar to Jane Doe, Inc., the NDVH, the FVPV, VAWnet, and others continue to minimize and ignore female initiation and male victimization, they are actually hindering and not helping in the construction of a gender-inclusive understanding of the issue of dating and domestic violence that will make both boys and girls safer (Straus, 2006).

The fact is that there are a growing number of young men who talk to each other about the need to intervene when they witness males hitting females. There are now dating violence prevention and intervention workshops in our public and private schools, as noted in the reference section of this book, that often address the fact that males should not hit females (Cascardi and Avery-Leaf, 2003; Foshee, 1996; Jackson, 1999; Matthews, 1984; O'Keefe, 2005; Rosenbluth, 2002).

However, perhaps because most domestic and dating violence interventions ignore female offending and male victimization, as their websites report, males being slapped or hit with objects by females is still publicly portrayed as being far less offensive that men hitting women. Just as troubling is the fact that in some instances this use of violence by females is still portrayed as being romantic or humorous (O'Keefe, 1997).

Though the majority of domestic violence organizations claim their goal is to protect females, not warning females about the consequences of their initiating physical assaults actually places those females in greater danger of being assaulted. What can the reasons be that the majority of domestic violence organization websites minimize or ignore male victimization and female offenses?

Dating violence interventions and prevention programs are important not only for teenage intervention but also because that behavior may replicate itself in adult relationships (O'Keefe, 2005). Replacing the myriad of causal factors that are often unique, situational and individual, with a one-gender-fits-all sexism and the oppression of women theory not only ignores reams of academic empirical studies to the contrary; this one-gender-fits-all is also a theory that can actually endanger, not protect, females (Finkelhor and Straus, 2006).

There appears to be a disturbing lack of logic and common sense in believing that child, sibling, dating, same-sex couple, and elder abuse have a myriad of complex causal factors whereas the abuse of adult heterosexual males and heterosexual females occurs exclusively or primarily because of sexism and the oppression of women. The issue of unequal power in familial abuse is not specific to adult heterosexual males and females (Chalk and King, 1998). Most children, regardless of gender, learn at an early age that parents, regardless of gender, have more physical and economic power than children. In fact, most family violence researchers recognize that the issue of power and control runs through child, sibling, spousal, intimate partner, and elder abuse (Crowell and Burgess, 1996). The issues of power and control are often the first lessons children, both male and female, learn from adults, both male and female.

It appears that the issues of power and control are the rules of adults that children are expected to learn to abide by. Spanking or other forms of coercive behavior are no more or less than one person using force or manipulative behavior to change or alter the behavior of another person (Straus, 2006).

Many teenagers and young adults have heard from their parents, regardless of gender, that as long as they live in their parents' house they must abide by their parents' rules. These are gender-neutral lessons we all learn as children from inside the family household, not from the outside social structure (Jaffee, Caspi, Moffitt, and Taylor, 2004).

The reasons stated for the majority of abuse in the dating violence studies referenced in this chapter are jealously, anger, stress, antisocial psychological behaviors, and a myriad of other intimate discords. It appears to be not only illusionary but also dangerous to believe that in the adulthood of heterosexual males and females that the myriad of causal factors of dating violence should be ignored or are only minimal factors that should be replaced with the one-size-fits-all patriarchal explanation (Updike, 1999).

Further, no empirical evidence-based studies can show that the abuse of heterosexual women is primarily caused because of sexism and the oppression of heterosexual women by heterosexual men and that heterosexual intimate partner abuse is dramatically different from other relationship abusive behavior.

Though some forms of partner manipulation, coercion, aggression, and abuse between boys and men can differ from that of girls and women, many if not most of those behaviors do not (Hamel, in press).

A growing number of studies show the "behavioral patterns of various forms of violence, such as male violence against women and men and female violence against men and women, may be similar" (Kruttschnitt et al., 2004, p. 100). The needs of one group of victims do not invalidate nor should they be more important than the needs of another. It is important that interventions, policies, and procedures are designed to reflect the perpetration and victimization of boys and young men and girls and young women.

An evaluation of school-based programs that primarily focus on males as the assaultive and aggressive perpetrators and females as docile and passive victims failed to change the beliefs or attitudes of the students toward the use of dating violence, and the evaluators suggest that programs should reflect data from the majority of empirical studies showing that both boys and girls can be either or both offenders or perpetrators of dating violence (Cascardi and Avery-Leaf, 2003).

One of the early and most respected researchers concerning dating violence reports that if the underlying problems of dating violence are not openly and honestly dealt with those same problems may very well reemerge in future relationships (Makepeace, 1987).

The failure of the majority of domestic violence organizations to recognize the victimization of boys by girls also hinder research and impede prevention studies that can help document a better understanding of risk factors that place both boys and girls at risk of physical victimization. The ignoring of female offending by domestic violence organizations increases the chances of victimization for both females and boys (Hamel, 2006).

What is it that causes our public policy makers, VAWA, and the majority of domestic violence organizations to minimize and ignore the victimization of boys by girls? Should not all these organizations be as equally concerned about our sons as they are about our daughters? Neither our sons nor daughters should need to report equal percentages of victimization before receiving equal compassion, empathy, education, and access to services and funding.

How do these domestic violence organizations expect to explain how or why these myriad of complex, multifaceted, and dramatically different reasons given by teenagers and young adults for their use of dating violence can all stunningly and mysteriously change to become sexism and the oppression of women the day our daughters become women and our sons become men? Why, given only very limited, if any, empirically based evidence, do our public policy makers and the majority of domestic violence organizations continue to claim or believe that 58% to 95% of domestic violence is committed by assertive and aggressive males against passive and docile females?

The opinions and beliefs of teenagers and young adults, regardless of gender or sexual orientation, are too important to be ignored. They must be allowed to become the instruments and tools that can break the cycle of violence that begins in the family, in childhood, and continues on into adulthood.

Everyone agrees that males must become more involved with the issue of dating and domestic violence. However, few of our public policy makers and even fewer dating and domestic violence advocates seem willing or able to understand that many, if not most, males avoid the issues of dating and domestic violence because ideological feminist domestic violence advocates have misidentified the problem.

Conclusion

First and foremost this chapter is far more concerned with the cause than the consequences of dating and domestic violence because prevention should always preclude intervention. *Cause* is generally defined as that without which an effect or a phenomenon would not exist. If we first can identify the causal factors and provide proper intervention and education, we will also be treating the consequences by lessening the number of abusers and the victims of their abuse. As always, it must be the horse and then the cart.

A visit to the websites of the vast majority of the nationally recognized dating and domestic violence websites reveals that the most of these organizations actively engage in minimizing or ignoring male victimization regardless of age. After reading the studies referenced in this chapter it should be difficult, if not impossible, to understand how federal funds for dating violence should be allocated to biased and prejudiced domestic violence organizations that adhere to dated 20th-century one-size-fits-all theories. These organizations continue to ignore the reams of empirically evidence-based studies showing that domestic or dating violence is a complex and multifaceted issue that requires interventions for both our sons and our daughters (Fiebert, 2005).

The NIJ research report "The Criminalization of Domestic Violence: Promises and Limits" (Fagan, 1996, p. 48) concludes:

> Let's not be embarrassed or embarrass ourselves by continuing on this frustrating path of fad-driven and nonsystematic policies with weak after-the-fact evaluations. Collaborative research to develop and test theoretically driven interventions and policies will make a significant contribution to the development of policies for legal interventions to protect battered women. A continuation of the research efforts of the past two decades will not.

The NRC report to Congress titled "Advancing the Federal Research Agenda on Violence Against Women" (Kruttschnitt et al., 2004, p. 100) also says, "Finally, there is emerging and credible evidence that the general origins and behavioral patterns of various forms of violence, such as male violence against women and men and female violence against men and women, may be similar."

The majority of dating violence studies show that physical violence in dating relationships is reciprocal. In fact many studies show that girls initiate and use nonsexual physical violence more than boys (O'Keefe, 2005). O'Keefe claims that most of the dating violence studies ignore the intention, circumstance, context, or consequence of this dating violence. Because of these limitations, O'Keefe and the domestic violence organizations claim the YRBS does not present the truth, the whole truth, and nothing but the truth. Yet, as this chapter reveals, almost each and every domestic or dating violence website contains the claim that it is a fact that 1 in 5 female high school students report being physically or sexually abused by a dating partner. However, the truth, as noted already, is that this ubiquitous "1 in 5" data so often cited as "fact" by domestic or dating violence websites was retrieved from a small, single, stand-alone state sample of the national YRBS report.

All domestic violence organizations that present data detailing female victimization and purposely ignoring male victimization overlook the fact that the YRBS data does not provide evidence for the intention, circumstances, context, or consequences of dating violence behavior; however, this does not prevent the data from appearing almost everywhere without a word of descent from advocates. If not for ideology, how can all of these nationally recognized domestic violence organizations, ethically or morally, continue to claim that the YRBS data is valid and should be believed when documenting female victimization and that the same YRBS data should be ignored and dismissed concerning male victimization? There seems to be little to no mention of this double standard in the literature concerning dating or domestic violence? For the safety of all victims regardless of age, gender, or sexual orientation, our public policy makers should become more concerned about this apparent double standard.

The fact is that females suffer more severe injury, seek more medical attention, are often emotionally distressed, and, because they are more fearful than boys, report incidents more often than boys. However, these behaviors are after-the-fact consequences. Further, because of physical differences in strength and contemporary cultural gender norms, females will most often suffer more long-term consequences and suffer more emotionally and economically than some males. Again, these are after-the-fact consequences and not causal factors (Straus, 2006).

For the safety of both our daughters and our sons, it is time for members of Congress to read the report "Advancing the Federal Research Agenda on Violence Against Women." The report notes a growing body of evidence that shows that the incidence of violence against both males and females may be similar. The authors of this report believe that our public policy makers need to become more concerned with empirically based studies and data and less concerned with ideologically held beliefs (Kruttschnitt et al., 2004).

As the studies referenced in this chapter show, there should be little doubt that some dating violence incidents are similar to some of the oppressive and violent relationships between some spouses or intimate partners. However, studies clearly point out that the majority of this behavior is not severe long-term violent behavior (O'Keefe, 2005; Tjaden and Thoennes, 2000a).

It should be obvious, for the safety of everyone involved, that it is time for dating and domestic violence organizations to stop concluding that female violence against males is most frequently in self-defense and that male victimization is often irrelevant because the after-effects are that females will suffer more physically and emotionally (Straus, 2006).

The dating violence studies referenced herein show that the majority of domestic and dating violence incidents are minor and that domestic and dating violence prevention will succeed only when advocates become open and inclusive of all victims regardless of age, gender, or sexual orientation.

An ever increasing number of empirically evidence-based studies now report the victimization of males at the hands of females. If domestic or dating violence organizations are to prevent or minimize dating or domestic violence regardless of age or sexual orientation they must begin to take the offending of females and the victimization of males more seriously than they presently do (O'Leary, 2000).

Public policy makers and domestic violence advocates must commit to a long-term holistic effort to provide prevention and intervention programs for teenagers and young adults regardless of gender. Although after-the-fact interventions for females remains greater than for males, the minimizing and marginalizing of male victimization has created negative, not positive, concerns for all victims (Straus, 2006). It is time we point our finger at our own heart and head and not at each other. It is time to begin at the beginning, not the end. We must place the cause before the consequence to effectively minimize or eliminate that consequence.

Discussion Questions

1. Imagine that you are a county district attorney and that you have the power to change laws in your jurisdiction. Upon reviewing all of the contemporary domestic violence studies from the U.S. Department of Justice would you continue with contemporary mandatory or preferred arrest policies or allow, after proper dating and domestic violence training, law enforcement officers to use the same discretionary arrest policies that they use for all other crimes? Explain why.

2. After law enforcement returns to discretionary arrest policies you discover that county, state, and national domestic violence organizations have mobilized a massive campaign to bring national attention to their opposition and they demand that you return to the mandatory dating and domestic violence arrest policies. What data and empirical evidence will you cite to document that for the safety and protection of those being abused, law enforcement should adhere to discretionary arrest policies?

3. Consider the assertion "that criminal justice statistics provide a measurement of only the behavior of a subset of the population and not the population in general" (Macionia, 1997). Does this fact undermine or support the general belief that males in general are prone to abusive behavior and females are prone to passive and docile behavior (Dorbash and Dorbash, 1979)? Explain why.

4. Does the LCI-commissioned TRAS (LCI, 2007) undermine or support the belief that, in dating relationships, males are almost always guilty of being the abuser and females most often only act out in self-defense? Is there any reason to believe that there is some age when boys and girls end dating violence and begin domestic violence behavior?

5. Recommend the best possible prevention policy to combat dating and domestic violence. These policies must be supported by evidence-based data and remain within both personnel and fiscal reality. Use one of the educational programs discussed in this chapter and some of the on-line references in this book to demonstrate how to use your limited resources to reduce both dating and domestic violence behavior among all the varied demographic populations within your jurisdiction.

The California Conundrum: Keeping the Promise

5

If we appeal to law, we sometimes call upon a Trojan horse; when we invite law in, law re-invites itself time and again, but on its own terms and with its own agenda.

—Renee Romken

Introduction

Hendricks, McKean, and Hendricks (2003, p. 178), in the college text *Crisis Intervention,* note the following:

> Currently, intimate partner violence is studied from a family violence perspective, a feminist [Duluth] perspective, and a social psychological perspective. If one reviews the research, commentaries, and debates between adherents of the three perspectives, it sometimes seems as if they are talking about different phenomenon.

The National Institute of Justice (NIJ) notes in many of its publications that it is "... the research, development, and evaluation agency of the U.S. Department of Justice (DOJ). NIJ provides objective, independent, evidence-based knowledge and tools to enhance the administration of justice and public safety."

This chapter uses California as an illustration of an ideological domestic violence intervention-based public policy. It seems, at least to me, that the reason so many researchers, advocates, and public policy makers seem to be talking about domestic violence as being different phenomena is because the majority of contemporary interventions, similar to California, appear to be using tools (policies) that too often appear to be driven by legislative constraints, considerations, and an inherent conflicts of interests from programs already in place rather than evidence-based knowledge provided by the DOJ (Kruttschnitt, McLaughlin, and Petrie, 2004).

The purpose of the National Research Council (NRC) is to advise the federal government concerning science and technology with the intent that their policy-related research will help the federal and in turn state government in developing legislation. Again, it appears that much of the legislation developed in California, and elsewhere in America, has often chosen to ignore the NRC advice in favor of contemporary domestic violence ideology that is sometimes based in late 20th-century dogma (Gelles, 2007).

The NRC report "Advancing the Federal Research Agenda on Violence Against Women" (Kruttschnitt et al., 2004, p. 6) notes:

> As a previous National Research Council committee found, the design of prevention and control strategies—programs and services available to victims and offenders that aim to decrease the number of new cases of assault or abusive behavior, reduce the risk of death or disability from violence, and extend life after a violent event—frequently is driven by ideology and stakeholders interests rather than by plausible theories and scientific evidence of causes.

The majority of public policy makers and most domestic violence agencies, as this book and their websites demonstrate, appear to have primarily embraced the Duluth perspective and have minimized or marginalized the family violence perspective and the social psychological perspective. It appears to me that they have done this because the latter two perspectives are too inclusive of male victimization. It is very clear that the majority of domestic violence agencies and advocates, as their websites clearly show, too often minimize, marginalize, and ignore male victimization.

For reasons that escape me, our public policy makers and the criminal justice system, more often than not, adhere to the single ideological domestic violence advocates theory at the expense of the family or social psychological theory.

The findings from the National Violence Against Women Survey (NVAWS) were presented in a report sponsored by NIJ and the Centers for Disease Control and Prevention (CDC) (Tjaden and Thoennes, 2000a). They write, "These findings support the theory that violence perpetrated against women by intimates is often part of a systematic pattern of dominance and control" (p. iv). However, Tjaden and Thoennes present no empirically based evidence of their subjective perspective in their NVAWS reports to the NIJ. From my research it appears that few to none from NIJ or the CDC noticed that Tjaden and Thoennes do not point out in the NVAWS that the intimate partner violence committed against a woman is actually a systematic pattern of dominance and control or patriarchal terrorism by males over females.

And what should have been just as troubling for the NIJ and the CDC is that Tjaden and Thoennes (2000a) may not be providing objective research. They do not offer any similar theories or in fact any theories at all about male victimization despite the fact that the NVAWS details that more than one of every three victims of intimate partner violence is male (ibid., p. 55).

Perhaps because of their personal and professionally held beliefs Tjaden and Thoennes (2000a) may have injected their personal and professional beliefs into the survey, as if their personally held beliefs were supported by their empirically evidence-based data. I have read and reread—and invite others to do the same—the findings from the NVAWS and can find little to no empirically evidence-based findings that support the claim made by Tjaden and Thoennes that intimate partner violence is exclusively or primarily caused by adult heterosexual men against adult heterosexual women because of their patriarchal attempt to control or dominant women.

Dominance and control, it seems, are just assumed by Tjaden and Thoennes (2000a) to be the primary causal factors of intimate partner violence, as nowhere do these researchers provide any empirical data to document their claim (Dutton, 2006; Gelles, 2007; Straus, 1998; Straus, in press).

What should be most troubling for the NIJ is that subjective, not objective, authors similar to Tjaden and Thoennes continue to drive both federal and local legislation and criminal justice intervention (Dutton, 2006).

Keeping the Promise (KtP)

Casey Gwinn is the chair of the California Attorney General Task Force on Local Criminal Justice Response to Domestic Violence. The task force report titled "Keeping the Promise" Victim Safety and Batterer Accountability is available on line on the California Attorney General Task Force (Gwinn et al., 2005).

The members of the task force seem to be a well-intentioned group of qualified professionals. However, it appears that most members have decided to ignore or are unaware of many recent DOJ-sponsored and privately funded studies concerning the issue of domestic violence. It appears that because of their intent to continue or increase contemporary policies and procedures, many task force members often are unaware of or have decided to disregard advice from the majority of scholars and researchers, both public and private, concerning contemporary domestic violence intervention, surveys, reports, data, and studies.

Many sociologists and criminologists believe that many of the recent policy-related research findings continue to be overlooked because the empirically based data disputes the ideological held beliefs of many domestic violence agencies and advocates (Fagan, 1996).

Ideological domestic violence advocates are people more concerned with women's rights than with victim or civil rights. Many, if not most, domestic violence advocates continue to claim that domestic violence is a crime of misogyny. They believe that domestic violence is caused by the hatred men have for women and that men use violence to control the behavior of women (Brownmiller, 1975; Dobash and Dobash, 1979).

However, reams of public and private data outline that most men do not abuse women. Ideological domestic violence advocates claim that though it is true that the majority of men are not violent—a fact that criminal justice data supports and advocates cannot deny—many advocates claim that because of the patriarchal structure of contemporary society, the majority of men silently condone violence against women (Hendricks et al., 2003). Hence, in the eyes of ideological domestic violence advocates, until proven innocent, all men are guilty of being the enemy of all women. This ideological philosophy is the foundation of the majority of domestic violence agencies, and those agencies have had a dramatic effect on both federal and state interventions. Thus, when this ideology is accepted as fact, these advocates must believe that men are the offenders and women their victims.

This Duluth theory makes it improbable, if not impossible, for these advocates to believe that women can actually be offenders and males their victims. Hence, when men present themselves as victims to domestic violence advocates, those men are seen first as offenders in the sheep's clothing of victims and when the facts of an individual incident do reveal the truth, some men will be accepted as the rare male victim (Walton, 2003, p. 18). This ignorance of male victimization permeates our public policies and drives federal and state intervention.

Permeating the System

The "Keeping the Promise" report (Gwinn et al., 2005) is a classic example of a one-solution-fits-all ideological domestic violence advocacy trumping scientific studies and research. This one-solution-fits-all intervention is not exclusive to California. Although this chapter concerns itself primarily with the "Keeping the Promise" report, this ideological domestic violence advocacy is the foundation for most federal and state domestic violence intervention in America.

A letter to the California attorney general for the State of California is at the beginning of "Keeping the Promise," and it claims in part that "this report should be read as a road map for addressing profound problems in the handling of domestic violence incidents in California." In reality, as this chapter shows, this report appears to be a rework of many of the failed polices of the 20th century. Though the numbers of all homicide victims regardless of relationship have dropped dramatically over the last 22 years, the number of white females who are murdered by their intimate partner remains virtually unchanged from 1976 to 2002 (Rennison and Welchans, 2000).

The greatest failing of the California "road map" appears to be that it is founded on criminalizing all acts of "family conflict" as if they were the same as "battering behavior." It is also predicated on a one-solution-fits-all ideological paradigm that lacks empirical evidence; hence, many of the KtP recommendations are profoundly out of date, and they ignore many of the recommendations provide by the DOJ studies.

One-Solution-Fits-All

Fagan (1996, p. 38) warns advocates and public policy makers in the DOJ-sponsored report "The Criminalization of Domestic Violence: Promises and Limits" that "assuming that the patriarchy and power relations alone cause of domestic violence leads us toward conclusions that do not consider a full array of explanatory variables from other disciplines."

Accepting the patriarchy (Duluth theory) as the single or primary cause of domestic violence has made many advocates and public policy makers believe that domestic violence is, in fact, violence against women and that the cause of domestic violence is primarily adult heterosexual men abusing adult heterosexual women. This single, ideological solution clouds the ability of many advocates, public policy makers, and criminal justice interveners to understand the complex and multifaceted issue that domestic violence is.

The 20th-century one-solution-fits-all ideological domestic violence advocate paradigm is the belief that every act of family conflict must be criminalized because they will always escalate and that all family conflict offenders must be treated as batterers (Gelles, 2007). Further, viewing domestic violence only or primarily through the lens of the patriarchy causes one to believe that men must be the abusers and women their victims. The KtP single solution ideology has caused the task force report to present microsolutions to a macrophenomenon.

Domestic Violence Is Not Treated the Same as Other Crimes

California, similar to all the others states, has not passed a battering law. What California and all the other states have done is to criminalize almost every act of family conflict. Domestic violence laws, most often, are similar or the same regardless of how minor, infrequent or chronic and serious the incident is. This may suit some advocates; however, there is an ever growing number of victims of violent chronic abuse and interveners who see little logic with a one-solution-fits-all intervention that treats the victims of minor family conflict the same as those who are violently and chronically abused (Huntley and Kilzer, 2005).

The NVAWS clearly shows that the majority of the alleged violence that both men and women report are incidents where they are pushed, grabbed, shoved, slapped, or hit (Tjaden and Thoennes, 2000a).

In some states only the fear that a physical conflict might occur is enough to issue a restraining order that often can lead to criminal justice intervention. When there is any violation of the restraining order, regardless of context or circumstances, those actions, regardless of how minor they are, will be considered criminal acts (Miller, 2005). The idea that any act of family conflict is equal to battering may be the most significant reason for the dramatic leap in the number of males and females being arrested. If the "Keeping the Promise" report were only concerned with battering behavior it may very well have been a promising road map.

Most domestic violence advocates claim, on one hand, that what they want is for the criminal justice system to treat domestic violence the same as all other crimes. However, their one-solution-fits-all intervention policies ignore the time-honored traditional difference between felonies (i.e., serious crimes) and misdemeanors (i.e., minor crimes). This has created a complex and multifaceted intervention process that mixes civil procedures with the criminal process. There are now domestic violence policies and procedures that make demands of the criminal justice system that are dramatically different and at times radically at odds with all other criminal justice training and interventions.

What sets the American criminal justice system apart from many other nations is the historic and time-honored belief that everyone must be assumed to be innocent until the facts and evidence in the case will produce a verdict of guilt or innocence.

However, everyone involved in the criminal justice system understands that the majority of contemporary domestic violence training is predicated on the belief that women are the victims and men their abusers. I have attended "training the trainer" domestic violence programs, and it is generally accepted by the trainers that offenders will be always be referred to as *he* and the victims referred to as *she*. It is also a fact that the vast majority of contemporary domestic violence training teaches criminal justice interveners that the vast majority of the time *she* will be the victim and that the vast majority of the time *he* will be the primary or dominant aggressor (Gladwell, 2005).

In case there is any confusion about the *he* and *she* in domestic violence prevention training, the training often notes that the person who is bigger and stronger should be considered the offender and that it is not important who assaulted who first. There should be little doubt that this training creates an unspoken biased association of guilt (men) and innocence (women) (Domestic Violence Arrests: Beyond the Obvious, 2000).

Battering Behavior

Most researchers agree that a "batterer" is a family member or intimate partner who with premeditation and malice aforethought repeatedly uses coercion, force, or violent physical assaults to manipulate and control the behavior of another family member or intimate partner. Research shows that most batterers are dangerous and violent people. Many batterers suffer from antisocial personality disorders or are people who use violence to resolve conflict, and it has been my experience that the vast majority of law enforcement officers I worked with and trained agree that batterers, regardless of gender or why they batter, should be arrested.

Family Conflict

Family conflict most often occurs without premeditation or malice aforethought and involves the use of threats or minor physical assault in a specific or isolated disagreement. This behavior is often the result of perceived misbehavior, financial matters, jealously, and animated and vocal disagreements.

What KtP and California law ignores is that although the issuance of restraining orders, mandatory arrest, no-drop-prosecutions, batterer intervention programs, and mandatory health practitioner reports can be positive and productive concerning battering behavior, they can also be negative and counterproductive concerning family conflict.

The Domestic Violence Problem

In chapter 1, on page 11 of the introduction of KtP under the heading "The Domestic Violence Problem," the task force informs the attorney general, "National studies show that 85 percent of reported cases of victimization by intimate partners were against women" (Gwinn et al., 2005). The citation that the task force provides is the DOJ-sponsored study "Extent, Nature, and Consequences of Intimate Partner Violence" (Tjaden and Thoennes, 2000a). However, that DOJ study makes no such claim. What it does report on page iii is that nearly 25% of surveyed women and 7.6% of surveyed men reported they were raped or physically assaulted by an intimate partner at least once in their lifetime. On the same page it also reports that 1.5% of women and 0.9% of men reported they were raped or physically assaulted by a partner in the previous 12 months. Why would the KtP report otherwise?

Why does the task force ignore the fact that the report it cites refutes, not supports, the 85% claim? One of the problems for some members of the task force, similar to most one-solution-fits-all ideologists, is that they are unwilling or unable to see or understand data that they do not agree with. The majority of the national studies actually show that the physical assault victimization of intimates range from 9% to 30% for women and from 13% to 16% for men. This differential is not the 85% to 15% differential that the task force claims that national studies document. There is only one national study that documents a 85% to 15% differential: the National Crime Victimization Survey (NCVS) (U.S. Department of Justice, Bureau of Justice Statistics, 2001). For reasons that escape me, many advocates simply choose to accept the NCVS as fact and ignore all the other studies.

The Fear Factor Gender Differential

Fear of being a victim is much higher in women than in men, although crime data shows that it is young males who suffer the majority of the victimization (Brody, Lovas, and Hay, 1995). One study documents that females are approximately three times more likely than males to be fearful of a physical assault from their abusive partner (Follingstad, Wright, and Sebastian, 1991).

The Bureau of Justice Statistics report "Intimate Partner Violence in the United States" states that 15.2% of women, compared with 2.5% for males, report being afraid of a reprisal concerning an intimate partner violence incident (Catalano, 2006). A number of studies show that females startle more easily than males and that females react more fearfully to stressful events than do males (Brizendine, 2006).

The 30th edition of the DOJ's *Criminal Justice Statistics Sourcebook* documents that females report they are more than twice as fearful as males to walk alone at night in their neighborhood (Maguire and Pastore, 2002). And the Australian Bureau of Statistics report "Personal Safety Survey 2005" shows that women are twice as fearful as men when walking alone in their neighborhoods after dark. This survey also shows that women are three times more likely than men to experience anxiety or fear concerning domestic violence incidents (Trewin, 2005).

Given the differences in physical size and strength between men and women, the latter are far more likely to fear their abusive partner, to experience injury, and to receive medical attention for their injuries, so it is reasonable for females to fear intimate partner violence more than men (Holtzworth-Munroe, 2005; Laroche, 2005).

Reporting

Females regardless of age who report they have been abused by an intimate partner are far more likely than males to report that they are afraid of their partner and to report that they have been injured (Hamberger and Guse, 2002; Johnson and Bunge, 2001; Morse, 1995; O'Keefe and Treister, 1998).

The task force ignores the fact that the NVAWS details that women (26.4%) are approximately twice as likely as men (13.4%) to report being victimized to law enforcement officers. The NVAWS reports that women are also more likely (51.9% of women v. 36.2% of men) to report being stalked to law enforcement.

The task force also overlooks the fact that the NVAWS documents that the police are approximately three times more likely to arrest or detain (36.4% for women v. 12.3% for men) an intimate partner perpetrator when the victim is female.

The gender differential of higher reporting for females holds true for same-sex victimization. Between 1993 and 1999 13,740 men reported being victimized by their male intimate partner as compared with 16,900 women who were victimized by their female intimate partner (Rennison, 2001). Family violence studies show that women are significantly more likely than men to call the police in response to a partner assault. The General Social Survey (GSS) of Canada documents that women are twice as likely as men to report their victimization to the police (AuCoin, 2005).

The NVAWS reports that more than half of all physical assaults by intimates are relatively minor and consist of pushing, grabbing, shoving, slapping, and hitting and that 1.3% of women and 0.9% of men are physically assaulted by an intimate partner annually (Tjaden and Thoennes, 2000b). The NCVS details that 50% of women and 32% of men who are assaulted by an intimate partner report suffering an injury (Bureau of Justice Statistics, U.S. Department of Justice, Office of Justice Programs, 2007a). The NVAWS outlines that 39.0% of women and 24.8% of men report being injured during their most recent physical assault. This survey includes both violent and minor intimate partner assaults.

The GSS statistics report that an estimated 7% of women and 6% of men in current or previous spousal relationship have been victimized. Although the Canadian data does show women are victimized more than men, it also shows that domestic violence against men occurs at rates similar to most national family violence surveys and studies. The GSS reveals that approximately 23% of women and 15% of men claim they were beaten, choked, or threatened by having a gun or knife used against them. Women are more than twice as likely to be injured, three times more likely to fear for their life, and more than six times more likely to seek medical attention.

The NVAWS data seems to say that if men and women did report their physical assaults at the same rate for crime surveys similar to the NCVS, more than one of every three intimate partner victims would be a man. The gender differential in these two surveys clearly documents that men are far more reluctant to view and report their victimization as a crime than are women.

The June 2005 DOJ report "Family Violence Statistics" (Durose et al. 2005) records that family violence accounts for only 11% of all reported and unreported violence and that the majority of family violence is simple assault.

The NCVS shows that only approximately one half of 1% of people, both men and women, who answered the survey report that they have been a victim of domestic violence (Bureau of Justice Statistics, U.S. Department of Justice, Office of Justice Programs, 2007a). The NCVS numbers do not represent the claim so often made by ideological advocates that domestic violence is a crime of epidemic proportions; hence, the NCVS data set is always ignored by the very same domestic violence advocates who then use the same NCVS data set to continue their claim that the 85% female victimization data from the very NCVS survey is absolutely true.

How can and why do domestic violence advocates, as well as the members of the KtP report, accept the 85% female victimization data presented by the NCVS as fact and then claim that the data in the NCVS reporting that only one half of 1% of people surveyed reported they have been victims of domestic violence data is fiction?

Dating Relationships

Dating relationships, by their very nature, fall under the legal umbrella covered by California domestic violence laws. The Centers for Disease Control and Prevention (CDC) Youth Risk Behavior Surveillance System (YRBS) monitors health-risk behaviors among youth and young adults (CDC, 2006).

Ideological domestic violence advocates, as their websites clearly reveal, universally ignore data from the YRBS unless and when it suits their agenda. The YRBS (CDC, 2006, p. 44) outlines that 9.3% of girls and 9.0% of boys report being hit, slapped, or physically hurt on purpose by a boyfriend or girlfriend. The same page of the YRBS also documents that 10.8% of girls and 4.2% of boys report being physically forced to have sexual intercourse.

When ideological domestic violence advocates, as their websites show, do use the data that the YRBS reports, they most often use only the information concerning the victimization of girls and ignore the data showing the victimization of boys.

In California, the data on the attorney general's website note that there is little difference between male and female students who report being victimized by their dating partner. Approximately 60% of students report they were the victims of dating violence (SafeState, 2006).

In Gwinn's hometown of San Diego in 2005, fewer girls (11.0%) than boys (11.8%) report being hit, slapped, or physically hurt on purpose by a girlfriend or boyfriend in the past 12 months. Is it logical to assume that this abuse differential magically changes to 85% versus 15% differential the day girls and boys become women and men? Also, 13.2% of the girls and 7.0% of the boys in San Diego report they were physically forced to have sexual intercourse. Gwinn and all of the other members of the task force must or should know that under California law that all those hits, slaps, and forced sexual behavior are all, by California statute law, acts of domestic violence.

These California teenagers may not be that far removed from the lessons they learn from their parents, regardless of gender. And the lesson many of them often learn at home is that physical force and economic coercion often works to control the behavior of others. The rights of parents or other adults almost always supersede those of children. People who possess more physical or economic power, regardless of gender, often use that power to get their own way.

This is not a lesson taught from outside the patriarchy; it is a lesson taught from inside the home by the family hierarchy and by both parents, regardless of gender. In homes the physical assaults between adults and the physical assaults against children teach many lessons to children. According to Straus et al. (1980) children most often learn these three lessons:

- Those who love you the most are also those that hit you.
- There is sometimes a moral right to hit other members of the same family.
- When all else fails, use violence.

Another study reports that a majority of children use physical assaults and coercion to resolve conflicts among siblings. In fact, a number of these studies reveal that sibling violence is the most common form of family violence in the United States (Wallace, 2002). After 21 years in law enforcement, I cannot remember any time when parents believed that it would be a good idea to call the police when there were minor incidents of siblings pushing, shoving, slapping, or hitting each other.

Domestic Violence Homicides

The task force notes that homicide is the most serious consequence of violence and that the number of domestic violence homicides is unacceptably high for women. It does not mention, however, that domestic violence homicides may be unacceptably high for men (Paulozzi, Saltzman, Thompson, and Holmgreen, 2001).

The DOJ report "Family Violence Statistics" (Durose et al., 2005) reports that females account for 58% of all family murder victims. Although male victims account for 42% of the victims KtP makes no mention of male homicide victimization.

Another DOJ report titled "Violence by Intimates" (Greenfeld et al., 1998) shows that between 1976 and 1996 of the 20,311 men who were intimate partner murder victims, 62% were killed by wives, 4% by ex-wives, and 34% by nonmarital partners such as girlfriends. Of the 31,260 women who were intimate partner murder victims, 64% were killed by husbands, 5% by ex-husbands, and 32% by nonmarital partners such as boyfriends.

Although murder is the most serious form of violence, criminal justice data claims that it is by far the least common. In 1999 murder accounted for only one tenth of 1% of the total reported crime reported to the Federal Bureau of Justice (FBI) (Hendricks, McKean, and Hendricks, 2003, pp. 187–188). The vast majority of people murdered are men murdered by other men. If we define *violence* as being murders, certainly there is no question that men are far more violent than women, both inside and outside the home.

As noted already, data show that more females than males are the victims of intimate partner homicides. However, the Bureau of Justice Statistics reports that homicides account for less than one half of 1% (0.3) of all family violence between 1998 and 2002 (Durose et al., 2005).

The FBI supplementary homicide report (National Center for Juvenile Justice, 2007) reveals that in California between 1990 and 2000 the number of acquaintance murders dropped by 53%. The number of strangers murdered dropped by 48%, and the number of family murders dropped by 28%.

Limited Understanding and a Lack of Knowledge

The California attorney general has two important reports that are predominately displayed on his website. One is the "California Intimate Partner Homicide Project." That report is based on the DOJ-sponsored study "Analysis of Unexamined Issues in the Intimate Partner Homicide Decline" (Wells and DeLeon-Granados, 2002), which concludes the following:

> Our findings imply that the net effect of arrests, convictions, and incarceration is not to reduce female victimization, but to ensnare more women in the criminal justice system net. Again, if we begin with the premise that much of the intended policy and enhancement in criminal justice system response to domestic violence has been designed with the chief goal of protecting women, then a "system backlash" effect may be taking place. Over the study period arrests for domestic violence of male suspects increased a total of 37% but females arrests increased 446%. (p. 21)

The task force report seems unable or unwilling to connect the dots that link mandatory arrest and no-drop prosecution with these problems. California laws now demand that officers not ignore the difference in the seriousness of the domestic violence incidents. The task force also seems unwilling to recognize that in California almost all acts of family conflict are defined by legislative laws as acts of domestic violence.

California domestic violence legislation shows that the assembly members apparently believe, concerning domestic violence incidents, that the criminal justice system should ignore the differences between felonies and misdemeanors and the dramatic and diverse needs and wants of domestic violence victims.

The foremost problem with "Keeping the Promise" is that it appears to continue with the 20th-century ideological advocate recommendations while ignoring the role of 21st-century empirically evidence-based research findings in the formulation of criminal justice domestic violence policy and procedure (Gelles, 2007). And ironically, some of the information found on the California attorney general's website warns against a one-solution-fits-all approach.

Research Ignored

Over the last 30 years the criminal justice system has and should continue to play a role concerning criminal domestic violence intervention. There is little question that many lives have been saved and that some families have been made safer because of the criminalization of domestic violence. I do not want to "push back" changes; I simply want to "pull" changes into the 21st century.

Some obvious and painful problems with contemporary criminal justice intervention are not being addressed concerning domestic violence policies and practices. Too often ideological domestic violence advocates and public policy makers ignore important empirically based policy and relevant findings from DOJ-sponsored studies. And much too often domestic violence advocates and public policy makers, as their websites and legislation show, are unaware of these studies or refuse to acknowledge their recommendations.

Mandatory

The National Institute of Justice (NIJ) report "Controlling Violence Against Women" (Ford, Bachman, Friend, and Meloy, 2002) should be read by all domestic violence advocates and public policy makers. It certainly should have been read by all of the KtP task force members. The report concludes the following:

Above all, they [public policy makers] need to know that their policies and practices will not endanger women. Unfortunately, there are too few preventive impact evaluations of policies already in place and fewer still that approach methodological standards insuring sound data for shaping policy. (p. 76)

It appears that the KtP task force has little knowledge of this report or it is unaware of the fact that there are no evaluations in place, no methodological standards, and no data to demonstrate that the mandatory domestic violence policies and the other mandatory practices it recommends will not endanger some families. This criminalization of all acts of family conflict, regardless of how minor, overlooks the needs, wishes, and desires of the victims. The fact is that many families are seeking solutions, not sanctions.

Further, Ford et al. (2002, p. 75) notes, "We still have much to learn about differences in offenders and differences in populations of victims to justify advocating one policy over another without qualifications." Without evaluations in place, with a lack of methodological standards, and with no data to show their effectiveness, U.S. public policy makers have ignored DOJ-sponsored studies and have chosen to pass legislation that has created, in many states, mandatory reporting procedures, mandatory arrest, and no-drop prosecution policies.

DOJ-sponsored studies report that mandatory intervention policies and practices can produce negative effects for some families. Mandatory legal policies and practices have silenced many domestic violence victims and have caused others to lose any and all control over their lives and the lives of their children. A 13-year study titled "The Decline of Intimate Partner Homicide" (Wells and Deleon-Granados, 2005) provides evidence that from 1987 to 2000, in 58 different California counties, there is no statistically significant relationship between criminal justice intervention and victimization for any gender, race. or ethnic group. This study reports that where domestic violence law enforcement intervention increased the arrests of males increased by 37% and for females it increased by 447%. Convictions for males increased by 131% and for females they increased by 1,207%. It seems as some of the negative effects have been catastrophic for females.

Many of the people on the task force seem not to understand that these policies are harming some female victims.

Helpful for Some, Harmful for Others

Many people agree that some of the changes in criminal justice policies and practices can save some lives and can make some violent families safer. This is particularly true for families at the lower end of the socioeconomic educational strata of society. However, many recent DOJ studies show how mandatory policies, practices, and one-solution-fits-all criminal justice intervention processes have produced many unintended negative consequences for many families.

The report "Forgoing Criminal Justice Assistance" (Hotaling and Buzawa, 2003) shows that rigid mandatory interventions disregard the diversity of the family desires and lack varied programs suited for the diverse characteristics of multiproblem offenders and can cause many victims to ignore the system designed to assist them. The report also says that some victims, after criminal justice intervention, will not report new victimizations to law enforcement. These findings seem to demonstrate that mandatory and aggressive, one-solution-fits-all criminal justice policies are, at least in some incidences, not only ineffective but also can prove to be more harmful than helpful to some families.

One Size Does Not Fit All

Many individual feminists and now some feminist organizations agree that one-solution-fits-all intervention is a 20th-century concept that can harm many families. The Ms. Foundation for Women (2003) concludes in its report "Safety and Justice for All" that contemporary public policy makers have in fact, put in place policies and practices that do endanger some victims. The foundation also concludes that those who are being endangered most by these policies and practices are the very same victims who need help the most. It believes that our public policy makers should abandon the use of mandatory legal practices such as mandatory reporting, mandatory arrest, and no-drop prosecution policies. The foundation also believes that these one-size-fits-all mandatory policies and practices have eroded the rights of many who have been arrested for minor violations and prosecuted against the wishes of the victim.

Ellen Pence, who pioneered the intervention process of arrest, prosecution, and treatment, now believes that today's one-size-fits-all VAWA funded programs are wrong and are not what she intended. Pence believes that those who commit minor acts of family conflict or one violent act are not batterers (Huntley and Kilzer, 2005).

Esta Soler is the founder and president of the Family Violence Prevention Fund (FVPF) (http://www.endabuse.org/). Soler asserts that certainly all violence is wrong regardless of who is the perpetrator. But Soler claims domestic violence is not one person pushing another person one time because a couple has gotten into an argument. Soler believes that domestic violence occurs when there is an ongoing pattern of fear, intimidation, and violent assault.

However, Soler, similar to so many members of the task force, seems unaware that California law pays no attention to the difference between battering behavior and family conflict. Regardless of what Soler thinks, in California one person pushing another is a domestic violence crime. The task force recommendations also equate a push with a pummeling. Restraining orders are issued, arrests are made, people are prosecuted, people are placed in battering programs, and health practitioners are required by statute law to notify law enforcement without distinguishing the differences between serious and minor incidents because all acts of family conflict have been criminalized.

All these one-size-fits-all and mandatory interventions do not take into account the vast diversity of the needs and wishes of family members. The state has become the victim, and many of the real victims are reduced to witnesses for the state and against their will.

Why Ignore These NIJ-Sponsored Reports

The DOJ-sponsored report "Effects of No-Drop Prosecution of Domestic Violence upon Conviction Rates" (Davis, Smith, and Davies, 2001) says the following:

> No-drop policies are expensive. Another potential cost is the effect upon citizens' willingness to call the police when they become the victims of domestic violence. It is not known whether no-drop increased victim safety or placed the victims in greater jeopardy.

Another DOJ-sponsored report that is important concerning legislation and that the KtP ignores is "The Exposure Reduction or Backlash? The Effects of Domestic Violence Resources on Intimate Partner Homicide," (Dugan, Nagin, and Rosenfeld, 2001, pp. 34–35), which suggests the following:

> The results for prosecutor willingness suggest that simply being willing to prosecute cases of protection order violations may aggravate already tumultuous relationships. . . Increases in the willingness of prosecutors' offices to take cases of protection order violation are associated with increases in the homicide of white married intimates, black unmarried intimates, and white unmarried females.

This verifies why some victims are hostile to mandatory prosecution and that members of the task force need to recognize the dangers mandatory polices can have on some families.

The National Research Council

At the heart and core of what is wrong with the task force report is that it overlooks the following. The NRC report "Advancing the Federal Research

Agenda on Violence Against Women" (Kruttschnitt et al., 2004, p. 56) notes that researchers and scholars who do not distinguish between violence, abuse, or battering may do more harm than good.

Although most scholars and researchers understand it is vital to recognize the difference between battering and family conflict, California criminal and civil laws, laws in the majority of the states, and, in fact, federal laws and the entire criminal justice system often ignore these important distinctions (Hendricks et al., 2003).

Justice for All

The Ms. Foundation for Women understands that some contemporary domestic violence policies and practices are having disproportionate and negative impacts on some families. Their report suggests that many policies and practices put in place by U.S. public policy makers ignore the fact that many families want reclamation, rehabilitation, redemption, and restoration rather than arrest and incarceration. Families want their voices heard, not silenced. Families want their needs heeded, not ignored.

Mandatory arrest and no-drop prosecution pay no heed to any of these. Ironically, while some people proclaim these policies are bringing justice to domestic violence victims, these policies are stripping some victims and offenders of the legal rights that are the very foundation of our justice system. Without a doubt mandatory arrest and no-drop prosecution and the "state knows best" policies have an Orwellian tone to them.

Many mandatory domestic violence policies and practices are eerily similar to mandatory drug policies and practices. In a mystifying and stunning reversal of logic many progressives and liberals who oppose mandatory drug arrests and mandatory sentencing policies and practices do not oppose mandatory domestic violence arrests, policies, and practices.

There are many public policy makers and domestic violence advocates, similar to the KtP, who are more than willing to take the credit for passing laws that make lives safer for some victims. However, are the same people willing to take the responsibility for passing legislation that removes due process from both offenders and victims, silences the voices of victims, and may endanger the lives of some family members?

Many believe that mandatory domestic violence policies and practices are necessary because if they save only one life their effort is worthwhile. What these very same people are unwilling or are unable to understand is that this philosophical belief demands that they must also acknowledge that if these same policies and practices take only one life, they may not be worth the effort.

Are not the families who may be harmed by mandatory domestic violence policies and practices as worthy of the same compassion and sympathy as those who may be helped? Underserved victims should not have to account for half of the victims to deserve either compassion or services.

Restraining Orders

Family Violence: Legal, Medical, and Social Perspective (Wallace, 2002), one of the most widely read college texts concerning domestic violence, notes that research and positive results concerning the efficacy of restraining orders remains allusive.

In the college text *Domestic Violence: The Criminal Justice Response* (Buzawa and Buzawa, 2002, p. 245), the authors acknowledge "… For the subpopulation of offenders with an extensive criminal history, it [a restraining order] has little or no positive impact. Regardless of that reality, one-solution-fits-all domestic violence restraining orders are widely used in the civil and criminal courts of the state of California and elsewhere in this nation, often without considering the context and circumstances of each individual order.

The Facts

The DOJ report "Civil Protection Orders" (Keilitz, Davis, Efkeman, Flango, and Hannaford, 1998) reports something that the task force and most professionals in the criminal justice and social support system are or should be aware of. Violations of these civil protection orders increase and their effectiveness decreases, as the criminal record of the offender becomes more serious.

Another DOJ study reveals that offenders with prior arrest records are seven times more likely to be rearrested for domestic violence incidents (Hirschel, Buzawa, Pattavina, Faggiani and Reuland, 2007). This report says that restraining orders and arrests are not effective against offenders who have histories of violent offenses or offenders who have a history of not heeding court orders. In fact, some DOJ studies reports that the problems for many plaintiffs will increase, not decrease.

The DOJ report "*Controlling Violence against Women*" (Ford et al., 2002) demonstrates how contemporary research and empirical evidence suggests that restraining orders are of limited value as a means of preventing violence against many plaintiffs.

There is a valid and growing concern that some plaintiffs in contentious divorce cases may request and are awarded restraining orders after presenting perceived or unsupported allegations of abuse or fear of abuse. In Massachusetts, Barbara Gray, a sponsor of the original restraining order statute, stated that, "I think judges grant the restraining orders without even asking too many questions" (Young, 1999, p. 129).

The Premise

The task force report claims that the premise in the issuance of orders from the family court is that a period of separation or regulated contact will help prevent a recurrence of abuse. This is a disingenuous and dangerous premise with little to no empirical support and no foundation of fact. It is in fact little more than a hunch and a hope. As the studies that follow show, the results remain very mixed.

A two-year study of a Massachusetts court (Klein, 1996) suggests that restraining orders have little deterrent effect on violent and abusive offenders who have histories of criminal behavior or patterns of chronic domestic abuse. This, of course, means that the most dangerous offenders are not deterred by restraining orders. Many criminal justice professionals understand that the positive or negative effect of restraining orders is something that will be decided by the defendant, not the victim or the state (Wallace, 2002).

Another California study (DeBecker, 1997) from Gwinn's hometown of San Diego, explains that almost half of the plaintiffs who received restraining orders reported that things became worse, not better. Empirical data shows that *some* people can be helped, not harmed, if the orders are properly researched and issued, through the use of restraining orders. However, there is no data that can support the claim made by the KtP that restraining orders are powerful tools that can prevent [all] people from being abused. Clearly, empirical studies and data document that *some* people are harmed by the issuance of restraining orders (Buzawa and Buzawa, 1996).

The truth is that many of the orders are being issued with little to no background information concerning individual socioeconomic, educational, cultural, and behavioral variables of either the plaintiff or defendant. These variables are vital because studies do demonstrate that arrest and restraining orders can deter some domestic violence for and by some by families; however, they may increase the violence with families where the abusers have histories of criminal behavior, have no stake in the community, and are unemployed (Sherman, 1992). In fact the KtP task force report claims that offenders in the family court are typically more dangerous than those subject to criminal protective orders. This juxtaposition of premise and reality seems to have been lost on many judges in the family courts who continue to issue these orders.

The first paragraph in the restraining orders section of KtP notes, "Restraining orders can be a powerful tool to prevent batterers from committing further domestic violence, so long as there is a credible threat that violators will be sanctioned." However, again there are little to no empirically evidence-based data for this claim. KtP then reveals that in most California courts restraining orders are being issued without a credible threat that violators will be sanctioned. The task force does not address who is responsible for putting in place this dangerous practice of placing the cart before the horse. For the safety of everyone involved the KtP task force needs some way, somehow, to acknowledge that some restraining orders may work well for some families, whereas others may not work well for other families, and that some of these orders actually have negative effects for some families.

Should not the context of the event, the characteristics of those involved, and the possible negative consequences be identified and acknowledged before the orders are issued? Individual characteristics and complex contexts have been ignored by the one-solution-fits-all issuance of these orders for more than a generation in California and, in fact, in most other states.

Deterrence

The NRC report "Advancing the Federal Research Agenda on Violence Against Women" (Kruttschnitt et al., 2004, pp. 78–79) says that individual and different interventions are needed for individual and different people:

> The literature on repeat intimate-partner violence demonstrates that legal sanctions do have deterrent effects, although modest in magnitude, but that these effects vary by the characteristics of perpetrators, their relationship with their partners, their stake in social conformity, and factors influencing the decision to impose sanctions while research shows that the collective actions of the criminal justice system exert a substantial deterrent effect on crime, this fact is of limited value in formulating policy for specific crime problems.

This shows that the promise made by the KtP task force has dramatic limitations concerning the universal efficacy of restraining orders. Among criminal justice professionals it is common knowledge, as studies show, that the most dangerous of offenders are repeat offenders. And studies also reveal that repeat offenders are rarely deterred by the threat of arrest (Buzawa and Buzawa, 1996, 2002; Gosselin, 2000; Sherman, 1992).

And more and more criminal justice data verify that the majority of chronic domestic violence offenders have histories of violent behavior toward intimates, acquaintances, and strangers alike (Kruttschnitt et al., 2004).

Connecting the Dots

Diane M. Stuart is director of the Office on Violence Against Women at the DOJ. Appearing before the Senate Committee on the Judiciary concerning the reauthorization of the Violence Against Women Act Stuart (2005) made the following statement:

Violence Against Women Act funded National Institute of Justice research reported in the *Journal of the American Medical Association,* has determined the effectiveness of protection orders, concluding that permanent orders are associated with a significant decrease in risk of violence reported to police. Such results can give criminal justice officials greater confidence in granting permanent protection orders, when effectively enforced.

Stuart (2005) is referring to a Seattle, Washington, study (Holt, Kernic, Lumley, Wolf, and Rivara, 2002) that, at least on its surface, seems to show that the restraining orders, in and of themselves, provide the demonstrated protection. The study Stuart refers to is systematic, scientific, empirical, and extensive, and it did provide some positive results. However, what the study actually reveals is evidence that restraining orders, with a coordinated community-wide response and social agency support, may provide some protection for some victims. It can be both disingenuous and dangerous to claim that restraining orders, in and of themselves, will protect women.

California has been issuing restraining orders for more than two decades with, as the task force report shows, little to no coordinated community-wide cooperation. What Stuart (2005) did not report to the Senate Committee is the fact that very few jurisdictions have a coordinated community-wide response that can produce the same positive results as the Holt et al. (2002) study.

The positive results in Seattle may have been accomplished through the infusion of hundreds of thousands, if not millions, of dollars from the VAWA, NIJ, and the Office of Community Oriented Policing Services (COPS) grants as well as a core of volunteers in the Seattle area. These volunteers and the grants provide support and resources for the plaintiffs that are not available in most communities across America. Stuart makes no mention of those facts.

The "Controlling Violence Against Women" report (Ford et al., 2002) notes that policy makers and practitioners should feel confident that research findings, when properly contextualized, can be used in decision making on preventing violence. However, this report also notes that above all, policy makers need to know that their policies and practices will not endanger the plaintiff. Stuart and the committee should be aware that few communities in America that have properly contextualized domestic violence intervention programs similar to Seattle.

The Cart and the Horse

The KtP task force report clearly shows that proper criminal justice safeguards and social support are not available in most California communities. However, this dangerous lack of resources and proper supportive safeguards to protect the plaintiffs has not stopped the California courts for more than a decade from issuing thousands upon thousands of these orders. Properly contextualized or not, they seem to be the rule of thumb in the California courts.

There seems to be little question, as documented by the KtP task force report, that California has and continues to put the cart (restraining orders) before the horse (coordinated criminal justice and community-wide social support). What is truly troubling is that the KtP task force report provides proof positive that many communities and, in fact, entire counties in California do not provide properly contextualized coordinated criminal justice intervention and community-wide social support. And in fact, as I write this chapter, the California courts continue to issue restraining orders with little to no understanding about what dramatically different effects these orders can have on different families.

Both Gwinn and Stuart should openly and honestly acknowledge that a restraining order, in and of itself, is only a piece of paper. For offenders who ignore the deterrent effect of arrest and in communities that lack an intensive coordinated community response, the restraining order itself is little more than an empty threat to many offenders and provides little to no protection for the plaintiff (Buzawa and Buzawa, 2002).

In fact, the NRC study "Violence in Families" reports that it is still premature to conclude the actual effectiveness of a coordinated community response on individual members of the very diverse U.S. society (Chalk and King, 1998). This report, similar to almost all DOJ-sponsored reports, notes that it is far to early to believe we have discovered any one-solution-fits-all intervention process that resembles a powerful tool or a silver bullet. As I discovered during my years in law enforcement, many restraining orders produce false promises, broken hearts, and shattered families.

As of June 6, 2003, there were 227,941 active restraining orders against adults in California. No one, including the judges that issue these orders, really understands the fact that these orders can and will have dramatically different effects for both the offenders and those who are granted the orders. A director of the Los Angeles County Domestic Violence Council (LACDVC) noted that because they have witnessed the failure of restraining orders to protect many victims and because sometimes restraining orders can actually endanger victims, many of the LACDVC members remain very cautious about recommending the use of these "powerful tools" (Davis, 1998).

People who profess it is their goal to protect the plaintiffs of these orders, along with their children, really need to read the studies, to rethink the issue, and then to tell the truth, the whole truth, and nothing but the truth. Half-truths are whole lies, and half-truths can hurt more than lies. It is important to recognize that though some of these policies may help some people, the very same policies may actually harm as many people as they help.

In "*Domestic Violence: The Criminal Justice Response*," Buzawa and Buzawa (2002, p. 259) acknowledge, "... The need for rigorous study to determine what works, for whom, under what conditions, and at what cost is clearly recognized."

It seems that this task force, many professionals in the criminal justice system, and many domestic violence advocates in the social support agencies in California are either unaware or ignore many DOJ studies that warn about one-solution-fits-all interventions. Perhaps it is time for someone in the California attorney general's office to read these studies and reports to the attorney general about their findings.

Prosecuting Domestic Violence Misdemeanors: Ignoring the Obvious

The task force report notes, "For example, victims are often hostile to the prosecution, and recant prior damaging statements about the defendant." Studies show that more than half of the domestic violence victims will recant their testimony (Buzawa and Buzawa, 2003). Perhaps part of the problem is the fact that not all family members who seek help are battered victims and that many of the offenders are not batterers. The KtP task force ignores the fact that California's one-solution-fits-all domestic violence laws make no distinction between battering and family conflict. Criminal justice interveners need to understand that domestic violence is a very complex and multifaceted problem.

The majority of California courts and social service agencies do not provide individualized attention to identifiable specific problems. California's mandatory arrest, no-drop policies and its one-solution-fits-all approach demands that criminal justice interveners ignore the wishes and needs of the families. On page 5, the task force report also notes that:

> A majority of the prosecutors' offices in the core counties, however, do not work with community-based victim advocates and agencies that provide such services, preferring instead to work only with their own victim advocates.

The task force report then suggests that the prosecutors' office should work with community-based victim advocates. That cooperation will not take place until the one-solution-fits-all practices of the 20th century are changed to reflect the complexities of domestic violence offenders and victims.

Many advocates do understand what the KtP task force ignores. Many of the policies that the KtP task force recommends may be right for the system; however, they may be wrong for many families. The one-solution-fits-all intervention will fail until programs are tailored to meet the needs of individual families.

The risk of death or further injury concerning many interventions depends on the proper understanding the context of the incident, the individual characteristics of the family, factors that affect the offender, and the methodology of the intervention provided (Dugan, Nagin, and Rosenfeld, 2003).

No-drop prosecution policies, by their very nature, place the need of the state and community ahead of families by ignoring the context of specific incidents and the needs of individual families. In no-drop prosecution the state actually becomes the victim, and the victim is reduced merely to an interested witness in the case (Wallace, 2002). And then the system questions why so many families are hostile to criminal justice prosecution policies that ignore all of these important factors.

An Imperfect Idea

As city attorney for San Diego, Gwinn was the architect of the policy of prosecuting misdemeanor domestic violence cases even when the victims were unwilling or unable to participate in the prosecution. This concept was labeled *no-drop prosecution*. The name is actually a misnomer, as no jurisdictions actually prosecute each and every domestic violence incident. However, the philosophy is used to overlook the needs and desires of families and to prosecute cases that appear winnable and often against the wishes and needs of both the offenders and those family members being abused.

The reasons the state should not aggressively prosecute many domestic violence misdemeanors against the wishes of families should be obvious to anyone familiar with the criminal justice system. The most telling and dangerous reason, outlined by a DOJ-sponsored study of homicide data, is that increased prosecution rates appear to have increased the death rate for many intimates in those jurisdictions that are pursuing no-drop prosecution policies (Dugan et al., 2001). This report also reveal s that increasing prosecution was associated with increasing the number of deaths of white married couples, black unmarried intimates, and white unmarried women. To ignore addressing this issue after the fact and not before putting no-drop prosecution in place is inexcusable.

Just as troubling is a study of the Quincy District Court in Massachusetts that found that aggressive prosecution policies in that court increased by 2.5 times the likelihood that victims, when abused again, would not report that incident to law enforcement (Buzawa and Buzawa, 2002). Perhaps the fact that the family's needs are minimized or ignored plays an important role in the family's decision-making process.

It's All about Choice

What is truly troubling about mandatory arrest and no-drop prosecution is that many domestic violence advocates, particularly those who work in conjunction with the prosecutor's office, continue to approve of these one-solution-fits-all policies.

At the heart and core of the domestic violence advocate movement is the belief that choice empowers women. How or why is it that many of these advocates cannot see that mandatory arrest and no-drop prosecution is about not being given a choice and disempowerment of women?

Choice is at the heart and core of all domestic violence advocacy agencies concerning when and how a woman chooses to seek assistance. Those who train the many volunteers who answer domestic violence hotlines and provide advocacy in the courts teach them to always remind the victims that the decision to, for example, leave their abuser or file criminal charges must be theirs and no one else's.

Volunteer advocates are reminded, consistently and constantly, never to advise the victim/survivor as to what course of action they should take. Empowerment derives from allowing the victim or survivor to make independent decisions. Removing choice is disempowering. Mandatory policies are all about removing choice. How or why is it, then, that so many prosecutors, domestic violence advocates, and members of the KtP task force are actively involved in the disempowerment of families by removing their right of choice through the process of forcing mandatory arrest and no-drop prosecutions on families?

What Not to Do

It is often reported that law enforcement officers have been and remain reluctant to make arrests in domestic violence incidents. Most of that law enforcement supposed reluctance is based on anecdotal stories, not empirical facts. In truth, many empirical studies show that there is often little difference in the arrests of intimates or strangers. Similar factors influence the decision to arrest both intimates and strangers (Hendricks et al., 2003).

It is my personal and professional experience that the context and circumstances of individual incidents are weighed by most officers in making the decision to arrest or not. Many officers make the decision not to arrest to comply with the circumstances of the event and the desire of the family. The officers understand that many families are seeking assistance and solutions, not arrest and sanctions. Many officers also believe that some people they arrest, with the consent of the person who was abused, will return home shortly after the arrest. Officers believe, rightly or wrongly, that many people after being arrested might take out their anger on the person who caused their arrest. This is particularly true of chronic offenders who are released before all of the officer's paperwork was complete.

Officers also understand that many offenders involved in minor or isolated family conflict incidents are not batterers. It is not always family members who call law enforcement. When some family conflicts rise to the level of physical assaults, a neighbor or someone who witnesses the conflict might call the police.

Many domestic violence advocates and responding officers know full well that often the system places itself first and families second. In fact, many families who find themselves ensnared in the contemporary arrest dragnet think that some arrests are made to ensure that the law enforcement agency will not be sued.

In the case of no-drop policies it appears that many people in the hierarchal criminal justice system believe they are intellectually superior and that their decisions are more just and more important than the family's or that of an individual family member.

This does not mean that arrests should never be made against the desires of the family. And again, it is simply illogical to treat all victims and all offenders as if they are some monolithic group. Anyone who has had face-to-face interactions with families and offenders, not after-the-fact research reviews of data sets, understands full well the diverse problems and even more dissimilar needs families have. Hunches and hopes that policies might work are not hypothesis, nor are they to be considered the foundation for knowable or scientific truth.

Read the Studies

After reviewing the growing number of DOJ-sponsored studies that report no-drop policies are not a good idea, the reader must conclude that the task force members are not aware of these studies or have made the choice to ignore them. Most empirically evidence-based studies conclude that the concept of dragging each and every family into court and prosecuting each and every family member against the will of other family members is not always a good idea. Finn (2004, p. 7) says:

> Our research findings suggest that prosecutors should re-assess whether coercing victims to assist in the prosecution of their abusive partners is worth the costs. Use of coercive actions has the effect of lowering victims' empowerment, and this should not be an acceptable outcome for prosecutors.

Hotaling and Buzawa (2003, p. 28) say the following:

> What is troublesome is that this research has found that despite the victim's experience with a "model" intervention program reporting was still a major concern as the majority of victims did not report subsequent offenses to the police. In fact this research adds credence to earlier expressed fears that a too aggressive criminal justice response that did not reflect diversity of victim desires might have had the unintended effect of deterring future reporting.

It is difficult to understand why the State of California, the KtP task force, or many other criminal justice professionals have made the decision to continue to ignore the following warning that appears in the National Criminal Justice Research Service abstract (Davis et al., 2001):

> Finally, we do not know whether no-drop increases victims safety or place the victims in greater jeopardy.... Before no-drop is embraced as a desirable policy, we owe it to victims to find out whether they are well-served by taking away their right to decide the extent to which they want to pursue a criminal justice solution to their problem.

In this same section of "Keeping the Promise" the task force reports, "Domestic violence victims who receive support and services are more likely to be and feel safe and thus more likely to cooperate with prosecutors" (Davis et al., 2001, pp. 55–56). There is little to disagree with here.

However, California laws that include mandatory arrest and no-drop prosecution policies for domestic violence can have just the opposite effect. As the KtP report clearly documents there is not now, nor has there ever been, universal support for victims in California. Further, mandatory policies by their very nature cause interveners to be unable to respond within the proper context of the incident and mandatory policies, by their very nature, overlook individual needs and desires. Many victims do not view these one-size-fits-all mandatory policies as being supportive of their needs; rather, these policies seem to be supportive of the advocates needs and desires.

Perhaps the task force members should have read the on-line review of Mills's (1998) article "Mandatory Arrest and Prosecution Policies for Domestic Violence":

> Recent data suggest that arrest may actually increase abuse for some women. The number of jurisdictions implementing mandatory prosecution has increased, even though data on the benefits and drawbacks of the policy are scarce.
>
> When batterers were arrested, victims experienced repeat abuse in 26 percent of the cases. When batterers were arrested and the victim perceived the police as concerned and willing to listen, the repeat abuse rated dropped to nine percent.

Mandatory policies do not allow police to be willing to listen. There seems to be little doubt among scholars and researchers, and this includes a growing number of domestic violence advocates that mandatory arrest and no-drop policies are not good ideas. In fact, recommending that the State of California should more draconically enforce the mandatory arrest dragnet and no-drop prosecution persecution web may very well have the effect of victimizing, once again, many family members whom the criminal justice engulfs.

Holding Batterers Accountable: Batterer Intervention Programs, Probation Departments, and the Courts

The Nexus of the Problem

On page 5 of the "Executive Summary" the task force reports, "Batterer intervention programs are at the center of California's criminal justice response to domestic violence." In the same paragraph the task force notes that a DOJ-sponsored study (Jackson et al., 2003) reports, "Even after 15 years of national evaluations, it is impossible to say how effective these programs are."

On page 26 of the NIJ report it notes, "The stakes for women's safety are simply too high to rely on batterer intervention programs without stronger empirical evidence that they work" (Jackson et al., 2003).

More troubling still, on page 63 of the KtP task force report the program executive director of a batterer intervention program in Oakland notes about their batterer intervention programs used for almost 25 years in California, "… One of my interests is to make sure that we actually study programs, batterers' programs, because the reality is that we do not know if programs work." It is elementary that having a program, any program, that cannot demonstrate if it is effective or not simply cannot or should not be the core or centerpiece of any policy or program.

Rather than further defending contemporary batterer intervention programs, the KtP task force should have questioned why scholars and researchers have failed for decades to show that batterer programs actually do work and then asked themselves why batterer programs should remain central to the California response to domestic violence.

Many millions of dollars have been spent with little to no documentation of positive outcomes for batterer programs. How can the KtP task force expect accountability from batterers if the programs themselves provide no documentation of their own accountability?

It Gets Worse

The DOJ-sponsored report "Batterer Programs: What Criminal Justice Agencies Need to Know" (Healy and Smith, 1998) warns against any cookie-cutter approach to intervention because research documents the need for diverse approaches. California has in place programmatic and administrative standards for its batterer intervention programs that clearly lack diversity.

The California standards demand that all batterer programs adhere to the Duluth perspective. Healy and Smith (1998) report, "Central to the [Duluth] perspective is a gender analysis of power, which holds that domestic violence mirrors the patriarchal organization of society. In this view, violence is one means of maintaining male power in the family" (p. 4).

Further, the California standards insist that group treatment is the intervention of choice for domestic violence perpetrators. Treatment programs may be open to accepting new members as the program continues or may be closed in structure. The groups may range from a minimum of 4 to a maximum of 12. A simple review of the California standards documents that they clearly lack diversity.

The NRC report *"Understanding Violence Against Women"* (Crowell and Burgess, 1996) details quite clearly what the majority of scholars and researchers believe. Diversity is a most important component of batterer intervention programs. The majority of scholars and researchers agree that batterer intervention needs to be tailored, within reason, to the individual and diverse behaviors of individuals placed in the program.

The criminal justice system is responding to all domestic violence incidents as if battering behavior is the same as family conflict incidents. The majority of researchers and professionals agree that multifaceted causes require different and distinct interventions. Research into the cause and consequences of domestic violence should not and cannot be limited by any single ideological theory or any one-solution-fits all intervention (Fagan, 1996).

Concluding outcomes before research is complete can limit focus and can establish a bias against evidence to the contrary. Age-specific or single-gender research ignores or minimizes the vast array of many exploratory and explanatory theories concerning domestic violence. A partial list of some of the theories that attempt to explain domestic violence are as follows (Wallace, 2002, pp. 9–15):

- Psychopathology theory
- Substance abuse theory
- Social learning theory
- Exchange theory
- Frustration-aggression theory
- Ecological theory
- Sociobiology or evolutionary theory
- Culture of violence theory
- Patriarchy theory
- General systems theory
- Social conflict theory
- Resource theory

And despite the fact that advocates and legislators in California seem to believe they have discovered that the Duluth model is the single correct answer, many thousands of people have been interviewed, tested, observed, and evaluated over the last few decades and to date there is no single theory that can or should predominate over all of the others (Wallace, 2002).

However, most researchers and professionals agree there are three primary models, and some contain many of the previously mentioned subgroupings that attempt to explain the reason why many who profess to love and care for each other often choose to neglect, abuse, and batter their spouse, partner, or child (Chalk and King, 1998; Crowell and Burgess, 1996; Dutton, 2006; Fletcher, 2002; Flowers, 2000; Gelles and Loseke, 1993; Gosselin, 2000; Hamel and Nicholls, 2007; Kruttschnitt et al., 2004; Mignon, Larson, and Holmes, 2002; Reiss and Roth, 1993; Wallace, 2002).

The Duluth or Cognitive-Behavioral Model

This approach explains that domestic violence mirrors the patriarchal organization of society and because of misogyny (the hatred of women by men) it is men who primarily use violence in order to maintain their traditional dominate role in the family. It is proffered that the behavior of the male batterer is a result of sexism and culturally learned masculine mores and norms.

This training prepares law enforcement officers and others in the criminal justice system for battering behavior at the expense of dismissing or not understanding all other forms of family violence. The message of the majority of contemporary criminal justice domestic violence training and education is that "domestic violence is battering behavior."

The Family Conflict Model

The abuse is the result of family stresses or the acceptance of conflict to resolve disputes both in the family and the neighborhood. Abusers strive for an important or predominant role in the family. In this view any family member may contribute to the escalation of violence.

The Psychotherapeutic Model

This model proffers that personality disorders, early traumatic life experiences, or other individual dysfunctions predispose some people to use violence in family relationships.

Even those with little to no expertise concerning batterer treatment understand that group treatment programs do not provide for individual, diverse, and specific needs. And the structure of these programs clearly show them to be designed around the premise that men, because of the patriarchy, are the offenders and women their victims.

In fact, there are no state guidelines that provide for any form of structured interventions for violent women in California. And state guidelines do exist to ensure that there is no structured intervention for male victims, despite the fact that the NVAWS (Tjaden and Thoennes, 2000b) clearly outlines domestic violence victimization to be a problem for both men and women.

And Worse Still

There is little to no empirical data that can show why batterer intervention programs should be the center of California's criminal justice response. Perhaps in an effort to provide some empirical justification for making battering programs central to California's criminal justice response, it is stated on page 63 of the KtP task force report that "more to the point, batterers who do not complete their programs are more likely to re-abuse their victims."

Studies show that this appears to be true. However, rather than justifying the KtP task force's premise, this citation presents yet again another reason why batterer intervention programs should not be central to California's criminal justice response domestic violence.

Current research documents that the most chronic and violent abusers are people with long histories of criminally violent behavior toward friends and family and they are not representative of the general population. These offenders are the most dangerous people who will wreak the most havoc, and they, as data show, are not deterred by threats of incarceration, let alone batterer programs (Buzawa and Buzawa, 2002).

In fact, there are two progressive agencies concerning batterer intervention programs in California: (1) the National Family Violence Legislative Resource Center (http://www.nfvlrc.org) and (2) the Family Interventions Project (http://www.familytx.org/). Both are working with community leaders and agencies toward development of effective prevention programs.

The KtP task force informs the attorney general that studies show that batterers who successfully complete or attend the majority of the programs classes are less likely to recidivate than batterers who do not. Data seem to validate this. What the task force does not reveal to the attorney general may be more important though, such as that studies also show that most batterers who are not assigned to treatment programs also do not reabuse the same victim. Studies also indicate that placing offenders in batterer programs may cause some victims to remain with these dangerous offenders who cannot be deterred and hence place them in more, rather than less, danger for further victimization (Klein, 2004).

If there is no empirical evidence that batterer programs actually work, how is it possible that they remain the pillar, the very foundation of California's criminal justice response?

Law Enforcement's Response to Health Practitioner Reports of Domestic Violence

Empirical Data, Not Hunches and Hopes

A 1998 NRC study funded by the Carnegie Corporation, the U.S. Department of Health and Human Services, and the DOJ (Crowell and Burgess, 1998) details that to avoid unintended negative consequences scientific research must precede intervention programs concerning mandatory health practitioner intervention and domestic violence. The California assembly has done just the opposite, and worse still, the KtP task force and the California assembly seems intent on turning a blind eye to the negative consequences of their legislation.

The studies reported in "Violence in Families" (Chalk and King, 1998, pp. 295–296) provide a clear warning to individual states about the implementation of passing a mandatory reporting laws:

> The committee recommends that states initiate evaluations of their current reporting laws addressing family violence to examine whether and how early case detection leads to improved outcomes for the victims or families and promote changes based on sound research. In particular, the committee recommends that states refrain from enacting mandatory reporting laws for domestic violence until such systems have been tested and evaluated by research. In dealing with family violence that involves adults, federal and state government agencies should reconsider the nature and role of compulsory reporting policies.

For reasons not articulated in KtP, the California assembly and the task force seem to have decided to ignore that sage and safe advice.

Look before You Leap

As noted already, one of the most widely read college texts concerning domestic violence is *Family Violence: Legal, Medical, and Social Perspectives* by Californian Harvey Wallace (2002). One of the reasons why the Wallace text is so popular with colleges is that it recognizes something that the advocates and legislators in California seem to lack. The issue actually is family violence and not primarily violence against women. In the first paragraph of the preface Wallace warns:

> The study of family violence is a complex, multifaceted experience. By its very nature, family violence involves physicians, nurses, psychiatrists, psychologists, family counselors, educators, social workers, attorneys, judges, and law enforcement officials. All professionals have expertise in their own area of specialization. However, they may not understand or appreciate the difficulties

experienced by others in their area of interest. For example, a member of the medical profession may be able to diagnose physical injuries but not understand the complexities of the courtroom. (p. xi)

As the task force notes this mandatory medical reporting section is the most controversial. Perhaps it is the most controversial because it is a bad idea and because the recommendations of many of the health-care practitioners are ignored. The California assembly seems not to appreciate the difficulties faced by many of the health-care practitioners and, more importantly, their patients concerning mandatory reporting.

Leaping without Looking

Concerning law enforcement's response to health practitioner reports of domestic violence, the task force reports on page 7 of the Executive Summary:

California's domestic violence reporting requirement for health practitioners has proven controversial. We did not attempt, however, to decide whether the requirement is a good one. Our focus, instead, was to find out how health practitioners are complying with their reporting obligations, and how law enforcement responds to these reports.

It is difficult, if not impossible, to understand how or why the members of the KtP task force decided to put the cart before the horse. If the reporting requirement was not a good one, it would be logical to assume that health practitioners and law enforcement would have difficulty complying with a requirement that might actually harm some individuals and families. It is difficult to understand how a single California assembly member who wrote or approved this mandatory reporting law—a law that could have such profound ramification on the lives of those involved—could do so not knowing if the law was a good or not.

I do not question that the majority, if not all, of people involved with California's domestic violence intervention policies are well intentioned. However, good intentions do not always produce good results. Wallace (2002) helps us understand why there is so much confusion among those who have been charged to enforce this law.

How does one accurately study or research a phenomenon if a definition cannot be agreed on because the definition of any act both sets limits and focuses research within certain boundaries? The lack of agreement in defining family violence has led to confusion and disarray in attempts to determine factors that cause or contribute to family violence (Wallace, 2002, p. 3). Very simply stated, in California and elsewhere in America, family violence somehow morphed into domestic violence, then into violence against women, and then into battering behavior. Any member of any family, including the California assembly member's family, should be able to acknowledge the tremendous confusion that the California assembly has created for Californians by criminalizing almost every act of family conflict as being similar to battering behavior (O'Leary, 2000).

Further, legislation that mandates that the health-care practitioners must ignore their sworn medical and ethical obligations of meeting the desires, needs, and confidentiality of individual patients at the expense of conforming to the one-solution-fits-all arrest law seems, at least to me, to clearly show that the legislation does not understand the difficulties faced by many professional interveners.

Autonomy and Confidentiality

In a bit of Orwellian logic it is suggested that health-care practitioners inform the battered patient that the report the health-care practitioners are mandated to take is to be kept confidential by the clinic and cannot be accessed by friends, family, or other third parties without the patient's consent.

First, although it is technically true that the specific report may be kept confidential, the patient is not informed that his or her confidentiality and autonomy will be ignored by the criminal justice system. The truth is that patient confidentially and personal autonomy will become subservient to the system that seems to engulf whoever and whatever it wants.

Second, though the patient may very well have been injured in an altercation with another family member, a one-time injury inflicted by another family member does not automatically and absolutely cause that specific family member to be a battered victim and the person who inflicted the injury to be a batterer. Many families might agree that a fight between siblings is not often, if ever, considered battering behavior. This mandated reporting law makes no distinctions between family conflict and battering behavior.

California Mandatory Reporting Law: A Summary

Health-care practitioners are mandated to report to law enforcement any patient who is "suffering from any wound or other physical injury inflicted upon the person where the injury is the result of assaultive or abusive conduct" (see Hyman, n.d. for a summary).

A fact that many of the California assembly members seem to be unaware of is that most families and siblings in particular, do at times push, shove, slap, or hit one another. This behavior, though it should not be acceptable behavior, is not considered battering behavior by family members or professionals. This mandatory legislation has, wittingly or unwittingly, transformed all acts of family conflict regardless of how minor into the equivalent of battering behavior.

If a wife slaps a husband and the husband loses his balance, falls, and injuries himself, he is now, under California law, a battered patient and his wife a batterer.

Why Confusion Reigns

A visit to the FVPF website documents that the FVPF is not actually concerned with family violence; it is concerned with violence against women. One example of many is that the FVPF presents advice on how society should respect women and girls with no mention of men or boys deserving respect. Further, as the FVPF website documents, the FVPF consistently presents men and boys as abusers and women and girls as their victims.

The FVPF is located in San Francisco. The 2005 YRBS documents that in San Francisco 9.3% of girls and 8.3% of boys report they were hit, slapped, or physically hurt on purpose by a girlfriend or boyfriend (CDC, 2006). Given these data, it is difficult to understand how the FVPF can conclude that girls are victims and boys their abusers; however, a visit to the FVPF website should be enough to convince anyone who takes the time to read it that it is precisely what Soler and the FVPF proffers.

Remember, the FVPF website links readers to a summary of the healthcare practitioner section of the California law. This is despite the fact that Soler has written, more than once, that although all violence is wrong regardless of who is the perpetrator, all physically assaultive acts are not acts of domestic violence. The California law does not make that distinction.

Again, it must be noted that Soler believes that domestic violence is not one person pushing another person one time because of jealously or anger. Soler believes that domestic violence occurs when there is an ongoing pattern of fear, intimidation, and violent assault. I agree with Soler; however, California law does not listen to either of us.

Soler also seems oblivious to the fact that California "laws" define *domestic violence* for the criminal justice system. In the world of the California criminal justice system, domestic violence does not require an ongoing pattern of fear, intimidation and violent assault. Any and all physical assaults regardless of the context of the act must be reported by practitioners.

In fact, there is not a single domestic violence law in this nation that matches Soler's definition of *domestic violence* (Miller, 2004, 2005). Not a single state has a law that requires an ongoing pattern of fear, intimidation, and violent assault. Hence, the confusion and disarray in California and elsewhere in this nation continues.

The Letter of the Law

In the Executive Summary of the KtP task force report is a letter to the California attorney general that seems to enforce the belief that the law is more important than research, logic, or common sense. It reads in part:

> Our report includes disturbing examples of agencies that have failed: to respond to domestic violence victims, to enforce the law, to comply with the law, and to work in necessary collaboration (Gwinn et al., 2005).

Perhaps the controversy among so many health-care practitioners is that they understand it is a bad law. The task force seems to be unable or unwilling to accept the fact that the reason there may be so much noncompliance is that often the law ignores the wants, needs, and desires of so many California families.

Perhaps many health-care practitioners, scholars, and researchers understand that attempting to arrest their way out of the problem of domestic violence is not going to work in California or elsewhere. Though it may seem to be an alluring and simple answer, criminalizing all acts of family conflict may very well may be creating as many problems as it deters. Rather than simply strengthening and enforcing the law on the books, the California assembly needs to question what sections of the law seem to be working well and what sections of the law seem not to be working as well and to discover the whys concerning those differences. Simply imposing harsher penalties than the ones that are not working very well could be a recipe for a disaster.

The definition of insanity, someone once said, is doing the same thing over and over again and expecting different results. Why do the members of the KtP task force avoid recognizing that doing the same thing over and over again is not going to provide different results? In their infinite wisdom the California assembly has made it a crime for practitioners not to comply with this law. Lost on these assembly members is the fact that they are using force and power to control the behavior of a group of people who disagree with them rather than persuasion, reason, and common sense. There are many domestic violence advocates who recognize that style of behavior.

A clear example of the California assembly members not understanding they have passed a fundamentally flawed law is that it appears, as far as I have been able to determine, that not a single law enforcement officer in the criminal justice system has yet to arrest a medical practitioner for noncompliance. That is a very strong nonvocal message to the assembly members that the law is not a good law. And, thankfully in California many health-care practitioners continue to understand the importance of placing patient autonomy and confidentiality before their blind compliance with the letter of this very flawed law.

This particular section of mandated domestic violence intervention, more clearly than the others, plainly details how the law places the state above families. In California the law has become triumphant in creating confusion and disarray involving both the victims it intends to serve as well as advocates and other interveners who truly want to help victims regardless of age, gender, or sexual orientation. Many health-care practitioners have failed to enforce or comply with the law because they can clearly recognize that this law very well can harm some of those it is intended to help.

On the FVPV website program manager Lisa James notes that their organization supports reporting domestic violence incidents to the police only with the patient's consent.

Again, it is a fundamental educational concept to recognize that the only dumb question is the question not asked. The fact that this task force did not think it was necessary to ask the National Coalition Against Domestic Violence or the FVPV why their organizations oppose mandatory reporting by health-care practitioners is almost a crime in itself.

Recommendations for KtP Change

There continues a seemingly endless, negative, faulty, and fruitless argument between many domestic violence advocates, women's and men's rights organizations, and individuals concerning domestic violence regarding the following:

1. The majority domestic violence victims are battered women, and males are their batterers.
2. Concerning domestic violence men and women are equally violent.

When data are collected from battered women's shelters or self-reporting criminal justice surveys, women do appear to be the primary victim. However, data collected from family violence surveys document that men and women report victimization at approximately the same rate.

From this disparate data the fine line that often separates science from politics becomes blurred by those who think that if you do not believe 100% that sexism, the oppression of women, and the patriarchy is the root cause for most domestic violence, you must be 100% against them. Far too often ideological scholars and researchers predetermine which position their research will support before their research actually begins. In general, sociologists agree that the subjectivity of personal values is a form of bias and, hence, should be avoided in favor of objectivity. Objectivity is a scholar's personal neutrality in conducting research (Macionis, 1997).

In the first paragraph on page 1 of the *"Full Report of the Prevalence, Incidence, and Consequences of Violence Against Women"* Tjaden and Thoennes (2000b, p. 1) write, "In unprecedented numbers, scholars trained in such diverse disciplines as philosophy, literature, law, and sociology examined violence against women in the context of feminist ideology." Hence, Tjaden and Thoennes, similar to many other ideological advocates who should be expected to provide objective, independent, evidence-based knowledge and tools to enhance the administration of justice and public safety for the NIJ, appear to have made the decision to change traditional scientific objective research to subjective ideological research that presents data in a manner that fosters their ideological preconceived position on domestic violence victimization.

Tjaden and Thoennes (2000b) are ideological advocates. They did not want men included in the NVAWS, and they had only women interview women whereas only half of the males were interviewed by men.

The NVAWS reports that more males 53.8% than females 40% experienced some type of physical assault by an adult caretaker as a child. The survey also documents that 1.3% of women and 0.9% of men were physically assaulted by any type of intimate partner annually. The latter, at face value, appears to be saying that women are the primary victims until you read that Tjaden and Thoennes (2000b) report that the survey also documents that women report their victimization more than twice as often as men. One does not need to be a scientist or a scholar to recognize the importance of this. Despite the fact that women report their victimization twice as often as men, Tjaden and Thoennes declare that women should be considered the primary or more important victim.

Their ideological held beliefs may have caused Tjaden and Thoennes (2000b) to present data and to reach conclusions that are not synonymous with the facts they report on pages 29–31 of their report. Tjaden and Thoennes, perhaps because of their ideology, seem willing to minimize, marginalize, or ignore much of the data they present about male victimization in the NVAWS.

Criminal Justice Data

Criminal justice data and general surveys do reveal that women suffer from greater physical injuries and exhibit more fear of their intimate partners than men. Criminal justice data also document that more men than women are violent criminals. It is undeniable that physical strength and contemporary gender and cultural mores play important roles in those differences (Felson, 2002).

When domestic violence occurs between men and women the coercion and physical assaults, more often than not, have the same intent, yet their results often appear to be very dissimilar in their harmfulness (Hendricks et al., 2003). However, regardless of this, if more harm is suffered by one gender than the other, are not each equally guilty of the same intent? Do not each share equal responsibility when initiating the incident?

A Central Premise

Although many domestic violence advocates frame the issue of intimate partner homicide as a gender issue (women are killed simply because they are women), the U.S. Bureau of Justice statistics data show otherwise. These data clearly demonstrate, given the context of the violence, that men in general are more violent than women; however, some women can be as violent as some men.

Men commit more homicides against men than against women. The patriarchy has little to do with homicides. Data document that men are far more violent against other men than they are violent against women (Fox and Zawitz, 2006).

The "Suicide Fact Sheet" (CDC, n.d.) outlines that men also kill themselves far more frequently than they kill women. The fact sheet also documents that though males are four time more likely to die from suicide than females, females are three times as likely to report attempting suicide as men. Homicide data reveal that more females than males are the victims of intimate partner homicides. It is generally accepted by scholars and researchers that the behavior of a populace in general cannot be predetermined from the aggregate data of the behavior of an extremely small subgroup of that population (Macionis, 1997). Intimate partner homicides are rare events. In fact the 0.3% includes all victims of family violence, not only intimate partners. Excluding homicides, females account for 58% of victims of family violence and males 42% (Durose et al., 2005).

The time has come for public policy makers to question the wisdom of pitting the victimization reported by women against the victimization reported by men. Public policy makers need to question why ideological domestic violence advocates, who often know little to nothing about the complexities of the criminal justice system, pit male and female domestic violence victims against each other.

Why is it expected by criminal justice interveners, domestic violence advocates, and public policy makers that men need to be the victims of physical injuries as often as women or men need to be as fearful as women to receive equal empathy and support? Why is male victimization so often minimized, marginalized, and ignored? If domestic violence is unacceptable, regardless of severity, why is it not equally intolerable and unacceptable for either gender to perpetrate abuse?

Though some domestic violence advocates and a few public policy makers claim they are equally concerned about male victimization, the fact is that billions of public and private funds are being spent on female victimization, and little to nothing is being spent concerning male victimization. Almost all ideological domestic violence websites that show dating violence report the number of female victims while they overlook male victimization. Are not our sons as worthy as our daughters?

An Emerging Awareness

Erin Prizzy founded the first shelter for the victims of domestic violence in England. Prizzy believes that many women can be just as violent as many men. Prizzy is not a misogynist.

Ellen Pence pioneered the Duluth model for domestic violence intervention in America. Pence believes that one-size-fits-all policies similar to those in California are wrong. She believes, as do I, that too often offenders are placed in programs that do not suit their needs. Pence also believes many people charged with domestic violence are not batterers (Huntley and Kilzer, 2005).

Pence designed her community-wide intervention to address the most violent of the predators and those who are chronic batterers. Pence believes that if her partner cheated on her and she, in a fit of anger, slapped her partner that does not make Pence a batterer (Huntley and Kilzer, 2005). Pence does not appear to be a misogynist.

From what was outlined earlier in the chapter regarding the Ms. Foundation for Women, no one is going to accuse them of being a misogynist organization.

Ellen Goodman (2004), in an article for the *Boston Globe,* acknowledges that women initiate violence nearly as often—though not as lethally—as men. Goodman writes that men and women are approximately equally caring and empathetic. Some men are more so than women and some women more so than men: "When the social constraints are off—surely when women are rewarded for violence—they can mimic the worst behavior of men." Goodman is not a misogynist.

Linda G. Mills, who is a domestic violence survivor and not a misogynist, is the author of *Insult to Injury* (2003). Mills believes that mandatory intervention assumes a false omnipotence. Mills notes that in California this false omnipotence grew from the paradoxical claim of Gwinn and former police sergeant Anne O'Dell that the way to help women is to remove their right of choice.

Recommendations for the California Attorney General

Recommendation One

Read and heed the research. Over the last decade there have been numerous important findings in many scientific empirical studies. Anyone working in or with the criminal justice and who continues to ignore the two U. S. Department of Justice sponsored reports that follow very well may be instrumental in harming as many victims as they are helping.

The NIJ report "Controlling Violence Against Women" (Ford et al., 2002) must be read by all domestic violence advocates or anyone who is truly concerned about domestic violence. The recommendations from the California task force may very well have been quite different if just a few of the members had read this report.

The prosecution policy found to protect victims in Indianapolis was to permit victims who initiated their complaints at the prosecutor's office to drop charges, a finding that has been interpreted as evidence of victim's empowerment or self-protection (Ford, 1993).

A study that must be read for all advocates is the NRC's "Advancing the Federal Research Agenda on Violence Against Women" (Kruttschnitt et al., 2004), which notes that researchers and scholars who do not distinguish among violence, abuse, or battering may do more harm than good. California, and in fact most federal or state legislators, ignore that important distinction. The report also notes:

> Without consistency in the use of terms across studies, research in this field will remain fragmented; new measurement instruments that have been developed may not receive adequate testing or experimental use in studies that can demonstrate their power, and accurate prevalence and incidence estimates, especially of severe violence, will remain elusive. (p. 97)

This research shows that legal sanctions do have a deterrent effect, although modest in magnitude, but that these effects vary by characteristics of perpetrators, their relationships with their partners, their stake in social conformity, and factors influencing the decision to impose sanctions (Kruttschnitt et al., 2004, p. 7).

Finally, there is emerging and credible evidence that the general origins and behavioral patterns of various forms of violence, such as male violence against women and men and female violence against men and women, may be similar (Kruttschnitt et al., 2004, p. 100).

As previous NRC committees have found, the design of prevention and control strategies—programs and services available to victims and offenders that aim to decrease the number of new cases of assault or abusive behavior, reduce the risk of death or disability from violence, and extend life after a violent event—frequently is driven by ideology and stakeholder interests rather than by plausible theories and scientific evidence of cause (Kruttschnitt et al., 2004, p. 6).

Without evaluations in place, lacking methodological standards, and with no data to show they would not be harmful to some domestic violence victims, the California assembly members have turned a blind eye to most unbiased contemporary scientific empirical studies and have passed legislation that created one-solution-fits-all mandatory policies and procedures that are based on little to no research that documents their effectiveness.

Worse still, the California assembly members are either unaware of or have decided to overlook studies that show that many of the policies they have passed may be more harmful than helpful to many families.

Recommendation Two

Do away with all mandatory policies. Mandatory legal policies and practices have silenced many domestic violence victims, have driven others away from seeking help, and have caused others to lose any and all control over their lives and the lives of their children.

In fact, many of our mandatory domestic violence policies and practices are eerily similar to the mandatory drug policies and practices. It is mystifying as to why progressives and liberals who so often oppose mandatory arrest and sentencing policies for drug abuse do not oppose mandatory domestic violence arrests, policies, and practices.

Recommendation Three

Do not have in place any one-solution-fits-all interventions. All domestic violence advocates researchers argue against any one-solution-fits-all interventions for women who are arrested for domestic violence because of the many negative consequences presented by that policy. If these ideological researchers could look at the issue objectively, they would then understand that the same is true for men.

Recommendation Four

Treat our sons the same way we treat our daughters. The majority of domestic violence organizations, similar to the NDVH—perhaps because of its ideological beliefs—notes that one in five female high school students (a daughter) reports being physically or sexually abused by a dating partner.

The American Sociologist Association has formal guidelines for conducting and presenting research. Very simply put the association believes that research must be both technically competent and unbiased. Researchers must release all their findings without omitting specific data that upholds only their position on an issue.

Conclusion

Perhaps if the KtP task force or the California attorney general would review at least some of the studies mentioned in this chapter, they might revise their recommendations, many of which seem to be based on ideological beliefs and not empirical data.

There is hardly a more contentious issue in the criminal justice system than the issue of domestic violence. This task force has decided to repackage the policies of the 20th century that have failed many victims and present them once again as answers to the dilemmas we face early in the 21st.

It appears that the task force, far too often, accepts ideological assumptions as fact and ignores empirical data and research to the contrary. It appears that members of this task force all too frequently did not attempt to connect the empirical research dots. Instead, they have presented their report in an ideological manner that separates the issue of male and female violence, as if one has little to do with the other and that is not supported by data, and they have disregarded the opportunity to review the reams of unbiased scientific analysis of the issue.

The NRC reports that evidence now documents that the patterns and forms of violence—male violence against women and men and female violence against men and women—may be similar. The NRC believes that both men and women must end the fragmented gender-separated understanding concerning the cause and consequences of violence. To minimize the effects of violence or abusive behavior both men and women must be viewed as offender, as victim, and sometimes as both (Kruttschnitt et al., 2004).

Given the importance of the issue and the continued controversy that surrounds this debate—one that far too often drowns out the needs, desires, and the voices of the families involved—it is time for an unbiased assessment of the data and research.

Finally, this report brings to mind the questions that are only infrequently asked and less frequently answered. It is understandable why ideological domestic violence agencies would want to ignore the issue of male victimization; it is their agenda. However, why is male victimization so often gone unheeded by our public policy makers and both the electronic and print media?

Why does the federal government spend billions on female victimization and at the same time take the position of claiming the neutrality of the Violence Against Women Act? Many females and most males also wonder why so many domestic violence advocates—as their websites show—minimize, marginalize, and ignore male victimization.

Stranger still, why is the safety of our daughters in dating relationships a major concern for domestic violence agencies while our sons are ignored?

Most domestic violence agencies, on their websites, show the abuse noted by the Youth Risk Behavior Surveillance System suffered by our daughters and take no notice of the abuse suffered of our sons.

Do the federal government, domestic violence advocates, or these domestic violence agencies think that parents grieve more when their daughters rather than their sons are abused? Do parents grieve more when their children are physically assaulted or sexually abused by a family member rather than by an acquaintance or stranger?

And why do the California assembly members and the KtP task force place information provided to them by domestic violence advocates and agencies before the relevance and importance of reading and understanding the reports and studies available through the U.S. Department of Justice?

Enlightening information concerning domestic violence studies and reports that are now only a mouse click away seem to have been discounted.

Discussion Questions

1. Does the reason for the decline of effectiveness of restraining orders with chronic offenders correlate with other forms of criminal behaviors that these offenders may possess? How should these factors affect policy makers, prosecutors, judges, and others involved in the criminal justice system?
2. Assume that you are a policy maker or a judge and you are presented with a plea from a group of several families who have family members awaiting prosecutions as a result of no-drop policy. The families, in their written requests, have varied reasons for requesting a dismissal of the offender's trial. List some of these potential reasons. How many of these reasons would you consider are genuinely origination out of fear or violence?
3. The importance of critical thinking is particularly important when one studies and interprets statistical data. The Tjaden and Thoennes (2000a, p. 50, 2000b) studies discussed in this chapter even concede that "women report their victimization twice as often as men." This illustrates the importance of study the data set of the population being surveyed while at the same time considering the conditions that may affect this population's choices and actions. Discuss ways the Tjaden and Thoennes studies could be revised to include this critical statistical consideration. Predict the differences in the reports outcome that occur after having done so. How does that that revision affect your perception of the victimization rate between men and women?
4. For now, do not consider the shortcomings of the Duluth model, the Family Conflict model, and any of the other scores of treatment philos-

ophies that form the core of so many battering intervention programs. Think about why batterers who do not complete their program are more likely to abuse their victims. What are the reasons for that failure? Suggest a policy that would best isolate the chronic violence abusers from the general populations set of abusers and, once you have done so, suggest a course of action that would best suit both the interests of the community and the needs and safety of the victimized families.

5. Is it possible that some of the so-called evidence cited by advocates who have a specific agenda regarding domestic violence policy has been tainted by their ideologically held beliefs? Recommendations for change are presented at the end of this chapter, but please identify the challenges to these changes, and recommend courses of action that would best counter these challenges with the evidence-based empirical data.

Rape and Sexual Assault

6

It is not the facts which guide the conduct of men, but their opinions about facts; which may be entirely wrong. We can only make them right by discussion.

—Norman Angell

Introduction

The on-line *Encyclopedia Britannica* defines rape as follows:

Act of sexual intercourse with an individual without his or her consent, through force or the threat of force. In many jurisdictions, the crime of rape has be subsumed under that of sexual assault, which also encompasses acts that fall short of intercourse. Rape was long considered to be caused by unbridled sexual desire, but it is now understood as a pathological assertion of power over a victim.

Those That Stand Accused

Often when researchers address the issue of male victimization and female offending, they are accused, as I have been on a number of occasions, of caring more about male victims than female victims and of having a hidden agenda (Dutton, 2006). The hidden agenda, as some advocates will claim, is the issue of gender symmetry concerning domestic violence offending and victimization.

Gender symmetry is suggesting that an equal number of men and women are the victims of domestic violence. Further, many advocates believe that the issue of gender symmetry has another hidden agenda, which is an attempt to undermine the progress made concerning violence against women (Dutton, 2006). This accusation stems from the irrational proposition that "if you are not 100% for me, you must be 100% against me."

I, as the father of three daughters and two sons, respect the fact that equal rights were the central theme of the 20th-century feminist movement. I was raised by my grandmother, who was born in 1886 and did not enjoy many more rights than women born 2,000 years before her. I respect the 20th-century feminist movement and am more than pleased that my daughters had far more rights than my grandmother; thus, I expect equal rights for my daughters and sons.

Again I assure the reader that my professional career and research have convinced me, along with many other domestic violence researchers often accused of being against violence against women, that that the majority of data shows and that most researchers agree that concerning violent domestic violence incidents the more serious, injurious, and violent assaults, both physical or sexual, are suffered by females (Wallace, 2002).

I also believe that because of some of the contemporary effects of both nature and nurture, "the harmful effects of all levels of violence are greater for women, physically, psychologically, and economically" (Straus and Medeiros, 2002, p. 22). Further, I believe, as the majority of studies and data outline (including many of those listed by Feibert, 2005), that more females than males are seriously injured, murdered, and report their suffering emotionally and economically from domestic violence incidents than do men (Straus and Ramirez, 2002).

In addition, I clearly understand that females overwhelmingly report rape as more traumatic than any other assault, even when there are no physical injuries from the rape (Boudreau, 2000). The majority of contemporary studies also document that the "primary victims" of rape are adult heterosexual females and children regardless of gender (Barlow and Kauzlarich, 2002; Boudreau, 2000; Flowers, 2000; Wallace, 2002).

However, in instances of rape, similarly to domestic violence, there is little to nothing positive in minimizing or marginalizing any victim or offender because of the victim's gender, age, or sexual orientation. When one victim is proclaimed the primary or most important victim, then the other victim, by virtue of that specific dissimilarity, is viewed to be only a minor or less important victim. This pitting one victim against another is as old and odious as time itself and is a process that is almost always negative.

Engaging Men

My expertise resides in domestic or familial violence and its intersection with the criminal justice system. Thus, my expertise in the area of rape or sexual assault is also only in its intersection with the criminal justice system. Without a doubt I and the majority of domestic violence advocates agree on the need to engage more men in the effort to minimize domestic violence, sexual assaults, and rape.

The most serious problem confronting proper domestic violence, rape, and sexual assault intervention is the continuing and unnecessary divisiveness created when researchers, domestic violence advocates, and domestic violence organizations minimize or ignore male victimization (Dutton, 2006). It should not be difficult to understand that trivializing male victimization is not an effective process intended to engage more men.

This chapter suggests the continuing *gender v. gender* and *nature v. nurture* debate about domestic violence, rape, and sexual assault that seems to have consumed and divided so many professionals is far more negative than positive.

I do not doubt for a moment that some women who are beaten, battered, and raped by some men will truly and perfectly fit into Susan Brownmiller's hypothesis. However, by painting all males with the same brush of guilt, Brownmiller and ideological advocates who blindly adhere only to the "patriarchy makes them do it" hypothesis have been reduced to little less than ideologues railing against ideologues.

The Brownmiller (1975) theory of rape and sexual abuse cannot explain the many incidents of child sexual abuse, male victims of sexual abuse, female perpetrators of child sexual abuse, sibling sexual abuse, child-care sexual abuse, ritual sexual abuse, sexual abuse of children, women and men sexually abused by the clergy, female adult sexual abuse of adult males, sexual abuse in dating relationships (regardless of age, gender, or sexual orientation), same-sex sexual abuse, and elder sexual abuse (Flowers, 2000; Mignon, Larson, and Holmes, 2002; Wallace, 2002).

The Brownmiller hypothesis (1975) requires one to ignore the fact that many complex factors contribute to domestic violence. Most researchers agree that no single correct hypothesis or theory exists and that most researchers should have a cursory understanding of the many theories that are presented (Wallace, 2002).

The following is a list of some of the most commonly accepted theories (Wallace, 2002, pp. 9–15, 20–24):

1. Psychiatric model: Encompasses the social-psychological theory and the substance abuse theory.
2. Social-psychological model: Includes the social learning theory, the exchange theory, the frustration-aggression theory, the ecological theory, and the sociobiology or evolutionary theory.
3. Sociocultural model: Contains the culture of violence theory, the patriarchy theory (it is here where the Duluth intervention program remains stuck), the general systems theory, the social conflict theory, and the resource theory.
4. Cycle of violence theory.

A Crime That Spawned a Center

On July 26, 1957, two young boys, John, age 12, and Paul, age 11, were reported missing after a summer outing at D.W. Field Park in Brockton, Massachusetts. After an extensive search their bodies were discovered the next day. They were nude and had been sexually assaulted; their assailant had attempted to burn them. It was a horrific violent sexual crime.

The boys had taken a bus from nearby Stoughton to the park in Brockton, which includes a swimming pond. The entire Brockton fire and police departments were called to duty in an attempt to locate them shortly after they were reported missing. Early on the morning of July 27, one of the firefighters noticed smoke rising from a gully near one of the ponds. He discovered the boys' charred bodies, which had been repeatedly stabbed in the chest and abdomen and bound together with a rope. Under the bodies the firefighter found a house key. The key belonged to a 21-year-old Brockton man who had been released from prison 7 weeks earlier, where he had been incarcerated since the age of 15 for a sex crime he committed in 1951. He was known to the Brockton Police Department, and the key fit his front door. When confronted, he confessed to the murders and provided the details to the police.

This horrible crime outraged area residents and public policy makers and fed support for a law authorizing a treatment center for sex offenders. Two years later, a treatment center for the sexually dangerous was opened at the Bridgewater Correctional Facility.

Ironically, the murderer, whose multiple offenses had prompted the opening of the center for the sexually dangerous, was ruled incompetent to stand trial for the murders and was committed to the Bridgewater State Hospital, where he died in 2003. On the 50th anniversary of the murders, the center held 559 patients and inmates.

One official who spent approximately 30 years working in the Massachusetts Department of Correction commented that many of the sex criminals actually understand that they are too dangerous to be released. He noted that the murderer was very docile, never created any problems, and almost seemed to enjoy being in the state hospital (Keene, 2007).

In August, 2007, a 20-year-old man abducted a 7-year-old girl who was his cousin and drove off in his grandmother's car. Law enforcement spotted the car, and after a chase the man was arrested. Inside the car, the officers discovered the little girl's body. She was naked and badly bruised and showed signs of sexual assault. She was beaten about the face and neck and had blood in her mouth; her legs were gray and discolored (Schworm and Hernandez, 2007).

It is perfectly clear, particularly to law enforcement officers, that some people—and they are far more often men than women—are sexually dangerous and that their sexually dangerous behavior does not appear to be learned.

Experts

Without a universally accepted definition for rape or sexual assault, anyone who claims to be or is deemed to be an expert concerning the cause of rape and sexual assault may actually be an ideologue in the guise of an expert. *Merriam-Webster* defines an ideologue as an impractical idealist or an often blindly partisan advocate or adherent of a particular ideology.

The Brownmiller (1975) book *Against Our Will: Men, Women and Rape* was chosen by the *New York Times Book Review* as one of the outstanding books of the year. In it, Brownmiller claims that rape is "... nothing more or less than a conscious process of intimidation by which *all* men keep *all* women in a state of fear" (p. 15, italics in original). Further, she writes:

> Once we accept as basic truth that rape is not a crime of irrational, impulsive, uncontrollable lust, but is a deliberate, hostile, violent act of degradation and possession on the part of a would-be conqueror, designed to intimidate and inspire fear. (p. 391)

What Brownmiller (1975) seems to ignore is that without some form of fulfillment for the behavior of any would-be conqueror, any deliberate, hostile, violent act of degradation and possession will not take place. In robbery, the reason for the act is not to instill fear for the purpose of instilling fear; the fear is the means, and the material goods are the end product. In rape, the fear is the means and sex is the end product.

Robbery is a deliberate, hostile, and violent act in which fulfillment of that behavior is most often the possession of material goods. Hence, the intimidation and fearful acts in robbery provide material goods, and the intimidation and fearful acts in rape produce sex. Without any end there would not be a means.

It was not long ago that most cognitive scientists believed that emotions interfered with rational thought. In the judicial system it is still believed that it is best for judges and juries to set aside their emotions to reach a rational decision because emotions interfere with the rational though process. However, now many cognitive scientists recognize that "it is only because our emotional brains work so well that our reasoning can work at all" (Lehrer, 2007).

This past inability to understand the need to engage both emotions and reason may be the cause for so many historic unjust decisions reached by the justice system. The separate but equal doctrine handed down by the U.S. Supreme Court is only one of a litany of unjust decisions handed down by the court (Brinkley, 2002). My 21 years in the criminal justice system and the research I have conducted over the last decade have led me to recognize that U.S. courts are far more concerned about the laws themselves than the court is about the people the law affects.

If we are to provide a cure, we must know the cause. The two horrific incidents involving the boys and the girl described at the outset of the chapter are both violent sexual crimes. To believe that rape is nothing more or less than a conscious process of intimidation by which all men keep all women in a state of fear can be both dangerous and disingenuous, and believing that the truth has already been discovered ends the search for the truth.

The two incidents involving the boys and girl, along with millions of others, clearly document that rape is a complex and multifaceted crime that sometimes can involve unbridled sexual pathological desires. Do not these two incidents document that it is not always logical that sexual desires and pathological need always be placed at the opposite ends of the rape paradigm? Is it progressive, in an educational sense, to simply accept that rapes are always assertions of power that never or rarely involve unbridled sexual desires? Should not all factors be explored rather than accepting the one-cause-fits-all contemporary belief?

Should not the realization that rape and sexual assaults are complex and multifaceted phenomena put the simplistic one-cause-fits-all victim domination theory to bed (Wallace, 2002)?

Law Enforcement Intervention

During the late 1970s and early 1980s Brownmiller and a number of other feminist authors convinced the majority of the members of the criminal justice system, public policy makers, and the media that rape is exclusively or primarily a violent crime and that rape—an act that most often by its very nature requires some form of sexual arousal to be performed to completion—has little to no relevancy concerning sexual arousal (Barlow and Kauzlarich, 2002; Roberson, 2000; Schmalleger, 2005).

These single-theory ideologues rejected and continue to reject that rape can ever be a sexual act, and the majority of the members of the criminal justice system also accept the Brownmiller theory as fact (Barlow and Kauzlarich, 2002; Brownmiller, 1975; Roberson, 2000; Thornhill and Palmer, 2000; Schmalleger, 2005).

Regardless of whether rape is *caused* by nature or nurture or not, it should be the duty of law enforcement—or, in fact, most professionals in the criminal justice system—to enforce the law. However, for intervention programs, and more importantly for educational programs in our schools, similarly to domestic violence the correct cause determines the correct path to a correct cure.

Just as in the general issue of domestic violence, here in the specific issue of rape and sexual assault, any one-size-fits-all-intervention or solution with a one-size-fits-all definition appears to be doomed to failure (Niehoff, 1999). In Boudreau (2000), Owen Jones, a law professor at Arizona State University proffers that:

Anything that has "nature vs. nurture" in its title is necessarily headed in the wrong direction, he says. There's a famous way of putting it that says, "to ask whether or not a given behavior is a function of nature or nurture is like asking whether the area of a rectangle is a product of its length or its width." These things cannot operate independently.

In a demeaning and derogatory review of *A Natural History of Rape* by Thornhill and Palmer (2000), Brownmiller (2000) degrades and depreciates those authors personally and labels as garbage a suggestion by Thornhill and Palmer that young men should take a short course in the evolution of rape when they apply for a driver's license so as to better understand their impulses.

I do not know for certain if the cause of rape is nature (Thornhill and Palmer, 2000) or nurture (Brownmiller, 1975); however, I do believe that an ounce of proactive prevention is worth a pound of reactive intervention.

Educational Intervention

Both males and females intuitively recognize, and studies document, that many if not most men have difficulty understanding how or why females suffer far more trauma from the crime of rape than they do from almost all other violent crimes (Boudreau, 2000). Many young people begin dating when they reach middle-school age, and studies document that aggressive sexual behavior and date rape also begin at that early age (O'Keefe, 2005). A gender-neutral educational process concerning date rape should be folded into health education classes. If the goal is to reduce sexual aggression, regardless of who exhibits it, there is a need to explore what motivates that sexual aggressive behavior. To exclude either learned motivations or sociobiological motivations could be as dangerous as it would be disingenuous.

Despite Brownmiller's (1975, p. 12) claims that "no zoologist, as far as I know, has ever observed that animals rape in their natural habitat, the wild," an educational program could begin by exploring why rape is an overwhelmingly male behavior in almost every species where it is observed. It may difficult to see any rape in the wild when that observation would question the truth that you have already arrived at. Research concerning rape among animals in the wild was ongoing for many years before Brownmiller made that claim, and it continues today. Thornhill and Palmer (2000) report that there are now more than 50 studies.

The majority of social scientists now agree that human behavior is due in part to evolution or genetic dispositions (nature) as well as grounded in environmental or learned dispositions (nurture) (Niehoff, 1999). It is difficult for me to understand why so many advocates, similar to Brownmiller, continue to believe they have already discovered the truth, the whole truth, and nothing but the truth.

The best way to engage men in understanding the social and cultural problems domestic violence, sexual assaults, and rapes present to women is to have women also recognize the social and cultural problems domestic violence, sexual assaults, and rapes present to men. There is a need for both men and women to act as positive role models for young men and young women, and in doing so they can both support and create public policies and legislative changes that are designed to help everyone regardless of age, gender, or sexual orientation.

Invisible Victims

Some writers in the developing field of feminist criminology believe that, until recently, women has been invisible or an afterthought in criminological analysis (Schmalleger, 2005). Historically there is some truth in that claim.

Data from the national Youth Risk Behavior Survey (YRBS) show that 10.8% of girls and 4.2% of teenage boys report on the survey being physically forced to have sexual intercourse against their will with a dating partner (CDC, 2006, p. 44).

Data from the "National Violence Against Women Survey" (NVAWS) (Tjaden and Thoennes, 2000b, p. 13) reports the following:

> ... 0.3 percent of women surveyed and 0.1 percent of men surveyed said they were raped in the previous 12 months. These findings equate to an estimated 302,091 women and 92,748 men who are forcibly raped each year in the United States.

Despite those findings, the Federal Bureau of Investigation (FBI) Uniform Crime Reports (UCR) continue to define rape as "the carnal knowledge of a female forcibly and against her will" (FBI, n.d.). Clearly, concerning rape victimization males appear to remain invisible or an afterthought to the criminal justice system and, until recently, to the mainstream media.

In the foreword of the report "Ending gender-based violence: A call for global action to involve men" is the call to engage men in ending gender-based violence, Sahlin (2004) writes, "It is time to put an end to the continual violation of women, which is not worthy of a society that is built on the conviction that all human beings are of equal worth" (Ferguson et al., 2004, p. 6). It is difficult to disagree with that statement. However, the above conference report shows that the majority of the participants are concerned only with ending men's violence against women, and there is no mention of ending women's violence against men. I'm not sure how ignoring male victimization demonstrates "equal worth."

It seems problematic for me, as it should be for everyone involved, to understand how anyone can possibly think that the way to engage men in preventing violence against women—and more men do need to be engaged in the issue of ending violence—is to simply blame men for causing all the problems.

Perhaps a "human beings are all equally worthy conference" that recognizes that the acts by women that result in physical, sexual or psychological harm to men would demonstrate to men that it is in actuality a conference built on the conviction that all human beings are of equal worth, rather than one that is built upon the belief that ending violence against women is more important than ending violence against men. Such a conference would have more luck in engaging men in antiviolence efforts than one where the finger of blame is simply pointed at all men.

What is needed is a conference that attempts to engage everyone, regardless of age, gender or sexual orientation. Perhaps if we end placing the victimization of one segment of society—adult heterosexual women—before the victimization of everyone else, more people would become engaged in the effort to end domestic violence.

Further Complications

The definition of *rape* or *sexual assault* varies from state to state and internationally. In some states and in some countries the definition of rape has actually been replaced by sexual assault. And, in fact, sexual assault can have quite different definitions in different states. Thus, this lack of agreement makes it difficult to address or document an issue that is not even defined as the same issue (Scalzo, 2007).

Individual state statutes are posted on the Commission for the Prevention of Violence Against Women website with an interactive map at http://www.ndaa-apri.org/apri/programs/vawa/state_rape_reportings_requirements.html. This interactive map provides state-by-state information concerning domestic violence statutes and links to other resources and statistics.

Rape Statistics

The 2006 Duke University rape incident brought to the fore once again the argument concerning the percentages of false accusations of rape (Meadows and Thomas, 2006). The numbers of false accusations, of course, depend on who is asked. The numbers from domestic violence advocates, who most often take the side of women, can be as low as 2%, and the numbers from organizations that most often take the side of men, claim it is as high as 41% (Spilbor, 2003).

The 2% statistic is most often attributed to Brownmiller (1975), who claims that the false accusations in New York City dropped to about 2% after the department began to use female police officers to interview victims who report being raped. The problem is that Brownmiller provides no citation for that particular claim. This 2% statistic is sometimes attributed to Allison and Wrightman (1993). However, Allison and Wrightman cited as their source Katz and Mazur (1979), who reported studies of false allegations that ranged from 1% to 25%. It appears that Allison and Wrightman decided to use only the study that documents the 2% data (Haws, 1997).

The 41% statistic is from a study conducted by Eugene J. Kanin (1994), who examined 109 rape complaints. This statistic is sometime reported, and most often without the warning from Kanin, that the 41% findings should not be extrapolated to other populations. I believe that, for reasons too long to list, the exact truth may be impossible to ascertain. The most important adjunct to that long unlisted list is never trust one source, and that is the problem with the Kanin study. All social scientists understand that the results of a single study should never be accepted as fact. The results of the Kanin study have never been replicated.

A 1996 report from the U.S. Department of Justice (Connors, Lundregan, Miller, and McEwen, 1996) seems to present, at least to me, the strongest case for data that should be considered valid:

> Every year since 1989, in about 25 percent of the sexual assault cases referred to the FBI where results could be obtained (primarily by State and local law enforcement), the primary suspect has been excluded by forensic DNA testing. Specifically, FBI officials report that out of roughly 10,000 sexual assault cases since 1989, about 2,000 tests have been inconclusive (usually insufficient high molecular weight DNA to do testing), about 2,000 tests have excluded the primary suspect, and about 6,000 have been "matched" or included the primary suspect. The fact that these percentages have remained constant for 7 years, and that the National Institute of Justice's informal survey of private laboratories reveals a strikingly similar 26 percent exclusion rate, strongly suggests that postarrest and postconviction DNA exonerations are tied to some strong, underlying systemic problems that generate erroneous accusations and convictions. (pp. 28–29)

Despite the high, low, or median number of false allegations, I also believe that concerning the criminal justice system, the exact number of false allegations should be irrelevant. Regardless of whether the numbers of false allegations are high, low, or somewhere in the middle, each and every allegation needs to be examined for its particular and peculiar context and circumstances. Each and every alleged victim needs to be viewed through the lens of innocence and believed to be telling the truth, and each and every suspect should be viewed the same way. It is time that perpetrators, regardless of age, gender, and sexual orientation, be treated with the same empathy shown by some researchers toward adult female heterosexual perpetrators (Edleson, 1998; Mignon et al., 2002; Swan and Snow, 2002; Swan, Gambone, and Fields, 2005; Swan, Gambone, Fields, Sullivan, and Snow, 2005).

Over the years I have never ceased to be surprised by complaints from so many domestic violence advocates about the low rates of convictions concerning rape. Brownmiller (1975, p. 370) complains, "Unless the rules of evidence can be met, a prosecutor cannot bring a case into court, even though he knows, the victim knows, and the rapist knows that a crime has been committed." The victim and the rapist know they were there, but how does Brownmiller suggest that the prosecutor knows if the accused is actually guilty until there is empirically based evidence that can document that a rape actually took place. Again, high or low statistical data should be irrelevant to a prosecutor. Prosecutors and defense attorneys are both charged with seeking the truth. "She said, he said" accusations and counterclaims are not empirically based evidence.

Although it sounds overly simplistic, most often rape by its very nature only involves two people. To make an arrest, law enforcement officers do not need enough evidence to prove a case; they need only to establish probable cause. Probable cause is more than "she said, he said" and most often requires the following (Schmalleger, 2005, p. 18):

> ... a set of facts and circumstances that would induce a reasonably intelligent and prudent person to believe that a particular other person has committed a specific crime. Also, reasonable grounds must be established to make or believe an accusation.

However, probable cause alone may not be enough for a judge or a jury to find the accused suspect guilty, and the reality of false claims, regardless of what the actually number is, is an ever present problem for the many true victims who have filed genuine rape charges. And despite the havoc false claims can wreak on those falsely charged, the courts and the media seem to be unconcerned.

It is common practice for the majority of newspapers not to print the name of the alleged victim while at the same time they print the name of the alleged perpetrator. There should be little to no question that this "conviction before trial" process sends the implicit message that anyone accused of rape is guilty and anyone who brings the charges of rape is innocent. If not, why the obvious double standard? If someone has been falsely charged and then is later cleared in court, the newspapers have already sullied and dishonored that person's reputation.

Conclusion

For a couple of generations now Americans have been led to believe that government is not the solution to many of their problems; government, Americans are often told, is the problem. Only a cursory visit to the majority of domestic violence websites should cause readers to discover that most often they are being led to believe that men cannot be the solution to the problem of rape and sexual assault until men—all men in general—understand and admit that they are the problem. That is not a formula for attracting more men to stand up and speak out against rape and sexual assault.

Discussion Questions

1. What causes so many advocates to continue to adhere to the Brownmiller (1975) hypothesis?
2. What causes some people to rape and sexually assault?
3. Why is it that adult heterosexual males do not express the same horror and exhibit the same trauma at the thought of being raped by an adult heterosexual female?
4. It is universally agreed that more men need to become involved in the issues of domestic violence, rape and sexual assault. What do you think the best process is?
5. Should newspapers continue to print the name of the person who is charged with rape and exclude the person who alleges the rape? If you agree they should not, what should the newspapers do?

Mandatory Domestic Violence Arrest Policies

7

> If we appeal to law, we sometimes call upon a Trojan horse; when we invite law in, law re-invites itself time and again, but on its own terms and with its own agenda.
>
> —**Renee Romken**

What Is *Domestic Violence?*

Domestic violence advocates, members of the academe, men's and women's rights advocates, public policy makers, and any number of other professionals continue to argue over domestic violence offending and victimization, while there continues to be no nationally recognized or accepted definition of domestic violence (Wallace, 2002).

I believe that arguing over something that lacks definition and hence that remains different things to different people is not only an exercise in futility; it is also akin to doing the same thing over and over again while expecting different results. In fact, Johnson (1995) suggests that researchers are actually researching and identifying different phenomena as if they are one and the same phenomenon. Depending on which specific definition of domestic violence is accepted by both researchers and domestic violence advocates, the national number of domestic violence victims ranges between 7.6 to 213 per 1,000 women and 1.5 to 124 men (Hendricks, McKean, and Hendricks, 2003, p. 228). In fact, a visit to many of the national recognized and sometimes federally funded domestic violence websites reveals that many claim that 1 in every 3 women will be a victims of domestic violence in their lifetime.

What the vast majority of these nationally recognized websites do not include is that the data they present as fact is generally gathered by using the Commonwealth Fund Survey definition of the term. Further, these nationally recognized domestic violence websites do not inform the reader that using the same methodology the number of domestic violence victims will be approximately the same for men. This misrepresentation of the number—100,000,000 of women and men as being victims of domestic violence—is a disservice to the actual victims, and it does more harm than good.

In most states, domestic violence can be quite different from the general population perception of an act of violence or the professional perception of a battered victim that produces injured victims with broken noses and blackened eyes. In fact, in all the states domestic violence is not violence; it is abuse.

And clearly, abuse can be in the eye of the beholder. The California domestic violence law includes a threat that produces a fear in someone that abusive behavior might take place. Research shows that, for a variety of valid reasons (much higher rates of injury, sexual assaults, and intimate partner homicides), women both fear and report domestic violence incidents to law enforcement far more often than men (Laroche, 2005; Tjaden and Thoennes, 2000). However, it is important to recognize that injuries, sexual assaults, and homicides are results of aberrant behavior and not necessarily the cause.

In California, *abuse* can be defined as "molesting, attacking, striking, stalking, threatening, sexually assaulting, battering, harassing, telephoning, including, but not limited to, annoying telephone calls as described in Section 653m of the California Penal Code, Section 639-6531, destroying personal property, contacting, either directly or indirectly, by mail or otherwise, coming within a specified distance of, or disturbing the peace of the other party." Clearly, in California, similar to domestic violence laws in all states, domestic violence abuse includes but is not limited to battering behavior.

Battering

Most researchers agree that a batterer is a family member or intimate partner who with premeditation and malice aforethought repeatedly uses coercion, force, or violent physical assaults to manipulate and control the behavior of another family member or intimate partner. Research documents that batterers are dangerous people and that they deserve to be arrested (Mignon, Larson, and Holmes, 2002).

Family Conflict

Family conflict most often, but not always, occurs between family members or intimate partners without premeditation or malice aforethought and involves the use of threats or minor physical assault in a specific or isolated disagreement. Studies document that domestic violence in family conflict is fairly common, yet it is most often neither chronic nor severe (Hendricks et al., 2002). This behavior is often the result of the perceived misbehavior of others, financial matters, jealousy, stress, or personality disorders (Wallace, 2002).

A review of California domestic violence laws and intervention programs reveals that there is little to no distinction between these two quite different behaviors.

The "National Violence Against Women Survey" (NVAWS) details that more than half of all physical assaults by intimates are relatively minor and consist of pushing, grabbing, shoving, slapping, and hitting and that 1.3 million women and 834,732 men reported being physically assaulted by an intimate partner in the 12 months preceding the survey (Tjaden and Thoennes, 2000a, p. 10).

A June 2005 U.S. Department of Justice (DOJ) report "Family Violence Statistics" (Durose et al., 2005) documents that family violence accounts for only 11% of all reported and unreported violence and that the majority of family violence is simple assault. Studies document that the majority of victims report they were not injured in the physical assault (Tjaden and Thoeenes, 2000a, p. 41).

Some of the millions of family members who engage in minor family conflict may require law enforcement intervention. However, a growing number of DOJ studies document that many families have discovered that mandatory arrests that ignore the context and circumstances of the incident can have unintended detrimental effects on families (Eng, 2003). In California mandatory arrest mandates that law enforcement officers not only ignore the severity of the incident but also that officers must ignore the context and circumstances of individual incidents.

A False Premise

In all nonfamilial assault cases, regardless of severity, law enforcement officers are trained to exam the context and circumstances of the individual incident. Officers are trained to listen to and understand the diversity of the needs and preferences of those who had been assaulted before they make a decision to arrest or to use a number of other criminal justice options.

This use of officer discretion is at the core of judicious community policing in democratic societies (Sherman, 1992). It is universally agreed that fairness and impartiality are the essential foundational principals of a community policing (Trojanowicz and Bucqueroux, 1992).

The indifference of law enforcement officers toward domestic violence victims is most often the reason given for the draconic use of mandatory arrest policies that are found almost exclusively in domestic violence laws. However, that premise is primarily based on widely told and believed anecdotal incidents that are not supported by data and by less than a handful of methodology flawed studies of varying rigor or range (Avakame and Fyfe, 2001; Miller, 2004; Sinden and Stephens, 1999; Toon, Hart, Welch, Coronado, and Hunting, 2005).

My professional and personal experience leads me to the opinion that the vast majority of law enforcement officers understand that arresting some domestic violence offenders is not only the right thing to do, but that some-times arrest is essential for immediate cessation of violence and does provide for temporary victim safety (Buzawa and Buzawa, 2002; Davis, 1998; Sinden and Stephens, 1999).

Allegations by domestic violence advocates and many researchers in some 20th-century studies suggest that law enforcement officers are reluc-tant to arrest women and that male officers are indifferent to the plight of female victims. However, the architect of the Minneapolis Domestic Vio-lence Experiment, Lawrence Sherman (1992), documents that law enforce-ment officers do not make arrests in the majority of violent crimes, regardless of gender, in which the evidence can justify an arrest.

Although advocates and many researchers proffer that some data show that law enforcement officers refuse to arrest domestic violence perpetrators, this criminal justice data, more often than not, do not include the context, circumstances and victim preference of these individual incidents. My years in law enforcement have convinced me that few people, regardless of gender, in America should expect or want law enforcement officers to make arrests each and every time they have the authority to do so.

The majority of domestic violence incidents, as both criminal justice data and general surveys document, are for the following reasons:

1. Minor or misdemeanor crimes without injury and in which the officers do not have the power of arrest
2. A situation in which the victims' families do not want an arrest to take place
3. Because many incidents provide little to no evidence of who hit who first. Initiation of an assaultive event is important and remains a central probable cause factor concerning responsibility of guilt in the criminal justice system.

The Rise in Arrests for Females

In 1999 women accounted for approximately 35% of all domestic violence arrests in Concord, New Hampshire. In Vermont, women accounted for 23% of all domestic violence arrests, and in Boulder County, Colorado, it was 23% (Goldberg, 1999).

A recent DOJ study documents that, in states where officers have pre-ferred (there is an allowance for discretion) arrest policies, the incidents of arrest in intimate partner incidents rose by 177% compared with states, simi-lar to California, where there are mandatory policies, in which arrests rose by 97% (Hirschel, Buzawa, Pattavina, Faggiani, and Reuland, 2007).

In 22 states and the District of Columbia, arrest is mandated regardless of how minor the assault. These mandated arrests ignore the desire and needs of families and must be made despite the fact that the incident may have been a single isolated act of minor family conflict not commonly associated with battering behavior (Eng, 2003; *Huntley and Kilzer, 2005*; Soler, 2007).

The number of women being arrested in California for domestic violence has dramatically increased since the introduction of mandatory arrest policies. In California, the number of males arrested for domestic violence has increased by 37% whereas female arrests increased by 446% (Wells and DeLeon-Granados, 2005). The Wells and DeLeon-Granados study also documents that the greatest rise has been in conviction rates. Convictions rose by 131% for males but by 1,207% for females. It is even greater for male Hispanics (126%) and for female Hispanics (1,650%). This conviction rate clearly refutes the claim made by domestic violence advocates who believe, without any evidence-based data, that the rise in female arrests is due to law enforcement officers not knowing whom to arrest.

Further, national data provide evidence that male victims are more than three times likely to be arrested in a dual arrests than females. This data disparity in arrest and conviction rates between males and females suggests that far more males than females are being arrested without proper probable cause (Wells and DeLeon-Granados, 2002).

Questioning Mandatory Arrest

The National Research Council (NCR) study "Advancing the Federal Research Agenda on Violence Against Women" notes that there are dangers in not distinguishing among an act of violence, abuse, or battering (Kruttschnitt, McLaughlin, and Petrie, 2004). In most states the mandatory arrest law is a one-size-fits-all law that makes no distinctions among these three.

The DOJ-sponsored study "Police Intervention and the Repeat of Domestic Assault" (Felson, Ackerman, and Gallagher, 2005) reports that sometimes police intervention is necessary; however, the effect of arrest is too small to have policy significance.

Nationally, the advocates and legislators have decided that mandatory intervention policies will lead and the research results will follow. Hence, for good or bad, we are all research subjects. Testing a hypothesis that may be as harmful for some as it may helpful for others is a clear violation of fundamental research ethics: "Virtually everyone agrees … that researchers must strive to protect the safety of [all] people involved in a research project" (Macionis, 1997, p. 40). Chalk and King (1998, p. 296) clearly state, "… States refrain from enacting mandatory reporting laws for domestic violence until such systems have been tested and evaluated by research."

Mandatory reporting, arrest, and prosecution policies have yet to be tested and evaluated for their safety. More troubling is the fact that most public policy makers seem to be unaware or unconcerned about the many DOJ-sponsored studies that document the dangers, up to and including homicides, of such mandatory policies (Dugan, Nagin, and Rosenfeld, 2001; Eng, 2003; Iyengar, 2007).

The DOJ report "Forgoing Criminal Justice Assistance" (Hotaling and Buzawa, 2003) reveals that for some families, mandatory intervention and one-solution-fits-all (Fagan, 1996) criminal justice policies can be more harmful than helpful. This study is just one of a growing number of studies that document the many unintended negative effects created by mandatory arrest policies.

The DOJ study "The Effects of Arrest on Intimate Partner Violence" (Maxwell, Garner, and Fagan, 2001) explains that officers and victims should have a voice and choice concerning arrest. Studies document that the majority of offenders discontinue their aggressive behavior without an arrest. The vast majority of advocates agree that a woman's right to choose is a newly found fundamental freedom. Therefore, it is difficult to understand how or why the same domestic violence advocates support mandatory arrest and prosecution polices, both of which deny women their right of choice. This study also notes that requiring arrest for every incident of domestic violence may reduce the resources of communities when they respond to chronic violent offenders and victims most at risk. I also believe that research needs to assess the benefits and costs of mandatory arrest before implementing mandatory arrest policies.

Outcomes

A recent DOJ-sponsored study by Wells and DeLeon-Granados (2005) that most public policy makers should be aware of shows that there is no statistically significant relationship between criminal justice response and victimization. The study also documents that an ever increasing number of women are being ensnared in a criminal justice system that is supposed to protect them and that women are being arrested, convicted, and incarcerated in numbers far higher than they were before the passage of a mandatory arrest law designed to provide for their safety (Wells and DeLeon-Granados, 2002, pp. 21–22). Again, that same study documents the conviction rate for females arrested is far higher than for males arrested, which shows that the officers are following the letter of the law.

The Violence Against Women Act (VAWA) has spent billions specifically on violence against women, yet with little money and no changes in policy the nonfatal victimization rates for female relatives, friends, acquaintances,

Table 7.1 Nonfatal Violent Victimization Rate: Rate per 1,000 Females Age 12 or Older

	Intimates	Other Relatives	Friends/Acquaintances	Strangers
1993	9.8	3.3	15.8	15.4
2004	3.8	1.4	5.3	6.3

and strangers have decreased by approximately the same rate as intimates (Table 7.1).

Though the ultimate goal of VAWA is to reduce or minimize the domestic violence homicides of females the greatest drop in intimate partner homicide over the last couple of decades has been for males. White females continue to suffer from a higher rate of intimate partner homicide than black females or males of either race (Rennison and Welchans, 2000).

Despite the promise of advocates that VAWA would reduce homicides, there has been no statistically significant change in the intimate partner homicide victimization for white females. In fact, in 1995 the Bureau of Justice Statistics data documents that the intimate partner homicide rate for all females began to rise again (Fox and Zawitz, 2006).

Conclusion

Concerning female offending a great many researchers now agree that one-size-fits-all interventions have proven to be harmful for women and that law enforcement officers and programs interventions must examine the context and circumstances of the individual incidents (Edelson, 1998; Swan and Snow, 2002; Swan, Gambone, and Fields, 2005).

I question why so many advocates or public policy makers seem unable or unwilling to understand that the same should be true for men. Regardless of gender, a growing number of DOJ studies document that mandatory arrest and no-drop prosecution are flawed one-size-fits-all policies (Buzawa and Buzawa, 2002; Coker, 2001; Davis, 1998; Dugan et al., 2001; Dutton, 2006; Eng, 2003; Fedders, 1997b; Felson, 2002; Finn, 2004; Holder, 2001; Hotaling and Buzawa, 2003; Kelly, 2003; Mills, 1998).

It is difficult for me to understand how or why so many advocates and public policy makers accept the arrest findings of the Minneapolis Domestic Violence Experiment, while at the same time they ignore the fact that the author of that same study warned against the use of mandatory arrest (Sherman, 1992).

Mandatory arrest is seen by some critics as a dangerous and simple answer provided by public policy makers who believe that they must do something about domestic violence (Davis, 1998; Finn, 2004). The problem is that public policy makers have placed their policies ahead of the research. And worse still, many relevant 21st-century research findings have yet to make their way into the hands and hearts of public policy makers (Clear and Frost, 2001).

Arrest is a reactive and not a proactive intervention, and it is not a panacea for domestic violence. However, given the proper context and circumstances of an incident and listening to the preference those being abused, arrest can be a useful and necessary response by law enforcement (Hendricks et al., 2003). My recommendations are primarily based on the Hendricks et al. (2003) college text:

1. The authority but not the mandate for officers to make arrests in witnessed and unwitnessed incidents should remain in place.
2. Mandatory arrest should remain in place for all incidents that result in severe injury or for offenders with a history of chronic violence regardless of relationships.
3. Mandatory arrest should remain in place for all felony cases. Felony cases most often include injuries and the use of weapons.
4. Officer discretion should be allowed for repeat calls or chronic complaints. Officers should always check their computer or with their dispatcher to see if there have been prior calls at the same address or for the same offender of victim. Officers should always check for outstanding warrants.
5. Officer discretion should be allowed for victim preference. This does not mean that officers should or must adhere to victim preference, only that victim preference should be considered within the context and circumstances of individual incidents.
6. Studies document that more often than not the offender is gone by the time law enforcement arrives. Officers should apply for arrest warrants where applicable.
7. In minor incidents where none of the previous factors are met and there are no witnesses, officers should record all of the pertinent information and request a court date whereby both parties involved would be compelled to appear before a judge or a magistrate who can then determine the proper criminal or civil intervention. A list of criminal justice and social service agencies should always be provided to everyone involved.

Discussion Questions

1. Is mandatory arrest a good idea; should it continue? Please explain what prompted you to reach that decision.
2. If mandatory arrest is not a good idea, what should replace it?
3. What is the best proactive program concerning domestic violence?

4. Are one-size-fits-all domestic violence interventions a good or bad idea and why?
5. What do you think are some of the reason so many advocates and public policy makers continue to agree with one-size-fits-all interventions?

The Colorado Star Chamber

8

In the rush to condemn, a community and a state lost the ability to see clearly.

—Roy Cooper, North Carolina Attorney General

Introduction

The American criminal justice system is based on the assumption that everyone is to be considered innocent until proven guilty and that the guilt of anyone must be proven beyond a reasonable doubt. These are the fundamental standards that must be met before anyone should be judged to be guilty.

The epigram at the outset of the chapter is taken from a statement made by North Carolina attorney general Roy Cooper after he dropped all the criminal charges against the three Duke University students who had been charged with rape by Durham County District Attorney Mike Nifong.

What appears to be beyond a reasonable doubt is the fact that Nifong, many Duke University students and professors, the majority of domestic violence advocates, and many reporters in both the electronic and print media (Johnson, 2006) overlooked the two fundamental standards of guilt concerning these three Duke students (Taylor and Johnson, 2007).

Cooper believes that Nifong, whom Cooper brands as a "rogue prosecutor," railroaded the Duke students in a "tragic rush to accuse." However, on the the same day as the Cooper announcement, at a news conference the three students accused law enforcement, the district attorney's office, Duke University, the news media, and the public in general of disregarding their presumption of innocence (Beard, 2007).

Though this incident received national and international media coverage, this process of a tragic rush to accuse and disregarding the presumption of innocence has been occurring in the fast track prosecution program in the 10th Judicial District in Pueblo, Colorado, since 1999 (Langeland, 2002; Uekert, 2003). And this program receives federal funds through the U.S. Department of Justice (DOJ) despite the fact that the DOJ sponsored a report concluding that much of the prosecutorial success the fast track project members claim to have achieved is "... based on incomplete data and anecdotal material" (Uekert, 2003, p. 26).

Other concerns expressed by Uekert (2003) are as follows:

1. There seems to be a lack of counsel at the pretrial conference and during the court appearance and the application of jail sentences.
2. Constitutionally, the application of jail sentences in the fast track program appears to be a particularly questionable practice.
3. The legalities of fast track prosecution are a matter for state and perhaps eventually federal authorities to decide.

The art of disregarding the presumption of innocence has reached perfection while being ignored by the majority of the mainstream media in the form of the fast track process. Chief deputy district attorney Doug Miles, who helped found the fast track domestic violence intervention, believes if only the people who have been arrested, before seeing defense council or appearing before a judge, will just admit that they are guilty, they can get treatment as soon as possible. That certainly seems like a presumption of guilt.

They are the defendants who have been arrested and charged with domestic violence. And *they*, it seems as far as Miles is concerned, are guilty simply because *they* have been charged with a crime. Mike Nifong, as far as I know, only attempted to railroad three Duke University students. Miles and everyone else involved with the fast track program have been railroading, with federal funds and the approval of the DOJ, hundreds of men and women in El Paso County since 1999.

The U.S. Department of Justice

The following mission statement below is from the DOJ's website (http://www.usdoj.gov/02organizations/):

> To enforce the law and defend the interests of the United States according to the law; to ensure public safety against threats foreign and domestic; to provide federal leadership in preventing and controlling crime; to seek just punishment for those guilty of unlawful behavior; and to ensure fair and impartial administration of justice for all Americans.

There ought to be little doubt that it is the responsibility of the DOJ to ensure the fair and impartial administration of justice for all Americans. And this should include all Americans, even those who can not afford high-powered, expensive lawyers to help them with their defense. Coercing people into admitting they are guilty before they have the chance to consult with a lawyer seems to be the opposite of anything that the DOJ should want to become involved with. However, coercing people into admitting they are guilty before they consult with a lawyer is at the heart and core of the fast track program.

The Star Chamber

The belief that government should not force or coerce individuals to give self-incriminating information to those prosecuting them was codified in England during the 17th century primarily because of the use of the Star Chamber.

The Star Chamber was the name given to an English court established in 1487 that was faster and less rigid than the common-law courts. It was used by the Stuart Kings to further their ideology and was used in the defiance of Parliamentary law. The Star Chamber also administered an oath requiring individuals to answer any question asked of them, including those that might demonstrate or document their own guilt.

After Parliament abolished the Star Chamber in 1641, English common law included, equally for all its citizens, the privilege of the right against coerced statements and behavior and in particular the use of confessions that can be used as self-incrimination (Bartleby.com, 2007). This basic protection of individual rights was adopted by the American colonies, and in fact it was included in the Bill of Rights of the Constitution of the United States in the Fifth, Sixth, and Fourteenth (Section 1) Amendments.

The Fifth Amendment

No person shall be held to answer for a capital or otherwise infamous crime, unless on a presentment or indictment of a Grand Jury, except in cases arising in the land or naval forces, or in the Militia, when in actual service in time of War or public danger; nor shall any person be subject for the same offence to be twice in jeopardy of life or limb; nor shall be compelled in any criminal case to be a witness against himself, nor be deprived of life, liberty, or property, without due process of law; nor shall private property be taken for public use without just compensation.

The Sixth Amendment

In all criminal prosecutions, the accused shall enjoy the right to a speedy and public trial, by an impartial jury of the State and district wherein the crime shall have been committed, with district shall have been previously ascertained by law, and to be informed of the nature and cause of the accusation;

to be confronted with the witnesses against him; to have compulsory process for obtaining witnesses in his favor, and to have the Assistance of Counsel for his defense.

The Fourteenth Amendment—Section 1

All persons born or naturalized in the United States, and subject to the jurisdiction thereof, are citizens of the United States and of the State wherein they reside. No State shall make or enforce any law which shall abridge the privileges or immunities of citizens of the United States; nor shall any State deprive any person of life, liberty, or property, without due process of law; nor deny to any person within its jurisdiction the equal protection of the laws.

Thus, these amendments offer that everyone, regardless of affluence or influence, should not "be compelled in any criminal case to be a witness against himself, nor be deprived of life, liberty, or property, without due process of law" and that everyone, regardless of affluence or influence, should have the assistance of counsel for his or her defense. It is expected that the duty of the DOJ is to enforce, to the best of its ability, these rights in a fair and equitable manner for everyone, regardless of affluence or influence.

Moral and Legal Rights

In his book *The Men They Will Become*, Eli Newberger (1999, pp. 148–150) writes about the important lessons we all learn from the U.S. Constitution and the Bill of Rights. These essential and fundamental rights are vital to our freedom and are of particular importance in the court of law when individuals face the might of the government. They are as follows:

1. The Constitution gives people the right to remain silent so that they will not be pressured to provide information that may affect them detrimentally when they appear before a court of law.
2. The burden of proof in court is on the prosecutor (district attorney) to discover the truth through a process of seeking evidence and listening to conflicting testimony.
3. The U.S. Supreme Court insists that the defendant understands what the potential consequences might be if they admit guilt without first having the opportunity of an attorney present to represent their rights. The prosecutor represents the rights of the state and cannot wear two hats.
4. The law values fact more than opinion. The law values the truth more than what a single individual believes to be the truth.

5. The laws final and most important personal safeguard concerning an individual's freedom is that—above all else—the law honors honesty. To be honest is to be just.

Like so many other rights guaranteed by the Constitution these rights have not always been upheld by the government for all of its citizens (Brinkley, 2008). However, regardless of race, color, creed, gender, or national origin, affluence and influence always plays an important role in seeking justice (Cole, 1999; Friedman, 1993; Rothwax, 1996).

Anyone without the resources or without political connections in the United States will not always receive the same constitutional rights afforded those of affluence and influence. Regardless of many U.S. Supreme Court decisions to the contrary, history documents that the government does not provide many people—most often those at the lower end of the socioeconomic and educational ladder—with many of the rights guaranteed by the Constitution. Constructing fair and just laws is not difficult. It is in the proper implementation of those laws where the difficulty seems to arise (Cole, 1999). Anyone remotely familiar with the American criminal and civil justice system is clearly aware that the best lawyers provide the best defense and that the best lawyers cost the most money (Rothwax, 1996).

Injustice Indeed

The 1932 Scottsboro case Powell v. Alabama (1932) demonstrates that the Sixth Amendment sounds and looks good but that it only worked for those with money to pay for their own defense. You were guaranteed the right to "have the Assistance of Counsel for his defence" only if you could afford it.

Nine young black men were accused of raping two white women on a freight train near Paint Rock, Alabama. They were arrested and railroaded through the criminal justice system. On March 25, 1931, they were indicted, and on March 31 they were arraigned. The trials for all nine men began and ended on April 6. All of the defendants were found guilty, and all but one were sentenced to death. None of the "Scottsboro Boys" were provided with adequate counsel.

The judgment was later reversed by the U.S. Supreme Court. The court ruled that "the right to be heard would be in many cases of little avail if it did not comprehend the right to be heard by counsel" (Rothwax, 1997). The DOJ should help ensure that the same is as true today as it was then.

Justice for many citizens at the lower end of the socioeconomic educational strata of society continued to be denied by the courts until 1938 when the U.S. Supreme Court ruled in *Johnson v. Zerbst* that the Sixth and Fourteenth Amendments required that indigent defendants in felony cases in federal courts must be appointed counsel. For the state courts it would be *Gideon v. Wainwright* in 1963 before all citizens were afforded the rights the Fifth and Sixth has promised those many years before. Again, these were for felony cases only. The Argesinger v. Hamlin case in 1972 required legal representation be provided to anyone for a felony or a misdemeanor facing imprisonment (Schmalleger, 1999).

The premise in all of these decisions is the basic commonsense rationale that defendants who cannot afford an attorney or defendants who have little to no idea of what their rights actually are under the Fifth and Sixth Amendments need and should be provided legal counsel to represent them. These rights must be given to everyone when they go to trial, even when they cannot afford it. However, for every rule on the books there seems to be a way around that rule.

Plea Bargain

Criminal justice convictions are most often the result of a plea bargain (Boland et al., 1982). Most criminal justice data documents that more than 90% of convictions are resolved through negotiated pleas. Of convictions, data document that only about 6% of convictions are the result of a criminal trial (Schmalleger, 2005).

A plea bargain is generally accepted by the courts as a criminal procedure that involves negotiations between the defendant and his or her attorney on one side and the prosecutor on the other. The defendant is allowed by the prosecution to plead guilty or no contest to a crime. Often, this is a result of the prosecution agreeing to lessen the severity of charges or the dismissal of some of the charges. This process is designed to be to the benefit of the defendant, the prosecution, and the defense attorney.

In *Santobello v. New York* the U.S. Supreme Court agreed that plea bargaining, if properly administered, is to be encouraged. In fact, there is general agreement that there are not the resources to provide constitutional guaranteed trials to all defendants. Although this circumvents the many defendants' rights guaranteed by the Constitution, few will argue that this process respects the Constitution and represents justice when it is being fairly and judicially administered.

Plea bargaining requires judicial consent concerning the procedure to ensure that it is properly, fairly, and equitably administered. Defense attorneys often advise their clients to agree to a plea bargain when they are sure that the defendant does not have a chance to win the case. Prosecutors are often willing to bargain because it clears their case load and provides them with a conviction.

However, because the U.S. Supreme Court has held that a guilty plea does constitute a conviction it has been generally accepted by the courts across the nation that defendants be allowed the opportunity to talk with an attorney before they admit guilt. What kind of judicial system would we have if the only attorneys the defendants ever see are those who are working against their rights and whose specific job it is to find them guilty? That system would be called the Arrest Program in Colorado's 10th Judicial District, Pueblo County (Langeland, 2002).

To protect defendants against hastily arranged or unjust pleas the Federal Rules of Criminal Procedure (U.S. Government Printing Office, 2004) requires that before a judge can accept a plea bargain he or she is assured that the defendants have been afforded their rights. The judge shall inform the defendant of the following:

1. The complaint against the defendant
2. Any affidavit filed therewith
3. The defendant's right to retain counsel or to request the assignment of counsel if the defendant is unable to obtain counsel
4. The general circumstances under which the defendant may secure pre-trial release
5. That the defendant is not required to make a statement and that any statement made by the defendant may be used against the defendant
6. Of the right to a preliminary examination
7. A reasonable time and opportunity to consult counsel
8. That he or she will be detained or conditionally released as provided by statute or in these rules

In 1973 the National Advisory Commission on Criminal Justice Standards and Goals recommended plea bargains be abolished (Schmalleger, 2005). There was concern that the process of entering a plea bargain might change the goal of the criminal justice system to be administered fairly and equitably. There was concern that those working within the criminal justice system may be interested in defending their institutional interests more than the rights of those who appear before them looking for justice.

Society continues to believe that the courts, first and foremost, seek justice. Society continues to believe that the court, above all else, honors honesty. Well, perhaps concerning our contemporary confrontational and adversarial criminal justice system society might want to think again (Elikann, 1996).

The 2002 Colorado Star Chamber

The August 10–12 edition of the weekly newspaper *Independent* in Colorado Springs features an article, "Railroaded for Domestic-Violence Defendants, El Paso County's 'Fast Track' May Not Always Lead to Justice," (Langeland,

2002). What should be astonishing (but is not) is that so few people seemed to be aware of just what is going on in El Paso County. Or perhaps they are aware of it, but they just do not have the time to care.

It, once again, documents that the fears about plea bargaining that worried the 1973 National Advisory Commission on Criminal Justice Standards and Goals were quite valid. It is "equal justice concept" gone awry on a grand scale that actually involves the U.S. Department of Justice. (Unless otherwise noted, the following is from the Langerland, 2002 article.)

In May 1999 the county of El Paso, Colorado, began what it calls the fast track program. This program is designed to provide swift justice to the perpetrators of domestic violence. The program is in part funded by a grant from the U.S. Department of Justice. This is the very same DOJ that has intervened in police departments across the country to assure that all defendants get fair and equitable treatment from their police departments. It is generally agreed that before the fast track system that all suspects of all crimes in Colorado were treated on a case-by-case basis. This, in fact, is the intent of the Constitution and its many amendments. Most people reasonably believe that equal justice for all is and should be the ultimate goal of the DOJ.

The premise of the fast track program is supposed to be that by holding domestic violence offenders immediately accountable for their crime, the system will be able to deter further and future offenses. Of course, those even remotely familiar with the criminal justice system have understood, for all these years, that the basic philosophic theory of deterrence is the reason for the existence of the contemporary criminal justice system. It is not only and specifically intended for domestic violence offenders. And, in fact, most people who have little to no understanding of the criminal justice system have been led to believe this is how the entire system works. This sure and swift intervention is supposed to be true for all crimes, not just a chosen few. Is not that same premise, the very bedrock of how the entire system is, supposed to work for all crime?

What may come as a surprise to many, including those who work in the criminal justice field, very limited empirical or anecdotal evidence exists to support this claim (Manning, 1993). Two recent case studies of the fast track system that were funded by the DOJ conclude that this fast track system may not be constitutional. After reading the fast track article any reasonable and prudent person remotely familiar with the U.S. Constitution might consider that to be an understatement of monumental proportions.

The fast track system is a process in which the defendants after being arrested appear before a magistrate or a judge and are advised of their rights. The district attorney's office then meets with defendants in a pretrial conference and offers them a plea bargain without a defense attorney or public defender present. The law does not require that a defense attorney be present until after this pretrial conference.

There are still some questions concerning whether what fast track does is legal; however, there seems to be little question that it is not an ethical, just, fair, or honest process. What few dispute—and what the district attorneys' office or others in the court system seem little concerned with—is the fact that the fast track system is not offered on a fair and equitable basis to all defendants of all crimes.

Simply put, the article claims, the district attorney informs the defendants of domestic violence offenses only—many who are still in jail uniforms with handcuffs on—that they might remain or end up in jail if they do not take the deal they are being offered. The defendant is told that if he or she is willing to accept on the spot the offer being made by the district attorneys' office, the defendant will not do any more jail time, will not have to hire a defense attorney, and will not have to appear in court anymore. If they immediately accept the offer everything will be all over instantly and in 2 years there will be no record of this offense.

There should be little doubt by any reasonable and prudent person that although fast track is legal, it appears a little less than honorable or fair. And it is, with little doubt, not an equitable treatment of people who are arrested, as the fast track procedure is used only on domestic violence arrests, and then only those who are arrested during the week.

Further, anyone who understands the criminal justice system knows that nowhere in the United States, without some type of legal pardon, does a person's criminal record disappear. That promise by the district attorney's office is just the first of many misrepresentations made by those in a court system that is supposed to be in the search for the truth. Despite what the district attorney's office claims, the record or those arrested will remain on the books.

In 2002 more than 3,300 people were prosecuted using the fast track program. Approximately 76% were men and 24% were women. In the movie *Inherit the Wind* (Kramer, 1960), William Jennings Bryan states, "I do not think about the things that I do not think about." Clarence Darrow then asks Bryan, "Do you ever think about the things that you do think about?" Suppose we think about this fast track program for more than a passing moment or two. Perhaps it would help if we think about it as something that may not remain an isolated program in El Paso but rather as a system that one of our family members might end up in someday.

The article quotes Cari Davis, the director of a local domestic violence prevention program, as being generally supportive of the fast track program. Though Davis states that she supports fast track, she admits that she is troubled by the number of women being arrested. She claims that according to national statistics only about 5% of domestic violence perpetrators are women. There is not now, nor has there ever been, any empirical scientific evidence that supports her 5% claim. What may be true is that Davis believes the 5% figure to be a fact.

If Davis believes that the 5% figure is true, the question then is how can she support a program that tramples unjustly and discriminatorily on the rights of 627 women who are wrongly and unfairly arrested and charged with being the perpetrators of domestic violence? The 5% figure would mean that only 165 of 792 women arrested have been honestly and fairly charged with domestic violence.

Using the figures presented in the article, how can Davis, or anyone else, accept the fact that the majority of women arrested are innocent and have been unfairly prosecuted? How can she claim to express concern only about a program that she believes may be unfairly prosecuting 627 women? Perhaps she has not really thought about what she is thinking about.

As the Langeland article demonstrates, Davis is not the only person in El Paso County who is not thinking about what they are thinking about. And I may note that Davis expresses no concern about the fact that some males might also be unfairly arrested and coerced into pleading guilty.

The Colorado Coalition against Domestic Violence notes that the fast track model has a "whole range of ramifications for female defendants." It notes that women are the primary caretakers of children without noting, or perhaps being aware of, that the 2000 census documents that almost one out of five primary caretakers of children are now men.

Does that organization believe that the fast track model has no ramifications for male defendants? The facts are that the websites of the most domestic violence intervention programs document they are based on the Duluth Model of domestic violence and, as their websites document, they most often minimize or marginalize male victimization. Many do express concerns that some women who are arrested should not have been. Many nationally recognized domestic violence organizations, as their websites reveal, support mandatory arrest and prosecution policies for male offenders; however, these same organizations, similar to Davis's statement in the Langeland article, often question the use of mandatory arrest and prosecution policies for female offenders.

Thinking and Nonthinking

Court magistrate Jeffrey Saufley is credited in the Langeland article as presenting the most persuasive argument against the critics of fast track. He claims that approximately 60% of defendants pled guilty at pretrial conferences before fast track was implemented and that there was no change in numbers after fast track was implemented.

The Bureau of Justice Statistics reports that crime has been dropping over the last 20 years. It is possible that the number of nondomestic violence pleas in El Paso County may have dropped and the number of domestic violence pleas may have gone up. The total percentage of pleas in El Paso would then be the same as prior to fast track. In any event, this simple percentage claim is not a persuasive argument until one examines what those percentages are really reflective of. This does not demonstrate that Saufley is right or wrong; it simply documents that no persuasive argument was made as suggested in the article.

Nevertheless, Saufley, who most often presides over the fast track program, appears to at least attempt to be fair. However, simply because he attempts to be fair does not mean he succeeds. Saufley claims that he goes beyond what he is legally required to tell the defendants about their rights. However, when the public defender's office asked if they could advise defendants of their rights, Saufley said no. Those individuals he does not want in court are officers of the court; they are the defense attorneys whom many of the people arrested for domestic violence never get to hear or see.

Saufley says if the defendant is in the military he will advise them that if they plead guilty there is a possibility the plea could lead to a discharge from the service. Perhaps Saufley does not know that under federal law if a person is guilty of any domestic violence offense he or she cannot possess a gun. Without a gun, and given the pressure by many women's rights organizations concerning domestic violence in the military, the *may* would most often seem to be a *most likely*. Should anyone doubt that change from a *may* to a *most likely*, the vast majority of these military defendants, regardless of gender, would ask if they could consult with someone whose job it is to defend their rights and not to take them away.

Miles, the El Paso County chief deputy district attorney, worries that without fast track domestic violence, victims might change their minds and not want their offending partner to go to jail. The fact is that Miles does not even know if their offending partners wanted them arrested let alone go to jail. Miles claims that these domestic violence offenders are very slick and that they tend to be extremely manipulative.

The Langeland article states that domestic violence experts note that once the victim begins to ponder the economic consequences of his or her partner going to jail they might change their mind. And it is noted that these characteristics are almost always attributed to men who batter women. Perhaps Miles and the domestic violence experts involved with fast track have not noticed that, first, almost one of every four people in the fast track program are women and, second, there is absolutely no attempt made to discover, document, or demonstrate that the male arrested exhibits any characteristics attributed to a male batterer. And as noted more than once in this book, batterers are dangerous people, and they need to be identified. Apparently there is not enough time to be bothered with the facts in this fast track approach.

What fast track demonstrates, besides being an unbelievably wrong style of intervention, is that listening to and acknowledging the desires of domestic violence victims or ignoring them altogether presents the paradox that is almost never spoken of. If a victim is abused and wants only to get a restraining order, regardless of the abuse they have suffered and physical abuse noted on their affidavit, the domestic violence advocates help the victim get the order. Do what the victim wants them to do is the message advocates hear.

Thousands upon thousands of restraining orders are issued that document that the victim has been physically assaulted, and the courts too often do little more than issue a restraining order (Davis, 1998). Advocates are trained to listen to the victim, as these can be very complex situations that may involve life and death. It is generally agreed, nationwide, by the vast majority of victims' rights groups that the voices of victims must be heard (Buzawa and Buzawa, 1996). Listening to the victims' voice is the mantra of most domestic violence advocates. A victim should not be forced into doing what she or he does not want to do. The majority of victims know when it is time to act. This is turned on its head when law enforcement officers are involved. The exact opposite is expected from law enforcement officers, who are told domestic violence is a crime against the state, who are instructed not do what they want, who are told to do what the law says they should do. Nationwide, the vast majority of domestic violence training for law enforcement tells them to ignore what the victim wants and to make the arrest. This often continues when the victim is in court.

The fast track process does not provide the district attorney's office with enough time to explore the complexities of these domestic violence incidents or the concerns of the families involved. Miles admits that their office does not spend more than a half hour to listen or attempt to contact the offenders or victims in these cases before they insist the offender make a decision about accepting a plea bargain (Langeland, 2002; Uekert, 2003).

About 20 years ago domestic violence advocates complained that the police should treat domestic violence just like they treat other physical assaults. I believed then as I do now that many domestic violence cases can be quite complex and cannot and should not simply be treated as being just another assault case. Most advocates now claim just the opposite and that these crimes need special and particular attention that is quite different from most crimes. Data seem to indicate that the latter is true. Taking the time to listen to and to understand each individual incident is something that most police officers and victims agree on (Sinden and Stephens, 1999; Toon, Hart, Welch, Coronado, and Hunting, 2005).

In fact, much of what Miles claims in the article, as he admits, demonstrates that he does not have the time to listen to anyone involved. Miles claims that the defendants are adults and that they are capable of making intelligent decisions on their own without a lawyer.

Miles claims that the defendants' options are presented to them very clearly (he does not add quickly) and that they are quite capable of making these decisions on their own. Again, it seems as if the National Advisory Commission on Criminal Justice Standards and Goals was correct to express their concerns about the proper use of the plea bargain procedure.

Unsubstantiated Beliefs

Detective Howard Black of the Colorado Springs Police Department has worked on domestic violence cases for 18 years, and he believes that the fast track system works as a deterrent. He admits that it is only a belief and that he, his department, and in fact no one have any data to document that fast track works any better than any other system anywhere else in the country. In fact, there are no long-range scientific empirically controlled studies to substantiate the theory that arrest can minimize crime or can act as a deterrent to those who may think about committing a criminal act (Manning, 1996). Although Black claims that he sees perpetrators being more responsive to domestic violence laws because of fast track, he offers no proof.

Data from El Paso County show that more than one out of every three who have been fast tracked will appear before court again. And it is difficult to understand how Black fails to make the connection among the dramatic rise in women being arrested, mandatory arrest laws, and a definition for domestic violence that makes no differential between family conflict and battering behavior.

Miles claims that statistics suggest that fast track is working and notes that in the first year there were 3,600 cases and that now the caseload is down to about 3,300. How is it that that Miles has not noticed the dramatic rise in arrests of women? What he does not note is that the general rate of all crime has dropped over the last decade. That drop in crime in general has been accomplished without any fast track programs.

Has Miles considered it is possible that anyone involved in domestic violence disputes in El Paso County may now hesitate, because of fast track, to call because they fear when they do call they may be arrested as the perpetrator? Does he think that some victims will not call because what they want is a solution to their problem not the arrest of their partner? Miles does not recognize that one out of every four people arrested is a woman who will be fast tracked just as quickly as the men are.

One defendant complained that the deputy district attorney never asked for his side of the story although he kept telling the deputy district attorney that he did not do what he was charged with. When he did get an attorney of his own, the district attorney's office agreed to reverse his plea. Miles, in strange and convoluted logic, denies that the deputy district attorneys do not listen to the defendant's side of the story while at the same time claiming that the deputy district attorneys don't have more than a half an hour to talk with every defendant.

The defendants may have to spend months if not years in jail, and the district attorney's office does not have half an hour to listen to a defendant? It is also extremely difficult for me to understand how it never occurs to Miles, as an attorney, that the defendants in these difficult positions should be offered an attorney who is concerned with their protection, has the time and is willing to listen for more than a half an hour and is interested in their defense, not their prosecution.

Justice is blind indeed in El Paso County. Not only is justice blind, but it is also deaf to the plight of those without the affluence or the influence who should be afforded the right to an attorney who actually cares about their defense. Very few people in El Paso County criminal justice system seem to understand that in their criminal justice system they have misplaced the middle name of *justice* with *fast track*.

A local judge who once presided over fast track cases believes that many of the defense attorneys do not want to become involved because of the complexity of many of these cases or that they simply do not have the time to provide a proper defense for some of the offenders (Langeland, 2002). How does that statement reflect on the fact that judges should be concerned about justice?

Perhaps the judge is not aware, as the article notes, that in the next county plea bargains are offered to defendants at court appearances and that both the prosecutors and the public defenders are present. In fact, there appears to be no reason why the defendants in El Paso County are not being afforded their rights, similar to those in the next county, other than the fact that El Paso has a federal grant, acknowledged by the DOJ, that allows those criminal justice system to experiment on the lives of individuals to test a theory.

The theory of deterrence is not a bad theory. If some people understand that if they commit a crime the sanctions will be swift, certain, and just, they may be deterred from committing the same crime. The fact is that very same concept is supposed to be fundamental to everyone in the criminal justice system. The fact is, as I am clearly aware, most defendants do not spend a lot of quality time thinking before they act, and they do not spend much time thinking about being caught (Elikann, 1996).

Logic and Common Sense

There is a logical and common sense way for most people to decide if the fast track program is justice or not. All people have to do is ask themselves what they believe anyone of the law enforcement officers, attorneys, probation officers, or judges involved with the fast track would do if they were arrested for a singular, isolated, minor incident of family conflict and not battering behavior. Colorado law makes no distinction between those behaviors. Would any of these criminal justice professionals admit to doing something they and their family know they did not do, or would they ask for an attorney?

The question everyone—and first and foremost the DOJ—who claim that fast track is a good system must ask themselves as they look into a mirror is why the prosecutors in Colorado seek to deny the very basic constitutional right for an attorney for these defendants that they would demand are basic constitutional rights for themselves or members of their family.

Discussion Questions

1. Do you believe that the supporters of the fast track program would advise their family members to admit being guilty without an attorney and without a trial or a hearing? If so, please explain why.
2. Do you believe that the supporters would advise their family member *not* to admit their guilt without the advice of an attorney? If so, please explain why.
3. What could cause the director of a domestic violence program (Davis) to express her concern about women who are fast tracked yet express no concern in the Langeland article about men who are being fast tracked?
4. Does it appear that the fast track program is concerned about the dramatic difference between family conflict and battering behavior or is fast track a one-size-fits-all intervention?
5. Should the criminal justice system provide fast tracked justice for domestic violence intervention while allowing other interventions to remain on a slow track? Explain.

Ain't I a Victim

9

> A large proportion of family violence is committed by people who do not see their acts as crimes against victims who do not know they are victims.

> —**U.S. Attorney General's Task Force on Family Violence, 1984**

Introduction

Betty Friedan wrote in 1963 in her book *The Feminine Mystique*, "The problem lay buried, unspoken for many years in the minds of American women." What Friedan writes about is the cultural, societal, and legal barriers that for so many years prevented the equality of women in society. There remain many physiological and biological differences between men and women that most people, male and female, believe cannot and should not be altered.

However, after 4,000 years of written history, it has become acknowledged by almost everyone in America that there must be an equity of behavior from everyone and toward everyone, regardless of age or gender. The vast majority of women and men in this nation must continue to work together to create and continue change concerning equality and equity of behavior between the genders.

Domestic Violence Awareness

Beginning in October 1981 each year October is proclaimed "Domestic Violence Awareness Month." The logical assumption for the majority of women, men, girls, and boys is that this month should be inclusive of all victims regardless of age, gender, or sexual orientation.

However, as each October passes, the collective hope for change remains elusive for many victims. Too often, domestic violence advocates, public policy makers, and members of the electronic and print media continue to ignore scientific research and empirical studies. Facts remain replaced by fiction, and misinformation is allowed to become the truth. Many politically empowered domestic violence advocates angrily hiss and sneer from their institutional and political shadow that some who claim victimization are not victims at all (Dutton, 2006).

171

The rays of progress and dawn of hope that once lightened the dark corners of so many violent families continue to be dimmed. Where there were once the collective voices of women, men, girls, and boys, raising the hopes of the helpless with a promise of a new future for all victims of family violence, there is now all too often a clear and icy silence of one gender toward the other.

Facts and events, both past and present, are being purposely misused to promote specific ideologies and political agendas for some victims at the expense and actual exclusion of others. Some of the newly empowered advocates, rather than presenting principled promises and hope for all victims, are proffering 21st-century cultural, societal, and legal barriers that minimize the needs of some victims.

The collective *us* for all domestic violence victims has been replaced with a newly structured *I* and *me* (Felson, 2002). Some victims—adult heterosexual females—are now considered by legislation predominantly sponsored by the Violence against Women Act to be the primary victims while adult heterosexual males continue to be marginalized (Tjaden, P. and Thoennes, N., 2000a and 2000b). The majority of nationally recognized domestic violence organizations, as their websites attest, no longer prefer to continue to be agents of change. Those recognized as primary victims by these organizations—adult heterosexual females—now receive the bulk of concern, legislation and intervention. The primary change many of these organizations now seem to be concerned with is more money for their programs (Dutton, 2006).

Equality and Equity

In the early 1970s, often because of feminist activism, women's rights groups, and the justified concerns of advocates who worked with battered women and rape victims, the issue of domestic violence was dragged kicking and screaming, primarily by these groups, from the back alleys of societal ignorance. The issues of child, sibling, spousal, intimate partner, and elder abuse emerged out of closets of shame and silence. Victims emerged from behind the closed doors that held ignorance in check, and from the crannies and dark corners of our homes came those who were rarely listened to and acknowledged. After years of hushed silence, family violence was beginning to see the bright light of justice for all.

There is no question that feminist activism fought and brought the issue of violence against women to the forefront. They demanded that intervention be placed, first and foremost, into the hands of the criminal justice system. Their intent was to have the criminal justice system protect battered and sexually abused women and to punish their male offenders. And concerning the battering and sexual abusive behavior by those offenders and the plight of many of their victims, regardless of age, gender, or sexual orientation, they were and remain absolutely correct.

There should be no question that anyone, regardless of age, gender, or sexual orientation, who will beat, batter, or sexually abuse his or her spouse or any other family member deserves to be arrested and sanctioned as the courts seem fit.

Abusive Not Violent Behavior

However, as we begin the 21st century, because of domestic violence advocate activism and federal and state laws, domestic violence has become much far more complex than beatings and battering behavior. Some interventions can become multifaceted and complex phenomena. And the single greatest reason for that complexity is the fact that there is no single definition of domestic violence that either professionals or laypersons seem willing to accept (Wallace, 2002).

Legislatively, domestic violence is domestic violence, regardless of the age, gender, or sexual orientation of either offender or victims. Domestic violence as noted throughout this book is rarely limited only and exclusively for battering of women or sexual abusive behavior. At the insistence and persistence of the vast majority of domestic violence advocates, domestic violence offenses, either in civil or criminal courts, now embrace and encompass and psychological abuse as well as physical assaults (Wallace, 2002). Hence, domestic violence laws are not limited to only protecting battered or sexually abused victims but now most often include all abusive acts against all family members, intimate partners, or often times, all people who live in the same household regardless of legal relationship, age, or gender (http://www.womenslaw.org).

Data obtained from restraining or protective order affidavits show that many thousands of restraining orders are being issued where the plaintiff has not made any claims about being battered or sexually abused (Basile, 2004; Young, 1999).

The "Experts" Cannot See Them

"The National Conference on Family Violence: Health and Justice" convened in March 1994, 10 years after the first Attorney General's Task Force on Family Violence demanded that the criminal justice system take the issue of family violence seriously (Witwer and Crawford, 1995). The 1994 conference noted that the problem of family violence in the United States is epidemic and estimated that the annual incidence of abuse of family members is at 2 to 4 million for children, nearly 4 million for women, and 1 to 2 million for elder adults. The conference experts did not note the discovery of a single male victim of domestic violence. At this conference there were 400 professionals and 80 national experts.

The original intention of the authors of the "National Violence Against Women Survey" (NVAWS) (Tjaden and Thoennes, 2000b) was not to ask about male victimization nor female offending against males (Straus, 1998). Apparently Tjaden and Thoennes did not think that male victimization or female offending would be relevant. In fact, they could have put to rest the controversy about initiation, or who hits who first; however, they apparently decided not to ask that question as it is not a survey question.

When the NVAWS did ask about male victimization, it estimated that as many as 830,000 men may be victims of some type of domestic abuse each year (Tjaden and Thoennes, 2000b). This would mean that every 37.8 seconds there would be an abusive act by an intimate partner against a male victim. How or why is it possible that these professionals or national domestic violence experts at the 1994 conference could not discover the victimization of men?

The National Institute of Justice (NIJ) and the Bureau of Justice Statistics report titled "The Sexual Victimization of College Women" (Fisher, Cullen, and Turner, 2000) surveyed 4,446 women who were attending a two- or four-year college or university. Though the NVAWS discovered 830,00 male victims (approximately one of every three victims), the sexual victimization survey will not find any male victims simply because Tjaden and Thoennes (2000b) simply decided not to ask about male victimization.

In the NIJ report "Reviewing Domestic Violence Deaths" Websdale (2003, p. 27) writes, "Every year in the United States, 1000 to 1,600 women die at the hands of their male partners." Throughout the report Websdale clearly shows his concern for female victimization and even mentions that many women's deaths are of their own doing because of intimate partner violence. Websdale excludes any mention of male deaths, either at the hands of a partner or by their own hands as a result of domestic violence. In the 10 years prior to the Websdale report, another NIJ report documents that 4,992 men died at the hands of an intimate partner (Fox and Zawitz, 2006).

Information from fatality review teams also reveal that as many as one in every three domestic violence deaths is a homicide or suicide. However, Websdale (2003), like many domestic violence researchers, simply cannot recognize that men can be the victims of domestic violence. He writes, "In short, a fatality review identifies relevant social, economic, and policy realities that compromise the safety of battered women and their children" (p. 27). Although their deaths are well documented, male homicides and suicides remain invisible to the eyes of many researchers. There seems to be little to no understanding that a review of male homicides and suicides might document some gaps in research and improve preventive interventions that would save both male and female lives.

In March 2007 more than 1,000 leading health and violence prevention experts from 30 countries meet for the 2007 National Conference on Health and Domestic Violence. The conference was held to involve lawmakers and fundraisers in efforts to find better ways to keep women and children safe. The conference also wanted to engage boys and men in efforts to understand that violence is always wrong. Information about the conference can be found at the Family Violence Prevention Fund (FVPF) website (http://www.enda-buse.org/health/conference/). I could not find any information on the FVPF website about wanting to engage girls and women in efforts to understand that violence is always wrong.

The Institute of Law and Justice (ILJ) partnered with the National Center for Victims of Crime (NCVC) for an NIJ report titled "National Evaluation of the Legal Assistance for Victims Program" (Institute of Law and Justice and National Center for Victims of Crime, 2005). At the top of the report is the following epigram:

> This report is dedicated to all the women who had the courage and opportunity to leave an abusive relationship and seek legal help and support; and to all the women who are still thinking about it.

The theme throughout the reports is the need to provide assistance for women at the lower end of the socioeconomic educations strata of society who are the victims of domestic violence and need help in seeking a divorce. The people involved in the interventions were either unwilling or unable to uncover a single male victim of domestic violence who needed their assistance.

The ILJ and NCVC report (Institute of Law and Justice and the National Center for Victims of Crime, 2005, p. 187) claims the following:

> The Legal Assistance to Victims (LAV) program has been a success. It has provided resources that have greatly improved the quantity and the quality of legal services that are available to low-income domestic violence victims.

A review of the report National Evaluation of the Legal Assistance for Victims Program reveals that the program did not provide assistance to male victims and, in fact, the report makes no mention of male victimization.

On its website (http://www. now.org/issues/violence) NOW notes:

> NOW is unique in its approach to the issue of violence against women, emphasizing that there are many interrelated aspects to the issue—domestic violence; sexual assault; sexual harassment; violence at abortion clinics; hate crimes across lines of gender, sexuality and race; the gender bias in our judicial system that further victimizes survivors of violence; and the violence

of poverty emphasized by the radical right's attacks on poor women and children—all of which result from society's attitudes toward women and efforts to "keep women in their place."

The website also notes that every day four women die in this country as a result of domestic violence, that two to four million women are battered each year and 132,000 women report they have been victims of rape or attempted rape. There is no mention of male victimization.

While it may be understandable that women's organizations similar to NOW ignore male victims of domestic violence, it seems that organizations similar to the National Center for Victims of Crime, which are intended to provide recognition to all victims of crime regardless of age, gener or sexual orientation, should not.

Why Male Victims Seem Invisible

Even a cursory visit to most domestic violence websites reveals that they are primarily concerned with female victimization. As their websites report, the majority of all national domestic violence organizations continue to believe that domestic violence is singularly or primarily caused by patriarchal sexism and the power and control men want to exhibit over women. This is the Duluth Model of domestic violence intervention (http://www.duluth-model.org/).

Perhaps the problem is that once a domestic violence advocate believes—truly and absolutely believes—that patriarchy is the cause of domestic violence, that person must believe women are victims and men offenders.

What some advocates seem to be doing, at least to me, is accepting male victimization only in the abstract, because the facts and reams of data about male victimization demand they must accept its reality. When advocates accept the Duluth Model of domestic violence (men abuse women because of oppression and sexism) as their primary or only model, that model's theory seems to negate or minimize the reality of male victimization.

Hence, for the majority of domestic violence advocates, males must first and foremost be the offenders. Further, to believe that domestic violence is only or primarily caused by sexism and the power and control men want to exhibit over women, demands that an individual must believe that women are not and cannot be domestic violence offenders. Once an individual accepts either belief, the other belief must necessarily precede or follow.

The Duluth Model has caused many domestic violence advocates, experts, and public policy makers to ignore the hundreds of public and private studies and reams of data that document that male victimization ranges between 5% and 50%. Advocates who hold on to this Duluth, or patriarchy, theory means that the findings from the NVAWS (Tjaden and Thoennes, 2000b) that document there may be approximately between 835,000 and 2.9 million men who are physically assaulted by an intimate partner annually must be ignored.

Regardless of what domestic violence advocates want to believe, no studies or data exist to prove that male victims of domestic violence are very rare. Accepting, as the majority of domestic violence websites document that the advocates have, that the patriarchy causes domestic violence in turn may have led the majority of the advocates to overlook the reality of male victimization.

Is it possible that the Duluth model also caused the professionals and experts who attended the 1994 family violence conference, the vast majority of domestic violence advocates, and the majority of the public policy makers to ignore or not be able to see that the men can be victims of domestic violence violence? In fact the report from the 1994 conference recognizes not a single adult male victim.

Facts Ignored

As a result of the National Conference on Family Violence and with funds from the Violence Against Women Act (VAWA), from November 1995 to May 1996 the NVAWS (Tjaden and Thoennes, 2000b, p. iii)—one of the most comprehensive domestic violence studies to date—was conducted. The survey sampled 8,000 U.S. women and 8,000 U.S. men. The findings from the survey report, "The data show that violence is more widespread and injurious to women's and men's health than previously thought—an important finding for legislators, policymakers, intervention planners, and researchers as well as the public health and criminal justice communities." This advice and data seem to have fallen on deaf ears and blind eyes

This unawareness of the issue includes the vast majority of the print and electronic media. How did this country go from the proclaimed zero male victims in 1984 to 2.9 million male victims in 2000 without the media ever noticing the difference? In fact, it seems that once empowered by public policy, many domestic violence advocates became exactly the same as the people they once railed against. They simply reversed the gender consideration and now often, as their websites document, are females who do not care about males.

The Search for the Whole Truth

The NIJ report "The Criminalization of Domestic Violence: Promises and Limits" (Fagan, 1996) contains a warning. Fagan says that one-size-fits-all research and interventions lead us to assume that patriarchy and power relations alone cause domestic violence. When we assume that patriarchy and power relations alone cause domestic violence, advocates, public policy makers, and the media then assume that men are the offenders and women their victims.

Worse still, this one-size-fits-all intervention has led us to premature conclusions that cause us to ignore the broad array of causations, solutions, and interventions available concerning domestic violence. It has become fashionable to have state standards that apply a cookie-cutter approach to interventions, and there is tremendous resistance to any suggestions of change (Healy and Smith, 1998).

What cannot be ignored is the hundreds of public and private studies that clearly show that many males can be victims of domestic violence and of many females offenders. It seems that, far too often, as websites and legislation report, these studies have fallen on deaf ears, blind eyes, and closed minds.

Can't They Handle the Truth?

On October 2, 2000, President Bill Clinton by press release (White House, 2000) once again established October as Domestic Violence Awareness Month. The press release in part asserts, "According to the National Violence Against Women Survey, each year in the United States approximately 1.5 million women are raped and/or physically assaulted by their current or former husbands, partners, or boyfriends."

On October 5, 2000, in a *Boston Globe* commentary on page A27, Judith E. Beals, the executive director of the Massachusetts organization Jane Doe, Inc., wrote, "According to a recent federal report, one in four American women are raped or battered by an intimate partner, resulting in 4.8 million rapes and physical assaults against US women every year."

These are two clear examples of deaf ears, blind eyes, and closed minds. The only thing the FVPF, Clinton, and Beals got right, at least in part, is that their data all came from the same report, "Extent, Nature, and Consequences of Intimate Partner Violence" (Tjaden and Thoennes, 2000a). This report was sponsored jointly by the NIJ and the Centers for Disease Control and Prevention (CDC). However, the president of the FVPF, Clinton, and Beals chose not to reveal the entire sentence they quoted from that report.

The complete statement by Clinton is, "According to these estimates, approximately 1.5 million women and 834,732 men are raped and/or physically assaulted by an intimate partner annually in the United States" (Tjaden and Thoennes, 2000b, p. iii). The complete sentence for Beals is in the same report and on the same page: "Thus approximately 4.8 million intimate partner rapes and physical assaults are perpetrated against U.S. women annually, and approximately 2.9 million intimate partner physical assaults are committed against U.S. men annually" (ibid.). What could possibly cause all these people to cut a sentence in half? Did they purposely choose to ignore male victimization? Is it a fact that no one in the electronic or print media were aware that the sentence had to be cut in half by these people to overlook male victimization? Is it not a fact that domestic violence advocates, then and now, rail against those who attempt minimize domestic violence victimization of women?

And What about Our Children?

In the October 27, 2002, issue of the *Globe*, Beals writes on the editorial page that the Massachusetts Youth Risk Behavior Study confirms that one in five Massachusetts high school girls suffers from sexual abuse by a boyfriend. What Beals does not write—what she must be well aware of—is that the same study also confirms that 18% of girls and 7% of boys report being physically or sexually hurt on a date. Beals does not write that 16% of girls and 6% of boys report that someone had sexual contact with them against their will.

The website of the FVPF, which touts *family* in its title, turns a blind eye to the plight suffered by boys; boys, as their website documents, are viewed by the FVPF almost always as abusers, not victims. The home page of the White Ribbon Campaign notes it is an organization of men working to end men's violence against women (http://www.whiteribbon.ca/). Is not the White Ribbon Campaign aware that now more than 100 studies report male victimization and female offending? Are these half truths the message we want to be sending to our children in our schools? And almost all of the dating violence studies in the reference section of this book show quite clearly that jealously is primary reason for the violence. Do these domestic violence organizations and advocates expect that parents of both girls and boys want their sons and daughters to be treated differently?

The Patriarchy Makes Them Do It

Nancy Scannell, legislative director of Jane Doe, Inc., is quoted in a *Boston Globe* article titled "A Search of Equality" (Stockman, 2002) as saying, "Domestic violence happens because of sexism and ... control of men over women in our society." Jealously, anger, or rage is rarely mentioned by the domestic violence agencies, as their websites document, as reasons for dating or domestic violence.

If, as the majority of ideological domestic violence advocates clearly believe, domestic violence is caused by sexism, oppression, and the control men have over women in society, female to male abuse needs to be minimized or ignored. In fact, Jane Doe, Inc., as well as the vast majority of domestic violence advocates, ignore almost all school-age dating violence studies reporting that the most common reason boys and girls give for hitting or being hit by a dating partner are the real or perceived emotional betrayals and jealousies exhibited by their partner.

Katherine Green, Jane Doe, Inc.'s public affairs director states in the *Globe* article (Stockman, 2002), "Sometimes it snows in Florida," quoting a Jane Doe board member's comment on male victims at an annual board meeting. "We can't ignore it, but we don't make public policy around it." This belief might also be summed up as female-to-male abuse is too rare for Jane Doe, Inc., to care. To those who have sons as well as daughters, that statement seems to be a rather sad, egotistical, cruel, and chilling philosophy for an organization that purports to be concerned about the victims of domestic violence.

In Cecil County, Maryland, a number of Domestic Violence Rape Crisis Center advocates left a meeting simply because the Family Violence Council was going to show a videotape of the ABC news show "20/20" that contained a segment showing men being abused by women. The advocates claimed that they did not want to watch the segment because it contained sensationalist material they claimed was based on misleading statistics, myths, and nonscientific research. The advocates claimed that over a year they had only 14 men ask for services compared with 300 women. However, it was pointed out to the advocates that so few males seek their service because their website states that they do not accept males over the age of 14 (Wordbridges, 2003).

The Invisible Victim

That domestic violence is primarily violence against adult heterosexual women philosophy, is supported by National Organization of Women, the vast majority of other women's rights organizations, most domestic violence advocates, and the Violence Against Women Office.

It is foolish and irresponsible to ignore the fact that some domestic or dating violence can or does occur because of sexism or dated gender roles that remain as truth in the minds of some males and females. However, how is it possible that so many domestic violence advocates and public policy makers remain convinced that most domestic violence against women will occur for entirely different reasons than other forms of family violence?

The majority of studies exploring all forms of violence that occur within the home conclude that the different forms of family violence are linked in some manner, shape, or form with each other (Brownstein, 2000; Chalk and King, 1998; Hendricks, McKean, and Hendricks, 2003; Kruttschnitt, McLaughlin, and Petrie, 2004; Mignon, Larson, and Holmes, 2002; Wallace,

2002). The idea of using physical force or coercion in relationships is a lesson everyone learns as children. This "economic or physical might makes right" is a lesson taught by both mothers and fathers.

To posit the theory that domestic violence is primarily violent and angry heterosexual adult males beating and battering helpless and hapless heterosexual adult females to oppress women has achieved little more than hindering the progress made towards the end of the 20th century concerning the recognition of the insidious nature of domestic violence (Young, 1999).

In 1994, Congress in the passage of the VAWA directed the National Research Council (NRC) to "develop a research agenda to increase the understanding and control of violence against women...." (Crowell and Burgess, 1996, p. 2). Over the next decade the NRC explored the similarities and differences between violence in general and violence against women in particular. In 2004 the NRC concluded the following (Kruttschnitt et al., 2004, p. 100):

> Finally, there is emerging and credible evidence that the general origins and behavioral patterns of various forms of violence, such as male violence against women and men and female violence against men and women, may be similar. The committee believes that while gender-based studies of violence against women are important, some level of integration of research is critical to advancing our understanding of the causes of violence against and by women.

We must value, not diminish, vigorous debate. We must welcome, not marginalize, those with differing views. We must stimulate, not stifle, thinking. We must encourage, not dissuade, dialogue. Progress toward minimizing violence in our homes is hindered, not helped, by the finger pointing of guilt away from one gender and toward others.

The "sexism and oppression of women theory" is a red herring that impedes proper progress concerning resources and assistance for all victims of domestic violence. It creates an atmosphere of ignorance and distrust. It is almost impossible for men to gain recognition, resources, and assistance when they are the victims of an abusive relationship (Dutton, 2006).

Though our public policy makers often profess that they do care about male victims of domestic violence, it is a fact that not a single penny—not one red cent—of the billions allocated through the VAWA has been spent an adult heterosexual male victim intervention program.

All data show and almost all researchers agree that in violence between men and women, in which the more serious, injurious, and sexual assaults are suffered, there is little question that women are the primary victims (Laroche, 2005). However, those are the results and not the cause. The cause needs to be addressed to minimize the results.

No one, regardless of age or gender, is immune from any form of family conflict, nor are they impervious from the more serious forms of domestic violence. All lower levels of family conflict are serious and can quickly escalate into much more violent behavior for all members of the family, regardless of age or gender, without proper and early intervention. And, as noted over and over again in this book, the vast majority of domestic violence laws make no distinction between battering behavior and family conflict abuse.

And The Truth Shall Set Us Free

Perhaps exploring the needs and desires of all victims might eliminate the barriers that divide us and serve to create rancorous disputes between women's and men's rights groups. Perhaps including all victims regardless of age, gender, and sexual orientation might place up back onto the path of proper progressive concerning family or intimate partner violence intervention. All unbiased domestic violence studies, both public and private, document that many females do engage in and initiate many minor forms of family conflict, including spanking, neglect, pushing, shoving, and slapping.

When family violence escalates to more serious violence and physical injury, women become the primary by not exclusive victims. When the assaults are sexually in nature, men are by far the primary aggressor. When we agree to acknowledge the truth—that victims come in all ages and both genders—the truth will prove to be rewarding for all victims of domestic violence.

Proper progress will be discovered with the inclusion, not exclusion, of all victims or abusers of domestic violence, regardless of age or gender. The fact is that some men do violently batter and sexually abuse women as adults. However, this event alone is a specific, exclusive, single event in the complex continuum that is domestic violence. All data document quite clearly that the vast majority of men do not violently batter or sexually abuse women.

All data collected by anyone, anywhere, at any time document that domestic violence has no single or exclusive perpetrator or victim. Domestic violence is child, sibling, spousal, intimate partner, and elder abuse regardless of age or gender. Once we agree that the truth is the truth, we might begin to resolve the issue of domestic violence rather than continue to contest it.

Although many advocates fought the last half of the 20th century for equal rights, concerning domestic violence the sounds of silence about male victimization, as the many domestic violence websites and public policies document, hinders and not helps all victims regardless of age, gender, and sexual orientation.

Discussion Questions

1. Why is it so difficult for professional and laypeople alike to recognize the issue of males being abused at the hands of females?
2. Why would the president of the United States, the director of a national recognized domestic violence organization, and the director of Jane Doe, Inc., cut a sentence in half so as not to mention male victimization?
3. What difference does it make to victims, regardless of their age, gender, or sexual orientation, what the age, gender, or sexual orientation of their abuser is?
4. Should domestic violence be recognized as violence against women, or should it be violence against children, siblings, spouses, and intimate partners (regardless of sexual orientation), and elders?
5. Why do so many domestic violence organizations continue to claim that domestic violence incidents against men are rare events?

In Memoriam

10

In my end is my beginning.

—**Mary Stuart, Queen of Scots**

Introduction

Each year on December 31 on its editorial page, the *Boston Globe* lists the names of people who have died that year as a result of domestic violence. In the December 31, 2006, "In Memoriam" editorial, the executive director of the Massachusetts Domestic Violence and Sexual Assault Agency reported that Jane Doe, Inc., had issued its first Massachusetts report reviewing domestic violence homicide cases (Lauby, McCarthy, Meade, and White, 2006).

Domestic violence homicides are the most extreme expression of violent or abusive behavior. I agree with the director of Jane Doe, Inc., that the 2003 Massachusetts Domestic Violence Homicide (MDVHR) report should shed light not only on the lives of those who have lost their lives as a result of domestic violence, but also on the causes of these homicides.

Implicit Bias

The Jane Doe, Inc., website reports, similar to the majority of the nationally recognized domestic violence organizations, that most domestic violence advocates continue to believe that domestic violence is caused by sexism and the oppression of heterosexual women by heterosexual men (Stockman, 2002):

> "Men are sometimes victims of domestic violence," said Nancy Scannell, legislative director of Jane Doe Inc., a Massachusetts-based domestic violence coalition. "But the attempt to be inclusive [of male victims] should never be interpreted to mean that the issue is gender-neutral. It does not change our mind about why [domestic violence] happens. It happens because of sexism and power and control of men over women in our society.

I believe that the lost lives listed yearly on December 31 in the *Boston Globe* clearly show that domestic violence is far more complex and multifaceted than the sexism of heterosexual men abusing heterosexual women to assert their dominance.

I suggest that those who hold preconceived perceptions about what a specific conclusion should or will be, before all of the valid and empirical information data is explored and analyzed, creates an implicit bias that hinders advocates' ability to reach the proper conclusions presented to them by that data (Barlow and Kauzlarich, 2002).

The 2003 Massachusetts Domestic Violence Homicide Report

In the introduction of the MDVHR it is noted that the purpose of this and future reports is to "identify improvements in current policy and practice that can reduce domestic violence homicides in Massachusetts and to honor the lives of the victims of domestic violence" (Lauby et al., 2006, p. 4). This is of particular interest to me, as a growing number of studies document that some contemporary policies and practices are having negative, and not positive, effects on many families (Buzawa and Buzawa, 2003; Dugan, 2003; Dugan, Nagin, and Rosenfeld, 2001; Dutton, 2006; Eng, 2003; Felson, 2002; Finn, 2004; Gelles, 2007; Hirschel, Buzawa, Pattavina, Faggiani, and Reuland, 2007; Straus, 1998; Straus and Gelles, 1990; Sherman, 1992).

Too often many researchers and advocates will discount new studies that contradict the theories or hypotheses they hold to be true. These researchers and advocates believe that they have already discovered the truth, the whole truth, and nothing but the truth. The only new studies they will accept as valid are those that support their beliefs. When the new studies do not agree with their theories or hypotheses they will simply include only new data that agree with their theories or hypotheses and will ignore the data that clearly contradict their beliefs (Dutton, 2006; Gellis, 2007; Straus, 1998).

The Silent Voices

The following accounts are taken from the 2003 Massachusetts Domestic Violence Homicide Report.

January 14, 2003

On the evening of January 13, 2003, Laurinda Gomes, her daughter Karina Barbosa, and her mother, Maria Gomes, were shot to death by Laurinda's longtime boyfriend and Karina's father, Pedro Barbosa. After fatally wounding them, Pedro turned the gun on himself and committed suicide. His 12-

year-old son from a previous relationship, Laurinda's 21-year-old son from a previous relationship, and a young male cousin of Pedro's were at home at the time of the homicides but were physically unharmed.

February 7, 2003

Stephen Reid was stabbed multiple times allegedly by his wife, Sara Navarro, on the morning of February 7, 2003, at their home in a Boston halfway house. Both Reid and Navarro had histories of mental illness and violence and were receiving state mental health services. Neighbors indicated that the police had visited the house on several occasions prior to the domestic violence homicide.

March 25, 2003

Amelia Gomez was stabbed to death allegedly by her estranged boyfriend, Cesar Rios Vellez, in the parking lot of her apartment building on the evening of Tuesday, March, 25, 2003. Gomez told friends and family that Vellez was stalking her and that she was planning to seek a restraining order against him but was afraid to leave her home. When she did go out to get into her car Vellez stabbed her repeatedly and slit her throat. Vellez tried to flee, and when he was prevented he stabbed himself multiple times.

March 31, 2003

Livia Hedda Rev-Kury was strangled to death by her husband, George Kury, who then committed suicide by means of a drug overdose. The couple was having financial problems, and Rev-Kury had put an estimated $400,000 of the couple's savings into a restaurant they owned. The wife's physical health was deteriorating, and the husband was not happy about his impending employment transfer from the medical examiner's Cape Cod office to Boston.

April 19, 2000

Sally Spry was stabbed to death by her husband, William Spry, in their home. After killing his wife, William committed suicide by hanging himself. Local law enforcement reported that the couple had been experiencing ongoing domestic problems over the last week, though there were no court records of any problems.

April 19, 2003

Berenice Tejeda was stabbed to death by her husband of four weeks, Euclides Ortiz. After Tejeda found out that another woman was pregnant by Ortiz, he stabbed her. Ortiz had a criminal history for assault and battery and assault with the intent to commit rape, and an outstanding warrant for failing to register as a sex offender.

June 1, 2003

Colleen Stone was fatally shot in the back by her husband, Christopher Stone, following an argument in the driveway of their home on the morning of June 1, 2003. Stone fled the scene and then committed suicide by shooting himself in the head.

June 11, 2003

Donavan Penrose died from a head injury inflicted by Steven Laramee, who was engaged to Penrose's ex-girlfriend Natalie Blanchette. Laramee had an argument with Blanchette outside her home on the evening of June 10 after he saw her drinking with Penrose and accused the two of having an affair. During the course of their argument Blanchette tried to leave, and Laramee tore her dress. Blanchette called to Penrose for help. Laramee punched Penrose in the face; Penrose fell and was killed when his head struck the ground.

June 16, 2003

Gilane Azor Saget was stabbed to death allegedly by her estranged boyfriend Jean Claude Jules. After stabbing her, Jules put her body in her car, drove it to less than a block from where she worked, and left her and the car there.

June 26, 2003

Baby Petitry was stabbed to death with a shard of glass from a broken window allegedly by his girlfriend, Solange Anestal. The local district attorney's office reported that the couple's relationship had been on rocky grounds since their 2-month-old baby and Anestal's 5-year-old child from a previous relationship were taken away by the Department of Social Services amid abuse allegations against their mother. Court records show that Anestal was arraigned in September 2004 on murder charges and was awaiting trial due to continuances and psychiatric evaluation at Taunton State Hospital.

June 29, 2003

Nelli Bessonova was stabbed to death in front of her 15-year-old daughter allegedly by her husband, Viktor Bessonova. The couple had a history of domestic violence. Viktor woke Nelli up while she was sleeping in her daughter's room and began to stab her. Nelli escaped, and Viktor began to stab his stepdaughter. When the police arrived they found Nelli critically injured and Viktor, who had slashed his wrists but survived. Viktor was not injured, but was civilly committed because of mental illness.

July 23, 2003

Amy Levesque was fatally stabbed by her estranged boyfriend and father of her children, William Murphy. Murphy and Levesque had an argument outside a pub. Murphy stabbed Levesque and later reported the crime to a friend, who called the police. A month before the murder Murphy had been arrested for assault charges against Levesque, and 3 days before that Murphy had reportedly attempted suicide.

October 2, 2003

Dawne Marie Brault was stabbed to death at the front door of her home by her ex-boyfriend Ralph Nesbitt. Brault worked as a nursing assistant that also employed Nancy Robinson, who was Nesbitt's ex-girlfriend and the mother of his five children. Nesbitt had previously threatened to kill Brault and a male coworker he believed was having an affair with her. Nesbitt had a history of mental illness.

October 28, 2003

Timothy Maguire was strangled to death by Nathan Miksch, his dating partner. At some point after the murder Miksch severed Maguire's left arm and stuffed his body in a closet. When Miksch was arrested he claimed that all he could remember about the night of Maguire's murder was that he had passed out after taking prescription drugs and drinking alcohol.

November 2, 2003

William Casavant was smothered to death allegedly by his girlfriend, Kathleen Ferreira. The couple had a history of violence. Casavant had been arrested for assaulting Ferreira on a number of other occasions; during one such occasion, he had a gun and was acting suicidal. Ferreira is undergoing psychological testing.

November 26, 2003

Mary Toomey was stabbed to death by her housemate, Anthony DiBenedetto. DiBenedetto had been living with Toomey for about 3 years after separating from his wife. Court records show that DiBenedetto had a history of assault and of having a number of restraining orders taken out against him. DiBenedetto was also taking some psychiatric medications. After murdering Toomey, DiBenedetto stored her body in her bedroom and scattered onions throughout the room to mask the odor.

December 1, 2003

Lori Ann Corbett was stabbed to death by her ex-boyfriend Jason Beals. He allegedly entered Corbett's home, took a knife from the kitchen, and walked upstairs to her bedroom, where he stabbed her repeatedly and slit her throat. He then went down to the basement and stabbed himself to death.

I agree with the authors of the MDVHR that we should be guided by these incidents and use them, as the report notes on page 4, to raise awareness among individuals, communities, systems and policy makers. The silent voices of these victims speak very loudly about the fact that these incidents are complex and multifaceted.

Implicit Bias

Implicit bias occurs when people maintain a conscious or unconscious preference for one specific group of people over another (Project Implicit, 2007). More than 250 Implicit Association studies have been published by organizations concerned about various types of discrimination or bias. These studies found that many people harbor conscious or unconscious negative associations in relation to other people (Bower, 2006).

There can be no question that Jane Doe, Inc., and the vast majority of other domestic violence organizations, as their websites clearly document, favor females over males, and many, if not most, intentionally minimize, marginalize, and ignore male victimization. Jane Doe, Inc., has its philosophic foundation in the theory espoused by the Duluth Model, as do the vast majority of all domestic violence organizations and interventions, both public and private. The Duluth Model has influenced the vast majority of batterer interventions programs. In fact, in a number of states intervention providers are forbidden to use any other form of intervention (Dutton, 2005; Healy and Smith, 1998).

The Duluth Model is a "gender analysis of power, which holds that domestic violence mirrors the patriarchal organizations of society" (Healy and Smith, 1998, p. 4). The "… patriarchy theory views society as dominated by males, with women in subordinate positions who are treated by men as possessions and things (Wallace, 2002, pp. 14–15). At the core of this model is the belief that heterosexual males use violence to maintain control over heterosexual females and other family members. The Duluth Model claims that male batterers are not violent outside the family and that they would be just as abusive even if they were not abusing alcohol and drugs. Further, the Duluth Model reasons that battering is a rational act and not an action affected or afflicted by psychological problems. The Duluth Model predicts that all men will be abusive (Healy and Smith, 1998).

In an experiment by psychologist Aiden P. Gregg (2006), each participant in the experiment read an account of how one group of people was depicted as savage and ruthless and the other was portrayed as civilized and peaceful. At the end of the experiment the students reported an implicit preference for one group over the other (Bower, 2006).

There is little to no question that over the last couple of decades the vast majority of domestic violence organizations present males as aggressive and assertive (negative reinforcement) and females as docile and passive (positive reinforcement). And many of the nationally recognized domestic violence organizations claim that they are concerned only about the abuse of women and children.

Lessons Ignored

The MDVHR tragically and painfully shows that most domestic violence homicides are complex events. Such tragic occurrences do not support the Duluth theory that suggests that domestic violence incidents, regardless of how horrific, are committed or condoned by rational heterosexual men for the purpose of exerting power and control over heterosexual women. Nor, because of their comparative rarity, should these events be used to accurately explain the majority of domestic violence incidents.

The MDVHR clearly explains that the majority of these murderers who kill and then often take their own lives do not represent a general cross-section of men. In fact, murderers do not represent a cross-section of criminals (Barlow and Kauzlarich, 2002; Macionis, 1997; Myers, 2004; Schmalleger, 2005). I agree with Lauby et al. (2006, p. 4) that "the human toll from domestic violence is grossly underestimated." However, to minimize or exclude male victimization obviously contributes to the problem of underestimating the toll domestic violence has on males.

The majority of domestic violence incidents, regardless of severity, are often multifaceted and complex events (Wallace, 2002). There is also evidence that the majority of domestic violence incidents are neither chronic nor severe. Though murder is the most extreme form of domestic violence it is also the least common form of violence (Hendricks, McKean and Hendricks, 2003).

It is as improbable, if not impossible, to attempt to attribute similar behaviors to petty thieves and murderers as it is to attempt to attribute the similar behaviors of domestic violence murderers with the behavior of minor family conflict offenders regardless of age, gender, or sexual orientation. In fact, it may be as dangerous as it is disingenuous to attempt to make those comparisons.

Hundreds of domestic violence studies plainly outline that there is no single cause or cure (Wallace, 2002). And there is growing evidence that the general origins and behavioral patterns of the various forms of violence are similar (Brownstein, 2000; Hendricks et al., 2003; Kruttschnitt, McLaughlin, and Petrie, 2004).

Domestic Violence Homicide Is Preventable

The MDVHR claims that domestic violence homicides are preventable events (Luby et al., 2006, p. 23). I know of no one, other than a small number of domestic violence advocates engaged in law enforcement, who make that claim. What is true is that in some incidents there is clear evidence of heightened risk factors that those being abused, family, friends, and society in general should be made aware of. However, most sociologists, psychologists, or criminologists agree that it is improbable to impossible to claim that any murders, domestic or otherwise, are actually predictable events.

The Campbell et al. (2003) study that the MDVHR refers to does not make the claim that domestic violence homicides are preventable. What the study does claim is this:

> A team of researchers studied the Danger Assessment and found that despite certain limitations, the tool can with some reliability identify women who may be at risk of being killed by their intimate partner. (p. 16)

I am not aware of any criminologist, or anyone else in fact, who has produced data proving that increased risk factors actually and acutely can predict that a murder will take place.

The Campbell et al. (2003, p. 16) study warns (and the MDVHR does not) that:

> Eighty-three percent of the women who were killed had scores of 4 or higher, but so did almost 40 percent of the women who were not killed. This finding indicates that practitioners can use the Danger Assessment (like all intimate partner violence risk assessment tools) as a guide in the process rather than as a precise actuarial tool.

The report "*When Domestic Violence Kills*" (Abrams, Belknap, and Melton, 2001, p. 47) warns that:

> The commonsense predictors for domestic violence homicide are particularly difficult to demonstrate. Specifically, possession of guns, previous severe vio-

lence, previous police contact and heavy drug use fail to statistically predict domestic homicide. Because these characteristics are so widespread in our society, they grossly over-predict domestic violence.

Perhaps the beliefs that some of the authors held before they published the MDVHR may have skewed their perceptions of what the MDVHR actually reports. On July 22, 2007, Jane Doe, Inc.'s website boasted the claim that "battering and abuse are learned behaviors" and that "key to ending these crimes is building a non-sexist society." I could find nothing in the MDVHR that supports this claim.

Lauby et al. (2006) are correct that we must provide proper context for domestic violence, regardless of its severity and that proper context will put an end to stereotypes and myths. There is nothing in the MDVHR documenting that any of the 2003 domestic violence homicides were actually predictable, nor are there any data showing that any of these homicides occurred because of learned behavior or sexist beliefs.

I agree with Campbell et al. (2003) that dangerous assessments should be used as guides and that they are not a precise actuarial tool that can actually predict domestic violence homicides. If the problem of domestic violence, in it most minor or more horrific forms, are to end, the proper causes must be discovered before the proper cures can occur.

Conclusion

I do not question for a moment, as criminal justice data clearly reveal, that men are involved in far more lethal violence than women inside and outside of their homes. However, criminal justice data and data from the Center for Disease Control and Prevention, detail that men murder other men and take their own lives far more often than they murder women. I also agree with Jane Doe, Inc., that females suffer more than males from the effects of domestic violence (Felson, 2002; Kimmel, 2002; Laroche, 2005; Mills, 2003; Straus and Gelles, 1990).

However, it appears that Lauby et al. (2006) believe that the newspaper reports of these horrific incidents misrepresent what has occurred. They write, "Salacious labeling and the failure to provide a context for the murders can mislead readers and perpetuate stereotypes and myths" (p. 19) and also, "We are otherwise left no further ahead in understanding how social norms contribute to promoting domestic violence but in fact are further behind in knowing how our families, communities and system can make a difference" (ibid.).

I have read and reread the MDVHR, and there are no specific data in the report showing just what social norms Lauby et al. (2006) are referring to or what unspecified or unacknowledged social norms may have contributed to any of these horrific events. What the MDVHR does clearly document is that there appears to be very little rational and reasoned behavior occurring in these tragic murders. Slitting throats, severing arms, dying from a single punch, and storing dead bodies in the basement are "unique events."

The context for most of the murders appears to be aberrant behavior, self-inflicted injuries, suicides, mental illness, criminal histories, psychiatric medications, jealousy, rage, and psychological problems (Lauby et al., 2006). **And when those factors are absent, the majority of experts agree that many of the men who kill their wives rather than divorcing them are sociopaths (Fletcher, 2002; O'Brien, 2007; Stout, 2005).**

Discussion Questions

1. Is sexism and power and control of men over women in our society the root cause of domestic violence, or is it much more complex than that?
2. Do you believe that society in general—not males specifically—continues to value the lives of males more than they do females? And if you agree that males are valued more than females, provide specific data, incidents, and reasons that support your belief.
3. Should or should not dangerousness assessments be used in both civil and criminal courts? Please state specific data, incidents, and reasons that support your belief.
4. Do you believe that the reasons adult heterosexual males abuse adult heterosexual females are different or the same reasons for child, sibling, same-sex intimate partner, and elder abuse?
5. What role does sexism play concerning domestic violence? Please explain the sexist roles both men and women play.

Rethinking
Victimization

11

The test of a first-rate intelligence is the ability to hold two opposed ideas in mind at the same time and still retain the ability to function.

—F. Scott Fitzgerald

Some Perspective

In early 1960, Dr. C. H. Kempe introduced the term *battered child syndrome*. Society, after many failed attempts, began to accept that the majority of child abuse was not committed by strangers, nor was it a problem only for those at the lower end of the socioeconomic educational strata. Most people guilty of abusing children are not strangers; they are parents, family members, or other caretakers in the home.

It is universally agree—and unbiased data show—that concerning child abuse, males and females perpetrate approximate equal levels of nonsexual physical abuse (Gelles and Loseke, 1993). This accord and acceptance of responsibility from both genders allows for a consensus that has helped facilitate progress (Wallace, 2002).

The complex and multifaceted enigma that was originally presented as family violence has become the Violence Against Women Act (VAWA). VAWA has been presented by the majority of domestic violence advocates and public policy makers and has been published in the print and electronic media as exclusively or primarily adult heterosexual women being victims and the men in contemporary patriarchal society who beat and batter women because of sexism and the desire to oppress them, making them out to be the perpetrators. The National Coalition Against Domestic Violence (NVADV) website plainly states that it is concerned only with violence against women and children, not men.

Despite the lack of empirical research studies detailing that adult heterosexual women actually comprise the majority of family violence victims, this patriarchal theory is most often accepted as fact by domestic violence advocates (Dutton, 2006).

The victims of domestic violence are most often thought of by the general public as women with broken bones and blackened eyes. Although many studies document that males and females abuse each other at the same rate, only a limited number of studies and little scientific data can empirically question the fact that females do suffer greater physically, financially, and emotionally as a result of those events (Mills, 2003; O'Keefe, 2005; Straus and Medeiros, 2002; Straus and Ramirez, 2002). Nevertheless, studies document that the issue of domestic violence intervention is a far more complex and problematic phenomenon than oppressed passive adult heterosexual females being beaten by dominant aggressive adult heterosexual males (Wallace, 2002).

Differing Domestic Violence Data

After centuries of not addressing the abusive behavior in families or intimate partner relationships, toward the end of the 20th century change began to take place. However, there continue to be numerous myths, misconceptions, and outright denial that fragment and divide proper understanding of the issue (Dutton, 2006). The enigma that is domestic violence remains unresolved, and deliberations often continue to be contentious rather than conciliatory.

Domestic violence advocates who work with battered women often claim that 95% of domestic violence victims are women. Data from the "National Crime Victimization Survey" (NCVS) (U.S. Department of Justice, Bureau of Justice Statistics, 2001) records that approximately 85% of the victims are women. The "National Violence Against Women Survey" (NVAWS) reports that approximately two thirds of victims are women and one third are men. The "National Family Violence Surveys" of 1975 and 1985 (Straus, Gelles and Steinmetz, 1980; Straus and Gelles, 1990) and a bibliography that lists 161 empirical studies and 48 reviews or analyses (Fiebert, 2005) show that the abuse is approximately 50–50.

How is it possible to have such a divergent number of offenders and victims? Wallace (2002, p. 3) writes:

> How does one accurately study or research a phenomenon if a definition cannot be agreed on because the definition of any act sets limits and focuses research with certain boundaries?

These differences are not actual facts. These data are simply reflections of the fact that the majority of researchers, professionals, and advocates do not acknowledge a universal definition of domestic violence and use different methodologies to collect data.

Having domestic violence advocates, researchers, and others argue about a phenomenon that remains a different phenomenon to different people who then measure that different phenomenon in different ways is illogical and irresponsible. And yet the debate continues.

There is little to no agreement on just what a family is or is not; there is disagreement on who intimate partners are or are not, and there is debate about what dating violence is or is not. Violence is sometimes accepted as the fear that some form of violence might occur; violence can be a one-time event of pushing, shoving, or hitting; chronic long-term violent battering; or a homicide. One-size-fits-all policies cannot and do not differentiate between any of these.

Despite professional disagreement, the legal definition of *domestic violence* in the majority of states say that it is not specifically or primarily violence against heterosexual women by heterosexual men or only or primarily battering behavior between adult heterosexual males and females. Regardless, the majority of domestic violence advocates and organizations, as their websites clearly document, continue to define domestic violence primarily as violence against women by men.

Because of the laws in all 50 states, it is in the interest of all advocates, victims, and offenders to acknowledge that domestic violence is not most often battering behavior. In fact, the NVAWS clearly documents that most physical assaults between family members and intimate partners are relatively minor (Tjaden and Thiennes, 2000a, p. 11).

Perhaps it is time to examine the wisdom of labeling all physical assaults between family members and intimate partners as criminal acts and to question the mandating arrest and prosecution for those behaviors (Eng, 2003; O'Leary, 2000).

Compromise

With compromise, many of these apparent differences may actually prove to be more complementary than they are contradictory. The majority of surveys that ask who initiates the assault in domestic violence incidents reveal that women initiate assaults as often or more often than men (Chrisler, 2005; Foshee, 1996; Stake, 2006).

However, data also reveal that when women do use assaultive behavior, some of it is self-defensive and that women are more likely than men to be hurt physically, psychologically, socially, and economically regardless of which partner initiates the abusive or assaultive behavior (Mills, 2003; O'Keefe, 2005; Straus and Medeiros, 2002; Straus and Ramirez, 2002). Further, although not all abusive or assaultive behavior in a family escalates, certainly some of it does.

The majority of researchers and professionals agree that there are multifaceted causes and consequences of domestic violence that require different and distinct interventions given the context and circumstances of an individual event. The total separation of violence against women from all other efforts to understand the causes, consequences, and prevention of violence in general has proven to be counterproductive (Kruttschnitt, McLaughlin, and Petrie, 2004).

There is general agreement among researchers and scholars that research into the cause and consequences of domestic violence should not and cannot be limited by any single ideological theory or a one-size-fits-all intervention (Fagan, 1996; Felson, 2002). Age- and gender-specific research studies that ignore or minimize the vast array of the many exploratory and explanatory variables, by their very nature, can only provide partial and imperfect answers.

Most researchers and professionals agree that three principle theories—although there are far more than three—attempt to explain the reason why many who profess to love and care for each other often choose to neglect, abuse, and beat their spouse, partner, parent, or child.

The Duluth Model

This approach explains that domestic violence mirrors the patriarchal organization of society and that it is men, alone or primarily, who use violence to create a dominate role in the family. The behavior of the male is a result of sexism and culturally learned mores and norms. The violence of men against women is condoned by society. This perspective emphasizes legal victim protection and criminal sanctions for the perpetrators.

The Family Conflict Model

The abuse is the result of family stresses or the acceptance of conflict to resolve disputes both in the family and the neighborhood. Abusers strive for an important or predominant role in the family. In this view any family member or intimate partner may contribute to the escalation of conflict. The emphasis here is to provide services to recognize everyone's needs and desires while holding the perpetrator accountable.

The Psychological Model

This perspective proffers that personality disorders, early traumatic life experiences, or other individual dysfunctions predispose some people to use violence in family relationships. This perspective emphasizes psychological and psychiatric intervention, sometimes for both the victim and the perpetrator.

A Complex and Multifaceted Issue

Studies (Tjaden and Thiennes, 2000a; Gelles and Loske, 1993; Johnson and Ferraro, 2000) show that given the specific context and circumstances of individual events there can be some support for any one of the three perspectives. It seems logical that the context and circumstances of each specific incident should dictate the proper intervention for the individuals involved. However, the majority of contemporary criminal justice and social service interventions are predicated upon the Duluth perspective that assumes all domestic violence incidents involve power, that control issues and all incidents are battering, and that battering is not distinct and different from other family conflicts (Dutton, 2006; Healy and Smith, 1998). However, most contemporary criminal justice and social service interventions are predicated on the Duluth perspective that assumes all domestic violence incidents involve power and control issue, that all domestic violence incidents involve battering behavior and that battering behavior is not distinct and different from all other forms of family conflict (Dutton, 2006; Healy and Smith, 1998; Wallace, 2000).

Many researchers who are funded by the VAWA examine criminal justice data only for violence against women. This causes researchers to conclude and write that women are being abused and that women are not receiving fair and just treatment from the criminal justice system. Though this may be true, the complete data reveal that this mistreatment is not gender specific. The gender-specific VAWA research has caused public policy makers to establish criminal justice intervention and pass laws that are based on incomplete and partial evidence. This myopic and gender-focused research, of course, produces gender-specific results. Gender-specific research creates a single set of actions based on a single or incomplete data set rather than creating complete actions or complete data sets.

A review of all victims in the criminal justice system reveals that many victims, regardless of gender, are victimized twice. First they are victimized by an offender, and then many are reoffended by an underfunded and overwhelmed criminal justice system driven by procedures, protocols, and laws and not individual needs and desires.

Impediments to progress concerning domestic violence have been created because most domestic violence advocates and many public policy makers (it is, after all, the Violence Against Women Act) view domestic violence as a problem only or primarily for heterosexual women and their children. Many advocates conclude, without any criminal justice background and with no empirical evidence, that violence against women is distinct and different from many other forms of family or intimate partner abuse.

Disagreement continues among many researchers, scholars, and domestic violence advocates who present radically disparate data garnered from dramatically different methodologies of behavior. This statistical war of numbers has created a specious argument between many women's and men's rights groups concerning domestic violence:

- Women's rights groups claim that it occurs because of sexism and the power and control men have over women.
- Men's rights groups claim that both men and women are equally violent.

Each of these positions contains some elements of the truth, but neither is the absolute or complete truth. Both are troubling red herrings that more often than not serve to impede proper progress concerning comprehensive assistance for all victims.

The truth is apparent. Studies documenting that men and women are equally physically abusive cannot be used to generalize the needs of the victims of long-term and controlling physical abuse. It is just as true that the studies by professionals who serve battered women cannot be used to generalize the needs of victims of individual intermittent episodes of minor physical or emotional abuse. Advocates for all victims of domestic violence regardless of age, gender, or sexual orientation deserve to have their voices heard. An equitable inclusion of all victims, and not the exclusion of some, will act as a catalyst for more concern, compassion, and support for all victims.

Policies mandating that all single or isolated familial or intimate partner physical assaults are criminal acts and that all these incidents must be treated the same as repeat or chronic offending may actually be more harmful than helpful. These mandatory and one-size-fits-all policies often reduce resources that would allow the criminal justice system and social service agencies to better serve the community at large by focusing on battered victims and chronic offenders.

The extensively researched National Institute of Justice (NIJ) report "The Effects of Arrest on Intimate Partner Violence" (Maxwell, Garner, and Fagan, 2001, p. 9) notes the following:

> During the 6-month follow-up, the 3,147 interviewed victims reported more than 9,000 incidents of aggression by the suspects since the initial incident. While most victims reported no new incidents of aggression, about 8% of them reported a total number of incidents that represented more than 82% of the 9,000 incidents.

Rather than a one-size-fits-all intervention, because of the lack of resources and personnel the criminal justice system should focus on chronic offenders whereas social service agencies should primarily provide support to victims regardless of age gender or sexual orientation who are marginalized by their socioeconomic and educational status or their lack of family or public resources and support.

Batterers

There is general agreement that the behavior of a batterer is not the isolated behavior of someone acting out of anger or loss of temper or because of a lack of control over his or her emotions. The general consensus among advocates, scholars, and researchers is that a batterer is a family member or an intimate partner who repeatedly and with malice aforethought uses coercion, force, or physical violence to purposely manipulate and control or alter the behavior of another family member or intimate partner.

Battering can and does occur without physical assaults. Battering behavior can exhibit itself through the unvarying and constant threat of assaultive behavior, through isolation from friends or family, and through the absence of economic power or emotional control. Any of these behaviors can cause a family member or intimate partner to alter his or her behavior out of the fear that the physical abuse or other manipulative behaviors may reoccur at any time. Regardless if there are any physical assaults or violent battering behavior, some family members can still feel abused and believe they are powerless.

Family Conflict

Many people who are married or who live in a familial or intimate partner relationship, regardless of age, gender, or sexual orientation, will occasionally struggle with individual or family problems. A lack of education and economic resources can create or exacerbate these problems.

Many types of psychological and physical tactics are employed by family members or intimate partners, regardless of age, gender, or sexual orientation, who attempt to get their way in a specific or general disagreement. Too often, too many in contemporary society accept this type of behavior as normal.

Family conflict does not always involve violent assaults, nor is it always the result of a specific, long-term, carefully crafted, well thought out pattern of controlling behavior. Data document that family conflict is often minor and mutually abusive behavior.

The majority of Americans still believe that it is appropriate for men and women—people who have the power and resources in the family—to hit (spank) their children to change or alter their behavior. Other legal and socially accepted acts of abuse are hitting children with belts or other objects, corporal punishment in our schools, and the subtle condoning of sibling violence as children "just being children" (Straus, 1991).

Though violence against women is now considered a serious issue, many minor acts of violence by women against men continue to be portrayed as humorous by the media and are viewed by domestic violence advocates with little to no vocal criticism.

Family conflict can evolve from or be exacerbated by anger, anxiety, grief, alcohol abuse or drug use, stress, work issues, difficult medical decisions, and depression. Abusive behavior is often limited to threatening, pushing, shoving, grabbing, slapping, and throwing things. Verbal abuse and manipulative behavior can hurt just as much as a physical assault and can escalate to physical assaults. Family conflict is not always frequent and does not specifically and always escalate to more serious and injurious physical assaults. This behavior is often not viewed as criminal behavior by any member of the family.

Family or intimate partner conflict most often does not involve a batterer or a battered victim. This family-styled conflict is the face of domestic violence that is often presented to the criminal justice system.

Assessments Needed

Some hospitals have discovered that a hospital bed—the location that will most likely guarantee the survival of patients who suffer a cardiac arrest—is not so safe. Approximately 80% of patients who code while in their hospital bed, surrounded by nurses, doctors, and life-saving medical equipment, die in that bed. The problem often is poor assessments. In many cases the hospital takes too long to recognize the proper warning signs in individual patients.

In domestic violence the process is often less effective. In the criminal justice system the assessment is complete before the offenders or the victims are seen. There are no individual assessments for divergent program placements. The intervention is a one-size-fits-all program. Before anyone is seen, the assessment is that the male offender is an aggressive batterer and that females are the passive battered victims.

The cause of the assault, according to the prevailing view, is sexism, misogynist beliefs, and the oppression of women by men or by a society that condones violence against women. Offenders and victims are most often both placed in a cookie-cutter intervention process (Healy and Smith, 1998).

The Value of Assessments

Because of the increased number of females being arrested, many scholars, researchers, and domestic violence advocates now recommend that assessments be made before program placements are made. This is important because of the context and circumstances concerning the use of individual abusive behavior and the needs of individual family members (Edleson, 1998; Swan, Gambone, and Fields, 2005)

Assessments include the following:

1. Women who use violence in self-defense or after someone else initiates the violence
2. Women who have histories of violence at the hands of prior partners, parents, or caretakers as children

3. Women who are primary aggressors and who use physical assaults or coercive behavior to control their partner's behavior

It is difficult to understand why scholars, researchers, and advocates do not understand the importance of making these same assessments for everyone regardless of age, gender, or sexual orientation before they are placed into programs.

A comprehensive review of 20 years of research reveals that because of the many distinctive psychological characteristics, the variety of behavioral patterns concerning the abuse of alcohol, and the many different substance abuse problems, a variety of assessments along with a variety of different approaches and individualized intervention are necessary (Chalk and King, 1998).

It is also important for the education of the entire community that spouses and intimate partners who engage in lower levels of family conflict be distinguished from those who engage in violent and chronic battering behavior (Kruttschnitt et al., 2004).

The Need for a More Objective View

Empirical studies document that women and men use coercive behavior and initiate domestic violence incidents on an equal basis. The only data presenting women as passive victims and men as violent offenders are criminal justice and clinical data from domestic violence shelters.

It is generally recognized and labeled a clinical fallacy by sociologists that data from a subset of the people cannot be generalized to reflect the behavior of the general population. No one can empirically dispute the fact that most men are not criminals and that most women are not battered. It has become impossible to empirically deny that some women can be as guilty as some men when initiating physical assaults (Fiebert, 2005). It is now universally acknowledged by scholars, researchers, and advocates that domestic violence, regardless of its severity, is harmful to children (Chalk and King, 1998).

The NIJ (2004) report "Violence Against Women: Identifying Risk Factors" verifies that women who initiate or engage in aggressive behavior (e.g., hitting, kicking, punching) are at increased risk of being severely abused by their partner. Both men and women are exhibiting behavior that may be replicated by their children. The same NIJ report notes that approximately 62% of the women report that they were the one that initiated the incident and 60% said that their physical assault was not used to protect themselves from imminent harm from their partner. Many of the women in the NIJ (2004) study report they were beaten by their mother as a child. They often engaged in delinquent behavior as a child and abused alcohol or drugs, and many reported that their parents were arrested when they were children. There is little doubt, as many studies document (if the NIJ study was not gender specific), that the same is true for male offenders (Fiebert, 2005).

Unbiased Reporting of Facts

The findings from the NVAWS (Tjaden and Thoennes, 2000a) report that nearly 4.8 million incidents of intimate partner violence occur each year among U.S. women age 18 and older and that 2.9 million occur among men. Most assaults are relatively minor and consist of pushing, grabbing, shoving, slapping, and hitting.

The findings from the NVAWS document that 1.3% of women and 0.9% of men were physically assaulted by a current or intimate partner in the previous 12 months and that 39.0% of the women and 24.8% of the men reported being injured in that assault (Tjaden and Thoennes, 2000b).

A study from the American Association of University Women (AAUW) documents that females (35%) and males (29%) on college campuses report that they have been assaulted physically by being touched, grabbed, or pinched in a sexual way (AAUW, 2006). Data from the "Youth Risk Behavior Survey" (YRBS) shows that 8.8% of girls and 8.9% of boys report being hit, slapped, or physically hurt on purpose by a boyfriend or girlfriend and that 11.9% of girls and 6.1% of boys were physically forced to have sexual intercourse (Grunbaum et al., 2004). The findings from the NVAWS say that 40% of women and 54% of men report being physically assaulted as a child by an adult caretaker (Tjaden and Thoennes, 2000a). A U.S. Bureau of Justice Statistics special report details that the annual average number of intimate partner victimization between same gender couples is 13,740 for males and 16,900 for females (Rennison, 2001).

Conclusion

The aforementioned studies show that the total number of child, sibling, spousal, and intimate partner abuse of men, elders, gay, and lesbian abuse is greater than the abuse of adult heterosexual women by adult heterosexual men. Violence against everyone, not only or primarily women, regardless of age, gender, and sexual orientation should be treated as a significant social problem.

Data show that there is a need to end the use of physical assaults and psychological abuse among family members and intimate partners regardless of age, gender, or sexual orientation; these should never be used as a measuring tool concerning individual rights. It is ill advised—and frankly it has become counterproductive—to generalize which gender is the most violent without defining violence. It is without question that men commit more murders than women. However, it also a fact that men murder men and kill themselves at rates that far exceed the murders of women. It is counterproductive and irresponsible to expect that because some men are more abusive than some women that arresting and sanctioning men without exploring the context and circumstances of the event and individually assessing them will resolve the problem.

The willingness of each gender to accept its share of responsibility of the use of abusive behavior created much progress concerning child abuse. This is not the case concerning adult abusive behavior. The willingness of each gender to blame the other has proven to be as dangerous as it is divisive. It will prove to be far more productive for the safety of all victims to determine which specific individual in each specific incident initiates causes or creates the violence and then to provide interventions based on those incidents, one incident and one individual at a time.

It is counterproductive to minimize, marginalize, or ignore any victim or to paint one victim as always passive and the other as always aggressive. All physical assaults that are specifically used to change or alter the behavior of another family member or intimate partner are wrong. All psychologically abusive behaviors used to change or alter the behavior of another family member or intimate partner are also wrong. The claim that one group (adult heterosexual women) is more important (the primary victims) than the others is to proclaim adult heterosexual women to be the primary victims, as that age- and gender begin anew the old and odious process of placing the rights of one group (English against Irish, Northerners against Southerners, White against Black, etc.) against those of another. It is also divisive to pass public policy that proclaims one theory superior to the other when there is no empirical evidence to prove this.

Domestic violence intervention must be free of stereotypical gender bias and must become more positive and inclusive of all victims and less negative and exclusive. Promoting equality and eradicating stereotypical gender bias was and should remain the heart and soul of the feminist movement.

Too often, too many advocates think only in zero-sum terms of another era and are only concerned about "their" victims. Too often, too many advocates seem unable or unwilling to recognize that their behavior is the very same chauvinistic behavior they once railed against. Everyone, as progressive feminists understand, regardless of age, gender, sexual orientation or percentage of victimization deserves to have their needs and concerns heeded not hidden.

Discussion Questions

1. To what extent do societal influences affect our perception of the belief that domestic violence is an act perpetrated primarily by heterosexual men against heterosexual women?
2. If one accepts the supposition that cultural factors greatly affect our individual perception of domestic violence abusers, can it be deduced that other countries with different cultural beliefs and institutions than America will have different rates and occurrences of domestic violence incidents and different gender rationales concerning perpetrators and victims? If so, why?
3. Political interest groups affect the broader education and perception of American society, particularly in regards to domestic violence. This public affairs activity in turn is intensified as the public perception is molded in favor of the interest groups messages. How can this cycle be broken?
4. Aside from a general physiological advantage, males and females are at a level of parity in regards to their ability to inflict harm on each other. Empirical domestic violence data prove this deduction to be correct. Do you believe that males are biologically or sociologically predisposed to be more violent that females? Please identify some factors that would prove this assertion correct, and extrapolate on their origins.
5. The vast majority of domestic violence victims are "double victims." If you were a policy maker charged with reforming contemporary U.S. overburdened intervention systems, where would you begin: with public education? The justice system? Federal and state laws? Which areas are most amenable to reform?

Afterword

12

William Jennings Bryan: I do not think about the things that I do not think about.

Clarence Darrow: Do you ever think about the things that you do think about?

—Inherit the Wind

Introduction

This chapter is intended to serve as an open letter to the members of the U.S. Congress.

The very weekend I intended to submit the manuscript for this book, I received an e-mail from http://www.mediaradar.org concerning the following congressional resolution, H.RES. 590, which was waiting the approval of the 110th Congress. I absolutely agree with the 110th Congress that it should become involved in raising awareness about the devastating effects domestic violence has on families and communities.

The most important goal of this book in general, and this chapter in particular, is to help our public policy makers think about the things they are thinking about when they think about domestic violence. If the members of Congress do not have enough time to read this book, I request that in the interest of raising awareness they find the time to read this short chapter.

When the members of the 110th Congress thought about domestic violence, they did think about women, and, as the bill clearly documents, they did not think about or report about men as victims. In the congressional resolution that follows, men are portrayed as abusers, not as victims; boys are portrayed as abusers, not as victims.

Although members of Congress claim they want to raise domestic violence awareness, in their resolution they simply ignore the victimization of men when they write, "Whereas one in four women will experience domestic violence sometime in her life."

The Resolution

110th CONGRESS, 1st Session, H. RES. 590

Supporting the goals and ideals of National Domestic Violence Awareness Month and expressing the sense of the House of Representatives that Congress should raise awareness of domestic violence in the United States and its devastating effects on families and communities.

IN THE HOUSE OF REPRESENTATIVES

July 31, 2007

Mr. POE (for himself, Mr. COSTA, Mr. AL GREEN of Texas, Mrs. MCCAR-THY of New York, Mr. MARKEY, Mr. MOORE of Kansas, Mr. COHEN, Mr. ORTIZ, Mr. HOLDEN, Mrs. MALONEY of New York, Mrs. TAUSCHER, Mr. FILNER, Mr. JEFFERSON, Ms. ROYBAL-ALLARD, Mr. MCDERMOTT, Mr. ELLISON, Mrs. DRAKE, Ms. GINNY BROWN-WAITE of Florida, Mr. ALLEN, Mr. CLEAVER, Mr. MICHAUD, Mrs. BIGGERT, Ms. DELAURO, Mr. BERMAN, Mr. REICHERT, Mr. BISHOP of Georgia, Mr. MORAN of Virginia, Mr. GENE GREEN of Texas, Mr. NADLER, Mr. BRALEY of Iowa, Mr. CARNEY, Mr. MILLER of Florida, Mr. WYNN, Mrs. CHRISTENSEN, Mr. CONYERS, Ms. MATSUI, Ms. LINDA T. SANCHEZ of California, Mr. RUPPERSBERGER, and Mr. SHAYS) submitted the following Resolution, which was referred to the Committee on Education and Labor.

Resolution

Supporting the goals and ideals of National Domestic Violence Awareness Month and expressing the sense of the House of Representatives that Congress should raise awareness of domestic violence in the United States and its devastating effects on families and communities. Whereas one in four women will experience domestic violence sometime in her life;

Whereas domestic violence affects people of all ages, racial, ethnic, economic, and religious backgrounds;

Whereas women ages 16 to 24 experience the highest rates, per capita, of intimate partner violence;

Whereas 13 percent of teenage girls who have been in a relationship report being hit or hurt by their partners and one in four teenage girls has been in a relationship in which she was pressured into performing sexual acts by her partner;

Whereas there is a need for middle schools, secondary schools, and post-secondary schools to educate students about the issues of domestic violence, sexual assault, dating violence, and stalking;

Whereas the annual cost of lost productivity due to domestic violence is estimated as $727,800,000 with over $7,900,000 paid workdays lost per year;

Whereas homicides were the second leading cause of death on the job for women, with 15 percent of the 119 workplace homicides of women in 2003 attributed to a current or former husband or boyfriend;

Whereas landlords frequently deny housing to victims of domestic violence who have protection orders or evict victims of domestic violence for seeking help, such as by calling 911, after a domestic violence incident or who have other indications that they are domestic violence victims;

Whereas 92 percent of homeless women experience severe physical or sexual abuse at some point in their lifetimes;

Whereas Americans suffer 2,200,000 medically treated injuries due to interpersonal violence annually, at a cost of $37,000,000,000 ($33,000,000,000 in productivity losses, $4,000,000,000 in medical treatment);

Whereas people aged 15 to 44 years comprise 44 percent of the population, but account for nearly 75 percent of injuries and 83 percent of costs due to interpersonal violence;

Whereas 40 to 60 percent of men who abuse women also abuse children;

Whereas male children exposed to domestic violence are twice as likely to abuse their own partners;

Whereas children exposed to domestic violence are more likely to attempt suicide, abuse drugs and alcohol, run away from home, and engage in teenage prostitution;

Whereas adolescent girls who reported dating violence were 60 percent more likely to report one or more suicide attempts in the past year;

Whereas 13.7 percent of the victims of murder-suicide cases were the children of the perpetrator and 74.6 percent were female while 91.9 percent of the perpetrators were male; in 30 percent of those cases the male perpetrator also committed suicide;

Whereas a 2001 study by the Centers for Disease Control and Prevention (CDC) on homicide among intimate partners found that female intimate partners are more likely to be murdered with a firearm than all other means combined;

Whereas according to one study, during court ordered visitation, five percent of abusive fathers threaten to kill their spouses, 34 percent of abusive fathers threaten to kidnap their children, and 25 percent of abusive fathers threaten to physically hurt their children;

Whereas homicide is the third leading cause of death for Native American women and 75 percent of Native American women who are killed are killed by a family member or an acquaintance;

Whereas 88 percent of men think that our society should do more to respect women and girls;

Whereas men say that the entertainment industry, government leaders and elected officials, the sports industry, schools, colleges and universities, the news media and employers should be doing more to prevent intimate partner violence;

Whereas there is a need to increase funding for programs carried out under the Violence Against Women and Department of Justice Reauthorization Act of 2005 (VAWA 2005), Public Law 109-162, aimed at intervening and preventing domestic violence in the United States; and

Whereas individuals and organizations that are dedicated to preventing and ending domestic

violence should be recognized:

Now, therefore, be it resolved that the House of Representatives:

1. Supports the goals and ideals of National Domestic Violence Awareness Month
2. Expresses the sense of the House of Representatives that Congress should continue to raise awareness of domestic violence in the United States and its devastating effects on families and communities.

Thinking about Thinking

I suggest that if the members of Congress want to raise the awareness of domestic violence and its devastating effects on families and communities the members of Congress need to become more aware of the complexities of domestic violence. This congressional bill demonstrates that members of Congress are unaware of or have chosen to ignore the data reported in the following studies funded by Congress.

Although the 110th Congress Resolution 590 claims that Congress wants to raise awareness of domestic violence, it actually demonstrates the lack of awareness the Congress has about male victimization, i.e., the Resolution claims that "one in four women will experience domestic violence sometime in her life."

This claim most likely comes from the NVAWS, which shows that nearly 25% of women report victimization. However, why does Resolution 590 make no attempt to raise awareness about the fact that 7.6% of surveyed men also report being domestic violence victims (Tjaden and Thoennes, 2000a, p. iii)? Congress is most likely not aware that the NVAWS also reports that women are twice as likely as men to report their victimization.

Resolution 590 also claims that "13% of teenage girls who have been in a relationship report being hit or hurt by their partner.' There is no reason to dispute that, but what the Resolution does not report is that claim most likely comes from the Teen Relationship Survey, which reports on the same page (11) that 17% of teenage boys report being hit or hurt by their partner. Is the 110th Congress not aware of that data, or has it chosen to raise the awareness of the victimization of our daughters while ignoring the victimization of our sons?

Resolution 590 does nothing to raise awareness that domestic violence can affect all people of all ages, racial, ethnic, economic, and religious backgrounds equally (Wallace, 2002). It does nothing to raise awareness that women who abuse men also abuse children (McDonald, Caetano, Green, Jouriles and Ramisetty-Mikler, 2006). In fact, a careful reading of the Resolution shows that it often reports male offending and rarely documents data that now report male victimization (Fiebert, 2005).

"Advancing the Federal Research Agenda on Violence Against Women"

The federal public policy makers and their staff, as I have previously noted, need to become aware of the report "Advancing the Federal Research Agenda on Violence Against Women" (Kruttschnitt, McLaughlin, and Petrie, 2004; see reference list for URL), for which Congress paid. The congressional resolution herein clearly documents that members of Congress have either ignored or are unaware of this report.

"The Exposure Reduction or Backlash? The Effects of Domestic Violence Resources on Intimate Partner Homicide"

A National Institute of Justice (NIJ)-sponsored study that Congress needs to be read is "The Exposure Reduction or Backlash? The Effects of Domestic Violence Resources on Intimate Partner Homicide" (Dugin, Nagin, and Rosenfeld, 2001). This report notes simply being willing to prosecute cases of protection order violations may aggravate already tumultuous relationships. As prosecution willingness increases, we observe increases in homicide for white spouses … . Also, more white females are killed by their boyfriends. The largest effect is for white married females … . As the willingness index increases by 1, the expected number of white wives killed nearly doubles.

Controlling Violence against Women: A Research Perspective on the 1994 VAWA's Criminal Justice Impacts

Congress also needs to be aware of the NIJ report "Controlling Violence against Women: A Research Perspective on the 1994 VAWA's Criminal Justice Impacts" (Ford, Bachman, Friend, and Meloy, 2002, p. 75; see reference list for URL), which concludes the following:

But strong evidence that one policy is more effective than another in address-ing recidivism is elusive. We still have much to learn about the differences in offenders and differences in populations of victims to justify advocating one policy over another without qualification.

On the next page it concludes that the following:

Above all, they [public policy makers] need to know that their policies and practices will not endanger women. Unfortunately, there are too few preven-tive impact evaluations of policies already in place and fewer still that approach methodological standards insuring sound data for shaping policy (p. 76).

The fact that there are no evaluations in place, no methodological stan-dards and no data to demonstrate that mandatory domestic violence policies and practices will not endanger some victims did not prevent federal and local public policy makers from implementing those policies.

Intimate Partner Violence (IPV): Overview

The members of the 110th Congress, particularly those who sponsored the resolution H.RES 590, provided in its entirety herein because it includes the victimization of females and excludes the victimization of males, need to become more aware of the findings from the National Violence Against Women Survey that is cosponsored by the National Institute of Justice and the Centers for Disease Control (Tjaden and Thoennes, 2000a). This research has been available to the members of Congress since July of 2000.

On page iii.

Intimate partner violence is pervasive in U.S. society. Nearly 25 percent of surveyed women and 7.6 percent of surveyed men said they were raped and/or physically assaulted by a current or former spouse, cohabiting partner, or date at some time in their lifetime; 1.5 percent of surveyed women and 0.9 percent of surveyed men said they were raped and/or physically assaulted by a part-ner in the previous 12 months. According to these estimates, approximately 1.5 million women and 834,732 men are raped and/or physically assaulted by an intimate partner annually in the United States. Because many victims are victimized more than once, the number of intimate partner victimiza-tion exceeds the number of intimate partner victims annually. Thus, approxi-mately 4.8 million intimate partner rapes and physical assaults are perpetrated against U.S. women annually, and approximately 2.9 million intimate partner physical assaults are committed against U.S. men annually. These findings suggest that intimate partner violence is a serious criminal justice and public health concern.

On page 24:

> For example, 40% of surveyed women and 54% of surveyed men said they were physically assaulted as a child by an adult caretaker.

On page 29:

> Research on violence in same-sex relationships has been limited to studies of small, unrepresentative samples of gay and lesbian couples. Results from these studies suggest that same-sex couples are about as violent as heterosexual couples.

On page 49:

> The survey found that women who were physically assaulted by an intimate were significantly more likely than their male counterparts to report their victimization to the police (26.7% and 13.5%, respectively).

On page 50:

> A comparison of police responses to reports of physical assault committed against women and men by intimates showed that police were significantly more likely to take a report and to arrest or detain the perpetrator if the victim was female.

And the final sentence in the report on page 57:

> Given these findings, criminal justice practitioners should receive comprehensive training about the safety needs of victims and the need to conduct community outreach to encourage victims of intimate partner violence to report their victimizations to the police.

Conclusion

As stated in the resolution the Congressional goal is to, "raise awareness of domestic violence in the United States and its devastating effects on families and communities," perhaps it is time that Congress become aware that domestic violence has devastating effects on children, siblings, spouses, intimate partners and the elderly regardless of gender or sexual orientation. Perhaps sometime in the 21st century Congress will become aware of the reams of data that document male victimization and female offending.

References

A Safe Place (1997). *Expect respect: Anti-bullying program.* Austin: A Safe Place.

Abelson, R.P. (1995). *Statistics as principled argument.* Hillsdale, NJ: Lawrence Erlbaum Associates, Inc.

Abrams, M.L., Belknap, J. and Melton, H.C. (2001). When domestic violence kills. Denver: Project Safeguard. Retrieved 22 July 2007 from http://home.aol.com/projectsafeguard/frcmanual.pdf.

Academy for Educational Development (AED) (2005). Boys' problems in schools a growing crisis, AED Report finds. Retrieved 16 May 2006 from http://www.aed.org/News/pressreleases/boys_release.html.

Ackard, D.M. and Neumark-Sztainer, D. (2002). Date violence and date rape among adolescents: Associations with disordered eating behaviors and psychological health. *Abuse and Neglect* 26, 455–473.

Adams, S. (1999). *Serial batterers.* Boston: Massachusetts Trail Court, Office of the Commissioner of Probation. Retrieved 16 July 2007 from http://www.mass.gov/courts/probation/pr121699.html.

Administration for Children and Families (2004). U.S. Department of Health and Human Services. Retrieved 31 March 2007 from http://www.acf.dhhs.gov/programs/cb/pubs/cm04/chapterthree.htm#perp.

Aizenman, M. and Kelley, G. (1988). The incidence of violence and acquaintance rape in dating relationships among college men and women. *Journal of College Student Development* 29, 305–311.

Aldridge, L., Friedman, C. and Gigans, P. (1993). In touch with teens: A relationship violence prevention curriculum. Los Angeles: Los Angeles Commission on Assaults Against Women. Retrieved 28 May 2006 from http://www.lacaaw.org/itwt.html.

Allegrini, E. (2003, August 24). Assistant D.A. warns family violence goes unreported. *The Enterprise*, p. B1.

Allison, J.A. and Wrightman, L.S. (1993). *Rape, the misunderstood crime.* Thousand Oaks, CA: Sage Publishing.

American Association of University Women (AAUW) (1993). Hostile hallways: The AAUW survey on sexual harassment in America's schools. Washington, DC: American Association of University Women Educational Foundation Retrieved 28 May 2006 from http://www.aauw.org/member_center/publications/HostileHallways/hostilehallways.pdf.

American Association of University Women (AAUW) (2006). Drawing the line: Sexual harassment on college campus 2006. Washington, DC: American Association of University Women. Retrieved 28 May 2006 from http://www.aauw.org/research/dtl.cfm.

American Medical Association (AMA) (2007). Featured report: AMA Data on violence between intimates. Retrieved 30 July 2007 from http://www.ama-assn.org/ama/pub/category/13577.html#intimate_partner_violence.

Anand, G. (1994, May 9). Killing of Malden woman ignites fight on bail reform. *Boston Globe*, p.1.

Anbarghalami, R., Yang, L., VanSell, S.L. and Miller-Anerson, M. (2007). When to suspect child abuse. RNWeb 70 (4), 34–38. http://www.rnweb.com/rnweb. Retrieved No. 24, 2007.

Archer, C., Dupree, C., Miller, N., Spence, D. and Uekert, B. (2002). National evaluation of the grants to encourage arrest policies program: Final report. *Institute for Law and Justice*. Alexandria, VA. Retrieved 25 January 2007 from http://www.ilj.org/publications/ArrestPolicies.pdf.

Archer, J. (1999). Assessment of the reliability of the conflict tactics scales: A meta-analytic review. *Journal of Interpersonal Violence* 14, 1263–1289.

Archer, J. (2000a). Sex differences in aggression between heterosexual partners: A meta-analytic review. *Psychological Bulletin* 126, no. 5, 209–216.

Archer, J. (2000b). Sex differences in physical aggression to partners: A reply to Frieze (2000), O'Leary (2000), and White, Smith, Koss and Figuerdo (2000). *Psychological Bulletin*, 126, 697–702.

Archer, J. (2006). Cross-cultural differences in physical aggression between partners: A social-structural analysis. *Personality and Social Psychology Review* 10, 133–153.

Archer, J. and Ray, N. (1989). Dating violence in the United Kingdom: A preliminary study. *Aggressive Behavior* 15, 337–343.

Arellano, C.M., Kuhn, J.A. and Chavez, E.L. (1997). Psychosocial correlates of sexual assault among Mexican American and White non-Hispanic adolescent females. *Hispanic Journal of Behavioral Sciences* 19, no. 4, 446–460.

Arias, I., Samios, M. and O'Leary, K.D. (1987). Prevalence and correlates of physical aggression during courtship. *Journal of Interpersonal Violence* 2, 82–90.

Arias, I. and Johnson, P. (1989). Evaluations of physical aggression among intimate dyads. *Journal of Interpersonal Violence* 4, 298–307.

Arnold, J. (2001, August). Early misconduct detection. *Law and Order*, pp. 80–86.

Arriaga, X.B. and Foshee, V.A. (2004). Adolescent dating violence. Do adolescents follow in their friends' or their parents' footsteps? *Journal of Interpersonal Violence* 19, 162–184.

Armstrong, T.G., Heideman, G., Corcoran, K.J., Fisher, B., Medina, K.L. and Schafer, J. (2001). Disagreement about the occurrence of male-to-female intimate partner violence: A qualitative study. *Family and Community Health* 24, no. 1, 55–75.

Associated Press, (1997, May 27). Prosecutor splits a bullet. *Boston Globe*, p. A11.

Associated Press (1999, June 8). Domestic violence deaths up in NH. *Boston Globe*, p.E11.

Associated Press (2002, August 1). Army wife charged in husband's slaying. *Boston Globe*, p. A28.

Associated Press, (2005, February 11). Representation of indigent defendants inadequate, study says. *Boston Globe*, p. A6.

AuCoin, K. (Ed.) (2005). Family violence in Canada: A statistical profile. Canadian Centre for Justice Statistics. Retrieved 18 May 2007 from http://www.statcan.ca/english/freepub/85-224-XIE/85-224-XIE2005000.pdf.

Avakame, E.F. (1998). How different is violence in the home? *Criminology* 36, no. 3, 601–632.

Avakame, E.F. and Fyfe, J.J. (2001). Differential police treatment of male-on-female spousal violence. *Violence against Women* 7, no. 1, 22–45.

Avery-Leaf, S., Cascardi, M. and O'Leary, K.D. (1994). Efficacy of a dating violence prevention project. Poster presented at the 102nd annual meeting of the American Psychological Association, Aug. 12–16. Los Angeles, CA.

Avery-Leaf, S., Cascardi, M., O'Leary, K.D. and Cano, A. (1997). The efficacy of a dating violence prevention program on attitudes justifying aggression. *Journal of Adolescent Health* 21, 11–17.

Babcock, J., Waltz, J., Jacobsen, N. and Gottman, J. (1993). Power and violence: The relation between communication patterns, power discrepancies, and domestic violence. *Journal of Consulting and Clinical Psychology* 61, no. 1, 40–50.

Bachman, R. and Saltzman, L.E. (1995). Violence against women: Estimates from the redesigned national crime victimization survey (NCJ-154348). Bureau of Justice Statistics, U.S. Department of Justice. Retrieved 28 May 2006 from http://www.ojp.usdoj.gov/bjs/abstract/femvied.htm.

Beals, J.E. (Oct. 5, 2000). Domestic violence is rising; we need to act. *Boston Globe*. P. A27.

Barkan, S.E. and Snowden, L.L. (2001). *Collective violence*. Boston: Allyn and Bacon.

Barlow, H.D. and Kauzlarich, D. (2002). *Introduction to criminology*. Upper Saddle River, NJ: Prentice Hall.

Barnett, R. and Rivers, C. (2004). *Same difference: How gender myths are hurting our relationships, our children, and our jobs*. New York: Basic Books.

Baron, R.A. and Richardson, D.R. (1994). *Human aggression*. New York: Plenum.

Barrett, D. (2002, September 18). Shooting victim ended affair, police say. *Boston Globe*, p. A5.

Barry, S. (2000, January 28). Batterer's past clouds present. *Union-News*, p. B3.

Bass, A. (1994, September 25). The war on domestic abuse. *Boston Globe*, p.1.

Bartleby.com (2005). Star chamber. *Columbia Encyclopedia*, 6th ed. Retrieved 14 March 2007 from http://www.bartleby.com/65/st/StarCham.html.

Basile, S. (2004). Comparison of abuse alleged by same and opposite gender litigants as cited in requests for abuse prevention orders. *Family Violence* 19, 59–58.

Baum, K. and Klaus, P. (2005). Violent victimization of college students, 1995–2002. Bureau of Justice Statistics, U.S. Department of Justice, Washington, DC. Retrieved 28 May 2006 from http://www.ojp.usdoj.gov/bjs/pub/pdf/vvcs02.pdf.

Beard, A. (2007, April 12). All charges dropped in Duke rape case. *Boston Globe*, p. 2.

Becker, O., Benbow, N., Campbell, J., Clemons, D., Coldren, J., Contreras, A. et al. (2001, October 25). The Chicago women's health risk study at a glance. State of Illinois. Retrieved 21 October 2007 from http://www.icjia.state.il.us/public/pdf/bulletins/at_a_glance2004.pdf.

Begun, R.W. and Huml, F.J. (1999). *Violence prevention skills: Lessons and activities for elementary students*. San Francisco: Jossey-Bass.

Belknap, J. and Melton, H. (2005). Are heterosexual men also victims of intimate partner abuse? VAWnet. Retrieved 7 March 2007 from http://new.vawnet.org/Assoc_Files_VAWnet/AR_MaleVictims.pdf.

Bennett, L. and Fineran, S. (1998). Sexual and severe physical violence among high school students: Power beliefs, gender, and relationship. *American Journal of Orthopsychiatry* 68, no. 4, 645–652.

Bennett, L. and Williams, O.J. (2003). Substance abuse and men who batter: Issues in theory and practice. *Violence against Women* 9, no. 5, 558–575.

Benson, M.L. and Fox, G.L. (2004). When violence hits home: How economics and neighborhood play a role. Washington, DC: Department of Justice, National Institute of Justice. Retrieved 7 March 2007 from http://www.ncjrs.gov/pdf-files1/nij/205004.pdf.

Bergman, L. (1992). Dating violence among high school students. *Social Work* 37, 21–27.

Berk, R. and Newton, P. (1985). Does arrest deter wife battery? An effort to replicate the findings of the Minneapolis spouse abuse experiment. *American Sociological Review* 50, 253–262.

Berlinger, J.S. (2004). Taking an intimate look at domestic violence. *Nursing 2004: The Journal of Clinical Excellence* 34, no. 10, 42–46.

Bernard, M.L. and Bernard, J.L. (1983). Violent intimacy: The family as a model for love relationships. *Family Relations* 32, 283–286.

Biden, J.R. (2005). Senate passes Violence Against Women Act of 2005. Retrieved 9 August 2007 from http://biden.senate.gov/newsroom/details.cfm?id=246960.

Billingham, R.E. and Sack, A.R. (1986). Courtship violence and the interactive status of the relationship. *Journal of Adolescent Research* 1, 315–325.

Bird, G.W., Stith, S.M. and Schladale, J. (1991). Psychological resources, coping strategies and negotiation styles as discriminators of violence in dating relationships. *Family Relations* 20, 45–50.

Black, M.C., Noonan, R., Legg, M., Eaton, D. and Breiding, M.J. (2006, May 19). Physical dating violence among high school students—United States, 2003. Centers for Disease Control, *Morbidity and Mortality Weekly Report* 55, no. 19, 532–535. Retrieved 27 May 2006 from http://www.cdc.gov/mmwr/preview/mmwrhtml/mm5519a3.htm.

Block, C.R., Engel, B., Naureckas, S.M. and Riordan, K.A. (2000). The Chicago women's health risk study at a glance. Retrieved 13 August 2007 from http://www.icpsr.umich.edu/NACJD/help/faq3002.html.

Bocko, S., Cicchetti, C.A., Lempicki, L. and Powell, A. (2004). Restraining order violators, corrective programming and recidivism. Boston: Massachusetts Trail Court. Retrieved 16 July 2007 from http://www.mass.gov/courts/probation/crostudy.pdf.

Boland, B., Logan, W., Stones, R., and Martin, W. (1987). The prosecution of felony arrests, 1982. Washington, DC: Department of Justice, Bureau of Justice Statistics.

Bookwala, J. (2002). The role of own and perceived partner attachment in relationship aggression. *Journal of Interpersonal Violence* 17, 84–100.

Bookwala, J., Frieze, I.H., Smith, C. and Ryan, K. (1992). Predictors of dating violence: A multivariate analysis. *Violence and Victims* 7, 297–311.

Boorstin, D.J. (1983). *The discoverers.* New York: Random House.

Bograd, M. (1994). Battering, competing clinical models, and paucity of research: Notes to those in the trenches. *Counseling Psychologist* 22, 593–597.

Boston Globe (2001, August 19). Communism's fall, p. D6.

Boston Globe (2003, March 18). DNA tests value, p. A22.

Boston Globe (2003, December 31). In memoriam, p. A14.

Boston Globe (2005, December 31). In memoriam.

Boudreau, D. (2000). Code to violate? Magazine of scholarship and creativity at Arizona State University. Retrieved 4 August 2007 from http://researchmag.asu.edu/stories/rape.html.

Bowen, M. (1999). *Black hawk down.* New York: Penguin.

Bower, B. (2006). The bias finders. *Science News Online* 169, no. 16. Retrieved 21 July 2007 from http://www.sciencenews.org/articles/20060422/bob9.asp.

Bribiescas, R.G. (2006). *Men: Evolutionary and life history.* Cambridge, MA: Harvard University Press.

Brinkley, A. (2008). *The unfinished nation: A concise history of the American people.* Boston: McGraw Hill.

Britannica.com (2000). http://www.britannica.com/bcom/eb/article/0/05716,24330.html.

Brizendine, L. (2006). *The female brain.* New York: Morgan Road Books.

Brody, L.R., Lovas, G.S. and Hay, D.H. (1995). Gender differences in anger and fear as a function of situational context. *Sex Roles* 32, 47–78. Retrieved Nov. 23, 2007 from http://findarticles.com/p/articles/mi_m2294/is_n1-2_v32/ai_17012182.

Broidy, L.M., Nagin, D.S., Tremblay, R.E., Brame, B., Dodge, K., Fergusson, D. et al. (2003). Developmental trajectories of childhood disruptive behavior disorders and adolescent delinquency: A six-nation replication. *Developmental Psychology* 39, 222–245.

Brown, B.B. (1999). You're going out with who? Peer group influence on adolescent romantic relationships. In W. Furman, B.B. Brown and C. Feiring (Eds.), *The development of romantic relationships in adolescence* (pp. 291–329). New York: Cambridge University Press.

Brown, G.R. (2004). Gender as a factor in the response of the law-enforcement system to violence against partners. *Sexuality and Culture* 8, 1–87.

Brown, J.B. (2001). WAST is effective tool for identifying domestic abuse of females—Womenabusescreeningtool.*AmericanFamilyPhysician*63,no.6.Retrieved13July 2007 from http://findarticles.com/p/articles/mi_m3225/is_6_63/ai_71579204.

Brownmiller, S. (1975). *Against our will: Men, women and rape.* New York: Fawcett Columbine.

Brownmiller, S. (2000). Thornhill: Rape on the brain. Retrieved 4 August 2007 from http://www.susanbrownmiller.com/susanbrownmiller/html/review-thornhill.html.

Brownstein, H.H. (2000). *The social reality of violence and violent crime.* Boston: Allyn and Bacon.

Burcky, W., Reuterman, N. and Kopsky, S. (1998). Dating violence among high school students. *School Counselor* 35, no. 5, 353–358.

Bureau of Justice Statistics. (2006). http://www.ojp.usdoj.gov/bjs/intimate/report/htm. Retrieved Dec. 7, 2007.

Bureau of Justice Statistics (n.d.). Sourcebook of Criminal Justice Statistics. Retrieved 23 October 2007 from http://www.albany.edu/sourcebook.

Bureau of Justice Statistics, U.S. Department of Justice, Office of Justice Programs (2007). FBI supplementary homicide reports. Retrieved 23 October 2007 from http://www.ojp.usdoj.gov/bjs/homicide/gender.htm.

Burke, P.J., Stets, J.E. and Pirog-Good, M.A. (1988). Gender identity, self-esteem, and physical and sexual abuse in dating relationships. *Social Psychology Quarterly* 51, 272–285.

Burman, B., John, R. and Margolin, G. (1992). Observed patterns of conflict in violent, nonviolent, and nondistressed couples. *Behavioral Assessment 14*, 15–37.

Burnham, T. and Phelan, J. (2000). Mean genes: From sex to money to food: Taming our primal instincts. New York: Perseus Publishing.

Busby, D. and Compton, S. (1997). Patterns of sexual coercion in adult heterosexual relationships: An exploration of male victimization. *Family Process 36*, 81–94.

Buzawa, E.S. and Buzawa, C.G. (Eds.) (1996). Do arrests and restraining orders work? Thousand Oaks, CA: Sage Publishing.

Buzawa, E.S. and Buzawa, C.G. (2002). *Domestic violence: The criminal justice response*. Newbury Park, CA: Sage Publishing.

Buzawa, E., Hotaling, G. and Klein, A. (1998). The response to domestic violence in a model court: Some initial finding and implications. *Behavioral Sciences and the Law 16*, 185–206

California Alliance Against Domestic Violence. Retrieved 28 May 2006 from http://www.caadv.org/about_us.html. (No longer on line.)

California Men's Centers San Diego (n.d.). Retrieved 30 May 2007 from http://www.californiamenscenters.org/.

Call, M.R., Tolman, R.M. and Saunders, D.G. (2003). Adolescent dating violence victimization and psychological well-being. *Journal of Adolescent Research 18*, no. 6, 664–681.

Campbell, J.C., Webster, D., Koziol-McLain, J., Block, C.R., Campbell, D., Curry, M.A. et al. (2003). *Assessing risk factors for intimate partner homicide*. Washington, DC: Department of Justice 250/November 14–19. Retrieved 22 July 2007 from http://www.ncjrs.gov/pdffiles1/jr000250e.pdf.

Cano, A., Avery-Leaf, S., Cascardi, M. and O'Leary, K.D. (1998). Dating violence in two high school samples: Discriminating variables. *Journal of Primary Prevention 18*, no. 4, 431–446.

Capaldi, D.M. and Clark, S. (1998). Prospective family predictors of aggression toward female partners for at-risk young men. *Developmental Psychology 34*, 1175–1188.

Capaldi, D.M. and Crosby, L. (1997). Observed and reported psychological and physical aggression in young, at-risk couples. *Social Development 6*, 184–206.

Capaldi, D.M., Dishion, T.J., Stoolmiller, M. and Yoerger, K. (2001). Aggression toward female partners by at-risk young men: The contribution of male adolescent friendships. *Developmental Psychology 37*, 61–73.

Capaldi, D.M., Kim, H.K. and Shortt, J.W. (2004). Women's involvement in aggression in young adult romantic relationships: A developmental systems model. In M. Putallez and K.L. Bierman (Eds.), *Aggression antisocial behavior, and violence among girls: A developmental perspective* (pp. 223–241). New York: Guilford Press.

Capaldi, D.M. and Owen, L.D. (2001). Physical aggression in a community sample of at-risk young couples: Gender comparisons for high frequency, injury, and fear. *Journal of Family Psychology 15*, 425–440.

Caputo, R.K. (1998). Police response to domestic violence. *Social Casework 69*, 81–87.

Carlson, B.E. (1987). Dating violence: a research review and comparison with spouse abuse. *Social Casework 68*, 16–23

Carney, M., Butell, F. and Dutton, D. (2006). Women who perpetrate intimate partner violence: A review of the literature with recommendations for treatment. *Aggression and Violent Behavior* 12, 108–115.

Carr, J.L. (2005, February). American College Health Association campus violence white paper. Baltimore: American College Health Association. Retrieved 28 May 2006 from http://www.acha.org/info_resources/Campus_Violence.pdf.

Carrado, M., George, M., Loxam, F., Jones, L. and Templar, D. (1996). Aggression in British heterosexual relationships: A descriptive analysis. *Aggressive Behavior* 22, 401–415.

Cascardi, M. and Avery-Leaf, S. (2003). Violence against women: Synthesis of research of secondary school officials. U.S. Department of Justice, Washington, DC. Retrieved 27 May 2006 from http://www.ncjrs.gov/pdffiles1/nij/grants/201342.pdf.

Cascardi, M., Avery-Leaf, S., Oleary, K.D. and Slep, A. (1999). Factor structure and convergent validity of the Conflict Tactics Scale in high school students. *Psychological Assessment* 11, no. 4, 546–556.

Cascardi, M., Langhinrichsen, J. and Vivian, D. (1992). Marital aggression: Impact, injury and health correlates for husbands and wives. *Archives of Internal Medicine* 152, 1178–1184.

Cascardi, M. and Vivian, D. (1995). Context for specific episodes of marital violence: Gender and severity of violence differences. *Journal of Family Violence* 10, 265–293.

Catalano, S. (2006). Intimate partner violence in the United States. Bureau of Justice Statistics, Washington, DC Department of Justice. Retrieved 5 February 2007 from http://www.ojp.usdoj.gov/bjs/intimate/ipv.htm.

Cate, R.M., Henton, J.M., Koval, J., Christopher, R.S. and Lloyd, S. (1982). Premarital abuse: A social psychological perspective. *Journal of Family Issues* 3, 79–90.

Caulfield, M.B. and Riggs, D.S. (1992). The assessment of dating aggression: Empirical evaluation of the Conflict Tactics Scale. *Journal of Interpersonal Violence* 4, 549–558.

Cellucci, P. (1997, December 20). Lets all join the war to stop domestic violence. *Boston Globe*, p. A11.

Centers for Disease Control and Prevention (CDC) (n.d.). National Center for Injury Prevention and Control, intimate partner violence: Fact sheet. Retrieved 27 May 2006 from http://www.cdc.gov/ncipc/factsheets/ipvfacts.htm.

Centers for Disease Control and Prevention (CDC) (n.d.). Web-based injury statistics query and reporting system. Retrieved 13 July 2007 from http://www.cdc.gov/ncipc/wisqars/.

Centers for Disease Control and Prevention (CDC) (2006). National Center for Injury Prevention and Control dating abuse fact sheet. Retrieved 30 May 2006 from http://www.cdc.gov/ncipc/dvp/DatingViolence.htm.

Centers for Disease Control and Prevention (CDC) (2005, June 9). Youth risk behavior surveillance—United States, 2005. *Morbidity and Mortality Weekly Report* 55, no. SS–5, 1–112. Retrieved 18 May 2007 from http://www.cdc.gov/mmwr/PDF/SS/SS5505.pdf.

Centers for Disease Control and Prevention (CDC), Office of Statistics and Programming, National Center for Injury Prevention and Control (2001, May 4). Table 2: Estimated number of nonfatal injuries treated in hospital emergency departments, by sex, intent, and mechanism of injury—United States, 2000. *Morbidity and Mortality Weekly Report* 50, 340–346. Retrieved 13 July 2001 from http://www.cdc.gov/mmwr/preview/mmwrhtml/mm5017a4.htm#tab2.

Chaiken, M.R., Boland, B., Maltz, M.D., Martin, S. and Tragonski, J. (2005). Prosecutors' programs ease victims' anxieties. *National Institute of Justice Journal* 252, 30–32. Retrieved 3 June 2007 from http://www.ncjrs.gov/pdffiles1/jr000252.pdf.

Chalk, R. and King, P. A. (Eds.) (1998). Violence in families. Washington, DC: National Academy Press. Retrieved 27 May 2006 from http://fermat.nap.edu/catalog/5285.html.

Chase, K.A., Trebous, D., O'Leary, K.D. and Strassberg, Z. (1998). Specificity of dating aggression and its justification among high-risk adolescents. *Journal of Abnormal Child Psychology* 26, no. 6, 467–473. Retrieved 28 May 2006 from http://www.findarticles.com/p/articles/mi_m0902/is_6_26/ai_53870348.

Chesney-Lind, M. (2002). Perspectives on youth. Retrieved 29 April 2007 from http://perspectivesonyouth.org/Pages-YT-BkReviews/Winter-2003-2.htm.

Choose Respect (2007). Choose respect. Retrieved 29 May 2007 from http://www.chooserespect.org/scripts/.

Clark, M.L., Beckett, J., Wells, M. and Dungee-Anderson, D. (1994). Courtship violence among African-American college students. *Journal of Black Psychology* 20, no. 3, 264–281.

Clear, T.R. and Frost, N.A. (2001). Criminology and public policy: A new journal of the American Society of Criminology. *Criminology and Public Policy* 1, no. 1, 1–3.

Close, S. (2005). Dating violence prevention in middle school and high school youth. *Journal of Child and Adolescent Psychiatric Nursing* 18, no. 1, 2–9.

Cochran, D. (1995, October 12). The tragedies of domestic violence: A qualitative analysis of civil restraining orders in Massachusetts. Boston: Office of the Commissioner of Probation, Massachusetts Trial Court.

Cohall, A. (1999). Strategies for health care providers to address adolescent dating violence. *American Medical Women's Association* 14, 144–145.

Coker, A.L., Davis, K.E., Arias, I., Desai, D., Sanderson, M., Brant, H.M. et al. (2002). Physical and mental health effects of intimate partner violence for men and women. *American Journal of Preventive Medicine* 23, no. 4, 260–268.

Coker, D. (2001). Crime control and feminist law reform in domestic violence law: A critical review. *Buffalo Criminal Law Review* no. 4, 1–860. Retrieved 17 June 2007 fromhttp://wings.buffalo.edu/law/bclc/bclrarticles/4(2)/cokerpdf.pdf.

Cole, D. (1999). *No equal justice: Race and class in the American criminal justice system*. New York: New Press.

Cook, P.W. (1997). *Abused men: The hidden side of domestic violence*. Westport, CT: Praeger/Greenwood.

Cooney, M. (2003, November). The privatization of violence. *Criminology* 41, no. 4. Committee on the Judiciary, United States Senate. Retrieved 27 May 2006 from http://judiciary.senate.gov/hearing.cfm?id=1570.

Commonwealth Fund (2007). 1998 women's and men's health survey. Retrieved 5 April 2007 from http://www.cmwf.org/surveys/surveys_show.htm?doc_id=228069.

Commonwealth v. O'Connor (1990). 407 Mass. 663.

Connors, E., Lundregan, T., Miller, N. and McEwen, T. (1996). Convicted by juries, exonerated by science: Case studies in the use of DNA evidence to establish innocence after trial. Washington, DC: U.S. Department of Justice Research Report. Retrieved August 8, 2007 from http://www.ncjrs.gov/pdffiles/dnaevid.pdf.

Cordova, J., Jacobsen, N., Gottman, J., Rushe, R. and Cox, G. (1993). Negative reciprocity and communication in couples with a violent husband. *Journal of Abnormal Psychology* 102, 559–564.

Craven, D. (1996). Female victims of violent crime. Washington, DC: U.S. Department of Justice, Bureau of Justice Statistics Retrieved 6 March 2007 from http://www.ojp.usdoj.gov/bjs/pub/pdf/fvvc.pdf.

Crowell, N.A. and Burgess, A.W. (Eds.) (1996). Understanding violence against women. Washington, DC: National Academy Press. Retrieved 6 March 2007 from http://www.nap.edu/books/0309054257/html/index.html.

Daly, M. and Wilson, M. (1988). *Homicide*. New York: Aldine De Gruyter.

Darves-Bornoz, J.M., Choquet, M., Ledoux, S., Gasquet, I. and Manfredi, R. (1998). Gender differences in symptoms of adolescents reporting sexual assault. *Social Psychiatry and Psychiatric Epidemiology* 33, no. 3, 111–117.

Davis, R.L. (1995). *Massachusetts General Law 209A: Abuse of another kind.* Cambridge, MA: Harvard University, Grossman Library.

Davis, R.L. (1998). *Domestic violence facts and fallacies.* Westport, CT: Praeger.

Davis, R.L. (2000). Domestic violence. In A.E. Kazdin (Ed.), *Encyclopedia of psychology.* New York: Oxford University Press.

Davis, R.L. (2005). Battering intervention for police families. *Law and Order,* 53(9), 117–122.

Davis, R. C., Smith, B.E. and Davies, H.J. (2001). Effects of no-drop prosecution of domestic violence upon conviction rates. *Justice Research and Policy* 3, no. 2, 1–13. Retrieved 22 May 2007 from http://www.ncjrs.gov/App/Publications/abstract.aspx?ID=193235.

Davis, R.C., Smith, B.E. and Taylor, B. (2003). Increasing the proportion of domestic violence arrests that are prosecuted: A natural experiment in Milwaukee. *Criminology and Public Policy* 2, no. 2, 263–282.

Dawson, J.M. and Langan, P.A. (1998). *Murder in families.* Retrieved 22 January 2007 from http://www.ojp.usdoj.gov/bjs/pub/pdf/mf.pdf.

Deal, J.E. and Wampler, K.S. (1986). Dating violence: The primacy of previous experience. *Journal of Social and Personal Relationships* 3, 457–471.

Dearwater, S.R., Coben, J.H., Campbell, J.C., Nah, G., Glass, N., McLoughlin, E. et al. (1998). Prevalence of intimate partner abuse in women treated at community hospital emergency departments. *Journal of the American Medical Association* 280, no. 5, 433–438.

DeBecker, G. (1997). *The gift of fear.* Boston: Little, Brown.

DeKeseredy, W.S. and Schwartz, M.D. (1998). *Woman abuse on campus: Results from the Canadian national survey.* Thousand Oaks, CA: Sage.

DeMarco, P. (2003, May 23). 2 teachers accused of assaults. *Boston Globe,* p. B2.

DeMaris, A. (1992). Male versus female initiation of aggression: The case of courtship violence. In E.C. Viano (Ed.), *Intimate violence: Interdisciplinary perspectives* (pp. 111–120). Bristol, PA: Taylor and Francis.

DeMaris, A. (1990). The dynamics of generational transfer in courtship violence. A biracial exploration. *Journal of Marriage and Family* 52, no. 1, 219–231.

deWeerth, C. and Kalma, A.P. (1993). Female aggression as a response to sexual jealousy: A sex role reversal? *Aggressive Behavior* 19, 265–279.

Ditson, J. and Shay, S. (1984). Use of home-based microcomputer to analyze community data from reported cases of child abuse and neglect. *Child Abuse and Neglect* 8, no. 4, 503–9.

Dobash, R.E. and Dobash, R.P. (1979). *Violence against wives: A case against the Patriarchy.* New York: Free Press.

Dobash, R.E. and Dobash, R.P. (1992). *Women, violence and social change,* New York: Routledge.

Dobash, R.E. and Dobash, R.P. (1998). Violent men and violent contexts. In R.E. Dobash and R.P. Dobash (Eds.), *Rethinking violence against women* (pp. 141–168). Thousand Oaks, CA: Sage.

Domestic Abuse Helpline for Men and Women (2007). Domestic abuse helpline for men and women. Retrieved 30 May 2007 from http://www.dahmw.org/pub/.

Domestic Violence Arrests: Beyond the Obvious. (2000). A new national training conference. Colorado Springs, CO: U.S. Department of Justice. http://www.transformcommunities.org/tctatsite/tools/dv_arrests_bto.html. Retrieved Nov. 25, 2007.

Domestic Violence Fatality Review Teams (2006). Domestic Violence Fatality Review Team 2006 annual report executive summary. Retrieved 14 July 2007 from http://www.fdle.state.fl.us/CitResCtr/Domestic_Violence/2006_DV_FRT.pdf.

Donziger, S.R. (1996). *The real war on crime: The report of the National Criminal Justice Commission.* New York: Harper Perennial.

Douglas, E.M. and Straus, M.A. (2003). Assault and injury of dating partners by university students in 19 countries and its relation to corporal punishment experienced as a child. *European Journal of Criminology* 3, 293–318. Retrieved 21 June 2007 from http://pubpages.unh.edu/~mas2/CP33y-ID33.pdf.

Dowd, L. (2001). Female perpetrators of partner aggression: Relevant issues and treatment. *Journal of Aggression, Maltreatment, and Trauma* 5, 73–104.

Dugan, L. (2003). Domestic violence legislation: Exploring its impact on the likelihood of domestic violence, police involvement, and arrest. *Criminology and Public Policy* 2, no. 2, 283–212.

Dugan, L., Nagin, N. and Rosenfeld, R. (2001). Exposure reduction or backlash? The effects of domestic resources on intimate partner homicide, final report. Washington, DC: U.S. Department of Justice, National Institute of Justice. Retrieved 10 March 2007 from http://www.ncjrs.gov/pdffiles1/nij/grants/186194.pdf.

Dugan, L., Nagin, D.S. and Rosenfeld, R. (2003, November). Do domestic violence services save lives? *National Institute of Justice Journal* no. 250, 20–25. Washington, DC: Department of Justice, National Institute of Justice. Retrieved 10 March 2007 from http://www.ncjrs.gov/pdffiles1/jr000250f.pdf.

Durose, M.R., Wolf Harlow, C., Langan, P.A., Motivans, M., Rantala, R.R. and Smith, E.L., (2005). Family violence statistics: Including statistics on strangers and acquaintances. Washington, DC: Bureau of Justice Statistics. Retrieved 28 May 2006 from http://www.ojp.usdoj.gov/bjs/pub/pdf/fvs.pdf.

Dutton, D., Kwong, M. and Bartholomew, K. (1999). Gender differences in patterns of relationship violence in Alberta. *Canadian Journal of Behavioural Science* 31, 150–160. Retrieved 4 July 2007 from http://findarticles.com/p/articles/mi_qa3717/is_199907/ai_n8869160.

Dutton, D. and McGregor, B. (1991). The symbiosis or arrest and treatment for wife assault: The case for combined intervention. In M. Stienman (Ed.), *Women battering: Policy responses* (pp. 131–154). Cincinnati: Anderson.

Dutton, D.G. (1988). Profiling of wife assaulters: Preliminary evidence for a trimodal analysis. *Violence and Victims* 3, 5–29.

Dutton, D.G. (1994). Patriarchy and wife assault: The ecological fallacy. *Violence and Victims* 9, no. 2, 167–182. Retrieved 11 April 2007 from http://www.dvmen.org/dv-40.htm.

Dutton, D.G. (1995). *The batterer: A psychological profile*. New York: Basic Books.

Dutton, D.G. (2006). *Rethinking domestic violence*. Vancouver: UBC Press.

Dutton, D.G. and Corvo, K. (2006). Transforming a flawed policy: A call to revive psychology and science in domestic violence research and practice. *Aggression and Violent Behavior* 11, no. 5, 457–483.

Dutton, D.G. and Nicholls, T.L. (2005). The gender paradigm in domestic violence research and theory: Part 1—The conflict of theory and data. *Aggression and Violence Behavior* 10, 680–714.

Dutton-Greene, L.B. and Straus, M.A. (2005, July). The relationship between gender hostility and partner violence and injury. Paper presented at the 9th International Family Violence Research Conference, Portsmouth, NH. Retrieved 10 March 2007 from http://pubpages.unh.edu/~mas2/PR5.pdf.

Ebbert, S. (1998, October 23). Domestic violence reports on rise more awareness linked to increase. *Boston Globe*, p. B1.

Edleson, J.L. (1995). Do batterers' programs work? Minnesota Center Against Violence and Abuse. Retrieved 22 January 2007 from http://www.mincava.umn.edu/papers/battrx.htm.

Edleson, J.L. (1998). Fact and fantasy: Violent women. Minnesota Center Against Violence and Abuse. Retrieved 13 March 2007 fromhttp://www.mincava.umn.edu/documents/factfantasy/factfantasy.html.

Egan, N. (n.d.). The police response to spouse abuse: An annotated bibliography. New York: John Jay College of Criminal Justice. Retrieved 23 October 2007 from http://www.lib.jjay.cuny.edu/research/spouse.html.

Ehrensaft, M.K., Cohen, P., Brown, J., Smailes, E., Chen, H. and Johnson, J.G. (2003). Intergenerational transmission of partner violence: A 20-year prospective study. *Journal of Consulting and Clinical Psychology* 71, 741–753.

Ehrensaft, M.K., Moffitt, T.E. and Caspi, A. (2004). Clinically abusive relationships in an unselected birth cohort: Men's and women's participation and developmental antecedents. *Journal of Abnormal Psychology* 113, 258–270.

Eilperin, J. (2007, March 28). New drive afoot to pass equal rights amendment. *Washington Post*, p. A1.

Eitzen, D.S. and Zinn, M.B. (2006). *Social problem,* 10th ed. Boston: Pearson.

Elikann, P.T. (1996). *The tough-on-crime myth*. New York: Insight Books.

Ellement, J. (1999, Apr. 5). Is spanking abuse? SJC to take up case. *Boston Globe*, B6.

Elliot, P. (Ed.) (1990). *Confronting lesbian battering: A manual for the battered women's movement*. St. Paul: Minnesota Coalition for Battered Women.

Elliot, D.S., Huizinga, D. and Morse, B.J. (1986). Self-reported violent offending: A descriptive analysis of juvenile violent offenders and their offending careers. *Journal of Interpersonal Violence* 1, no. 4, 472–514.

Elsea, W.R., Napper, G. and Sikes, R.K. (1990, August 10). Current trends and other intimate assaults—Atlanta, 1984. Centers for Disease Control and Prevention, *Morbidity and Mortality Weekly Report* 39, no. 31, 525–529. Retrieved 11 July 2007 from http://www.cdc.gov/mmwr/preview/mmwrhtml/00001707.htm.

Ely, G. (2004). Dating violence. In L. Rapp-Paglicci, C. Dulmus and J. Wordarski (Eds.), *Handbook of preventive interventions for children and adolescents* (chapter 19). Hoboken, NJ: John Wiley and Sons.

Elze, D.E. (2002). Against all odds: The dating experiences of adolescent lesbian and bisexual women. *Journal of Lesbian Studies* 6, no. 1, 17–29.

Eng, P. (2003). Safety and justice for all: Examining the relationship between the women's anti-violence movement and the criminal legal system. *Ms. Foundation for Women*. http://www.ms.foundation.org/user-assets/pdf/program/safety_justice.pdf. Retrieved July 30, 2006.

Estrich, S. (2000). *Sex and power*. New York: Riverhead Books.

Evans, P.E. (1996). *The verbally abusive relationship*. Holbrook, MA: Adams Media.

Fagan, J. (1996). The criminalization of domestic violence: promises and limits. Washington, DC: U.S. Department of Justice, National Institute of Justice. Retrieved 3 June 2006 from http://www.ojp.usdoj.gov/nij/pubs-sum/157641.htm.

Fagan, J. and Browne, A. (1994). Violence between spouses and intimates: Physical aggression between women and men in intimate relationships. In A.J. Reiss and J.A. Roth (Eds.), *Understanding and preventing violence: Volume 3: Social influences*. Washington, DC: National Academy Press (pp. 115–292). Retrieved 23 October 2007 from http://books.nap.edu/openbook.php?record_id=4421&page=115.

Faludi, S. (1999). *Stiffed*. New York: William Morrow and Company.

Farrell, W. (1988). *Why men are the way they are*. New York: Berkley Books.

Farrell, W. (1999). *Women can't hear what men don't say*. New York: Putnam.

Fedders, B. (1997a). Lobbying for mandatory-arrest polices; Race, class and the politics of the battered women's movement. *New York University Review of Law and Social Change*. 23, 291–296.

Fedders, B. (1997b). Mandatory arrest for domestic violence: A universal solution? Retrieved 25 July 2007 from http://academic.udayton.edu/health/01status/violence02.htm.

Feder, L. and Forde, D.R. (2000). Test of the efficacy of court-mandated counseling for domestic violence offenders: The Broward Experiment, executive summary. Washington, DC: U.S. Department of Justice. Retrieved 20 June from http://www.ncjrs.gov/pdffiles1/nij/grants/184631.pdf.

Feder, L. and Henning, K. (2005). A comparison of male and female dually arrested domestic violence offenders. *Violence and Victims* 20, no. 2, 153–171.

Federal Bureau of Investigation (FBI) (n.d.). Uniform crime reports. Retrieved 4 August 2007 from http://www.fbi.gov/ucr/ucr.htm.

Feingold, R. (2005). Statement of U.S. Senator Russ Feingold at the senate judiciary committee hearing for the reauthorization of the violence against women act. Retrieved 9 August 2007 from http://judiciary.senate.gov/hearing.cfm?id=1570.

Feiring, C., Deblinger, E., Hoch-Espada, A. and Haworth, T. (2002). Romantic relationship aggression and attitudes in high school students: The role of gender, grade, and attachment and emotional styles. Journal of Youth and Adolescence 31, no. 5, 373–385.

Felson, R.B. (2002). *Violence and gender reexamined.* Washington, DC: American Psychological Association.

Felson, R.B., Ackerman, J.M. and Gallagher, C. (2005). Police intervention and the repeat of domestic assault. Washington, DC: Department of Justice. Retrieved 27 June 2007 fromhttp://www.ncjrs.gov/pdffiles1/nij/grants/210301.pdf.

Felson, R.B. and Cares, A.C. (2005). Gender and the seriousness of assaults on intimate partners and other victims. *Journal of Marriage and Family* 67, 182–195.

Felson, R.B. and Messner, S. (1998). Disentangling the effects of gender and intimacy on victim precipitation in homicide. *Criminology* 36, no. 2, 405–424.

Felson, R.B. and Messner, S.F. (2000). The control motive in intimate partner violence. *Social Psychology Quarterly* 63, no. 1, 86–94.

Feltey, K.M., Ainslie, J.J. and Geib, A. (1991). Sexual coercion attitudes among high school students: The influence of gender and rape education. *Youth and Society* 23, no. 2, 229–250.

Ferguson, H., Hearn, J., Holter, O.G., Jalmert, L., Kimmel, M., Lang, J. et al. (2004). *Ending gender-based violence: A call for global action to involve men.* Sida. Retrieved 5 August 2007 from http://www.sida.se/sida/jsp/sida. jsp?d=118anda=3108andlanguage=en_US.

Fering, C. and Furman, W.C. (2000). When love is just a four letter word: Victimization and romantic relationships in adolescence. *Child Maltreatment* 5, no. 4, 293–298.

Ferraro, K.J. and Pope, L. (1993). Irreconcilable differences: Battered women, police, and the law. In N.Z. Hilton (Ed.), *Legal responses to wife assault* (pp. 96–121). Newbury Park, CA: Sage Publications.

Fiebert, M.S. (1996). College students' perception of men as victims of women's assaultive behavior. *Perceptual and Motor Skills* 82, 49–50.

Fiebert, M.S. (2005). References examining assaults by women on their spouses or male partners: An annotated bibliography. Retrieved 17 June 2005 from http:// www.csulb.edu/~mfiebert/assault.htm.

Fiebert, M.S. and Gonzales, D.M. (1997). College women who initiate assaults on their male partners and the reasons offered for such behavior. *Psychological Reports* 80, 539–579.

Finkelhor, D. and Straus, M. (2006). Bibliography of the family research laboratory. Retrieved 22 January 2007 from http://pubpages.unh.edu/~mas2/vp-bib.htm.

Finn, M.A. (2004). Effects of victims' experiences with prosecutors on victim empowerment and re-occurrence of intimate partner violence, final report. Washington, DC: Department of Justice. Retrieved 22 May 2007 from http://www.ncjrs.gov/pdffiles1/nij/grants/202983.pdf.

Finn, M.A. and Bettis, P. (2006). Punitive actions or gentle persuasion. *Violence against Women* 12, no. 3, 268–287.

Finn, M.A., Blackwell, B.S., Stalans, L.J., Studdard, S. and Dugan, L. (2004). Dual arrest decisions in domestic violence cases: The influence of departmental policies. *Crime and Delinquency* 50, 565–589.

Fisher, B.S., Cullen, F.T. and Turner, M.G. (2000). The sexual victimization of college women. Washington, DC: Department of Justice. Retrieved 1 July 2007 from http://www.ncjrs.gov/pdffiles1/nij/182369.pdf.

Fisher, M., Florsheim, P. and Sheetz, J. (2005). That's not my problem: Convergence and divergence between self- and other-identified problems among homeless adolescents. *Child and Youth Care Forum* 34, 393–403.

Fletcher, A. (1995). *Gender, sex and subordination in England, 1500–1800.* New Haven, CT: Yale University Press.

Fletcher, C. (1996, Summer). What cops know. *On Patrol,* pp. 44–50.

Fletcher, G. (2002). *The new science of intimate relationships.* Malden, MA: Blackwell Publishing.

Flowers, R.B. (1999). *Drugs, alcohol and criminality in American society.* Jefferson, NC: McFarland and Company, Inc.

Flowers, R.B. (2000). *Domestic crimes, family violence and child abuse.* Jefferson, NC: McFarland and Company, Inc.

Follingstad, D.R. (2007). Rethinking current approaches to psychological abuse: Conceptual and methodological issues. *Aggression and Violent Behavior* 12, 439–458.

Follingstad, D., Bradley, R., Helff, C. and Laughlin, J. (2002). A model for predicting dating violence: Anxious attachment, angry temperament and a need for relationship control. *Violence and Victims* 17, no. 1, 35–47.

Follingstad, D.R., Rutledge, L.L., Berg, B.J., Hause, E.S. and Polek, D.S. (1990). The role of emotional abuse in physically abusive relationships. *Journal of Family Violence* 5, 107–120.

Follingstad, D.R., Wright, S. and Sebastian, J.A. (1991). Sex differences in motivations and effects in dating violence. *Family Relations* 40, 51–57.

Foo, L. and Margolin, G. (1995). A multivariate investigation of dating aggression. *Journal of Family Violence* 10, 351–377.

Ford, D.A. (2003). Coercing victim participation in domestic violence prosecutions. *Journal of Interpersonal Violence* 18, 669–684.

Ford, D.A., Bachman, R., Friend, M. and Meloy, M. (2002). Controlling violence against women: A research perspective on the 1994 VAWA's criminal justice impacts. Retrieved 23 January 2007 from http://www.ncjrs.gov/pdffiles1/nij/grants/197137.pdf.

Foshee, V.A. (1996). Gender differences in adolescent dating abuse prevalence, types and injuries. *Health Education Research* 11, no. 3, 275–286. Retrieved 27 May 2006 from http://her.oxfordjournals.org/cgi/content/abstract/11/3/275-a.

Foshee, V.A., Bauman, K.E., Arriaga, X.B., Helms, R.W., Koch, G.G. and Linder, G.F. (2000). The safe dates project. *Prevention Researcher* 7, no. 1, 5–7.

Foshee, V.A., Bauman, K.E., Ennett, S.T., Linder, G.F., Benefield, T. and Suchindran, C. (2004). Assessing the long term effects of the safe dates program and a booster in preventing and reducing adolescent dating violence victimization and perpetration. *American Journal of Public Health* 94, no. 4, 619–625.

Foshee V.A., Bauman, K.E., Ennett, S.T., Suchindran, C., Benefield, T. and Linder. F.G. (2005). Assessing the effects of the dating violence prevention program "Safe dates" using random coefficient regression modeling. *Prevention Science* 6, no. 3, 245–258.

Foshee, V.A., Bauman, K.E., Greene, W.F., Koch, G.G., Linder, G.F. and MacDougall, J.E. (2000). The safe dates program: 1-year follow-up results. *American Journal of Public Health* 90, no. 10, 1619–1622.

Foshee, V.A., Bauman, K.E. and Linder, G.F. (1999). Family violence and the preparation of adolescent dating violence: Examining social learning and social control processes. *Journal of Marriage and Family* 61, no. 2, 331–342.

Foshee, V.A., Linder, G.F., Bauman, K.E. and Langwick, S.A. (1996). The safe dates project: Theoretical basis, evaluation design, and selected baseline findings. *American Journal of Preventive Medicine* 12, 39–46.

Fox, J.A. and Zawitz, M.W. (2006). Homicide trends in the United States: 1996–2004. Washington, DC: Department of Justice, Bureau of Justice Statistics. Retrieved 23 January 2007 from http://www.ojp.usdoj.gov/bjs/homicide/homtrnd.htm.

Fredrick, A. (2001, October). Adolescent dating violence. *Nursing Spectrum* 20, 12–15.

Freedner, N., Freed, L.H., Yang, Y.W. and Austin, S.B. (2002). Dating violence among gay, lesbian, and bisexual adolescents: Results from a community survey. *Journal of Adolescent Health* 21, 469–474.

Friedan, B. (1963). *The Feminine Mystique.* New York: Dell.

Friedman, L.M. (1993). *Crime and punishment in American history.* New York: Basic Books.

Frieze, I.H. (2005). *Hurting the one you love.* Belmont, CA: Thompson/Wardsworth.

Gage, M.J. (1980). *Women, church, and state.* Watertown, MA: Persephone Press.

Ganley, A.L. (1998). Improving the health care response to domestic violence: A trainer's manual for health care providers. Family Violence Prevention Fund. Http://www. endabuse.org/programs/healthcare/files/healthtrainer.pdf.

Garbarino, J. (1999). *Lost boys.* New York: Free Press.

Gelles, R.J. (1980). Violence in the family: A review of research in the seventies. *Journal of Marriage and the Family* 42, 873–885.

Gelles, R.J. (1995). Domestic violence factoids. Minnesota Center against Violence and Abuse. Retrieved 23 January 2007 from http://www.mincava.umn.edu/papers/factoid.htm.

Gelles, R.J. (2001). The missing persons of domestic violence: Male victims. Retrieved 23 January 2007 from http://www.breakingthescience.org/RichardGelles_MissingPersonsOfDV.php.

Gelles, R.J. (2007). The politics of research: The use, abuse, and misuse of social science data—The case of intimate partner violence. *Family Court Review* 45, no. 1, 42–51.

Gelles, R.J. and Loseke, D.R. (1993). *Current controversies on family violence.* Newbury Park, CA: Sage Publications.

Gelles, R.J. and Straus, M.A. (1988). *Intimate violence.* New York: Simon and Schuster.

Ghiglieri, M.P. (1999). *The dark side of man.* Reading, MA. Perseus.

Gladwell, M. (2005). *Blink.* New York: Little, Brown and Company.

Glasser, W. (1984). *Control theory.* New York. Harper and Row.

Globe Staff (2000, April 13). Brave talk on rape. *Boston Globe,* p. A26.

Goldberg, C. (1999, November 22). Spouse abuse crackdown, surprisingly, nets many women. *New York Times,* p. A16.

Goldsmith, S. (Ed.) (1993, Winter). Prosecutors perspective. National District Attorneys Association.

Gondolf, E. (1996). Characteristics of batterers in a multi-site evaluation of batterer intervention systems. Retrieved 4 July 2007 fromwww.mincava.umn.edu/documents/gondolf/batchar.html.

Gondolf, E.W. (1990). Who are those guys? Toward a behavioral typology of batterers. *Violence and Victims* 3, 187–293.

Gondolf, E.W. (1997). Batterer programs; What we know and need to know. *Journal of Interpersonal Violence* 12, no. 1, 83–98.

Goodenow, C.S. (personal communication, 4 January 2002) in reference to *The 1999 Massachusetts Youth Risk Behavior Survey.*

Goodman, E. (2004, September 23). Tender terrorists? *Boston Globe*, OpEd page.

Gordis, E. (2001). Alcohol and violence. *National Institute on Alcohol Abuse and Alcoholism* 25, no. 1. Retrieved 9 August 2007 from http://pubs.niaaa.nih.gov/publications/arh25-1/3-4.htm.

Gosselin, D.K. (2000). *Heavy hands: An introduction to the crimes of domestic violence.* Upper Saddle River, NJ: Prentice Hall.

Graham-Bermann, S. and Edleson, J. (2001). *Domestic violence in the lives of children.* Washington, DC: American Psychological Association.

Graham-Kevan, N. and Archer, J. (2003). Intimate terrorism and common couple violence: A test of Johnson's predictions in four British samples. *Journal of Interpersonal Violence* 18, 1247–1270.

Graham-Kevan, N. and Archer, J. (2005). Investigation three explanations of women's relationship aggression. *Psychology of Women Quarterly* 29, 270–277.

Grana, S.J. (2002) *Women and (in) justice.* Boston: Allyn and Bacon.

Grandin, E. and Lupri, E. (1997). Intimate violence in Canada and the United States: A cross-national comparison. *Journal of Domestic Violence* 12, 417–443. Retrieved 27 June 2007 from http://www.fact.on.ca/Info/dom/grandi97.htm.

Grandin, E., Lupri, E. and Brinkerhoff, M.B. (1998). Couple violence and psychological distress. *Canadian Journal of Public Health* 89, 43–47.

Grauwiler, P. and Mills, (2004, March). *Moving beyond the criminal justice paradigm: A radical restorative justice approach to intimate abuse. Journal of Sociology and Social Welfare.* Retrieved 15 July 2006 from http://www.findarticles.com/p/articles/mi_m0CYZ/is_1_31/ai_n6065939/print.

Gray, H.M. and Foshee, V.A. (1997). Adolescent dating violence: Differences between one-sided and mutually violent profiles. *Journal of Interpersonal Violence* 12, 126–141.

Greenfeld, L.A., Rand, M.R., Craven, D., Klaus, P.A., Perkins, C.A., Ringel, C. et al. (1998). Violence by intimates: Analysis of data on crimes by current or former spouses, boyfriends, and girlfriends. Washington, DC: Department of Justice, Bureau of Justice Statistics. Retrieved 23 January 2007 from http://www.ojp.usdoj.gov/bjs/pub/pdf/vi.pdf.

Greenfeld, L.A. and Snell, T.L. (1999). Women offenders. Washington DC: Bureau of Justice Statistics. Retrieved 3 January 2007 from http://www.ojp.gov/bjs/pub/pdf/wo.pdf.

Grisso, J.A., Wishner, A.R., Schawarz, D.F., Weene, B.A., Holmes, J.H. and Sutton, R.L. (1991). A population-based study of injuries in inner-city women. *American Journal of Epidemiology* 134, no. 1, 59–68.

Groopman, J. (2007). *How doctors think.* Boston: Houghton-Mifflin.

Grunbaum, J.A., Kann, L., Kinchen, S., Ross, J., Hawkins, J., Lowry, R., et al. (2004, May 21). Youth Risk Behavior Surveillance—United States, 2003. *Morbidity and Morality Weekly Report* 53 no. SS-2. Retrieved 13 March 2007 from http://www.cdc.gov/mmwr/PDF/SS/SS5302.pdf.

Gryl, F.E., Stith, S.M. and Bird, G.W. (1991). Close dating relationships among college students: Differences by use of violence and by gender. *Journal of Social and Personal Relationships* 8, 243–264.

Gwinn, C., Bell, E., Berger, L., Cervantes, A., Edwards, L., Gomez, J. et al. (2005). Keeping the promise: Victim safety and batterer accountability. Retrieved 18 May 2007 from http://www.safestate.org/documents/DV_Report_AG.pdf.

Haber, J., Leach, A.M., Schudy, S.M. and Sideleau, B.F. (1978). *Comprehensive psychiatric nursing.* New York: McGraw-Hill.

Halpern, C.T., Oslak, S.G., Young, M.L., Martin, S.L. and Kupper, L.L. (2001). Partner violence among adolescents in opposite-sex romantic relationships: Findings from the National Longitudinal Study of Adolescent Health. *American Journal of Public Health* 4, no. 3, 467–482.

Hamberger, L.K. (1997). Female offenders in domestic violence. A look at actions in their context. *Journal of Aggression, Maltreatment and Trauma* 1, no. 1, 117–129.

Hamberger, L.K., Lohr, J. and Bonge, D. (1994). Intended function of domestic violence is different for arrested male and female perpetrators. *Family Violence and Sexual Assault Bulletin* 10, 40–44.

Hamberger, L.K., Lohr, J., Bonge, D. and Tolin, D. (1997). An empirical classification of motivations for domestic violence. *Violence against Women* 3, 401–423.

Hamberger, L.K. and Guse, C.Ec (2002). Men's and women's use of intimate partner violence in clinical samples. *Violence Against Women,* 8 (11), 1301–1331.

Hamel, J. Intimate partner violence research and theory: Toward a gender-inclusive conception. *International Journal of Men's Health.* (in press).

Hamel, J. and Nicholls, T.L. (Eds.) (2007). *Family interventions in domestic violence.* New York: Springer.

Hammock, G.S. and Richardson, D.R. (1992). Predictors of aggressive behavior. *Aggressive Behavior* 18, 219–229.

Hankin, B.L., Abramson, L.Y., Moffit, T.E., Silva, P.A., McGee, R. and Angell, K.E. (1998). Development of depression from preadolescence to young adulthood: Emerging gender differences in a 10-year longitudinal study. *Journal of Abnormal Psychology* 107, 128–140.

Hanson, R.F., Kievit, L.W., Saunders, B.E., Smith, D.W., Kilpatrick, D.G., Resnick, H.S. et al. (2003). Correlates of adolescent reports of sexual assault: Findings from the National Survey of Adolescents. *Child Maltreatment* 8, no. 4, 261–272.

Harbert, R. (2006, February 15). Stopping the violence. *Old Colony Memorial* p. A1.

Harders, R.J., Struckman-Johnson, C., Struckman-Johnson, D. and Caraway, S.J. (1998). Verbal and physical abuse in dating relationships. Paper presented at the meeting of American Psychological Association, San Francisco.

Harned, M.S. (2002). A multivariate analysis of risk markers for dating violence victimization. *Journal of Interpersonal Violence* 17, 1179–1197.

Harris, M.B. and Knight-Bohnhoff, K. (1996). Gender and aggression: Perceptions of aggression. *Sex Roles* 112, 1–25.

Hart, J. (2000, May 30). Statistics say abuse hits close to home. *Boston Globe,* p. B1.

Haws, D. (1997). The elusive numbers on false rapes. *Columbia Journalism Review.* Retrieved 8 August 2007 from http://backissues.cjrarchives.org/year/97/6/rape.asp.

Health, Inc. (2006). Dating violence: Why does it occur and how does it fit in the cycle of violence? http://www.Athealth.com/consumer/disorders/datingviolence.html. Retrieved May 16, 2006.

Healy, K.M. and Smith, C. (1998). Batterer programs: What criminal justice agencies need to know. Washington DC: U.S. Department of Justice. Retrieved 24 January 2007 fromhttp://www.ncjrs.gov/pdffiles/171683.pdf.

Heise, L., Ellsbert, M. and Gottemoeller, M. (1999). Ending violence against women. *Population Reports* 20, no. 11. Baltimore: John Hopkins University School of Public Health, Population Information Program. Retrieved 13 July 2007 from http://www.infoforhealth.org/pr/l11/violence.pdf.

Hemenway, D., Prothrow-Stith, D. and Browne, A. (2005). Report of the 2004 Boston youth survey. Harvard School of Public Health, Harvard Youth Violence Prevention Center, Boston. Retrieved 10 March 2007 from http://www.cityof-boston.gov/humanservices/pdfs/youthsurvey2004.pdf.

Hendricks, J.E., McKean, J. and Hendricks, C.G. (2003). *Crisis intervention*. Springfield, IL: Thomas Publishers, Ltd.

Hendy, H.M., Weiner, K., Bakerofskie, J., Eggen, D., Gustitus, C. and McLeod, K. C. (2003). Comparison of six models for violent romantic relationships in college men and women. *Journal of Interpersonal Violence* 18, 645–665.

Henning, K. and Renauer, B., (2005). Prosecution of women arrested for intimate partner abuse. *Violence and Victims* 20, no. 3, 171–189.

Henning, K., Renauer, B. and Holdford, R. (2006). Victim or offender? Heterogeneity among women arrested for intimate partner violence. *Journal of Family Violence* 26, 351–368.

Henry, B., Caspi, A., Moffitt, T.E. and Silva, P.A. (1996). Temperamental and familial predictors of violent and non-violent criminal convictions: From age 3 to age 18. *Developmental Psychology* 32, 614–623.

Henton, J., Cate, R., Koval, J., Lloyd, S. and Christopher, S. (1983). Romance and violence in dating relationships. *Journal of Family Issues* 4, 467–482.

Herrera, V.M. and McCloskey, L.A. (2003). Sexual abuse, family violence, and female delinquency: Findings from a longitudinal study. Violence and Victims 18, no. 3, 319–335.

Hewitt, J.P. (1999, April 29). Trying to make sense of the senseless. *Boston Globe*, p. A25.

Heyman, R.E. and Schlee, K.A. (1997). Toward a better estimate of the prevalence of partner abuse: Adjusting rates based on the sensitivity of the Conflict Tactics Scale. *Journal of Family Psychology* 11, 331–338.

Heyman, R.E. and Slep, A.M.S. (2002). Do child abuse and interparental violence lead to adulthood family violence? *Journal of Marriage and Family* 64, no. 4, 864–870.

Hilton, N.Z., Harris, G.T. and Rice, M.E. (1998). On the validity of self-reported rates of interpersonal violence. *Journal of Interpersonal Violence* 13, no. 1, 58–72.

Hilton, N.Z., Harris, G.T., Rice, M.E., Krans, T.S. and Lavigne, S.E. (1998). Antiviolence education in high schools: Implementation and evaluation. *Journal of Interpersonal Violence* 13, no. 6, 726–742.

Himelein, M.J., Vogel, R.E. and Wachowiak, D.G. (1994). Nonconsensual sexual experiences in pre-college women: Prevalence and risk factors. *Journal of Counseling and Development* 72, 411–415.

Hines, D.A. and Saudino, K.J. (2003). Gender differences in psychological, physical, and sexual aggression among college students using the revised Conflict Tactics Scales. *Violence and Victims* 18, no. 2, 197–217.

Hirschel, D., Buzawa, E., Pattavina, A., Faggiani, D. and Reuland, M. (2007). Explaining the prevalence, context, and consequences of dual arrest in intimate partner cases. Washington, DC: U.S. Department of Justice. Retrieved 19 May 2007 from http://www.ncjrs.gov/pdffiles1/nij/grants/218355.pdf.

Hirschel, J.D. and Dawson, D.J. (2003). Violence against women: Synthesis of research for law enforcement officials. Washington, DC: U.S. Department of Justice. Retrieved 31 May 2007 from http://www.ncjrs.gov/pdffiles1/nij/grants/198372.pdf.

Hogben, M., Byrne, D. and Hamburger, M.E. (1996). Coercive heterosexual sexuality in dating relationships of college students: Implications of differential male–female experiences. In E.S. Byers and L.F. O'Sullivan (Eds.), *Sexual coercion* (pp. 69–78). New York: Haworth.

Holder, R. (2001). Domestic and family violence: Criminal justice intervention. University of New South Wales Sydney: Australian Domestic and Family Violence Clearinghouse. Retrieved 27 June 2007 from http://www.austdvclearinghouse.unsw.edu.au/PDF%20files/issuespaper3.pdf.

Holmes, W.C. and Sammel, M.D. (2005). Brief communication: physical abuse of boys and possible associations with poor adult outcomes. *Annals of Internal Medicine* 143, no. 8, 581–589. Retrieved 7 February 2007 from http://www.annals.org/cgi/reprint/143/8/581.pdf.

Holt, V.L., Kernic, M.A., Lumley, T., Wolf, M.E. and Rivara, F.P. (2002). Civil protection orders and risk of subsequent police-reported violence. *Journal of the America Medical Association* 288, 589–594.

Holtzworth-Munroe, A. (2005). Male versus female intimate partner violence: Putting controversial findings into context. *Journal of Marriage and Family* 67, 1120–1125. Retrieved 23 June 2007 from http://www.personal.psu.edu/mpj/2005%20JMF%20Holtzworth-Munroe.pdf.

Holtzworth-Munroe, A., Meehan, J.C., Herron, K. Rehman, U. and Stuart, G.L. (2000a). Do subtypes of martially violent men continue to differ over time? *Journal of Consulting and Clinical Psychology* 71, 728–740.

Holtzworth-Munroe, A., Meehan, J.C., Herron, K. Rehman, U. and Stuart, G.L. (2000b). Testing the Holtzworth-Munroe and Stuart (1994) batterer typology. *Journal of Consulting and Clinical Psychology* 68, 1000–1019.

Hotaling, G.T. and Buzawa, E.S. (2003). Forgoing criminal justice assistance: The non-reporting of new incidents of abuse in a court sample of domestic violence victims. Washington DC: U.S. Department of Justice. Retrieved 25 January 2007 fromwww.ncjrs.org/pdffiles1/nij/grants/195667.pdf.

Houts, L.A. (2005). But was it wanted? Young women's first voluntary sexual intercourse. *Journal of Family Issues* 26, 1082–1102.

Howard, D.E. and Wang, M.Q. (2003a). Psychosocial factors associated with adolescent boys' reports of dating violence. *Adolescence* 38, no. 151, 519–533. Retrieved 16 May 2006 from http://www.findarticles.com/p/articles/mi_m2248/is_151_38/ai_113304957.

Howard, D.E. and Wang, M.Q. (2003b). Risk profiles of adolescent girls who were victims of dating violence. *Adolescence* 38, no. 149, 1–14. Retrieved 16 May 2006 from http://www.findarticles.com/p/articles/mi_m2248/is_149_38/ai_103381757.

Howard, D.E. and Wang, M.Q. (2005). Psychosocial correlates of U.S. adolescents who report a history of forced sexual intercourse. *Journal of Adolescent Health* 36, 372–379.

Hoyle, C. (1998). *Negotiating domestic violence.* Oxford: Clarendon Press.

Huntley, S. and Kilzer, L. (2005, February 5). First in a series: Battered justice. Rocky Mountain Times. Retrieved 22 May 2007 from http://www.rockymountainnews.com/drmn/news/article/0,1299,DRMN_3_3523667,00.html.

Hyde, J.S. (1984). How large are gender differences in aggression? A developmental meta-analysis. *Developmental Psychology* 20, 722–736.

Hyman, A. (preparer) (n.d.). California's Domestic Violence & Mandatory Reporting Law: Requirements for health care practitioners. Bay Area Legal Aid for the Family Violence Prevention Fund. Retrieved from http://endabuse.org/health/mandatoryreporting/california.pdf.

Institute for Law and Justice National Center for Victims of Crime (2005). National evaluation of the legal assistance for victims program Retrieved 25 January 2007 from http://www.ilj.org/publications/LAV_FINAL_FINAL_RPT.pdf.

Irwin, C.E. and Rickert, V.I. (2005). Coercive sexual experiences during adolescence and young adulthood: A public health problem. *Journal of Adolescent Health* 36, 359–361.

Isely, P.J., Busse, W. and Isely, P. (1998). Sexual assault of males in late adolescence: A hidden phenomenon. *Professional School Counseling* 2, no. 2, 153–160.

Iyengar, R. (2007, August 7). The protection battered spouses don't need. *New York Times,* OpEd page.

Jackson, N.A. (2007). *Encyclopedia of domestic violence.* New York: Routledge.

Jackson, S., Feder, L., Forde, D.R., Davis, R.C., Maxwell, C.D. and Taylor, B.G. (2003). Batter intervention programs: Where do we go from here? Washington, DC: National Institute of Justice. Retrieved 25 January 2007 from http://www.ncjrs.gov/pdffiles1/nij/195079.pdf.

Jackson, S.M. (1999). Issues in the dating violence research: A review of the literature. *Aggression and Violent Behavior* 4, no. 2, 233–247.

Jackson, S.M., Cram, F. and Seymour, F.W. (2000). Violence and sexual coercion in high school students' dating relationships. *Journal of Family Violence* 15, 23–36.

Jacobson, N. and Gottman, J. (1998). *When men batter women.* New York: Simon and Schuster.

Jacobson, N., Gottman, J., Waltz, J., Rushe, R., Babcock, J. and Holtzworth-Munroe, A. (1994). Affect, verbal content, and psychophysiology in the arguments of couples with a violent husband. *Journal of Consulting and Clinical Psychology* 62, no. 5, 982–988.

Jaffee, S.R., Caspi, A., Moffitt, T.E. and Taylor, A. (2004). Physical maltreatment victim to antisocial child: Evidence of an environmentally-mediated process. *Journal of Abnormal Psychology* 113, 44–55. Retrieved 15 July 2006 from http://opr.princeton.edu/seminars/jaffeeS05.pdf.

Jaffe, P.G., Sudermann, M., Reitze, D. and Killip, S.M. (1992). An evaluation of a secondary school primary prevention program on violence in intimate relationships. *Violence and Victims* 7, 129–146.

James, W.H., West, C., Deters, K.E. and Armijo, E. (2000). Youth and dating violence. *Adolescence* 35, no. 139, 455–465. Retrieved 10 March 2007 from http://www.findarticles.com/p/articles/mi_m2248/is_139_35/ai_68535843.

Jan, T. (2006, April 16). 2 injured in hub in separate stabbings by girls. *Boston Globe*, p. B3.

Jane Doe Inc. Retrieved 28 May 2006 from http://www.janedoe.org/.

Janelle, C. (2006). Domestic violence starting in teenage years. WorldNow. Retrieved 26 April 2006 from http://www.wistv.com/Global/story.asp?S=4816793.

Johnson, H. and Bunge, V. (2001). Prevalence and consequences of spousal assault in Canada. *Canadian Journal of Criminology*, 43 (1), 27–45.

Johnson, K.C. (2006). Press in action. Durham-in-Wonderland. Retrieved 9 July 2007 from http://durhamwonderland.blogspot.com/2006/09/press-inaction.html.

Johnson, M.P. (1995). Patriarchal terrorism and common couple violence: Two forms of violence against women. *Journal of Marriage and the Family*, 57 (2), 283–294.

Johnson, M.P. (2000). Conflict and control: Images of symmetry and asymmetry in domestic violence: In A. Booth, A. Crouter, and M. Clements (Eds.), *Couples in conflict*. Hillsdale, NJ: Lawrence Erlbaum. Retrieved 25 January 2007 from http://www.personal.psu.edu/faculty/m/p/mpj/boothfinal2.htm.

Johnson, M.P. (2005). Domestic violence: It's not about gender—Or is it? *Journal of Marriage and Family* 67, 1126–1130. Retrieved 31 March 2007 from http://www.personal.psu.edu/mpj/2005%20JMF%20Johnson.pdf.

Johnson, M.P. (2006a). A "general" theory of intimate partner violence: A working paper. Sociology and Women's Studies, Penn State. Retrieved 23 June 2007 from http://www.personal.psu.edu/mpj/2006%20TCRM.doc.

Johnson, M.P. (2006b). Conflict and control. Gender symmetry and asymmetry in domestic violence. *Violence against Women* 12, 1003–1018. Retrieved 23 June 2007 from http://www.personal.psu.edu/mpj/2006%20VAW.pdf.

Johnson, M.P. (2006c). Gendered communication and intimate partner violence. In B.J. Dow and J.T. Wood (Eds.), *The sage handbook of gender and communication* (pp.71–87). Thousand Oaks, CA: Sage. Retrieved 23 June 2007 fromhttp://www.personal.psu.edu/mpj/in%20press%20Dow%20and%20Wood.doc.

Johnson, M.P. and Ferraro, K.J. (2000). Research on domestic violence in the 1990's: Making distinctions. *Journal of Marriage and the Family* 62, 948–963. Retrieved 21 June 2007 from http://www.personal.psu.edu/mpj/2000%20JMF%20Johnson%20and%20Ferraro.pdf.

Jones, L.E. (1987). School curriculum project evaluation report. St. Paul: Minnesota Coalition for Battered Women.

Judicial Council of California (2007). California courts self-help center. Retrieved 22 October 2007 from http://www.courtinfo.ca.gov/selfhelp/.

Jurkowitz, M. (2002, November 21). TV, radio and online. *Boston Globe*, p. D12.

Kaczor, B. (2002, September 7). Sons convicted of murdering father. *Boston Globe*, p. A2.

Kaczor, B. (2002, September 9). Verdict on Florida teens debated. *Boston Globe*, p. A12.

Karmen, A. (1996). *Crime victims*. Boston: Wadsworth Publishing.

Kanin. E.J. (1994). False rape allegations. *Archives of Sexual Behavior* 23, no. 1. Retrieved 8 August 2007 from http://www.sexcriminals.com/library/doc-1002-1.pdf.

Kantor, G.K. and Jasinski, J.L. (Eds) (1997). *Out of the darkness*. Thousand Oaks, CA: Sage.

Kasian, M. and Painter, S. (1992). Frequency and severity of psychological abuse in a dating population. *Journal of Interpersonal Violence* 7, no. 3, 350–364.

Katz, J., Kuffel, S.W. and Coblentz, A. (2002). Are there gender differences in sustaining dating violence? An examination of frequency, severity, and relationship satisfaction. *Journal of Family Violence* 17, 247–271.

Katz, S. and Mazur, M.A. (1979). *Understanding the rape victim*. New York: John Wiley and Sons.

Kaura, S.A. and Allan, C.M. (2004). Dissatisfaction with relationship power and dating violence perpetration by men and women. *Journal of Interpersonal Violence* 19, 576–588.

Keene, K. (2007, July 29). 50 years ago: A crime that spawned center. *Boston Globe* p. 57.

Keilitz, S.L., Davis, C., Efkeman, H.S., Flango, C. and Hannaford, P.L. (1998). Civil protection orders: Victims' views on effectiveness. Washington, DC: National Institute of Justice. Retrieved 25 January 2007 from http://www.ncjrs.gov/pdf-files/fs000191.pdf.

Kelling, G., Pate, T., Dieckman, D. and Brown, C. (1974). The Kansas City preventive patrol experiment. Washington, DC: Police Foundation. Retrieved 25 January 2007 from http://www.policefoundation.org/pdf/kcppe.pdf.

Kelly, L. (2003). Disabusing the definition of domestic abuse. *Florida State University Law Review*, 30, no. 4, 791–855. Retrieved 7 March 2006 from http://www.law.fsu.edu/Journals/lawreview/downloads/304/kelly.pdf.

Kelly, W. (1998). *Pogo*, vol. 1. Seattle: Fantagraphics Books.

Kernsmith, P. (2005). Exerting power or striking back: A gendered comparison of motivations for domestic violence perpetration. *Violence and Victims* 20, no. 2, 173–185.

Kilpatrick, D.G., Acierno, R., Saunders, B., Resnick, H.S., Best, C.L. and Schnurr, P.P. (2000). Risk factors for adolescent substance abuse and dependence: Data from a national sample. *Journal of Consulting and Clinical Psychology* 68, no. 1, 19–30.

Kimmel, M.S. (2002). Males victims of domestic violence: A substantive and methodological research review. Retrieved 25 January 2007 from http://www.xyonline.net/downloads/malevictims.pdf.

King, J.I. (2001). *All but my soul*. Scottsdale, AZ: Mind Matters Publishing.

Kinsley, M. (2002, September 9). How to live a rational life. *Time*, p. 113.

Kittredge, C. (2002, August 8). Domestic violence groups doubt researcher's study. *Boston Globe*, p. 1.

Klaus, P. (2005). Crime and the nation's households, 2005. Washington, DC: Department of Justice, Bureau of Justice Statistics. Retrieved 9 May 2007 from http://www.ojp.usdoj.gov/bjs/pub/pdf/cnh05.pdf.

Klaus, P. and Rennison, C.M. (2002). Age patterns in violence victimization, 1976–2000. Washington, DC: Department of Justice, Bureau of Justice Statistics. Retrieved 7 March 2007 from http://www.ojp.usdoj.gov/bjs/pub/pdf/apvv00.pdf.

Klein, A. (1996). Re-abuse in a population of court restrained male batterers. In E. Buzawa and C. Buzawa (Eds.), *Do arrest and restraining orders work?* (pp. 192–213). Thousand Oaks, CA: Sage.

Klein, A. (2000). Dear readers. *National Bulletin on Domestic Violence Prevention* 6, no. 6. Boston.

Klein, A.R. (2004). *The criminal justice response to domestic violence.* Belmont, CA: Wadsworth/Thomson Learning.

Klinger, D.A. (1995). Policing spousal assault. *Journal of Research in Crime and Delinquency* 32, no. 13, 308–324.

Koss, M.P. and Dinero, T. (1989). Discriminant analysis of risk factors for sexual victimization among a national sample of college women. *Journal of Consulting and Clinical Psychology* 57, no. 2, 242–254.

Kramer, S. (director) (1960). *Inherit the Wind.* Los Angeles: United Artists.

Kranish, M. (2005, August 15). Flaws are found on validating medical studies. *Boston Globe*, p. A1.

Kreiter, S.R., Krowchuk, D.P., Woods, C.R., Sinal, S.H., Lawless, M.R. and DuRant, R.H. (1999). Gender differences in risk behaviors among adolescents who experience date fighting. *Pediatrics* 104, no. 6, 1286–1292.

Kropp, P.R., Hart, S.D., Webster, C.D. and Eaves, D. (1995). *Manual for the spousal assault risk assessment guide,* 92nd ed. Vancouver: British Columbia Institute Against Family Violence.

Kruger, R.F., Caspi, A. and Moffitt, T.E. (2000). Epidemiological personology: The unifying role of personality in population-based research on problem behaviours. *Journal of Personality* 68, 967–998.

Kruttschnitt, C., McLaughlin, B.L. and Petrie, C.V. (Eds.) (2004). Advancing the federal research agenda on violence against women. Washington, DC: National Academies Press. Retrieved 2 May 2007 from http://www.nap.edu/catalog/10849.html.

Kyriacou, D.N., Anglin, D., Taliaferro, E., Stone, S., Tubb, T., Linden, J.A. et al. (1999). Risk factors for injury to women from domestic violence. *New England Journal of Medicine* 341, no. 25, 1892–1898.

Kyriacou, D.N., Anglin, D., Taliaferro, E., Stone, S., Tubb, T. Linden, J.A., Muelleman, R., Barton, E. and Kraus, J.F. (1999). Risk factors for injury to women from domestic violence. *New England Journal of Medicine* 341, no. 25, 1927–1929.

Lane, K. and Gwartney-Gibbs, P.A. (1985). Violence in the context of dating and sex. *Journal of Family Issues* 6, 45–49.

Laner, M.R. (1990). Violence or its precipitators: Which is more likely to be identified as a dating problem? *Deviant Behavior* 11, 329–329.

Laner, M.R. and Thompson, J. (1982). Abuse and aggression in courting couples. *Deviant Behavior* 3, 229–244.

Langan, P.A. and Dawson, J.M. (1995). Spouse murder defendants in large urban counties. Washington, DC: Department of Justice, Bureau of Justice Statistics. Retrieved 3 February 2007 from http://www.ojp.usdoj.gov/bjs/pub/pdf/spousmur.pdf.

Langeland, T. (2002, August 15–21). Railroaded for domestic violence defendants, El Paso County's "fast track" may not always lead to justice. *Colorado Springs Independent.* Retrieved 23 October 2007 from http://csindy.com/csindy/2002-08-15/cover.html.

Langford, L., Isaac, N.E. and Kabat, S. (1999). Homicides related to intimate partner violence in Massachusetts, 1991–1995. Boston Peace at Home. Retrieved 20 July 2007 from http://www.peaceathome.org/pdfs/homrepo.pdf.

Langhinrichsen-Rohling, J., Neidig, P. and Thorn, G. (1995). Violent marriages: Gender differences in levels of current violence and past abuse. *Journal of Family Violence* 10, no. 2, 159–175.

Langhinrichsen-Rohling, J., Palarea, R., Cohen, J. and Rohling, M. (2000). Breaking up is hard to do: Unwanted pursuit behaviors following the dissolution of a romantic relationship. *Violence and Victims* 15, no. 1, 73–89.

Laroche, D. (2005). Aspects of the context and consequences of domestic violence—Situational couple violence and intimate terrorism in Canada in 1999. Quebec, Canada, Institut de la Statistique du Quebec. Retrieved 4 February 2007 from http://www.stat.gouv.qc.ca/bul/conditions_vie/AspectViolen_an.pdf.

LaRosa, P. (2006). *Tacoma confidential.* New York: Signet.

Lattimore, P.K., Riley, K.J., Trudeau, J., Leiter, J. and Edwards, S. (1997). Homicide in eight U.S. cities: Trends, context, and policy implications. Washington, DC: Department of Justice, National Institute of Justice. Retrieved 6 March 2007 from http://www.ncjrs.gov/pdffiles/167263.pdf.

Lauby, M., McCarthy, K., Meade, J. and White, L.S. (2006). 2003 Massachusetts domestic violencehomicide report. Boston: Jane Doe Inc. Retrieved Nov. 23 2007 from http://www.janedoe.org/know/2003%20MA%20DV%20Homicide%20. Report.pdf.

Lauritsen, J.L. and White, NA. (2001). Putting violence in its place: The influence of race, ethnicity, gender, and place on the risk for violence. *Criminology and Public Policy* 1, no. 1, 37–59.

Lavoie, F., Vezina, L., Piche, C. and Boivin, M. (1995). Evaluation of a prevention program for violence in teen dating relationships. *Journal of Interpersonal Violence* 10, 516–524.

Leahy, P. (2005). Statement of Senator Patrick Leahy on the reauthorization of the Violence Against Women Act. Retrieved 9 August 2007 from http://leahy.senate.gov/press/200507/071905.html.

Lehrer, J. (2007, April 29). Hearts and minds. Boston Globe, p. E1. Retrieved 8 August 2007 from http://www.boston.com/news/education/higher/articles/2007/04/29/hearts__minds/.

Lerman, L.G. (1992). The decontextualization of domestic violence. *Journal of Criminal Law and Criminology* 83, no. 1, 217–240.

Lerner, G. (1986). *The creation of patriarchy.* New York: Oxford University Press.

Lerner, H.G. (1988). *Women in therapy.* New York: Harper and Row.

Levey, B. (1990). Abusive teen dating relationship: An emerging issue for the 90s. *Response to the Victimization of Women and Children* 13, no. 1, 59.

Levy, B. (1984). Skills for violence free relationships: Curriculum for young people ages 13–18. St Paul: Minnesota Coalition for Battered Women.

Liptak, A. (2003, August 23). Ethics inquiry clears lawyer whose stories were at odds. *New York Times,* p. A12.

Liz Claiborne, Inc. (LCI) (2006). It's Time to Talk Day. Retrieved 30 May 2007 from http://www.loveisnotabuse.com/itstimetotalk/.

Liz Claiborne, Inc. (LCI) (2007). Teen dating abuse survey 2005. Retrieved 30 May 2007 from http://www.loveisnotabuse.com/pdf/Liz%20Claiborne%20Mar%2006%20Relationship%20Abuse%20Hotsheet.pdf.

Lo, W.A. and Sporakowski, M.J. (1989). The continuation of violent dating relationships among college students. *Journal of College Student Development* 30, 432–439.

Lockwood, D. (1978). Sexual aggression among male prisoners. Unpublished dissertation, University Microfilms International, Ann Arbor, MI.

Lottes, I.L. and Weinberg, M.S. (1996). Sexual coercion among university students: A comparison of the United States and Sweden. *Journal of Sex Research* 34, 67–76.

Luci, P. and Galloway, J. (1994). Sexual jealousy: Gender differences in response to partner and rival. *Aggressive Behavior* 20, 203–211.

Lupri, E. (2004). Institutional resistance to acknowledging intimate male abuse. Retrieved 4 February 2002 from http://garscontent.com/Quotidiens/Quotidiens_412/Alberta.pdf.

Lynam, D.R. (1997). Pursuing the psychopath: Capturing the fledgling psychopath in a nomological net. *Journal of Abnormal Psychology* 106, 425–438.

Lynam, D.R., Caspi, A., Moffitt, T.E., Wikstrom, P., Loeber, R. and Novak, S. (2000). The interaction between impulsivity and neighborhood context on offending: The effects of impulsivity are stronger in poorer neighborhoods. *Journal of Abnormal Psychology* 10, 563–574.

Macionis, J.J. (1997). *Sociology.* Upper Saddle River, NJ: Prentice Hall.

Macgowan, M.J. (1997). An evaluation of a dating violence prevention program for middle school students. *Violence and Victims* 12, 223–235.

Macmillan, R. and Kruttschnitt, C. (2005). Patterns of violence against women: Risk factors and consequences. Washington, DC: Department of Justice. Retrieved 14 July 2007 from http://www.ncjrs.gov/pdffiles1/nij/grants/208346.pdf.

MacNeil, G. and Newell, J. (2004). School bullying: Who, why and what to do. *Prevention Researcher* 11, no. 3, 115–117.

Magdol, L., Moffit, T.E., Caspi, A., Newman, D.L., Fagan, J. and Silva, P.A. (1997). Gender differences in partner violence in a birth cohort of 21-years-olds: Bridging the gap between clinical and epidemiological approaches. *Journal of Consulting and Clinical Psychology* 654, 68–78.

Magdol, L. Moffitt, T.E., Caspi, A. and Silva, P.A. (1998). Developmental antecedents of partner abuse: A prospective-longitudinal study. *Journal of Abnormal Psychology* 107, 375–389.

Maguire, K. and Pastore, A.L. (Eds.) (2002). *Bureau of Justice Statistics Sourcebook of Criminal Justice Statistics—2002*, 30th ed. Washington, DC: U.S. Department of Justice.

Makepeace, J.M. (1981). Courtship violence among college students. *Family Relations* 30, 97–102.

Makepeace, J.M. (1986). Gender differences in courtship violence victimization. *Family Relations* 35, 383–388.

Makepeace, J.M. (1987). Social factors and victim-offender differences in courtship violence. *Family Relations* 36, 87–91.

Malik, S., Sorenson, S.B. and Aneshensel, C.S. (1997). Community and dating violence among adolescents: Perpetration and victimization. *Journal of Adolescent Health* 21, 291–302.

Mann, C. (1988). Getting even? *Justice Quarterly* 5, 33–51.

Manning, P.K. (1993). The preventive conceit. *American Behavioral Scientist* 36, no. 5, 639–650.

Margolin, G., John, R. and Gleberman, L. (1988). Affective responses to conflictual discussions in violent and nonviolent couples. *Journal of Consulting and Clinical Psychology* 56, no. 1, 24–33.

Marshall, L.L. and Rose, P. (1987). Gender, stress and violence in the adult relationships of a sample of college students. *Journal of Social and Personal Relationships* 4, 299–316.

Martin, D. (1976). *Battered wives*. San Francisco: Glide Publications.

Maryland Network Against Domestic Violence (2001). Maryland domestic violence statistics. Retrieved 4 February 2007 from http://www.mnadv.org/.

Maslow, A.H. (1971). *The farther reaches of human nature*. New York: Viking.

Massachusetts Office for Victim Assistance (2000). Training manual for civilian domestic violence victim advocates in police departments.

Mattaini, M.A. and McGuire, M.S. (2006). Behavioral strategies for constructing nonviolent cultures with youth: A review. *Behavior Modification* 30, 184–224.

Matthews, W. J. (1984). Violence in college couples. *College Student Journal* 18, 150–158.

Maxwell, C.D., Garner, J.H. and Fagan, J.S. (2001). The effects of arrest on intimate partner violence: New evidence from the spouse assault replication program. Washington, DC: Department of Justice, National Institute of Justice. Retrieved 4 February 2007 from http://www.ncjrs.gov/pdffiles1/nij/188199.pdf.

McCoy, D. (2006). *The manipulative man*. Avon, MA: Adams Media.

McCuller, W.J., Sussman, S., Holiday, K., Craig, S. and Dent, C.W. (2002). Tracking procedures for locating high-risk youth. *Evaluation and the Health Professions* 25, 345.

McDonald, R., Caetano, R., Green, C.E., Jouriles, E.N. and Ramisetty-Mikler, S. (2006). Estimating the number of American children living in partner-violent families. *Journal of Family Violence* 20, 137–142. Retrieved 14 July 2006 from http://www.smu.edu/experts/study-documents/family-violence-study-may2006.pdf.

McKinney, K. (1986). Measures of verbal, physical and sexual dating violence by gender. *Free Inquiry in Creative Sociology* 14, 55–60.

McNamara, E. (1998, October 18). Battered wives let down by law. *Boston Globe*, p. B1.

McNamara, E. (2002, July 28). He dares to question. *Boston Globe*, p. B1.

McNamara, E. (2003, August 6). A lesson in openness. *Boston Globe*, p. B1.

Meadows, S. and Thomas, E. (2006). A troubled spring at Duke. Msnbc.com: Newsweek. Retrieved 8 August 2007 from http://www.msnbc.msn.com/id/12115147/site/newsweek/.

Meloy, J. and Boyd, C. (2003). Female stalkers and their victims. *Journal of American Academy of Psychiatry and Law* 31, 211–219. Retrieved 5 July 2007 from http://www.jaapl.org/cgi/reprint/31/2/211.pdf.

Merriam-Webster OnLine (2007). Violence. Retrieved 28 May 2006 from http://www.m-w.com/dictionary/violence.

Merrill, L.L., Hervig, L.K., Milner, J.S. and Newell, C.E. (1998). Intimate partner conflict resolution in a navy basic trainee sample. *Military Psychology* 10, 1–15.

Migon, S.I. and Holmes, W.M. (1995). Police response to mandatory arrest laws. *Crime and Delinquency* 41, no. 4, 430–442.

Mignon, S.I., Larson, C.J. and Holmes, W.M. (2002). *Family abuse: Consequences, theories, and responses.* Boston: Allyn and Bacon.

Mihalic, S., Irwin, K., Elliot, D., Fagan, A. and Hansen, D. (2001). Blueprints for violence prevention. Washington, DC: Department of Justice, Office of Juvenile Justice and Delinquency Prevention. Retrieved 10 March 2007 fromhttp://www.ncjrs.gov/html/ojjdp/jjbul2001_7_3/contents.html.

Mingus, N.I. (1990). Elder abuse. Ottawa: National Clearinghouse on Family Violence. Retrieved 27 June 2007 from http://www.phac-aspc.gc.ca/ncfv-cnivf/familyviolence/pdfs/elderab.pdf.

Millbank, S., Riches, M. and Prior, B. (2000). Reducing repeat victimisation of domestic violence: The NDV Project. Retrieved 4 February 2007 from http://www.aic.gov.au/conferences/criminality/riches.pdf.

Miller, J. (2001). *One of the guys: Girls, gangs and gender.* New York: Oxford University Press.

Miller, N. (2004). Domestic violence: A review of state legislation defining police and prosecution duties and powers. Alexandria, VA: Institute for Law and Justice. Retrieved 25 January 2007 from http://www.ilj.org/publications/DV_Legislation -3.pdf.

Miller, N. (2005). What does research and evaluation say about domestic violence laws? Alexandra, VA: Institute for Law and Justice. Retrieved 25 January 2007 from http://www.ilj.org/publications/dv/DomesticViolenceLegislationEvaluation.pdf.

Mills, L.G. (1998). Mandatory arrest and prosecution policies for domestic violence: A critical literature review and the case for more research to test victim empowerment approaches. *Criminal Justice and Behavior* 25, no. 3, 306–318. Retrieved from http://www.nvaw.org/policy/mandarrest.

Mills, L.G. (2003). *Insult to injury: Rethinking our responses to intimate abuse.* Princeton, NJ: Princeton University Press.

Minnesota Coalition for Battered Women (2007). Understanding men who batter. Retrieved 17 July 2007 from http://www.mcbw.org/pdf/menwhobatter.pdf.

Minnesota Program Development Inc. (n.d.). Duluth model. Retrieved 5 July 2007 from http://www.duluth-model.org/.

Moffitt, T.E. (1993). Adolescence-limited and life-course-persistent antisocial behavior: A developmental taxonomy. *Psychological Review* 100, no. 4, 674–701.

Moffitt, T.E. and Caspi, A. (1999). Findings about partner violence from the Dunedin Multidisciplinary Health and Development Study. Washington, DC: Department of Justice, National Institute of Justice. Retrieved 4 February 2007 from www.ncjrs.gov/pdffiles1/170018.pdf.

Moffitt, T.E., Krueger, R.F., Caspi, A. and Fagan, R.W. (2000). Partner abuse and general crime: How are they the same? How are they different? *Criminology* 38, no. 1, 199–232.

Moffitt, T.E., Robins, R. and Caspi, A. (2001, November). A couples analysis of partner abuse with implications for abuse prevention policy. *Criminology and Public Policy* 1, 5–36.

Molidor, C. and Tolman, R.M. (1998). Gender and contextual factors in adolescent dating violence. *Violence against Women* 4, 180–194.

Molidor, C., Tolman, R.M. and Kolber, J. (2000, February). Gender and contextual factors in adolescent dating violence. *Prevention Researcher* 7, no. 1, 1–4.

Moretti, M.M. and Jackson, M. (2004). *Girls and aggression*. New York: Springer.

Morse, B. (1995). Beyond the Conflict Tactics Scale: Assessing gender differences in partner violence. *Violence and Victims* 10, no. 4, 251–269.

Ms. Foundation for Women (2003). Safety and justice for all: Examining the relationship between the women's anti-violence movement and the criminal legal system. Retrieved 30 July 2006 from http://www.ms.foundation.org/user-assets/PDF/Program/safety_justice.pdf.

Muehlenhard, C. and Cook, S. (1988). Men's self-reports of unwanted sexual activity. *Journal of Sex Research* 24, 58–72.

Mulroney, J. and Chan, C. (2005). Men as victims of domestic violence. *Australian Domestic and Family Violence Clearinghouse.* Retrieved 20 June 2007 from http://www.austdvclearinghouse.unsw.edu.au/topics/topics_pdf_files/Men_as_Victims.pdf.

Murphy, J.E. (1988). Date abuse and forced intercourse among college students. In G.P. Hotaling, D. Finkelhor, J.T. Kirkpatrick and M.A. Straus (Eds.), *Family abuse and its consequences: New directions in research* (pp. 285–296). Newbury Park, CA: Sage.

Myers, D.G. (2004). *Psychology.* New York: Worth Publishers.

National Archive of Criminal Justice Data (NACJD). University of Michigan, http://www.icpsr.umich.edu/NACJD/.

National Center for Injury Prevention and Control, Intimate Partner Violence: Overview. Retrieved 30 May 2007 from http://www.cdc.gov/ncipc/factsheets/ipvfacts.htm.

National Center for Juvenile Justice (2007). Supplementary homicide reports: 1980–2004. Retrieved 18 May 2007 from http://ojjdp.ncjrs.org/ojstatbb/ezashr/.

National Center for Victims of Crime (2004). Dating violence resource center. Retrieved 6 July 2006 from http://www.ncvc.org/ncvc/main.aspx?dbID=DB_DatingViolenceResourceCenter101.

National Coalition of Anti-Violence Programs (NCAVP) (2006). Anti-lesbian, gay, bisexual and transgender violence in 2005. Retrieved 4 June 2007 from http://www.coavp.org/documents/2005NationalHVReport.pdf.

National Crime Victimization Survey. (2003). http://www.ojp.usdoj.gov/bjs/abstract/ntmc.htm. Retrieved Nov. 23, 2007.

National Institute of Justice (NIJ) (2004). Research in Brief—Violence against women: Identifying risk factors. Washington, DC. Retrieved 13 August 2006 from http://www.ncjrs.gov/pdffiles1/nij/197019.pdf.

NDVH (National Domestic Violence Hotline). 2007. http://www.ndvh.org. Retrieved Nov. 17, 2007.

Newberger, E.H. (1999). *The men they will become.* Reading, MA: Perseus Books.

Niehoff, D. (1999). *The biology of violence.* New York: Free Press.

O'Beirne, K. (2006). *Women who make the world worse.* New York: Sentinel.

O'Brien, K. (2007, July 22). Why do men kill their wives? *Boston Globe Magazine*, pp. 28–31.

O'Keefe, M. (1997). Predictors of dating violence among high school students. *Journal of Interpersonal Violence* 12, 546–568.

O'Keefe, M. (1998). Factors mediating the link between witnessing interparental violence and dating violence. *Journal of Family Violence* 13, 39–57.

O'Keefe, M. (2005). Teen dating violence: A review of risk factors and prevention efforts. VAWnet of the National Resource Center on Domestic Violence Resources. Retrieved 18 May 2007 from http://new.vawnet.org/Assoc_Files_ VAWnet/AR_TeenDatingViolence.pdf.

O'Keefe, M. and Treister, L. (1998). Victims of dating violence among high school students: Are the predictors different for males and females? *Violence Against Women*, 4(2), 195–223.

O'Leary, K.D. (1988). Physical aggression between spouses: A social learning theory perspective. In V.B. Van Hasselt, R.L. Morrison, A.S. Beeeack and M. Hersen (Eds.), *Handbook of family violence* (pp. 31–55). New York Plenum.

O'Leary, K.D. (2000). Are women really more aggressive than men in intimate relationships? Comment on Archer (2000). *Psychological Bulletin* 126, no. 5, 685–689.

O'Leary, K.D., Barling, J., Arias, I., Rosenbaum, A., Malone, J. and Tyree, A. (1989). Prevalence and stability of physical aggression between spouses: A longitudinal analysis. *Journal of Consulting and Clinical Psychology* 57, 263–268.

O'Sullivan, L., Byers, E. and Finkleman, L. (1998). A comparison of male and female college students' experiences of sexual coercion. *Psychology of Women Quarterly* 22, 177–195.

Patten, P. (2000). Dating violence: Why does it occur and how does it fit in the cycle of violence? Retrieved 16 May 2006 from http://www.athealth.com/Consumer/ disorders/datingviolence.html. (Originally published in *Parent News* [online] 6, no. 4)

Paulozzi, L.J., Saltzman, L.E., Thompson, M.P. and Holmgreen, P. (2001, October 12). Surveillance for homicide among intimate partners—United States, 1981–1998. *Surveillance Summaries* 50, no. SS03, 1–16. Retrieved 18 May 2007 fromhttp://www.cdc.gov/mmwr/preview/mmwrhtml/ss5003a1.htm.

Pearson, P. (1997). *When she was bad: Violence women and the myth of innocence*. New York: Viking.

Pedersen, P. and Thomas, C.D. (1992). Prevalence and correlates of dating violence in a Canadian University sample. *Canadian Journal of Behavioural Science* 24, 490–501.

Pence, E. and Das Dasgupta, S. (2006). Re-examining "battering": Are all acts of violence against intimate partners the same. Retrieved 16 July 2007 from http://data.ipharos.com/praxis/documents/FINAL_Article_Reexaming_Battering_082006.pdf.

Peterson, K.S. (2003, June 22). Studies shatter myth about abuse. *USA Today*. Retrieved 9 July 2007 from http://www.usatoday.com/news/health/2003-06 -22-abuse-usat_x.htm.

Pizzy, E. (1971). *Quietly or the neighbours will hear*. London: Penguin Books.

Pizzy, E (1998). *The emotional-terrorist and the violence prone*. London: Commoners Pub.

Plass, M.S. and Gessner, J.C. (1983). Violence in courtship relations: A southern sample. *Free Inquiry in Creative Sociology* 11, 198–202.

Pleck, E. (1989). Criminal approaches to family violence, 1640–1980. In L. Ohlin and M. Tonry, *Family violence, vol. 2: Crime and justice: A review of research.* Chicago: University of Chicago Press.

Police-Stress.com (2005). Police pre-employment evaluations, training and programs. Retrieved 18 May 2007 from http://www.police-stress.com/.

Pollack, W. (1998). *Real boys.* New York: Random House.

Postmus, J.L. and Severson, M. (2006). Violence and victimization: Exploring women's histories of survival. Washington, DC: U.S. Department of Justice. Retrieved 13 July 2007 from http://www.ncjrs.gov/pdffiles1/nij/grants/214440.pdf.

Powell v. State of Alabama (1932). 287 U.S. 45. Findlaw.com. Retrieved 14 March 2007 from http://caselaw.lp.findlaw.com/scripts/getcase.pl?court=US&vol=287 &invol=45.

Power, J. and Kerman, E. (2006). Research facts and findings. Retrieved 28 July 2007 from http://www.actforyouth.net/documents/Feb06.pdf.

Project Implicit (2007). Retrieved 21 July 2007 from http://www.projectimplicit.net/ index.php.

Prothrow-Stith, D. and Spivak, H.R. (2005). *Sugar and spice and no longer nice: How we can stop girls' violence.* Hoboken, NJ: Jossey-Bass.

Ptacek, J. (1998). *Battered women in the courtroom.* Boston: Northeastern University Press.

Rakowsky, J. (2002, September 18). Bail ruling is seen adding to jail crowding. *Boston Globe,* p. 34.

Ranalli, R. and Rosenwald, M. (2002, May 30). Shooting leaves 1 dead, 1 injured. *Boston Globe,* p. B1.

Rand, M. (1998). Criminal victimization 1997. Washington, DC: Department of Justice, Bureau of Justice Statistics. Retrieved 13 February 2007 from http://www. ojp.usdoj.gov/bjs/abstract/cv97.htm.

Rand, M. (1997). Violence-related injuries treated in hospital emergency departments. Washington, DC: Department of Justice, Bureau of Justice Statistics. Retrieved 13 February 2007 from http://www.ojp.usdoj.gov/bjs/pub/pdf/ vrithed.pdf.

Reed, C. (2003, May 23). Veteran teacher faces sexual assault charges. *Boston Globe,* p. B2.

Regents of the University of Michigan (2007). National survey of adolescents. Retrieved 10 March 2007 from http://webapp.icpsr.umich.edu/cocoon/ICPSR-STUDY/02833.xml.

Reiss, A.J., Jr. and Roth, J.A. (1993). Understanding and preventing violence. Washington, DC: National Academy Press Retrieved 24 May 2007 from http://www. nap.edu/catalog/1861.html#toc.

Renetti, C.M. and Maier, S.L. (2002). "Private" crime in public housing: Violent victimization, fear of crime and social isolation among women in public housing residents. *Women's Health and Urban Life* 2, 46–65. Retrieved 13 February 2007 from http://www.utsc.utoronto.ca/~socsci/sever/journal/1.2/Renzetti.pdf.

Rennison, C.M. (1998). Criminal victimization 1998. Washington, DC: Bureau of Justice Statistics, Department of Justice. Retrieved 13 February 2007 from http://www.ojp.usdoj.gov/bjs/abstract/cv98.htm.

Rennison, C.M. (2001). Intimate partner violence and age of victim, 1993–1999. Washington, DC: Bureau of Justice Statistics, Department of Justice. Retrieved 13 February 2007 from http://www.ojp.usdoj.gov/bjs/pub/pdf/ipva99.pdf.

Rennison, C.M. (2002). Criminal victimization 2001. Washington, DC: Bureau of Justice Statistics, Department of Justice. Retrieved 13 February 2007 from http://www.ojp.usdoj.gov/bjs/abstract/cv01.htm.

Rennison, C.M. (2003). Intimate partner violence, 1993–2001. Washington, DC: Bureau of Justice Statistics, Department of Justice. Retrieved 27 July 2006 from http://www.ojp.usdoj.gov/bjs/pub/pdf/ipv01.pdf.

Rennison, C.M. and Welchans, S. (2000). Intimate partner violence. Washington, DC: Bureau of Justice Statistics, Department of Justice. Retrieved 18 May 2007 from http://www.ojp.usdoj.gov/bjs/pub/pdf/ipv.pdf.

Respecting Accuracy in Domestic Abuse Reporting (RADAR) (2007). http://www.mediaradar.org/docs/radardocument-agenda-forvawa-reform.pdf. Retrieved Nov. 29, 2007.

Richardson, D.S. (2005). The myth of female passivity: Thirty years of revelations about female aggression. *Psychology of Women Quarterly* 29, no. 3, 238–247. Retrieved 31 May 2007 from http://www.blackwell-synergy.com/doi/abs/10.1111/j.1471-6402.2005.00218.x.

Richardson, D.S. and Hammock, G.S. (2007). Social context of human aggression: Are we paying too much attention to gender? *Aggression and Violent Behavior* 12, no. 4, 417–426.

Riggs, D.S. and Caulfield, M. (1997). Expected consequences of male violence against their female dating partners. *Journal of Interpersonal Violence* 12, 229–240.

Riggs, D.S. and O'Leary, K.D. (1989). A theoretical model of courtship aggression. In M.A. Pirog-Good and J.E. Stets (Eds.), *Violence in dating relationships: Emerging social issues* (pp. 53–70). New York: Praeger.

Riggs, D.S. and O'Leary, K.D. (1996). Aggression between heterosexual dating partners: An examination of a causal model of courtship aggression. *Journal of Interpersonal Violence* 11, 519–540.

Riggs, D.S., O'Leary, K.D. and Bresline, B.F. (1990). Multiple correlates of physical aggression in dating couples. *Journal of Interpersonal Violence* 5, 61–73.

Roberson, C. (2000). *Introduction to criminal justice.* Incline Village, NV: Copperhouse.

Roberts, K. (2004). The myth of gender symmetry. Peace at Hand, Maine Coalition to End Domestic Violence.

Roberts, T.A. and Klein, J. (2003). Intimate partner abuse and high-risk behavior in adolescents. *Archives of Pediatrics and Adolescent Medicine* 157, no. 4, 375–380.

Robertson, T. (2002, September 22). Judge questions whether visit to Afghan camp broke law. *Boston Globe*, p. A25.

Robinson, A.L. and Chandek, M.S. (2000). The domestic violence arrest decision: Examining demographic, attitudinal and situational variables. *Crime and Delinquency* 46, 18–38.

Roscoe, B. and Callahan, J.E. (1985). Adolescents self-report of violence in families and dating relations. *Adolescence* 79, 545–553.

Roscoe, B. and Kelsey, T. (1986). Dating violence among high school students. *Psychology* 23, 53–59.

Rosen, L. and Fontaine, J. (Eds.) (2007). Violence and victimization research division's compendium of research on violence against women, 1993–2006. Retrieved 21 May 2007 from http://www.ojp.usdoj.gov/nij/vawprog/vaw_portfolio. pdf.

Rosenbluth, B. (2002). *Expect respect: A school based program promoting health relationships for youth.* National Resource Center on Domestic Violence: NRCDV Publications. Retrieved 23 October 2007 from http://new.vawnet.org/Assoc_ Files_VAWnet/NRC_Expect-full.pdf.

Rothwax, H.J. (1997). *Guilty: The collapse of criminal justice.* New York: Warner Books.

Rouse, L.P. (1988). Abuse in dating relationships: A comparison of blacks, whites, and Hispanics. *Journal of College Student Development* 29, 312–319.

Rouse, L.P., Breen, R. and Howell, M. (1988). Abuse in intimate relationships: A comparison of married and dating college students. *Journal of Interpersonal Violence* 3, 414–429.

Ryan, K.A. (1998). The relationship between courtship violence and sexual aggression in college students. *Journal of Family Violence* 13, 377–394.

Sack, A.R., Keller, J.F. and Howard, R.D. (1982). Conflict tactics and violence in dating situations. *International Journal of Sociology of the Family* 12, 89–100.

SafeState (2006). California student survey. Retrieved 18 May 2006 from http:// www.safestate.org/index.cfm?navid=254.

Sagrestano, L.M., Heavey, C.L. and Christensen, A. (1999). Perceived power and physical violence in marital conflict. *Journal of Social Issues* 55, no. 1, 65–79.

Saunders, D. (1986). When battered women use violence. *Violence and Victims* 1, no. 1, 47–60.

Saunders, D.G. and Hamilton, R. (2003). Violence against women: Synthesis of research on offender intervention. Final report. Washington, DC: Department of Justice. Retrieved 15 July 2007 from http://www.ncjrs.gov/pdffiles1/ nij/grants/201222.pdf.

Saunders, D.G. (1998). Wife abuse, husband abuse, or mutual combat. In K. Yllo and M. Bograd (Eds.), *Feminist perspectives on wife abuse.* Thousand Oaks, CA: Sage. 90–113.

Sax, L. (2005). *Why gender matters.* New York: Doubleday.

Scalzo, T. (2007). Rape and sexual assault reporting laws. *American Prosecutors Research Institute* 1, no. 3. Retrieved 28 July 2007 from http://www.ndaa-apri.org/apri/ index.html. (For a print copy email ncpvaw@ndaaapri.org or call 703-549-9222)

Schmalleger, F. (2007). *Criminal justice today* 9th ed. Upper Saddle River, NJ: Prentice Hall.

Schmalleger, F. (2005). *Criminal justice today* 8th ed. Upper Saddle River, NJ: Prentice Hall.

Schmidt, J.D. and Sherman, L.W. (1993). Does arrest deter domestic violence? *American Behavioral Scientist* 36, 601–609.

Schwartz, M., O'Leary, S.G. and Kendziora, K.T. (1997). Dating aggression among high school students. *Violence and Victims* 12, no. 4, 294–305.

Schworm, P. and Hernandez, J. (Aug. 7, 2007). Kin says suspect has troubled past. *Boston Globe*, p. B1.

Selekman, J. and Praeger, S.G. (2006). Violence in schools. In J. Selkmen (Ed.), *School nursing: A comprehensive text* (p. 934). Philadelphia: F.A. Davis Company.

Shakil, A., Smith, D., Sinacore, J.M. and Krepcho, M. (2005). Validation of the HITS domestic violence screening tool with males. *Family Medicine* 37, no. 3, 193–198. Retrieved 13 July 2007 from http://www.stfm.org/fmhub/fm2005/March/Amer193.pdf.

Sharpe, D. and Taylor, J.K. (1999). An examination of variables from a social-developmental model to explain physical and psychological dating violence. *Canadian Journal of Behavioural Science* 31, no. 3, 165–175.

Sherman, L.W. (1992). *Policing domestic violence: Experiments and dilemmas.* New-York: Free Press.

Shook, N.J., Gerrity, D.A., Jurich, J. and Segrist, A.E. (2000). Courtship violence among College students: A comparison of verbally and physically abusive couples. *Journal of Family Violence* 15, 1–22.

Shupe, A., Stacey, W. and Hazlewood, L. (1987). *Violent men, violent couples: The dynamics of domestic violence.* New York: John Wiley and Sons.

Sigelman, C.K., Berry, C.J. and Wiles, K.A. (1984). Violence in college students' dating relationships. *Journal of Applied Social Psychology* 5, 530–548.

Silverman, J.G., Raj, A., Mucci, L.A. and Wathaway, J.E. (2001). Dating violence against adolescent girls and associated substance use, unhealthy weight control, sexual risk behavior, pregnancy, and suicidality. *Journal of the American Medical Association* 286, no. 5, 572–579.

Simmons, R. (2002). *Odd girl out: The hidden culture of aggression in girls.* New York: Harcourt Inc.

Simonelli, C.J. and Ingram, K.M. (1998). Psychological distress among men experiencing physical and emotional abuse in heterosexual dating relationships. *Journal of Interpersonal Violence* 13, 667–681.

Simonelli, C.J., Mullis, T., Elliot, A.N. and Pierce, T.W. (2002). Abuse by siblings and subsequent experiences of violence within the dating relationship. *Journal of Interpersonal Violence* 17, 103–121.

Simons, R.L., Lin, K.H. and Gordon, L.C. (1998). Socialization in the family of origin and male dating violence: A prospective study. *Journal of Marriage and the Family* 60, no. 2, 467–478.

Sinden, P.G. and Stephens, B.J. (1999). Police perceptions of domestic violence: the nexus of victim, perpetrator, event, self and law. *An International Journal of Police Strategies and Management* 22, no. 3, 313–327.

Smith, J.P. and Williams, J.G. (1992). From abusive household to dating violence. *Journal of Family Violence* 10, 153–165.

Smith, P.H., White, J.W. and Holland, L.J. (2003). A longitudinal perspective on dating violence among adolescent and college-age women. *American Journal of Public Health* 93, no. 7, 1104–1109.

Snell, T.L. (1994). *Women in prison.* Washington, DC: Department of Justice, Bureau of Justice Statistics.

Snyder, H.N. and Sickmund, M. (2006). Juvenile offenders and victims: 2006 national report. Washington, DC: U.S. Department of Justice, Office of Justice Programs, Office of Juvenile Justice and Delinquency Prevention. Retrieved 28 May 2006 from http://ojjdp.ncjrs.gov/ojstatbb/nr2006/.

Soler, E. (2007). Backlash study. Family violence prevention fund. Retrieved 3 April 2007 From http://www.endabuse.org/programs/display.php3?DocID=241.

Sommer, R. (1994). Male and female perpetrated partner abuse. Doctoral dissertation, University of Manitoba. Retrieved 5 July 2007 from http://fathersforlife. org/reena_sommer/reena_sommer_DV_toc.htm.

Sommers, C.H. (2000). *The war against boys*. New York: Simon and Schuster.

Sontag, D. (2002, November 17). Fierce entanglements. *New York Times*, Sunday Magazine.

Sousa, C.A. (1999). Teen dating violence: The hidden epidemic. *Family and Conciliation Courts Review* 27, no. 3, 356–374.

Spence, D.L. (2000). Brockton, Massachusetts, arrest policies project. Washington, DC: U.S. Department of Justice. Retrieved 29 July 2007 from http://www.ncjrs. gov/pdffiles1/nij/grants/201874.pdf.

Spencer, G.A. and Bryant, S.A. (2000). Dating violence: A comparison of rural, suburban and urban teens. *Journal of Adolescent Health* 25, no. 5, 302–305.

Spilbor, J.M. (2003). What if Kobe Bryant has been falsely accused? Retrieved 8 August 2007 from http://writ.news.findlaw.com/commentary/20030811_spilbor.html.

Spitzberg, B. and Rhea, J. (1999). Obsessive relational intrusion and sexual coercion victimization. *Journal of Interpersonal Violence* 14, no. 1, 3–20.

Stacy, C., Schandel, L., Flannery, W., Conlon, M. and Milardo, R. (1994). It's not all moonlight and roses: Dating violence at the University of Maine. *College Student Journal* 28, 2–9.

Stacey, W., Hazelwood, L. and Shupe, A. (1994). *The violent couple*. Westport, CT: Praeger.

Stanko, E. (1992). Domestic violence. In G.W. Cordner and D.H. Hales (Eds.), *What works in policing: Operations and administration examined* (pp. 49–61). Cincinnati: Anderson.

Stark, E. and Flitcraft, A. (1985). Spouse abuse. In *Source book: Surgeon general's workshop on violence and public health* (np). Washington, DC: Centers for Disease Control and Prevention.

Stark and Flitcraft. (1985). Spouse Abuse. Surgeon General's Workshop on Violence and Public Health: Sourcebook, 1985. Centers for Disease Control, 1986: ASI-SA 43.

Steinmetz, S. (1981). A cross-cultural comparison of sibling violence. *International Journal of Family Psychiatry* 2, no. 3–4, pp. 337–351.

Stets, J.E. (1991). Psychological aggression in dating relationships: The role of interpersonal control. *Journal of Family Violence* 6, 97–114.

Stets, J.E. and Henderson, D.A. (1991). Contextual factors surrounding conflict resolution while dating: Results from a national study. *Family Relations* 40, 29–40.

Stets, J.E. and Pirog-Good, M.A. (1987). Violence in dating relationships. *Social Psychology Quarterly* 50, 237–246.

Stets, J.E. and Pirog-Good, M.A. (1989a). Patterns of physical and sexual abuse for men and women in dating relationships: A descriptive analysis. *Journal of Family Violence* 4, 63–76.

Stets, J.E. and Straus, M.A. (1989b). The marriage license as a hitting license: A comparison of assaults in dating, cohabiting and married couples. *Journal of Family Violence* 4, 161–180.

Stewart, A. (1999). Domestic violence: Deterring perpetrators. Paper presented at the 3rd National Outlook Symposium on Crime in Australia, Canberra, Australia. Retrieved 25 January 2007 from http://www.aic.gov.au/conferences/outlook99/stewart.pdf.

Stockman, F. (2002, October 28). A search of equality. *Boston Globe*, p. B1.

Stout, M. (2005). *The sociopath next door*. New York: Broadway Books.

Straus, M. (1993). Physical assaults by wives: A major social problem. In R. Gelles and D. Loseky (Eds.), *Current controversies on family violence* (pp. 67–87). Newbury Park, CA: Sage.

Straus, M.A. (1979). Measuring intrafamily conflict and violence: The conflict tactics (CT) scales. Retrieved 6 February 2007 from http://pubpages.unh.edu/~mas2/CTS41%20(CTS2x-Abridged).pdf.

Straus, M.A. (1991). *Beating the devil out of them*. New York: Lexington Books.

Straus, M.A. (1998, February 28). The controversy over domestic violence by women: A methodological, theoretical, and sociology of science analysis. Paper presented at the Claremont Graduate University, Claremont, CA. Retrieved 5 February 2007 from http://pubpages.unh.edu/~mas2/CTS21.pdf.

Straus, M.A. (2001). Prevalence of violence against dating partners by male and female university students worldwide. *Violence against Women* 10, 790–811. Retrieved 6 February 2007 from http://pubpages.unh.edu/~mas2/ID16.pdf.

Straus, M.A. (2006). Dominance and symmetry in partner violence by male and female university students in 32 nations. Paper presented at conference on Trends in Intimate Violence Intervention, New York University. Retrieved 28 May 2006 from http://pubpages.unh.edu/~mas2/ID41E2.pdf.

Straus, M.A. (2007). Conflict tactics scales. In N.A. Jackson (Ed.), *Encyclopedia of domestic violence* (pp. 190–197). New York: Routledge. Retrieved 29 March 2007 from http://pubpages.unh.edu/~mas2/CTS44G.pdf.

Straus, M.A. (in press). Future research on gender symmetry in physical assaults on partners. *Violence against Women*. Retrieved 18 April 2006 from http://pubpages.unh.edu/~mas2.

Straus, M.A. and Gelles, R.J. (1990). *Physical violence in American families: Risk factors and adaptations to violence in 8,145 families*. New Brunswick, NJ: Transaction.

Straus, M., Gelles, R. and Steinmetz, S. (1980). *Behind closed doors: Violence in the American family*. Newbury Park, CA: Sage.

Straus, M.A., Hamby, S.L., Boney-McCoy, S. and Sugarman, D.B. (1996). The revised conflict tactics scales (cts2): Development and preliminary psychometric data. *Journal of Family Issues* 17, 283–316. Retrieved 27 June 2007 from http://pubpages.unh.edu/~mas2/CTS15.pdf.

Straus, M.A. and Medeiros, R.A. (2002, November). Gender differences in risk factors for physical violence between dating partners by university students. Paper presented at annual meeting of the American Society for Criminology, Chicago. Retrieved from http://pubpages.unh.edu/~mas2/ID28W.pdf.

Straus, M.A. and Ramirez, I.L. (2002, July). Gender symmetry in prevalence, severity, and chronicity of physical aggression against dating partners by university students in Mexico and USA. Paper presented at the 15th World Meeting of the International Society for Research on Aggression, Montreal. Retrieved 18 May 2006 from http://pubpages.unh.edu/~mas2/.

Straus, M.A. and Scott, K. (2007). Gender symmetry in partner violence: The evidence, the denial, and the implications for primary prevention and treatment. Retrieved 11 July 2007 from http://pubpages.unh.edu/~mas2/V70%20version%20N3.pdf.

Straus, M.A. and Stewart, J.H. (1998). Corporal punishment by American parents: National data on prevalence, chronicity, severity, and duration, in relation to child and family characteristics. Paper presented at the 14th World Congress of Sociology, Montreal. Retrieved from http://pubpages.unh.edu/~mas2/CP36.pdf.

Straus, M.A. and Yodanis, C.L. (1996). Corporal punishment in adolescence and physical assaults on spouses later in life: What accounts for the link? *Journal of Marriage and the Family* 58, 825–841. Retrieved 27 June 2007 from http://pubpages.unh.edu/~mas2/CP23.pdf.

Stuart, D. (2005). Statement of Diane M. Stuart director of the Office on Violence against Women. Retrieved 9 August 2005 from http://www.usdoj.gov/ovw/docs/testimony07192005.pdf.

Stuart, G., Moore, T., Gordon, K., Hellmuth, J., Ramsey, S. and Kahler, C. (2006). Reasons for intimate partner violence perpetration among arrested women. *Violence against Women* 12, 609–621.

Sugarman, D.B. and Hotaling, G.T. (1989). Dating violence: Prevalence, context, and risk markers. In M.A. Pirog-Good and J.E. Stets (Eds.), *Violence in dating relationships: Emerging social issues* (pp.3–32). New York: Praeger.

Surette, R. (1998). *Media, crime, and criminal justice*. Boston: West/Wadsworth.

Swan, S., Gambone, L. and Fields, A. (2005). Technical report for an empirical examination of a theory of women's use of violence in intimate relationships. Washington, DC: Department of Justice. Retrieved 13 March 2007 from http://www.ncjrs.gov/pdffiles1/nij/grants/208611.pdf.

Swan, S., Gambone, L., Fields, A., Sullivan, T.P. and Snow, D.L. (2005). Women who use violence in intimate relationships: The role of anger, victimization and symptoms of posttraumatic stress and depression. *Violence and Victims* 20, no. 3, 267–285. Retrieved 30 July 2007 from http://people.cas.sc.edu/swansc/anger.pdf.

Swan, S. and Snow, D. (2002). A typology of women's use of violence in intimate relationships. *Violence against Women* 8, 286–319.

Swisher, K.L. (Ed.) (1996). *Domestic violence*. San Diego: Greenhaven Press.

Task Force on Local Criminal Justice Response to Domestic Violence (2005). Keeping the promise: Victim safety and batterer accountability. Retrieved 25 January 2007 from http://www.safestate.org/documents/DV_Report_AG.pdf.

Tatara, T., Kuzmeskus, L.B., Duckhorn, E., Bivens, L., Thomas, C., Gertig, J. et al. (1998). The National Elder Abuse Incidence Study: Final report. Washington, DC: Administration for Children and Families and the Administration on Aging in the U.S. Department of Health and Human Services. Retrieved 30 June 2007 from http://www.aoa.gov/eldfam/Elder_Rights/Elder_Abuse/ABuseReport_Full.pdf.

Taylor, S. and Johnson, K.C. (2007). *Until proven innocent: Political correctness and the shameful injustices of the Duke lacrosse rape case*. New York: Thomas Dunne Books.

Texas Council on Family Violence (n.d.). National domestic violence hotline. Retrieved 30 May 2007 from http://www.ndvh.org/.

Thompson Jr., E.H. (1990). Courtship violence and the male role. *Men's Studies Review* 7, no. 3, 1, 4–13.

Thompson Jr., E.H. (1991). The maleness of violence in data relationships: An appraisal of stereotypes. *Sex Roles* 24, 261–278.

Thompson, M., O'Neill Grace, C. and Cohen, L.J. (2001). *Best friends, worst enemies: Understanding the social lives of children.* New York: Ballantine Books.

Thornhill, R. and Palmer, C.T. (2000). *A natural history of rape.* Cambridge, MA: MIT Press.

Tjaden, P. and Thoennes, N. (2000a). Extent, nature, and consequences of intimate partner violence. Washington, DC: Department of Justice, National Institute of Justice. Retrieved 18 May 2006 from http://www.ncjrs.gov/txtfiles1/nij/181867. txt. (Paper copies may be ordered by calling 800-851-3420.)

Tjaden, P. and Thoennes, N. (2000b). Full report of the prevalence, incidence, and consequences of violence against women. Washington, DC: Department of Justice, National Institute of Justice. Retrieved 28 May 2006 from http://www. ncjrs.org/pdffiles1/nij/183781.pdf.

Tontodonato, P. and Crew, B.K. (1992). Dating violence, social learning theory, and gender: A multivariate analysis. *Violence and Victims* 7, 3–14.

Toon, R., Hart, B., Welch, N., Coronado, N. and Hunting, D. (2005). Layers of meaning: Domestic violence and law enforcement attitudes in Arizona. Arizona State University, Morrison Institute for Public Policy. Retrieved 1 July 2007 from http://www.morrisoninstitute.org:80/.

Traux, N. (2002). *Silent blue tears.* New York: Milo House Press.

Trewin, D. (2005). *Personal safety survey.* Australian Bureau of Statistics. Retrieved 18 May 2007 from http://www.abs.gov.au/.

Trojanoqicz, R. and Bucqueroux, B. (1992). *Community policing: A contemporary perspective.* Englewood Cliffs, NJ: Prentice Hall.

Tyre, P. (2006, January 30). The trouble with boys. *Newsweek.* Retrieved 28 May 2006 from http://www.msnbc.msn.com/id/10965522/site/newsweek/.

Uekert, B.K. (2000). Lake County, California, arrest polices project. Washington, DC: U.S. Department of Justice. Retrieved 29 July 2007 from http://www.ncjrs. gov/pdffiles1/nij/grants/201874.pdf.

Uekert, B.K. (2003). Process evaluation of the Pueblo domestic violence project: July 1998. Pueblo, CO. Washington, DC: U.S. Department of Justice. Retrieved 14 March 2007 from http://www.ncjrs.gov/pdffiles1/nij/grants/201885.pdf.

University of New Hampshire (2007). The Conflict Tactics Scales. Retrieved 13 March 2007 from http://pubpages.unh.edu/~mas2/ctsb.htm.

Updike, N. (1999, May–June). Hitting the wall. *Mother Jones.* Retrieved 31 May 2007 from http://www.motherjones.com/news/outfront/1999/05/updike.html?welcome= true.

U.S. Department of Health and Human Services (2007). Who typically abuses children? Retrieved 30 May 2007 from http://faq.acf.hhs.gov/cgi-bin/acfrightnow. cfg/php/enduser/std_adp.php?p_faqid=70.

U.S. Department of Health and Human Services, Children's Bureau (1998). Child maltreatment 1996: Reports from the states to the National Child Abuse and Neglect Data System. Washington, DC: Government Printing Office. Retrieved 30 June 2007 from http://www.acf.hhs.gov/programs/cb/pubs/ncands96/ index.htm.

U.S. Dept. of Justice (2000). Domestic violence arrests: Beyond the obvious. Training project. http://www.transformcommunities.org/tctatsite/tools/dv_arrexts_bto .html. Retrieved Nov. 18, 2007.

U.S. Department of Justice, Bureau of Justice Statistics (2001). National crime victimization survey. Retrieved 30 May 2007 from http://www.ojp.usdoj. gov/bjs/cvict_rd.htm.

U.S. Government Printing Office (2004). Federal rules of criminal procedure. Washington, DC: U.S. Government Printing Office. Retrieved 14 March 2007 from http://judiciary.house.gov/media/pdfs/printers/108th/crim2004.pdf.

VAWNet (2003). National Online Resource Center on Violence Against Women (VAWnet) Interventions for Batterers. Retrieved 16 July 2007 from http://new. vawnet.org/category/index_pages.php?category_id=559.

Vennochi, J. (2000, November 17). Oh, what a plot the politicians are weaving in Florida. *Boston Globe*, p. A27.

Violence Against Women and Department of Justice Reauthorization Act (2005). House of Representatives 3402 (109th Congress). Retrieved 3 June 2007 from http://www.govtrack.us/congress/bill.xpd?bill=h109-3402.

Violence Against Women Resource Guide (2007). National Archive of Criminal Justice Data. Retrieved 22 June 2007 from http://www.icpsr.umich. edu/NACJD/vaw/.

Violence Policy Center (2006). American roulette: Murder-suicide in the United States. Washington, DC. Retrieved 22 May 2007 from http://www.vpc.org/ studies/amroul2006.pdf.

Waiping, A.L. and Sporakowski, M.J. (1989). The continuation of violent dating relationships among college students. *Journal of College Student Development* 30, 432–439.

Waldner-Haugrind, L.K. and Magruder, B. (1995). Male and female sexual victimization in dating relationships: Gender differences in coercion technique and outcomes. *Violence and Victims* 10, no. 3, 203–215.

Wallace, H. (2002). *Family violence: Legal, medical, and social perspectives.* Boston: Allyn and Bacon.

Walton, S. (2003). *When violence hits home: Domestic abuse and families.* Washington, DC: National Conference of State Legislatures.

Websdale, N. (2003). Reviewing domestic violence deaths. Washington, DC: Department of Justice 250, 26–31. Retrieved 29 June 2007 from http://www.ncjrs.gov/ pdffiles1/jr000250g.pdf.

Wekerle, C. and Wolfe, D.A. (1999). Dating violence in mid-adolescence: Theory, significance, and emerging prevention initiatives. *Clinical Psychology Review* 19, no. 4, 435–456.

Wells, W. and DeLeon-Granados, W. (2002). Analysis of unexamined issues in the intimate partner homicide decline: Race, quality of victim services, offender accountability and system accountability, final report. Washington, DC: Department of Justice. Retrieved 21 May 2007 from http://www.ncjrs.gov/pdf-files1/nij/grants/196666.pdf.

Wells, W. and DeLeon-Granados, W. (2004). California Intimate Partner Homicide Project. http://www.safestate.org/documents/dh-ca%20iph%20graphs4.pdf. Retrieved Nov. 18, 2007.

Wells, W. and DeLeon-Granados, W. (2005). The decline of intimate partner homicide. *National Institute of Justice Journal*. 252, 33–34. Retrieved 21 May 2007 from http://www.ncjrs.gov/pdffiles1/jr000252.pdf.

Weston, R., Temple, J.R. and Marshall, L.L. (2005). Gender symmetry and symmetry in violent relationships: Patterns of mutuality among racially diverse women. *Sex Roles* 53, no. 7–8,553–571.

Wetendorf, D. (1998). Police perpetrated domestic violence. Paper presented at the annual conference of the National Center for Women and Policing, Las Vegas, NV.

Wetendorf, D. (2007). Abuse of power. Retrieved from http://www.abuseofpower. info/index.htm.

Whitaker, D.J., Haileyesus, T., Swahn, M. and Saltzman, L.S. (2007). Differences in frequency of violence and reported injury between relationships with reciprocal and nonreciprocal intimate partner violence. *American Journal of Public Health* 97, 941– 947.

White House (2000, October 2). National domestic violence awareness month, Office of the Press Secretary. Retrieved 30 June 2007 from http://clinton4.nara. gov/WH/new/html/Tue_Oct_3_100650_2000.html.

White, J., Merrill, L. and Koss, M. (2001). Predictors of courtship violence in a Navy recruit sample. *Journal of Interpersonal Violence* 5, 61–73. Retrieved 5 July 2007 from http://stinet.dtic.mil/cgi-bin/GetTRDoc?AD=ADA370104andLoc ation=U2anddoc=GetTRDoc.pdf.

White, J.W. and Huphrey, J.A. (1994a). Female aggression in heterosexual relationships. *Aggressive Behavior* 20, 195–202.

White, J.W. and Koss, M.P. (1991). Courtship violence: Incidence in a national sample of higher education students. *Violence and Victims* 6, 247–256.

White, J.W. and Smith, P.H. (2001). Developmental antecedents of violence against women: A longitudinal perspective. Washington, DC: Department of Justice. Retrieved 28 March 2007 from http://www.ncjrs.gov/pdffiles1/nij/grants/ 187775.pdf.

White, M., Goldkamp, J. and Campbell, S. (2005). Beyond mandatory arrest: Developing a comprehensive response to domestic violence. *Police Practice and Research* 6, no. 3, 261–278.

Williams, K.R. (2005). Arrest and intimate partner violence: Toward a more complete application of deterrence theory. *Aggression and Violent Behavior* 10, 660–679.

Williams, S.L. and Frieze, I.H. (2005). Patterns of violence relationship, psychological distress, and marital satisfaction in national sample of men and women. *Sex Roles* 52, 771–785. Retrieved 27 June 2007 from http://findarticles. com/p/articles/mi_m2294/is_11-12_52/ai_n15395186.

Witkin, Stanley L. (2001, July). Complicating causes. *Social Work* 46, no. 3, 197–200.

Witwer, M.B. and Crawford, C.A. (1995). A coordinated approach to reducing family violence: Conference highlights. Washington, DC: Department of Justice, National Institute of Justice Retrieved 6 March 2006 from http://www.ncjrs. gov/pdffiles/redfam.pdf.

Wolf, K.A. and Foshee, V.A. (2003). Family violence, anger expression styles, and adolescent dating violence. *Journal of Family Violence* 18, 309–316.

Wolfe, D.A., Wekerle, C. and Scott, K. (1997). *Alternatives to violence: Empowering youth to develop health relationships.* Thousand Oaks, CA: Sage.

Wolfe, D.A., Wekerle, C., Scott, K., Straatman, A., Grasley, C. and Reitzel-Jaffe, D. (2003). Dating violence prevention with at-risk youth: A controlled outcome evaluation. *Journal of Consulting and Clinical Psychology* 71, no. 2, 279–291.

Wolfgang, M. (1958). *Patterns of criminal homicide.* Philadelphia: University of Pennsylvania Press.

Wolfgang, M. and Ferracuti, F., (1967). *The subculture of violence.* London: Tavistock.

Wolfgang, M., Figlio, R. and Sellin, T. (1987). *Delinquency in a birth cohort.* Chicago: University of Chicago Press.

Wong, D.S. (1994, May 10). Weld backs new bail measure tougher rules considered in wake of revere killing. *Boston Globe*, p. 21.

Wong, D.S. (1994, May 17). Weld administration called hypocritical on bail issue. *Boston Globe*, p. 26.

Wordbridges (2003). *Is there anti-male bias in domestic violence services? Adult Abuse Review* 2, no. 3. Retrieved 8 July 2007 from http://www.wordbridges. net/elderabuse/AAR/Vol2Issue3/antimaledv.html.

Wordes, M. and Nunez, M. (2002, May). Our vulnerable teenagers: Their victimization, its consequences and directions for prevention and intervention. The National Center for Victims of Crime and the National Council on Crime and Delinquency. http://www.ncvc.org/ncvc/main/aspx?dbID=DB_Teens453. Retrieved Nov. 17, 2007.

WorldNow and WISTV (2006). Domestic violence starting in teenage years. Retrieved 28 May 2006 from http://www.wistv.com/Global/story.asp?S=4816793.

Wrangam, R. and Peterson, D. (1996). *Demonic males.* Boston: Houghton Mifflin Co.

Yochelson, S. and Samenow, S.E. (1976). *The criminal personality.* New York: Jason Aronson.

Young, C. (1994). Abused statistics: domestic violence; like hydra heads or spreading kudzu, the false statistics keep proliferating. *National Review.* Retrieved 13 July 2007 from http://findarticles.com/p/articles/mi_m1282/is_n14_v46/ai_15674702.

Young, C. (1999). *Ceasefire! Why women and men must join forces to achieve true equality.* New York: Free Press.

Young, C. (2000, October 13). Looking at violence. *Boston Globe*, p. C7.

Young, C. (2002, September 23). A lawyer's obligation when client is guilty. *Boston Globe*, p. A15.

Young, C. (2003, May 23). Girls, violence and us. *Boston Globe*, p. All.

Young, C. (2006. August 14). At 40, is NOW what it set out to be then? *Boston Globe.* op ed page.

Zawitz, M.W. (1994). *Violence between intimates.* Washington, DC: Department of Justice, Bureau of Justice Statistics. Retrieved 29 June 2007 from http://www. ojp.usdoj.gov/bjs/pub/pdf/vbi.pdf.

Zepp, J. (1996). Domestic and sexual violence data collection: A report to congress under the Violence Against Women Act. Washington, DC: Department of Justice. Retrieved 29 June 2007 from http://www.ncjrs.gov/pdffiles/alldom.pdf.

Zuger, A. (1998, July 28). A fistful of hostility is found in women. *New York Times.* Retrieved 29 June 2007 from http://www.samsloan.com/fistful.htm.

Recommendations

I prefer the company of peasants because they have not been educated sufficiently to reason incorrectly.

—Michel de Montaigne

The following are some recommended changes. These recommendations mirror the changes I suggested in my first book a decade ago. Sadly, 10 years, later few of the recommendations I made then have been put in place.

A mantra found on the majority of domestic violence websites is that violence toward women crosses racial and income barriers and battering [without defining the difference between battering and abuse] and knows no color other than black and white (Gelles, 2007).

Too often domestic violence advocates, when they comb criminal justice statistics, discover the inequities in that system (and there are many to be discovered) and then report only the inequities faced by adult heterosexual women because the system supports the agenda of violence against women while excluding the obvious fact that the same inequities are faced by most disadvantaged and minority family members regardless of age, gender, or sexual orientation.

Although advocates proffer the claim that violence against women crosses all racial and income barriers, they have only recently discovered what criminologists have known for decades. Data from the Bureau of Justice Statistics quite clearly documents that the same is true for all crimes regardless of age, gender, or sexual orientation.

What is equally true, and should be more important concerning proper intervention, is that there is no question that though domestic violence victims are not limited to those at the lower end of the socioeconomic educational strata of society, there is also little doubt that those who live at the disadvantaged strata of society need more help than those who are affluent and educated.

Recommendation One

In these first years of this 21st century our public policy makers must play a role in returning us to the goals of the 1984 U.S. Attorney General's Task

Force on Family Violence. What began almost a generation ago as intervention programs to help all family members has become in this 21st century intervention directed primarily toward the needs of adult heterosexual women. And there is no question that the needs of adult heterosexual women must be met; however, we must not replicate the mistakes of the past and brush aside the requests of others by minimizing, marginalizing, and ignoring their needs.

The National Research Council (NRC) in its report "Advancing the Federal Research Agenda on Violence Against Women" has informed the president and the Congress that there are far more similar than dissimilar characteristics connecting the issues of violence in general, familial violence, and violence against women.

The president, Congress, and domestic violence advocates have ignored the advice of the NRC and have continued in the 21st century with underresearched, untried, or unproven 20th-century policies and programs. Most, if not all, of these interventions are founded on value-based (stakeholder interest) rather than value-free (evidence-based) research, and many programs and policies are using the population in general as experimental research subjects (e.g., mandatory arrest, restraining orders, Duluth styled battering programs) to test the Duluth hypothesis of domestic violence (Kruttschnitt, McLaughlin, and Petrie, 2004).

The NRC task force recommended that our public policy makers must become more involved in understanding the empirical-based data that they have funded researchers to produce when confronting the issue of domestic violence. The findings from the National Violence Against Women Survey document that annually 4.8 million women and 2.9 million men are victims of intimate partner violence (Tjaden and Thoennes, 2000b).

As their websites clearly document, the majority of domestic violence organizations, many partially funded by Violence Against Women grants and often supported by public policy makers, minimize, marginalize or ignore those 2.9 million men. In California and many other states those 2.9 million men are minimized, marginalized, or ignored by legislative statute law.

Domestic violence in all 50 states is not defined as violence against adult heterosexual women; it is most often defined as child, sibling, spousal, intimate partner, and elder abuse. Despite that definition, legislation, domestic violence intervention is now most often presented by Congress as violence against women and girls and not boys and men.

The majority of researchers agree that more females are victims of physical and sexual assaults than males; however, males need not be minimized, marginalized, or ignored to provide the proper support for females. Recognizing male victimization may very well engage more men in the effort to end or minimize domestic violence.

Recommendation Two

End legislation that mandates "one-size-fits-all" (Duluth-styled) domestic violence intervention programs.

There is little to no scientific empirical data or evidence that documents that men in general are motivated by patriarchal sexist desires to oppress women and that men in general use or condone violence against women in an attempt to control their behavior. However, at the same time, there is evidence that some men do abuse some women because of a sexist desire to oppress women (Fletcher, 2002).

There are no scientific empirical studies, data, or evidence that document that the Duluth-styled batterer intervention programs work and are better than other interventions or sanctions (Jackson et al., 2003). This does not mean that battering programs need to be ended; they simply need to provide diverse and individual assessments that will allow interveners to provide effective intervention that will better reflect the proper context and circumstance that may have caused the individual abusive incidents (Dutton, 2006; Edleson, 1998; Hamel and Nicholls, 2007).

Recommendation Three

Mandatory education is proactive (i.e., stop it before it happens) whereas mandatory arrest is reactive not preventative.

One of the most popular college texts concerning domestic violence is *Family Violence: Legal, Medical, and Social Perspectives* (Wallace, 2002, p. xi):

> The study of family violence is a complex, multifaceted experience. By its very nature family violence involves physicians, nurses, psychiatrists, psychologists, family counselors, educators, social workers, attorneys, judges, and law enforcement officials. All of these professionals have expertise in their own area of specialization. However, they may not understand or appreciate the difficulties experienced by others in their areas of interest. For example, a member of the medical profession may be able to diagnose physical injuries, but not understand the complexities of the courtroom.

There has been much progress made concerning domestic and family violence in the legal, social, and educational fields as we begin life in the 21st century. However, many studies have documented the lack of preparedness by many physicians, nurses, psychiatrists, psychologists, family counselors, educators, social workers, attorney, judges, and law enforcement with respect to domestic and family violence (Jackson, 2007). This lack of adequate institutionalized training concerning domestic and family violence and its dynamics should be a concern. Domestic violence, either as battering or abusive behavior, will impact every nuclear or extended family in America.

In 1995 the NRC established the Panel for Research on Violence Against Women. This was at the specific request of Congress after the Violence Against Women Act (VAWA) was passed in 1994. The purpose of this panel was to report to Congress the success of intervention, causes, and consequences of violence against women.

After extensive research and workshops the panel produced a report of their findings titled "Understanding Violence against Women" (Crowell and Burgess, 2006). The first paragraph of the study reports in part, "Since the mid 1970s the body of research on violence against women has grown, yet misinformation abounds, and we seem little closer to ending violence against women now than 20 years ago" (p. v).

R. Barri Flowers (2000, p. 1) writes in *Domestic Crimes, Family Violence and Child Abuse*, "This secretive nature of family and intimate violence makes it all the more frightening—and all the more necessary that we uncover, understand, and prevent it."

In the "Full Report of the Prevalence, Incidence, and Consequences of Violence Against Women," Tjaden and Thoennes (2000b, p. v) write, "Despite this outpouring of research many gaps exist in our understanding of violence against women."

In America, almost on a weekly basis newspapers report following a family or domestic violence homicide or suicide that "family and friends were shocked to learn" or "the murder stunned neighbors" or "they were such nice people, I can't believe it."

A 20-year study of criminal justice intervention, "Exposure Reduction or Backlash? 1976–1996," documents that some domestic violence resources provided are associated with more killings than less for some victim types (Dugan, Nagin, and Rosenfeld, 2001).

There is no question that we must learn more about the issue of family and domestic violence. In Massachusetts in 1992 then governor William Weld and lieutenant governor Paul Cellucci declared a state of emergency in Massachusetts concerning domestic violence. I live in Massachusetts, and to the best of my knowledge no governor since then has rescinded that order.

Senators Edward Kennedy and John Kerry both agree that many families face the horror of domestic violence, and Congressman Martin Meehan has declared that we must recognize the silent epidemic of domestic violence.

In her heart-wrenching book, *All But My Soul*, Jeanne I. King (2001), who is a clinical psychologist with 20 years of clinical experience, laments that if she had understood the dynamics of domestic violence she would have been better prepared to respond to it.

We all need to understand it: Colleges and universities should require students to complete a fully credited college course about family and domestic violence before they graduate. The course would allow all professionals who deal with victims and perpetrators and those who develop family and domestic violence curricula for children as young as elementary school age to have the experience of a college or university education concerning family and domestic violence.

There is no better place to open the channels of communication and the light the beacons of understanding than our universities and colleges. To the best of my knowledge not a single state has such an initiative or requirement. These professionals with lanterns of knowledge illuminated through the flame of education will be the ones who will spread optimism where before there was, too often, many false hopes and broken promises.

Recommendation Four

The issuance of restraining orders for the most minor of family conflicts has, more than anything else, trivialized the original intent of these orders, which was to support—not replace—criminal charges and to inform law enforcement and the criminal justice system of the serious nature of the offense of domestic violence.

Restraining and protective orders have become one-situation-fits-all interventions that trivialize the original intention of the orders. If the orders to continue to be issued in the millions each year there needs to be, at the very least, two types of orders.

When there are no criminal charges alleged, a civil restraining order should be issued. A noncriminal violation of that order should be heard in civil court, not criminal court. A simple noncriminal violation of this order (e.g., custody dispute, nonthreatening phone call, visitation rights violations) should be heard in civil courts.

When there are, for example, serious criminal charges, a physical assault, or threats to murder, a criminal order of protection should be issued. Any criminal violation of that criminal restraining order should be heard in criminal courts.

Most states make no distinction in the restraining and protective orders they issue. Some are for the most minor of instances. In many states there need not be any crime committed for an order to issue (Buzawa and Buzawa, 1996; Miller, 2004, 2005; Young, 1999).

The California courts offer an on-line self-help center that informs Californians that judges cannot give custody to a person who committed domestic violence. Under California Family Code Section 3044 Californians can now receive a restraining order and sole custody of their children if they believe that the other parent of the child has disturbed their peace.

The California legislature has not only trivialized the importance of restraining and protection orders, originally intended for battered victims; it has also trivialized the rights of a parents who can be denied custody because the other parent has been issued an order where there are no criminal charges alleged because no crime has been alleged.

Recommendation Five

Police officers should be empowered not mandated to make arrests.

The original intent of domestic violence laws were intended to protect victims who were being battered. Few people, including the many domestic violence advocates, continue to believe that mandating arrests for any and all incidents of family conflicts between any and all family members is a productive intervention process.

In 21 years of law enforcement I responded only once to a call for a fight between siblings in which the parents wanted to have one of their children arrested for fighting with the other.

I also discovered that many family members who call for law enforcement intervention expect to be helped, not made to feel helpless. In the most extensive study undertaken concerning domestic violence and arrest the following results produced little to no support for arrest and none for mandatory arrest in the majority of law enforcement interventions (Maxwell, Garner, and Fagan, 2001):

- The findings provided systematic evidence supporting the argument that arresting male batterers may, independent of other criminal justice sanctions and individual processes, reduce subsequent interment partner violence. This is the strongest of the findings and most often when researchers insert *may* it is because there is no actually finding that the actual can or does support the proposition (i.e., arrest) being made. *May*, by inference, must also mean *may not*.
- The findings showed that though arrest reduced the proportion of suspects who reoffended and the frequency with which they reoffended, arrest did not prevent all batterers from continuing their violence against their intimate partners. Although this might sound positive, the findings also document that a small number of victims had chronically aggressive partners who may be the most violent and were not deterred.
- Although the previous findings may seem somewhat positive, they also demonstrated that a majority of suspects discontinued their aggressive behaviors even without arrest. Hence, this finding had an effect on the finding above it.

- The findings suggest that policies requiring mandatory arrest for all suspects may unnecessarily take a community's resources away from identifying and responding to the worst offenders and victims most at risk.
- Future research in this area (i.e., mandatory arrest) needs to assess the benefits and costs of arresting all suspects before there can be a systematic conclusion of preferred or mandatory arrest policies.

To build on this finding a more recent U.S. Department of Justice study concluded that in states with preferred arrest policies that still allowed for some officer discretion, the increase in the arrest rates were 80% higher than states with mandatory arrest (Hirschel, Buzawa, Pattavina, Faggiani, and Reuland, 2007).

Recommendation Six

There is a need to separate those who are truly violent from those who are not.

In a follow-up study of 3,147 interviewed victims, one report documents that about 8% of the victims reported a total number of incidents representing more than 82% of the 9,000 incidents. The same 8% also accounted for 28% of the 1,387 incidents recorded by the police (Maxwell et al., 2001, p. 9).

It is not a complicated task, using court records, for U.S. courts to recognize quite easily some people who are at high risk of being a chronic or repeat abuser and those that present a heightened danger to the community if they are released without being placed on probation or somehow having their behavior monitored.

A Massachusetts studied reported that 91% of chronic offenders has previously been arraigned on criminal or delinquency charges. Two thirds of them have a history of being arraigned on violence crimes and delinquency charges. At least 60% of them have a history of alcohol and drug abuse (Adams, 1999).

Chronic or repeat abusers are dangerous people, and they should not be bailed. If they are eligible for bail they should be placed on extensive and strict probation or affixed with an electronic monitoring device. Any criminal violation while on probation or while being electronically monitored should provide for immediate revocation of bail, and the offender should remain under lock and key until they are tried.

Recommendation Seven

There should be child endangerment laws that monitor the children and victims of repeat offenders.

Though domestic violence organizations are often given credit for bring the attention of domestic violence to the forefront, the fact is that it was the recognition that most child abusers were parents or caretakers of children. In 1961 C. H. Kempe first introduced the term *battered child syndrome* (Wallace, 2002, p. 30). In the early 1970s, advocates for abused women simply replaced child with women.

Despite the dramatic changes for intimate partner violence, little has changed since the early 1960s concerning physical assault against children. All courts in America continue to uphold the right of a parent to spank a child. In Massachusetts the courts have ruled many times that parents or guardians not only can spank children; they can also beat them with a belt or other implement.

One Massachusetts case involved a school-age boy with attention deficit disorder (Ellement, 1999). The "spanking" administered was not a tap on the wrist or a thump on the bottom of a diapered toddler. The child was hit so hard with a belt that the red bruise marks were visible when he attended school the next day. The teacher who noticed the marks notified the Division of Social Services (DSS) as required by law in Massachusetts. The state, as it has many times in the past, condoned the physical assault against the child. The court criticized DSS for bringing the charges against his father and asserted that the child had suffered only temporary pink marks and had been hit with the soft end of a belt. One judge concluded that the jurists did not even think the case was close enough to be brought before the court.

Spanking or the corporal punishment of children is legal in every state. In fact there are many states that continue to allow those in authority who are not parents or guardians to use corporal punishment against children. The majority of people, both adult males and adult females, continue to condone the spanking of children. Spanking is an incident whereby one person uses physical assault in an attempt to alter or control that person's perceived improper behavior.

When a law enforcement officer responds to a home where a parent has spanked or hit a 16-year-old child, he or she is trained to disregard domestic violence training. Officers have been informed that spanking is legal and that spanking is a "family problem."

The nexus of spanking and many domestic violence incidents is that many spankers or abusers believe their physical behavior is not meant to harm. In fact, most domestic violence between adults begins with threats and low levels of violence such as pushing, shoving, slapping, or grabbing.

Domestic violence abusers often believe that their partner has behaved inappropriately and the use of physical force is for "for their own good," as do parents who spank their children. Often the spankers or abusers believe their intent is to alter the improper behavior of their children or partners.

The battering of partners and the spanking of children are not simply physical aggressions but are physical aggressions intended to function as a method of control, subjugation, and intimidation. Many children learn this lesson before they can speak. Many domestic violence clinicians have heard the excuse from adult abusers that their behavior was for the victim's own good. Coincidently, that seems to be society's justification for spanking and the corporal punishment of children.

A public social service agency should ensure that all children receive proper follow-up counseling after any and all governmental domestic violence interventions. These public social service agencies should ensure that services are available for all children who are at greatest risk of living in a chronically abusive household.

It has become socially and legally unacceptable for adults to use physical assaults to change or alter the behavior of each other; we have the responsibility of informing our children why it remains socially and legally acceptable to use physical assaults against them to changer or alter their behavior. It should be, but somehow seems not to be, the responsibility of adults to understand that there can not be one magic calendar day when ethically and morally physical assaults no longer are acceptable behavior.

Recommendation Eight

Abuse of alcohol does not cause domestic violence, but it does exacerbate the risk.

There should be a specific national tax affixed to the sale of all alcoholic beverages for money that should be dedicated to help funding domestic violence education, shelters, and intervention programs.

Though few, if any, social scientists claim that alcohol or drug abuse actually causes domestic violence, criminal justice data clearly document that a strong relationship exists among alcohol, drug abuse, and violence, and data also show that the abuse of alcohol and drugs plays a significant role in child, sibling, spousal, intimate partner, and elder abuse (Durose et al., 2005; Flowers, 1999, 2000; Gordis, 2001; Wallace, 2002).

Recommendation Nine

The Family Violence Act

The VAWA should be restructured and renamed the Family Violence Act. Funds should be made available for services to all victims regardless of age, gender, or sexual orientation.

Recommendation Ten

The purpose of the NRC is furthering knowledge and advising Congress. The most important of all the recommendations is that all public policy makers need to sit down and read the NRC report, "Advancing the Federal Research Agenda on Violence Against Women" (Kruttschnitt, McLaughlin, and Petrie, 2004). This report is free and available on line. Although it is often not logical to begin anything in the middle, it might be insightful for U.S. public policy makers to begin with pages 48 and 49 in the report (Table R.1).

Unaware of the Data?

At the 2005 reauthorization of the VAWA (Biden, 2005) Senator Russ Feingold noted that one in four women are physically assaulted by an intimate partner during their adult lives and that 1.5 million women are raped or physically assaulted by an intimate partner each year. Feingold did not mention male victimization.

At these hearing Senator Orrin Hatch noted that many women live in fear and lack the resources they need and deserve. Senator Hatch did not mention male victimization.

Senator Arlen Specter noted that the legislation demonstrates the U.S. commitment to combat violence against women. Senator Specter did not mention male victimization.

Senator Patrick Leahy (2005) noted that in 1976 there were 1,600 women killed as a result of domestic violence. Leahy did not mention that in the same year there were 1,357 males victims of domestic violence.

Senator Joe Biden, the author of the VAWA, noted that the act is critical to ensuring the safety and well-being of the women and children in the United States. Senator Biden made no mention about ensuring the safety and well-being of men in the United States.

At the VAWA hearings Senator Biden pointed to Department of Justice data, which shows that 85% of intimate partner offenders are men. Diane Stuart, the director of the office on Violence Against Women, corrected him and claimed that the Department of Justice data actually indicates that the percentage of male offenders is 88%. Stuart (2005) noted that more than $5 million of VAWA money is spent on research efforts.

I agree with Stuart when she noted that the government's efforts to reduce violence against women must continue. I know only too well that in most American families violence (i.e., physical assaults and coercive behavior) begins at home.

The very purpose of this book and my hope is that perhaps before the next reauthorization of VAWA—if Stuart and all of these senators are still

Table R.1

Survey	Sample	Percentage of Female Victims	Percentage of Male Victims
National Surveys of Family Violence 1975	Households containing cohabiting (married or nonmarried couple)	12.1% overall 3.8% severe	11.6% overall 4.6% severe
National Surveys of Family Violence 1985	Households containing cohabiting (married or nonmarried couple)	11.3% overall 3.0% severe	12.1% overall 4.4.5% severe
National Alcohol and Family Violence Survey 1992	Married and cohabiting persons aged 18+	9.1% overall 1.9% severe	9.5% overall 4.5% severe
National Alcohol Survey 1995	Married and cohabiting couples	5.2% to 13.6%	6.22% to 18.21%
National Violence Against Women Survey 1995–1996	Persons age 18+	1.3%	0.9%
National Violence Against Women Survey 1995–1996	Married and cohabiting persons age 18+	1.1%	0.6%
National Crime Victimization Survey 2001	Persons aged 12+	0.43%	0.08%
Dunedin 1993–1994 Multidisciplinary Health and Development Study	Study participants age 21 who were in romantic relationships and their partners	40.9%	47.4%
Dunedin 1993–1994 Multidisciplinary Health and Development Study	Study participants age 21 who were married or cohabiting	38.8%	55.8%
Dunedin 1993–1994 Multidisciplinary Health and Development Study	Study participants age 21 who were married, cohabiting or dating	27.1% overall 12.7% severe	34.1% overall 21.2% severe
National Youth Survey 1992	Study participants who were married or cohabiting	20.2% overall 5.7% severe	27.9% 13.8% severe

available—that by these next hearings they might have read the aforementioned NRC report. Congress might also consider asking the NRC, the organization Congress has entrusted to keep them informed about domestic violence, about the issue of male victimization, about female initiation, and about how to get more men involved. And a recent meta-analysis reports that a woman's initiation or perpetration of violence is the strongest predictor of her being a victim (Whitaker, Haileyesus, Swahn, and Saltzman, 2007).

I must assume that the only reason Stuart, none of senators, and all but one witness at the VAWA hearings expressed any concern about male victimization is that they were apparently unaware of the actual scope of male victimization as documented in Kruttschnitt et al. (2004, pp. 48–49) or intimate partner violence reported by the Centers for Disease Control and Prevention.

Selected Resources

The National Domestic Violence Hotline (NDVH)
Website: http://www.ndvh.org/
(800) 799-SAFE (7233)
(800) 787-3224 (TTY for Deaf, Deaf-Blind and Hard of Hearing)

The NDVH is available 24 hours a day, 365 days a year. Advocates are available for victims or anyone calling on their behalf for crisis intervention, safety planning, information, and referrals to agencies in all 50 states, Puerto Rico, and the U.S. Virgin Islands. Assistance is available in English and Spanish with access to more than 140 languages through interpreter services.

Action Ohio Coalition for Battered Women
P.O. Box 15673
Columbus, OH 43215
(614) 221-1255 Fax: (614) 221-6357
(888) 622-9315 In State
Website: http://www.actionohio.org
Email: actionoh@ee.net

Alabama Coalition Against Domestic Violence
P. O. Box 4762
Montgomery, AL 36101
(334) 832-4842 Fax: (334) 832-4803
(800) 650-6522 Hotline
Website: http://www.acadv.org
Email: acadv@acadv.org

Alaska Network on Domestic and Sexual Violence
130 Seward Street, Room 209
Juneau, AK 99801
(907) 586-3650 Fax: (907) 463-4493
Website: http://www.andvsa.org

Arizona Coalition Against Domestic Violence
100 W. Camelback Suite 109,
Phoenix, AZ 85013
(602) 279-2900 Fax: (602) 279-2980
(800) 782-6400 Nationwide
Website: http://www.azcadv.org
Email: acadv@azadv.org

Arkansas Coalition Against Domestic Violence
1401 W. Capitol Avenue, Suite 170
Little Rock, AR 72201
(501) 907-5612 Fax: (501) 907-5618
(800) 269-4668 Nationwide
Website: http://www.domesticpeace.com
Email: kbangert@domesticpeace.com

California Partnership to End Domestic Violence
P. O. Box 1798
Sacramento, CA 95812
(916) 444-7163 Fax: (916) 444-7165
(800) 524-4765 Nationwide
Website: http://www.cpedv.org
Email: info@cpedv.org

Colorado Coalition Against Domestic Violence
P. O. Box 18902
Denver, CO 80218
(303) 831-9632 Fax: (303) 832-7067
(888) 788-7091
Website: http://www.ccadv.org

Connecticut Coalition Against Domestic Violence
90 Pitkin Street
East Hartford, CT 06108
(860) 282-7899 Fax: (860) 282-7892
(800) 281-1481 In State
(888) 774-2900 In State DV Hotline
Website: http://www.ctcadv.org
Email: info@ctcadv.org

DC Coalition Against Domestic Violence
1718 P Street, Suite T-6
Washington, DC 20036
(202) 299-1181 Fax: (202) 299-1193
Website: http://www.dccadv.org
Email: help@dccadv.org

Delaware Coalition Against Domestic Violence
100 W. 10th Street, #703
Wilmington, DE 19801
(302) 658-2958 Fax: (302) 658-5049
(800) 701-0456 Statewide
Website: http://www.dcadv.org
Email: dcadv@dcadv.org

Florida Coalition Against Domestic Violence
425 Office Plaza
Tallahassee, FL 32301
(850) 425-2749 Fax: (850) 425-3091
(850) 621-4202 TDD
(800) 500-1119 In State
Website: http://www.fcadv.org

Georgia Coalition Against Domestic Violence
P.O. Box 7532, Athens, GA 30604
Atlanta, GA 30354
(404) 209-0280 Fax: (404) 766-3800
Website: http://www.gcadv.org

Hawaii State Coalition Against Domestic Violence
716 Umi Street, Suite 210
Honolulu, HI 96819-2337
(808) 832-9316 Fax: (808) 841-6028
Website: http://www.hscadv.org

Idaho Coalition Against Sexual & Domestic Violence
815 Park Boulevard, #140
Boise, ID 83712
(208) 384-0419 Fax: (208) 331-0687
(888) 293-6118 Nationwide
Website: http://www.idvsa.org
Email: domvio@mindspring.com

Illinois Coalition Against Domestic Violence
801 S. 11th Street
Springfield, IL 62703
(217) 789-2830 Fax: (217) 789-1939
Website: http://www.ilcadv.org
Email: ilcadv@ilcadv.org

Indiana Coalition Against Domestic Violence
1915 W. 18 th Street
Indianapolis, IN 46202
(317) 917-3685 Fax: (317) 917-3695
(800) 332-7385 In State
Website: http://www.violenceresource.org
Email: icadv@violenceresource.org

Iowa Coalition Against Domestic Violence
515 28th Street, #104
Des Moines, IA 50312
(515) 244-8028 Fax: (515) 244-7417
(800) 942-0333 In State Hotline
Website: http://www.icadv.org

Kansas Coalition against Sexual and Domestic Violence
634 SW Harrison Street Topeka, KS 66603
(785) 232-9784 Fax: (785) 266-1874
Website: http://www.kcsdv.org
Email: coalition@kcsdv.org

Kentucky Domestic Violence Association
P.O. Box 356
Frankfort, KY 40602
(502) 209-5381 Fax: (502) 695-2488
Website: http://www.kdva.org

Louisiana Coalition Against Domestic Violence
P.O. Box 77308
Baton Rouge, LA 70879
(225) 752-1296 Fax: (225) 751-8927
Website: http://www.lcadv.org

Maine Coalition to End Domestic Violence
170 Park Street
Bangor, ME 04401
(207) 941-1194 Fax: (207) 941-2327
Website: http://www.mcedv.org
Email: info@mcedv.org

Maryland Network Against Domestic Violence
6911 Laurel-Bowie Road, #309
Bowie, MD 20715
(301) 352-4574 Fax: (301) 809-0422
(800) 634-3577 Nationwide
Website: http://www.mnadv.org
Email: mnadv@aol.com

Jane Doe, Inc./Massachusetts Coalition Against Sexual Assault and Domestic Violence
14 Beacon Street, #507
Boston, MA 02108
(617) 248-0922 Fax: (617) 248-0902
TTY/TTD: (617) 263-2200
Website: http://www.janedoe.org
Email: info@janedoe.org

Michigan Coalition Against Domestic & Sexual Violence
3893 Okemos Road, #B-2
Okemos, MI 48864
(517) 347-7000 Fax: (517) 347-1377
TTY: (517) 381-8470
Website: http://www.mcadsv.org
Email: general@mcadsv.org

Minnesota Coalition for Battered Women
1821 University Avenue West, #S-112
St. Paul, MN 55104
(651) 646-6177 Fax: (651) 646-1527
Crisis Line: (651) 646-0994
(800) 289-6177 Nationwide
Website: http://www.mcbw.org
Email: mcbw@mcbw.org

Mississippi Coalition Against Domestic Violence
P.O. Box 4703
Jackson, MS 39296
(601) 981-9196 Fax: (601) 981-2501
Website: http://www.mcadv.org

Missouri Coalition Against Domestic Violence
718 East Capitol Avenue
Jefferson City, MO 65101
(573) 634-4161 Fax: (573) 636-3728
Website: http://www.mocadv.org
Email: mcadv@sockets.net

Montana Coalition Against Domestic & Sexual Violence
P.O. Box 818
Helena, MT 59624
(406) 443-7794 Fax: (406) 443-7818
(888) 404-7794 Nationwide
Website: http://www.mcadsv.com
Email: mcadsv@mt.net

Nebraska Domestic Violence and Sexual Assault Coalition
825 M Street, #404
Lincoln, NE 68508
(402) 476-6256 Fax: (402) 476-6806
(800) 876-6238 In State
Website: http://www.ndvsac.org
Email: info@ndvsac.org

Nevada Network Against Domestic Violence
220 S. Rock Blvd. Suite 7,
Reno, NV 89502-2355
(775) 828-1115 Fax: (775) 828-9911
(800) 500-1556 In State
Website: http://www.nnadv.org

New Hampshire Coalition Against Domestic and Sexual Violence
P.O. Box 353
Concord, NH 03302
(603) 224-8893 Fax: (603) 228-6096
(866) 644-3574 In State
Website: http://www.nhcadsv.org

New Jersey Coalition for Battered Women
1670 Whitehorse Hamilton Square
Trenton, NJ 08690
(609) 584-8107 Fax: (609) 584-9750
(800) 572-7233 In State
Website: http://www.njcbw.org
Email: info@njcbw.org

New Mexico State Coalition Against Domestic Violence
200 Oak NE, #4
Albuquerque, NM 87106
(505) 246-9240 Fax: (505) 246-9434
(800) 773-3645 In State
Website: http://www.nmcadv.org

New York State Coalition Against Domestic Violence
350 New Scotland Avenue
Albany, NY 12054
(518) 482-5464 Fax: (518) 482-3807
(800) 942-6906 English-In State
(800) 942-6908 Spanish-In State
Website: http://www.nyscadv.org
Email: nyscadv@nyscadv.org

North Carolina Coalition Against Domestic Violence
115 Market Street, #400
Durham, NC 27701
(919) 956-9124 Fax: (919) 682-1449
(888) 232-9124 Nation wide
Website: http://www.nccadv.org

North Dakota Council on Abused Women's Services
418 E. Rosser Avenue, #320
Bismark, ND 58501
(701) 255-6240 Fax: (701) 255-1904
(888) 255-6240 Nationwide
Website: http://www.ndcaws.org
Email: ndcaws@ndcaws.org

The Office of Women Advocates
Box 11382
Fernandez Juancus Station
Santurce, PR 00910
(787) 721-7676 Fax: (787) 725-9248

Oklahoma Coalition Against Domestic Violence and Sexual Assault
3815 N. Santa Fe Ave., Suite 124
Oklahoma City, OK 73118
(405) 524-0700 Fax: (405) 524-0711
Website: http://www.ocadvsa.org

Oregon Coalition Against Domestic and Sexual Violence
380 SE Spokane Street, #100
Portland, OR 97202
(503) 230-1951 Fax: (503) 230-1973
Website: http://www.ocadsv.com

Pennsylvania Coalition Against Domestic Violence
6400 Flank Drive, #1300
Harrisburg, PA 17112
(717) 545-6400 Fax: (717) 545-9456
(800) 932-4632 Nationwide
Website: http://www.pcadv.org

Rhode Island Coalition Against Domestic Violence
422 Post Road, #202
Warwick, RI 02888
(401) 467-9940 Fax: (401) 467-9943
(800) 494-8100 In State
Website: http://www.ricadv.org
Email: ricadv@ricadv.org

South Carolina Coalition Against Domestic Violence and Sexual Assault
P.O. Box 7776
Columbia, SC 29202
(803) 256-2900 Fax: (803) 256-1030
(800) 260-9293 Nationwide
Website: http://www.sccadvasa.org

South Dakota Coalition Against Domestic Violence & Sexual Assault
P.O. Box 141
Pierre, SD 57501
(605) 945-0869 Fax: (605) 945-0870
(800) 572-9196 Nationwide
Website: http://www.southdakotacoalition.org
Email: sdcadvsa@rapidnet.com

Tennessee Coalition Against Domestic and Sexual Violence
P.O. Box 120972
Nashville, TN 37212
(615) 386-9406 Fax: (615) 383-2967
(800) 289-9018 In State
Website: http://www.tcadsv.org
Email: tcadsv@tcadsv.org

Texas Council on Family Violence
P.O. Box 161810
Austin, TX 78716
(512) 794-1133 Fax: (512) 794-1199
(800) 525-1978 In State
Website: http://www.tcfv.org

Women's Coalition of St. Croix
Box 2734
Christiansted
St. Croix, VI 00822
(340) 773-9272 Fax: (340) 773-9062
Website: http://www.wcstx.com
Email: wcscstx@attglobal.net

Utah Domestic Violence Council
205 North 400 West,
Salt Lake City, 84103
(801) 521-5544 Fax: (801) 521-5548
Website: http://www.udvac.org

Vermont Network Against Domestic Violence and Sexual Assault
P.O. Box 405
Montpelier, VT 05601
(802) 223-1302 Fax: (802) 223-6943
Website: http://www.vtnetwork.org
Email: vtnetwork@vtnetwork.org

Virginians Against Domestic Violence
2850 Sandy Bay Road, #101
Williamsburg, VA 23185
(757) 221-0990 Fax: (757) 229-1553
(800) 838-8238 Nationwide
Website: http://www.vadv.org
Email: vadv@tni.net

Washington State Coalition Against Domestic Violence
101 N. Capitol Way, #302
Olympia, WA 98501
(360) 586-1022 Fax: (360) 586-1024
Website: http://www.wscadv.org
Email: wscadv@wscadv.org

West Virginia Coalition Against Domestic Violence
4710 Chimney Drive, #A
Charleston, WV 25302
(304) 965-3552 Fax: (304) 965-3572
Website: http://www.wvcadv.org

Wisconsin Coalition Against Domestic Violence
307 S. Paterson Street, #1
Madison, WI 53703
(608) 255-0539 Fax: (608) 255-3560
Website: http://www.wcadv.org
Email: wcadv@wcadv.org

Wyoming Coalition Against Domestic Violence and Sexual Assault
P.O. Box 236
409 South Fourth Street
Laramie, WY 82073
(307) 755-5481 Fax: (307) 755-5482
(800) 990-3877 Nationwide
Website: http://www.wyomingdvsa.org
Email: Info@mail.wyomingdvsa.org

The Domestic Abuse Helpline for Men and Women (DAHMW)
Website: http://www.dahmw.org
(888) 743-5754
(888) 7HELPLINE

The DAHMW helpline is available 24 hours a day, 365 days a year. A number of studies show, as this book has noted, that the NDVH and many of the local advocacy agencies still primarily adhere to the Duluth philosophy. By its very nature, men are the perpetrators and women their victims; these advocates continue to be more weary than receptive about the victimization of adult heterosexual males.

The NDVH website notes that there will be a national conference held with the goal to create a unified national movement aimed toward ending domestic violence. That same paragraph notes, "In response to the 33 million American women who experience domestic violence, our challenge is to take another major step forward." The summit notification on the NDVH takes care to not mention a single male victimization.

This exclusion or minimization, noted throughout this book, of male victimization is the reason the DAHMW was established in 2000. DAHMW provides a positive and supportive model for male victims of spousal and intimate partner violence. The DAHMW also provides the support for female heterosexual and same-sex relationships. The DAHMW collaborates, whenever possible, with traditional domestic violence agencies. However, as of this date, the Maine Coalition Against Domestic Violence has refused to allow DAHMW to join that statewide effort.

Stop Abuse for Everyone (SAFE)
Website: http://www.safe4all.org/info

SAFE is a human rights organization that provides services, publications, and training to serve those who have typically been underserved. SAFE promotes services for all victims—whether straight men, gays and lesbians, teens, and the elderly—and accountability for all perpetrators.

At http://www.safe4all.org/resource-list/ there are links to 674 resources worldwide. Anyone who registers on the SAFE website can add resources to this list and comment on existing resources. SAFE's international headquarters are in Portland, Oregon.

National Child Abuse Hotline
Website: http://www.childhelp.org/get_help
(800) 4-A-CHILD
(800) 422-4453

The Childhelp National Abuse Hotline is available 24 hours a day, 7 days a week in the United States, Canada, Puerto Rico, Guam, and the U.S. Virgin Islands. Childhelp focuses its efforts on advocacy, prevention, treatment, and community outreach. If a child, parent, adult caretaker, or neighbor needs help or has any questions about child abuse or child neglect they can call the number listed above and then push 1 to talk to a counselor. The call is free and anonymous. The Hotline counselors don't know who the callers are, and the callers don't have to tell them. If possible do not use a mobile phone or a cell phone.

Elder Abuse Helpline
Website: http://www.elderabusecenter.org/default.cfm?p=statehotlines.cfm
(800) 677-1116

The Helpline is available Monday through Friday for information and referral. The Elder Abuse Helpline website is always available, and it provides detailed information about state and local listings. In case of an emergency call 911 or your local law enforcement agency.

National Teen Dating Abuse Helpline (NTDAH)
Website: http://loveisrespect.org/
(866) 331-9474
(866) 331-8453 (TTY for Deaf, Deaf-Blind and Hard of Hearing)

At the NTDAH you can find support and information about dating abuse. You can talk with a trained advocate 24 hours a day, 365 days a year. The website also offers a live chat site that is available from 4 p.m. to 2 a.m. central time. There is also a blog and a profile at the social networking site at http://www.myspace.com/ntdah.

The Gay, Lesbian, Bisexual and Transgender (GLBT) National Hotline
Website: http://www.glnh.org/hotline/index.html
(888) THE-GLNH
(888) 843-4564)

The GLBT is available Monday through Friday from 1 p.m. to 9 p.m. pacific time and Saturday from 9 a.m. to 2 p.m. pacific time.

The GLBT provides peer counseling and local resources for cities and towns across the United States. The GLBT will inform callers about coming-out issues, relationship concerns, HIV/AIDS anxiety, and safer sex. It also maintains the largest resource database of its kind, with more than 18,000 listings.

Family Nonviolence Inc. (FNI)
Website: http://www.familynonviolence.org/index.html

I have been the vice president of FNI since its inception. Although FNI is specifically concerned with the issue of domestic violence in Massachusetts, it does contain a number of original articles and links to other relevant and useful resources. You may contact FNI at into@familynonviolence.org.

Index

A

AAUW. *see* American Association of
    University Women (AAUW)
Aberrant behavior, 13
Abuse
    California definition, 146
    homeless women, 209
    NDVH definition, 56
Abusive behavior not violent behavior, 173
Academy for Educational Development
    (AED), 69
Acquaintance killings, 21
Action Ohio Coalition for Battered Women,
    273
Adams, John, 47
Adams, Samuel, 47
Advancing Federal Research Agenda on
    Violence Against Women, 211
Advancing the Federal Research Agenda
    on Violence Against Women,
    102–103, 106, 127, 149
Adversaries *vs.* partners, 11
AED. *see* Academy for Educational
    Development (AED)
African Americans
    annual assault rates, 15
    female injuries, 35
    risk factors, 18
    spousal killings, 20
Against Our Will: Men, Women and Rape,
    137
Age risk factors, 18
Aggravated assault, 19
Aggression, 70–71
Aggressive prosecution policies, 110
Alabama Coalition Against Domestic
    Violence, 267
Alaska Network on Domestic and Sexual
    Violence, 267
Alcohol abuse, 22

teenagers, 67
Alcoholic beverages tax affixed, 263
All But My Soul, 258
Ambition, 10
American Association of University
    Women (AAUW), 69, 204
American College of Health Association, 69
American Sociologist Association, 127
Anestal, Solange, 188
Anger, 27
April 19, 2000, 187
April 19, 2003, 187–188
Arizona Coalition Against Domestic
    Violence, 267
Arkansas Coalition Against Domestic
    Violence, 268
Arrests
    defined, 152
    increasing abuse, 113
Arson, 19
Assault
    African Americans, 15
    male *vs.* female involvement, 19
    men, 15
    women, 15
Assaultive behavior by women, 197
Assessments
    include, 202–203
    needed, 202
    value, 202–203
Attention deficit disorder, 262
Attorneys, 6
Autonomy and confidentiality, 119–120
Awareness, 171–172

B

Barbosa, Karina, 186–187
Barbosa, Pedro, 186–187
Battered child syndrome, 3, 6, 195
Battered Wives, 4

Batterer intervention programs
  diversity, 115
  effectiveness, 115–116
  KtP, 114–115
Batterer Programs: What Criminal Justice
    Agencies Need to Know
  DOJ, 114
Batterers, 200–201
Battering, 146
  behavior, 50, 93
  vs. family conflict, 103–104
  law, 91
  victims, 41
Beals, Jason, 190
Beals, Judith E., 178
Bessonova, Nelli, 188–189
Bessonova, Viktor, 188–189
Bias, 34
Biden, Joseph, 264
  VAWA, 75
Biological children killings, 20
Bisexual community, 5
BJS. see Bureau of Justice (BJS)
Black, Howard, 167
Blanchette, Natalie, 188
Boston Youth Survey 2004, 67
Bowdoin, James, 47
Boy victimization, 76
Brault, Dawne Marie, 189
Brownmiller, Susan, 137
  theory of rape and sexual abuse, 135
Bureau of Justice (BJS), 30
  Intimate Partner Violence, 37
  violence-related injuries, 36–37
Bureau of Justice Statistics, 164–165
Bureau of Justice Statistics Sourcebook, 30
Burglary, 19

C

CAADV. see California Alliance Against
    Domestic Violence (CAADV)
California
  abuse definition, 146
  conundrum, 87–131
  domestic violence law, 146
  Duluth perspective, 114
  family conflict, 93
  Family Interventions Project, 115–116
  group treatment, 115

  ideological domestic violence
      intervention-based public policy,
      87
  laws on domestic violence, 121
  mandatory reporting law, 120–121
  murder incidence, 98
  National Family Violence Legislative
      Resource Center, 115–116
California Alliance Against Domestic
    Violence (CAADV), 65
California Attorney General Task Force on
    Local Criminal Justice Response
    to Domestic Violence, 89
California Intimate Partner Homicide
    Project, 98–99
California Partnership to End Domestic
    Violence, 268
Canada
  GSS, 95
Capaldi, Deborah, 26
Casavant, William, 189
Cause
  aberrant behavior, 13
  defined, 82
  domestic violence, 5, 148
CDC. see Centers for Disease Control and
    Prevention (CDC)
Centers for Disease Control and Prevention
    (CDC), 36
  dating violence, 78–79
  homicide among intimate partners, 209
  Injury Statistics Query and Reporting
      System, 36–37
  website, 36–37
  YRBS, 96–97
Change, 28–29
Child abuse, 2
  by acquaintances, 3
  criminalization, 3
  gender, 4, 24
  power and control dynamics, 4–5
  statistics, 26
Child advocacy movement, 3
Child endangerment laws, 261
Children, 179–180
  counseling after domestic violence, 263
  exposed to domestic violence, 209
  killings, 20
  physical assault protection, 8
  power and control, 26
Choice empowering women, 111
Chronic criminals shared behavior, 27

Chronic offenders, 29
Chronic or repeat abusers, 261
Cigarettes, 67
Circumstances, 75–76
Civil procedures mixed with criminal
    process, 92
Civil Protection Orders, 104
Civil rights movement, 3
Clinton, Bill, 178
Clinton, Hillary Rodham, 56
Coercion, 4, 13
    criminal behavior, 5
Cognitive-behavioral model, 115
College campus dating abuse, 68–69
Colorado Coalition Against Domestic
    Violence, 164, 268
Colorado Star Chamber, 155–168
Common sense, 168–169
Commonwealth Fund Survey, 145
Community Oriented Policing Services
    (COPS), 107
Compassion, 27
Complex and multifaceted issue, 198–200
Compromise, 197–198
Confessions, 157
Confidentiality, 119–120
Conflict Tactics Scales (CTS), 26, 39–40
Congressional resolution, H.RES 590,
    207–210
Connecticut Coalition Against Domestic
    Violence, 268
Context, 75–76
Control, 2
    female behavior, 23
Controlling Violence Against Women, 107,
    211–212
    DOJ, 104
    NIJ, 99–100
COPS. *see* Community Oriented Policing
    Services (COPS)
Corbett, Lori Ann, 190
Counterfeiting, 19
Courts, 114–115
Crime
    family conflict, 6–7
    male *vs.* female involvement, 19
    statistics, 19–20
    variety, 13
Criminal behavior
    coercion, 5
    economic control, 5
    physical power, 5

Criminalization of Domestic Violence,
    177–178
Criminal justice impacts, 211–212
Criminal Justice Statistics Sourcebook
    fear factor gender differential, 94
Criminal Personality, 27
Crisis Intervention, 49, 87
CTS. *see* Conflict Tactics Scales (CTS)
Cycle of violence theory, 135

D

DAHMW. *see* Domestic Abuse Helpline for
    Men and Women (DAHMW)
Data unaware, 264–265
Date rape
    Massachusetts Youth Risk Behavior
        Study, 179
    YRBS, 141
Dating abuse, 47–85
    college campus, 68–69
    defined, 55–56
    gender bias, 54
    one-solution-fits-all, 52
    reciprocal physical violence, 83
    risk factors, 51–52
    underlying problems, 81
    women's rights research, 52–53
Dating violence, 50–51
    CDC, 78–79
    females, 79
    gender, 72–73
    intervention and prevention, 80
    males, 79
    male victimization, 84–85
    NCVC, 77
    reasons, 82
    safety, 79–82
    VAWA, 64–65
Davis, Cari, 163
December 1, 2003, 190
Decline of Intimate Partner Homicide, 100
Delaware Coalition Against Domestic
    Violence, 268
Delinquency in a Birth Cohort, 27
Del Martin, 4
Department of Justice (DOJ)
    Batterer Programs: What Criminal
        Justice Agencies Need to Know,
        114
    Civil Protection Orders, 104

Controlling Violence Against Women, 104
Effects of Arrest on Intimate Partner Violence, 150
Effects of No-Drop Prosecution of Domestic Violence upon Conviction Rates, 102
Family Violence Statistics, 147
Forgoing Criminal Justice Assistance, 150
mission statement, 156–157
Police Intervention and the Repeat of Domestic Assault, 149
Depression, 22
DIAP. see Duluth Abuse Intervention Project (DAIP)
DiBenedetto, Anthony, 189–190
Differing domestic violence data, 196–197
Disparate data
domestic violence, 9
Disraeli, Benjamin, 33
District of Columbia Coalition Against Domestic Violence, 269
Diversity
batterer intervention programs, 115
DOJ. see Department of Justice (DOJ)
Domestic Abuse Helpline for Men and Women (DAHMW)
helpline, 277
website, 277
Domestic violence
Commonwealth Fund Survey definition, 145
defined, 7–8, 145–146, 182, 256
disagreement about definitions, 9
disparate data, 9
fallacious argument, 25–26
initiated on equal basis, 203
legal definition, 197
multifaceted phenomenon, 6, 191
NDVH definition, 1
21st century, 8–9
variety, 13
Domestic Violence: The Criminal Justice Response, 104, 108–109
Domestic Violence Awareness Month, 171
Dugan, Laura, 43
Duke University rape incident 2006, 141–142
Duke University students, 155
Duluth Abuse Intervention Project (DAIP), 6–7

Duluth model, 126, 176–177, 190, 198
Duluth perspective, 115
California standards, 114
Duluth theory, 90
primary cause of domestic violence, 91
Dutton, Donald, 26, 33

E

Economics
abuse, 2
control, 4
criminal behavior, 5
gender abuse, 25
jail consequences, 165
risk factors, 18
Edleson, Jeffrey L., 42–43
Educators, 6
Effects of Arrest on Intimate Partner Violence
DOJ, 150
NIJ, 200
Effects of No-Drop Prosecution of Domestic Violence upon Conviction Rates, 102
Elder abuse, 2, 4–5
Elder Abuse Helpline, 278
Embezzlement, 19
Emotional abuse, 59
Emotions, 137
Empathy, 27
Empowering women, 111
Equality and equity, 172–173
Equal Rights Amendment, 3
Equal risk theory, 38
Expenditures of VAWA, 150
Exposure Reduction or Backlash? Effects of Domestic Violence Resources on Intimate Partner Homicide, 102, 211, 258
Extend, Nature, and Consequences of Intimate Partner Violence, 178

F

Facts, 36–37
Facts ignored, 177
Fagan, Jeffery, 26
Fallacious argument, 25–26
False accusations, 141–142

False premises, 147–148
Familial homicides, 2
Family conflict, 50–51, 146–147, 201–202
   vs. battering, 103–104
   California, 93
   criminalization, 6–7, 91
   KtP, 93
   model, 115, 198
Family counselors, 6
Family Interventions Project
   California, 115–116
Family member abuse incidence, 15
Family Nonviolence Inc. (FNI), 279
Family Research Laboratory, 8
Family violence
   escalation, 182
   vs. violence by strangers, 6
Family Violence: Legal, Medical, and Social
   Perspective, 104, 118, 257
Family Violence Act, 263–264
Family Violence Prevention Fund (FVPF),
   65, 101, 121, 175
Family Violence Statistics, 147
Fast track program, 166
   premise, 162
Fatality review teams, 174
FBI. *see* Federal Bureau of Investigation
   (FBI) Supplemental Homicide
   Report
Fear factor gender differential, 94
February 7, 2003, 187
Federal Bureau of Investigation (FBI)
   Supplemental Homicide Report,
   14
Feingold, Russ, 264
Felonies *vs.* misdemeanors, 92
Females
   annual assault rates, 15
   assaultive behavior, 197
   behavior, 23
   biological children killings, 20
   initiating domestic and dating violence,
     79
   injuries, 35
   intimate partner victims, 21
   murdered by family members of
     acquaintances, 20
   offending, 79–80
   physical assaults, 2
   propensity to commit crimes, 19
   rights research, 52–53
   rise in arrests, 148–149

   sibling killings, 20
   societal role, 19
   spousal killings, 20
   victimization, 129
   victims, 196
Feminine Mystique, 171
Feminist movement, 3
Ferreira, Kathleen, 189
Fifth Amendment, 157
Florida Coalition Against Domestic
   Violence, 269
FNI. *see* Family Nonviolence Inc. (FNI)
Foregoing Criminal Justice Assistance, 101
Forgery, 19
Forgoing Criminal Justice Assistance, 150
Foshee, V.A., 71
Fourteenth Amendment, 158
Fraud, 19
Friedan, Betty, 171
FVPF. *see* Family Violence Prevention Fund
   (FVPF)

G

Gay, Lesbian, Bisexual and Transgender
   (GLBT) National Hotline, 279
Gay community, 5
Gelles, Richard, 26
Gender
   agenda, 61
   analysis of power, 190
   bias in dating abuse, 54
   blame, 53–54
   child abuse, 4, 24
   dating violence, 72–73
   economic abuse, 25
   equality, 3–4, 9
   interpersonal control, 71
   neutral ambition, 10
   psychological injuries, 25
   sexual assaults, 4
   specific funding of VAWA, 14
   specific VAWA research, 199
   symmetry, 63–64
   victims, 24
   violence, 24
General Social Survey (GSS), 95
Georgia Coalition Against Domestic
   Violence, 269
Gideon v. Wainwright, 160
Girl victimization, 76

GLBT. *see* Gay, Lesbian, Bisexual and Transgender (GLBT) National Hotline
Gomes, Laurinda, 186–187
Gomes, Maria, 186–187
Gomez, Amelia, 187
Goode, William, 24
Goodman, Ellen, 20, 126
Governmental domestic violence interventions, 263
Gray, Barbara, 104–105
Green, Katherine, 180
Gregg, Aiden P., 191
Group treatment, 115
GSS. *see* General Social Survey (GSS)
Gwinn, Casey, 89

H

Habitual offenders, 27
Harvard Youth Violence Prevention Center, 67
Hatch, Orrin, 264
Hawaii State Coalition Against Domestic Violence, 269
Head injury, 188
Health care workers, 6
Heterosexual females victimization, 34
Heterosexual male victimization, 34
HITS. *see* Hurt, Insulted, Threaten, Scream (HITS)
Homeless women abuse, 209
Homicide among intimate partners, 209
Homicide in Eight U.S. Cities: Trends, Context, and Policy Implications, 21
Homicides, 20–21, 185
    domestic violence, 42
    familial, 2
    preventable, 192–193
Homicide-suicide, 22
Homosexual domestic violence, 34
Hurt, Insulted, Threaten, Scream (HITS), 39
Husbands *vs.* wives physical abuse, 8

I

Idaho Coalition Against Sexual and Domestic Violence, 269
Ideological domestic violence advocates, 89

Ideological red herrings, 13
Ideological research, 34
Ideologue defined, 137
Ideology
    domestic violence training, 92
    skewing public policy, 76–77
ILJ. *see* Institute of Law and Justice (ILJ)
Illinois Coalition Against Domestic Violence, 269
Implicit bias, 185–186, 190–191
Incidence family member abuse, 15
Indiana Coalition Against Domestic Violence, 270
Individual rights, 157
Injury Statistics Query and Reporting System, 36–37
Injustice, 159–160
In memoriam, 185–194
Institute of Law and Justice (ILJ), 175
Insult to Injury, 126
Interpersonal control, 71
Interpersonal violence injuries cost, 209
Intimate or family members defined, 14
Intimate partner abuse, 1
    annual rate, 15
    power and control dynamics, 4–5
Intimate partner killings, 20–21
Intimate partner violence (IPV), 212–213
    BJS, 37
    changes, 262
    as percentage of total violence against females, 21
Invisible victim, 180–182
Iowa Coalition Against Domestic Violence, 270
IPV. *see* Intimate partner violence (IPV)
It's Time to Talk Day, 59–60

J

Jail economic consequences, 165
James, Lisa, 123
Jane Doe, Inc., 54–55, 74, 179, 180, 185, 271
    favoritism, 190
January 14, 2003, 186–187
Job injuries *vs.* violence, 36
Johnson v. Zerbst, 159
Jones, Owen, 138
Journal of the American Medical Association, 107
Judges, 6

Jules, Jean Claude, 188
June 1, 2003, 188
June 11, 2003, 188
June 16, 2003, 188
June 23, 2003, 189
June 26, 2003, 188
June 29, 2003, 188–189
Justice, 168
Juvenile violence, 66–67

K

Kanin, Eugene J., 142
Kansas Coalition Against Sexual and
        Domestic Violence, 269
Keeping the Promise (KtP), 89–90
    autonomy and confidentiality, 119–120
    batterer intervention programs, 114–115
    cart and horse, 107–109
    central premise, 125–126
    choice, 110–111
    confusion, 121–122
    connecting dots, 106
    courts, 114–115
    criminal justice data, 124–125
    dating relationships, 96–97
    deterrence, 106
    domestic violence homicides, 97–98
    domestic violence problem, 93–94
    emerging awareness, 126–127
    empirical data, 118–119
    facts, 104
    family conflict, 93
    fear factor gender differential, 94
    holding batterers accountable, 114–115
    ignoring NIJ reports, 102–103
    ignoring research, 99
    imperfect idea, 110
    law enforcement's response to health
        practitioner domestic violence
        reports, 118–130
    leaping without looking, 118–119
    letter of law, 122
    limited understanding, 98–99
    looking before leaping, 118–119
    mandatory interventions, 99–100
    NRC, 102–103
    one size does not fit all, 101–102
    probation departments, 114–115
    prosecuting domestic violence
        misdemeanors, 109–110
    read studies, 112–113
    recommendations for California
        Attorney General, 126–128
    recommended changes, 123–124
    reporting, 94–95
    restraining orders, 104
    restraining orders premise, 105–106
    what not to do, 111–112
Kempe, C.H., 3, 195
Kennedy, Edward, 258
Kentucky Domestic Violence Association,
        269
Kerry, John, 258
King, Jeanne I., 258
KtP. see Keeping the Promise (KtP)
Kury, George, 187

L

LACDVC. see Los Angeles County
        Domestic Violence Council
        (LACDVC)
Laramee, Steven, 188
Larceny, 19
LAV. see Legal Assistance to Victims (LAV)
        program
Law enforcement officers
    adversaries vs. partners, 11
    intervention, 11–12
Law enforcement officials, 6
LCI. see Liz Claiborne, Inc. (LCI)
Leahy, Patrick, 264
Legal Assistance to Victims (LAV)
        program, 175
Legislation
    domestic violence, 6
Lesbian community
    power and control dynamics, 5
Lessons ignored, 191–192
Levesque, Amy, 189
Liz Claiborne, Inc. (LCI), 56–58
    emotional abuse, 59
    power and control, 58–59
    silence, 61
Logic, 168–169
Los Angeles County Domestic Violence
        Council (LACDVC)
    restraining orders failure, 108
Louisiana Coalition Against Domestic
        Violence, 270

M

Maguire, Timothy, 189
Maine Coalition to End Domestic Violence, 270
Males
    annual assault rates, 15
    initiating domestic and dating violence, 79
    intimate partner victims, 21
    murdered by family members of acquaintances, 20
    physical assaults, 2
    reluctance to report assaults, 17
    VAWA, 9–10
Male victimization, 14–15, 15
    dating violence, 84–85
    vs. female victimization, 129
    ignoring, 16, 79–80, 82–83
    invisible, 176–177
    recognition, 256
Mandatory arrest, 7, 43, 145–153
    domestic violence, 7
    false omnipotence, 126
    ignoring family desires, 101
    NIJ, 51
    warnings against, 118
Mandatory education, 257
Manslaughter, 19
March 13, 2003, 187
March 25, 2003, 187
Marginalizing victims, 42–43
Marijuana, 67
Maryland Network Against Domestic Violence, 271
Massachusetts Coalition Against Sexual and Domestic Violence, 271
Massachusetts Coalition Against Sexual Assault and Domestic Violence, 54
Massachusetts Constitution, 47–48
Massachusetts Domestic Violence Homicide Report (MDVHR), 185, 191
Massachusetts Youth Risk Behavior Study, 179
MDVHR. see Massachusetts Domestic Violence Homicide Report (MDVHR)
Measuring tools, 39–40
Men. see Males
Men They Will Become, 158

Michigan Coalition Against Sexual and Domestic Violence, 271
Miksch, Nathan, 189
Miles, Doug, 156
    fast track, 167
Mills, Linda, 26, 126
Minneapolis Domestic Violence Experiment, 148
Minnesota Coalition for Battered Women, 271
Misdemeanors vs. felonies, 92
Mississippi Coalition Against Sexual and Domestic Violence, 271
Missouri Coalition Against Domestic Violence, 272
Misunderstanding, 7, 13
MMWR. see Morbidity and Mortality Weekly Report (MMWR)
Moffitt, Terrie, 26
Montana Coalition Against Sexual and Domestic Violence, 272
Moral and legal rights, 158–159
Morbidity and Mortality Weekly Report (MMWR), 35
Motor vehicle theft, 19
Ms. Foundation for Women Safety and Justice for All, 101
Multiple stabbing, 187
Murder
    incidence, 98
    male vs. female involvement, 19
    model, 22
    by strangers, 21
Murphy, William, 189
Myths, 7

N

NACJD. see National Archive of Criminal Justice Data (NACJD)
Narcissism, 22
National Advisory Commission on Criminal Justice Standards and Goals, 161
National Archive of Criminal Justice Data (NACJD), 24
National Center for Victims of Crime (NCVC), 61, 175, 176
    dating violence, 77
National Child Abuse Hotline, 278

National Coalition Against Domestic
  Violence (NCADV)
  domestic violence cause, 5
  violent crimes, 37
  women only, 195
National Coalition of Anti-Violence
  Programs (NCAVP), 5
National Conference on Family Violence,
  15, 173
National Conference on Health and
  Domestic Violence 2007, 175
National Council on Crime and
  Delinquency (NCCD), 61
National Crime Victimization Survey
  (NCVS)
  data acceptance, 16–18
  violent crimes, 37
  women victims, 196
National Domestic Violence Awareness
  Month, 208
National Domestic Violence Hotline
  (NDVH), 15, 267
  abuse defined, 56
  domestic violence definition, 1
National Evaluation of the Legal Assistance
  for Victims Program, 175
National Family Violence Legislative
  Resource Center, 115–116
National Family Violence Surveys, 196
National Institute of Justice (NIJ), 16–18
  Controlling Violence Against Women,
    99–100
  Criminalization of Domestic Violence,
    177–178
  Effects of Arrest on Intimate Partner
    Violence, 200
  mandatory arrest, 51
  mission, 87
  Reviewing Domestic Violence Deaths,
    174
  Sexual Victimization of College Women,
    174
National Online Resource Center on
  Violence Against Women
  (VAWnet), 65–66
National Organization for Women (NOW),
  52–53
National Research Council (NRC), 28–29,
  76–78
  Advancing the Federal Research Agenda
    on Violence Against Women,
    102–103, 106, 127, 149
  advising Congress, 264
  purpose, 87–88
  research agenda, 181
  Understanding Violence Against Women,
    115
  Violence in Families, 108
National Survey on Drug Use and Health,
  67
National Teen Dating Abuse Helpline
  (NTDAH)
  website, 278
National Violence Against Women Survey,
  5, 8
  male victims in intimate partner
    violence, 88
National Violence Against Women Survey
  (NVAWS), 14
  domestic violence defined, 19
  job injuries vs. violence, 36
  minor domestic violence incidents, 49,
    92, 147
  original intention, 173
  rape, 141
  reporting, 94–95
National Youth Risk Behavior Survey, 68
National Youth Violence Prevention
  Resource Center, 70
Natural History of Rape, 139
Navarro, Sara, 187
NCADV. see National Coalition Against
  Domestic Violence (NCADV)
NCAVP. see National Coalition of Anti-
  Violence Programs (NCAVP)
NCCD. see National Council on Crime and
  Delinquency (NCCD)
NCVC. see National Center for Victims of
  Crime (NCVC)
NCVS. see National Crime Victimization
  Survey (NCVS)
NDVH. see National Domestic Violence
  Hotline (NDVH)
Nebraska Domestic Violence and Sexual
  Assault Coalition, 272
Nesbitt, Ralph, 189
Nevada Network Against Domestic
  Violence, 272
Newberger, Eli, 158
New England Journal of Medicine, 35–36
New Hampshire Coalition Against Sexual
  and Domestic Violence, 272
New Hampshire University Family
  Research Laboratory, 8

New Jersey Coalition for Battered Women, 272
New Mexico Coalition Against Domestic Violence, 273
New York Coalition Against Domestic Violence, 273
Nifong, Mike, 155, 156
NIJ. see National Institute of Justice (NIJ)
No-drop prosecution policies, 110
    ineffectiveness, 113
Non-facts, 35–36
    becoming facts, 33–35
Nonfatal violent victimization rate, 151
North Carolina Coalition Against Domestic Violence, 273
North Dakota Council on Abused Women's Services, 273
November 2, 2003, 189
November 26, 2003, 189–190
NOW. see National Organization for Women (NOW)
NRC. see National Research Council (NRC)
NTDAH. see National Teen Dating Abuse Helpline (NTDAH)
Numbers game, 37–38
Nurses, 6
NVAWS. see National Violence Against Women Survey (NVAWS)

O

Objectivity, 123
    need for, 203–204
October 2, 2003, 189
October 28, 2003, 189
O'Dell, Anne, 126
Offenders, 27
Office of Community Oriented Policing Services, 107
Office of Women Advocates, 274
O'Keefe study, 70–73
Oklahoma Coalition Against Domestic Violence and Sexual Assault, 274
One size does not fit all, 101–102
One-size-fits-all intervention, 91–92, 200
    dating abuse, 52
    ending legislation, 257
    permeating system, 90–91
    warning against, 99
One-solution-fits-all ideological domestic violence advocate paradigm, 91

On-line self-help center, 259
Oregon Coalition Against Domestic and Sexual Violence, 274
Ortiz, Euclides, 187–188

P

Pathological jealousy, 22
Patriarchal dominance, 5, 90, 179–180
Patriarchy
    causes domestic violence theory, 5
    empirical documentation, 4
    wife beating, 4
Patterns in Criminal Homicide, 2
Pence, Ellen, 101, 126
Pennsylvania Coalition Against Domestic Violence, 274
Penrose, Donavan, 188
Permanent protection orders effectiveness, 107
Petitry, Baby, 188
Physical abuse, 2
    husbands *vs.* wives, 8
Physical assaults
    between adult males and females, 2
    among siblings, 2
    children protection, 8
    statistics, 15
Physical power, 4
    criminal behavior, 5
Physicians, 6
Plea bargains, 160–161
Police Intervention and the Repeat of Domestic Assault, 149
Police officers
    adversaries *vs.* partners, 11
    empowered not mandated, 260
Powell v. Alabama, 159
Power and control dynamics, 2, 22–23
    bisexual community, 5
    child abuse, 4–5
    children, 26
    elder abuse, 4–5
    female behavior, 23
    gay community, 5
    intimate partner abuse, 4–5
    LCI, 58–59
    lesbian community, 5
    sibling abuse, 4–5
    theory, 4
    transgendered community, 5

TRAS, 58–59
Preferred arrest laws, 7
Prescription drug abuse, 67
Private family matter *vs.* social problem,
    2–3
Prizzy, Erin, 126
Probation departments, 114–115
Protective orders, 259
Psychiatric model, 135
Psychiatrists, 6
Psychological injuries, 25
Psychological model, 198
Psychological pain, 17
Psychologists, 6
Psychotherapeutic model, 115–116
Ptacek, James, 38–39
Public policy makers involvement, 256
Pummeling, 102
Pushing, 102

Q

Questioning mandatory arrest, 149–150

R

Rape, 133–153
    accused, 133–134
    crime spawning center, 135–136
    defined, 133, 141
    emotional intervention, 139–140
    engaging men, 134–135
    experts, 136–137
    invisible victims, 140–141
    law enforcement intervention, 138–139
    male *vs.* female involvement, 19
    nature *vs.* nurture, 138–139
    NVAWS, 141
    state statutes, 141
    statistics, 141–142
Rational thought, 137
Reason, 137
Recommendations, 255–263
    bail not allowed, 260–261
    behavior modifications, 261–263
    education and data availability, 264
    one-size-fits-all intervention ending
        legislation, 257
    on-line self-help center, 257–259
    police officers empowered not
        mandated, 259–260
    policy maker involvement, 255–256
    separation, 261
    specific tax for funding, 263
    VAWA restructured and renamed, 263
Reid, Stephen, 187
Rennison, Callie Marie, 37
Resources, 267–279
Restraining orders, 8, 92
    effectiveness, 105
    issuance, 259
    LACDVC failure, 108
    limited value, 104
Rethinking victimization, 195–205
Reviewing Domestic Violence Deaths, 174
Rev-Kury, Livia Hedda, 187
Rhode Island Coalition Against Domestic
    Violence, 274
Risk factors, 18
    dating abuse, 51–52
    offending, 23
    victimization, 23
Rivers, Caryl, 20
Robbery, 19
Romantic relationships, 1–2

S

SAFE. *see* Stop Abuse for Everyone (SAFE)
Safety and dating violence, 79–82
Saget, Gilane Azor, 188
Same Difference, 20
Samenow, Stanton E., 27
San Francisco FVPF, 121
Santobello v. New York, 160
Saufley, Jeffrey, 164
Scannell, Nancy, 54, 179, 185
Schism, 13
Scientific objectivity, 34
Scottsboro case (1932), 159
Search of Equality, 179
Self-defense aggression, 70–71
Self-incrimination confessions, 157
Self-interest, 13
Separate but equal doctrine, 137
Sexism and oppression of women theory,
    181
Sexual assault, 133–153
    crime spawning center, 135–136
    defined, 141

engaging men, 134–135
experts, 136–137
gender, 4
law enforcement intervention, 138–139
Sexual Victimization of College Women,
174
Sexual violence statistics, 26
Sherman, Lawrence, 148
Shot to death, 186–187, 188
SHR. *see* Supplemental Homicide Report
(SHR)
Siblings
abuse, 10
killings, 20
physical assaults, 2
power and control dynamics, 4–5
Silence
LCI, 61
TRAS, 61
Silent voices, 186–190
Sinden, P.G., 11
Sixth Amendment, 157–158
Smoking, 67
Smothered to death, 189
Social-psychological model, 135
Social workers, 6
Sociocultural model, 135
Soler, Esta, 101
South Carolina Coalition Against Domestic
Violence and Sexual Assault, 274
South Dakota Coalition Against Domestic
Violence and Sexual Assault, 275
Spanking, 25, 80, 262
Specter, Arlen, 264
Spousal killings, 20
Spray, Sally, 187
Spray, William, 187
Stabbed to death incidences, 187–190
Star Chamber, 157
Stephens, B.J., 11
Stevens, Pat, 38
Stone, Christopher, 188
Stone, Colleen, 188
Stop Abuse for Everyone (SAFE), 277
Strangers, 2
Strangers *vs.* family violence, 6
Strangled to death, 187, 189
Stuart, Diane M., 106, 107, 264
Substance abuse, 22
Suicide, 22
Supplemental Homicide Report (SHR),
29–30

Survey
female and male victim percentage, 265
Sutton, Willie, 24

T

Teenagers
alcohol abuse, 67
cigarettes, 67
marijuana, 67
opinions and beliefs, 82
victimization, 61–63
Teen Dating Abuse Survey (TRAS), 56–58
emotional abuse, 59
power and control, 58–59
silence, 61
Teen Relationship Survey, 211
Tejeda, Berenice, 187–188
Tennessee Coalition Against Domestic
Violence and Sexual Assault, 275
Texas Council on Family Violence, 275
Theft, 19
Thinking about thinking, 210–211
Thinking and nonthinking, 164–167
Toomey, Mary, 189–190
Training, 92
Transgendered community, 5
TRAS. *see* Teen Dating Abuse Survey
(TRAS)
Truth, 34, 178–179, 182

U

Unbiased fact reporting, 204
Understanding Violence Against Women,
14, 115
Unequal power and control, 2
Unequal treatment compared to other
crimes, 91–92
University of New Hampshire Family
Research Laboratory, 8
Unsubstantiated beliefs, 167–168
Utah Domestic Violence Council, 275

V

Valentine's Day, 48–49
VAWA. *see* Violence Against Women Act
(VAWA)

VAWnet. *see* National Online Resource Center on Violence Against Women (VAWnet)
Vellez, Cesar Rios, 187
Vermont Network Against Domestic Violence and Sexual Assault, 275
Victimization
  boys, 76
  girls, 76
  risk factors, 23
  teenagers, 61–63
Victims, 27–28, 171–183, 261
  battering behavior, 41
  gender, 24
Violence
  begetting violence, 10
  BJS, 36–37
  causes, 17–19
  in families, 108
  gender, 24
  location, 29–30
  against males by females, 14
  private family matter *vs.* social problem, 2–3
  related injuries, 36–37
  separation of parties, 261
Violence Against Women, 203
Violence Against Women Act (VAWA), 1, 9, 52–54, 75, 172
  comprehensiveness, 177
  criminal justice impacts, 211–212
  dating violence, 64–65
  expenditures, 150
  gender-specific funding, 14
  men, 9–10
  restructured and renamed, 263
  women only, 195
Violence Against Women Office, 14
Violent crimes
  male *vs.* female, 19
  NCVS, 37
Virginians Against Domestic Violence, 276

W

Wallace, Harvey, 118
Washington State Coalition Against Domestic Violence, 276
WAST. *see* Woman Abuse Screening Tool (WAST)
Welchans, Sarah, 37
West Virginia State Coalition Against Domestic Violence, 276
When Domestic Violence Kills, 192–193
White Ribbon Campaign, 179
Whole truth search, 177–178
Wife beating, 4
Wisconsin Coalition Against Domestic Violence, 276
Wives *vs.* husbands
  physical abuse, 8
Wolfgang, Marvin, 2
Woman Abuse Screening Tool (WAST), 39
Women. *see* Females
Women's Coalition of St. Croix, 275
Women's Equality Amendment, 3
Wyoming Coalition Against Domestic Violence and Sexual Assault, 276

Y

Yochelson, Samuel, 27
Young adults opinions and beliefs, 82
Youth Risk Behavior Study, 179
Youth Risk Behavior Surveillance System (YRBSS), 26, 55–56
Youth Risk Behavior Survey (YRBS), 68, 83–84
  CDC, 96–97
  date rape, 141
YRBSS. *see* Youth Risk Behavior Surveillance System (YRBSS)